Introduction to African American Studies

Introduction to African American Studies

A Reader

Edited by Stephen Balkaran

Central Connecticut State University

Bassim Hamadeh, CEO and Publisher
John Remington, Executive Editor
Gem Rabanera, Project Editor
Casey Hands, Associate Production Editor
Jess Estrella, Senior Graphic Designer
Trey Soto, Licensing Coordinator
Natalie Piccotti, Director of Marketing
Kassie Graves, Vice President of Editorial
Jamie Giganti, Director of Academic Publishing

Copyright © 2020 by Cognella, Inc. All rights reserved. No part of this publication may be reprinted, reproduced, transmitted, or utilized in any form or by any electronic, mechanical, or other means, now known or hereafter invented, including photocopying, microfilming, and recording, or in any information retrieval system without the written permission of Cognella, Inc. For inquiries regarding permissions, translations, foreign rights, audio rights, and any other forms of reproduction, please contact the Cognella Licensing Department at rights@cognella.com.

Trademark Notice: Product or corporate names may be trademarks or registered trademarks and are used only for identification and explanation without intent to infringe.

Cover images: Copyright © 2016 Depositphotos/Igor_Vkv.
Copyright © 2016 iStockphoto LP/duncan1890.

Printed in the United States of America.

Contents

Introduction vii

PART I Introduction to the African American Experience — 1

1. The Continuing Significance of Race: An American Dilemma — 2
   by Stephen Balkaran

2. A Blueprint for Africana Studies: An Overview of African/African American/African Caribbean Studies — 7
   by Marquita Pellerin

PART II African Americans in America, 1619–1800 — 27

3. Africans in the Americas — 28
   by Anthony B. Pinn

4. Why an Atlantic Slave Trade? — 42
   by Claudius Fergus

5. Slavery and States' Rights in the Early Republic — 59
   by Jeffrey Rogers Hummel

6. Slavery and the Problem of Democracy in Jeffersonian America — 74
   by Padraig Riley

PART III African Americans and the Meaning of Freedom, 1865–1900 — 91

7. Jim Crow — 92
   by Kenneth T. Walsh

8. Public Rights, Social Equality, and the Conceptual Roots of the *Plessy* Challenge — 108
   by Rebecca J. Scott

9. The Question of Color-Blind Citizenship: Albion Tourgée, W.E.B. Du Bois and the Principles of the Niagara Movement — 133
   by Mark Elliott

PART IV African American Literature, Arts, and Culture: The Harlem Renaissance, 1927–1940 — 153

10. Black Voices: Themes in African-American Literature — 154
    by Gerald Early

11	Baldwin's Reception and the Challenge of His Legacy by Lynn Orilla Scott	168
12	Poet-Translators: Langston Hughes to Paul Blackburn by Jonathan Mayhew	182
13	Harlem and the Renaissance: 1920–1940 by Cary D. Wintz	188
14	Reading the Harlem Renaissance into Public Policy: Lessons from the Past to the Present by Renata Harden, Christopher K. Jackson, and Berlethia J. Pitts	204

PART V The Civil Rights Movement, 1955–1970 — 219

15	The Origins and Causes of the Civil Rights Movement by David Levering Lewis	220
16	Civil Rights Reform and the Black Freedom Struggle by Clayborne Carson	231
17	Dr. Martin Luther King, Jr. and the African-American Religious Origins of the Beloved Community by Anthony E. Cook	241

PART VI Post-Racial America in the Age of Barack Obama — 253

18	Race and Multiraciality: Barack Obama to Trayvon Martin by Reginald Daniel	254
19	Analyzing the Dream: Racism and America's Social Cancer by Stephen Balkaran	270
20	Black Lives, the Flag, and the Continued Racial Hatred by Stephen Balkaran	283
21	Letter from the Birmingham Jail by Dr. Martin Luther King	292

Conclusion   305
About the Author   307

INTRODUCTION

> "African-Americans have contributed in every avenue of American life, since the inception of this great country economically, socially, and politically; they have carved their contribution into the American society. Militarily, African-Americans continue to play a vital role in every conflict, in every war, in every battle, and on every battlefield. African-Americans have put their lives on the line to protect freedom, liberty, and democracy in the Revolutionary War, Civil War, World War I and II, Korea, Vietnam, and the present day war in Iraq-Afghanistan. African-Americans have always met the challenge of serving America with great pride, commitment, and admiration."
>
> —Stephen Balkaran, Author. Published in the *New Haven Registrar*, February 15, 2007.

Famed African American author Ralph Ellison once posed an intriguing question on what America would be like without blacks. Not only did Ellison articulate the socioeconomic and cultural contributions of African Americans, but he also questioned what America would have been had Africans and their descendants not shaped and defined the past, new, and evolving America. Ellison eloquently showed that America's historical, political, economic, and cultural history was clearly shaped by African Americans and their experiences, and he also reminded us that America has continued to evolve with the black experience, through its music, literature, politics, art, and history.

The African American experience can be defined simply as the 300-year struggle against racism and oppression in a country that still today refuses to acknowledge or apologize for its wrongdoing. As we reflect on this struggle against racism and oppression, we must acknowledge that African Americans were an integral part of shaping American history, and our country would not be the same without the black experience. From the arrival of the first Africans in 1619 to the election of the nation's first African American president in 2008, the African American experience has been one of despair, struggle, hope, and triumph. No ethnic group in our history has defined, shaped, and influenced all segments of society as African Americans. Whether it is the social, cultural, economic, or political impact, the African American experience remains closely interwoven with the basic fabric of America. Due to ignorance and racial censorship, American history refuses to remind us of black inclusion in many of America's historical evolutions.

Our history books have deleted the fact that one of George Washington's closest confidants was an African American named Samuel Fraunces, who advised him on many of his battles, and that Crispus Attucks a fugitive slave in Massachusetts, became the first martyr of the American Revolution. Atticus became the first victim of the 1776 Revolutionary War in Bunker Hill; ironically, this war advocated life, liberty, and freedom, a contradiction to the newly formed nation, wherein the majority of African Americans were embedded in the institution of slavery. The African American slave trade played a key economic role in the American Revolutionary war and built large-scale economies in England, America, Holland, and many other European countries. European societies benefited from the African American slave industry, both directly and indirectly, while many of them also personally engaged in one of the world's social ills, the enslavement of black people.

The contributions of African Americans are far-reaching in American history: they include that of civil rights leaders, educators, architects, inventors, scientists, musicians, sports heroes, and others. Yet despite their commitment to America, there has remained a deep uncertainty as to who African Americans really are. Color becomes the tool that we use to gauge the black presence and define who and what they stand for. Legalized and systemic racism continues to haunt our country; segregation, Jim Crow, exclusion, oppression, and other discriminatory techniques remain a stark reminder of a sad time in American history when only white ethnic groups were allowed to benefit from our country's wealth and prosperity. As a result of this exclusion, African Americans remained second-class citizens, haunted by American terrorism.

How did the African American experience come to be defined by the concept of color? The answer to that question remains embedded in the historical context of our nation's history. The history of America has been closely pegged with racism and discrimination against African Americans; it is an issue that our founding fathers struggled to address in the early stages of this great nation, and as a result, it has continued to haunt our society, manifesting in slavery, Jim Crow segregation, the Civil Rights movement, and modern-day legalized and systemic racism. Retracing our history will show that, since the inception of America, the house of democracy has been plagued with cracks of racism and discrimination against African Americans, minority groups, and women. During the last 300 years, we have made little attempt to fix these cracks; hence, we and America have struggled with a defective foundation—a concept we call Race! The African American experience, whether manifested in politics, history, literature, art, music, civil rights, or other segments, has in one way or another been defined by historic and present-day racial experiences.

One of the foremost legacies of the African American experience is the struggle for civil rights, equality, and respect in America. This is a movement aimed primarily at advancing opportunities for African Americans, guaranteeing their constitutional rights, and eradicating legalized and systemic racism in the Jim Crow south, but more so, aimed at leveling the playing field for everyone in America. The Civil Rights movement has always been defined as one of the world's greatest social movements and has become the foundation of modern-day social movements around the world, which echo the works of Dr. Martin Luther. King and his nonviolence philosophy. The result of this famed movement led to The Civil Rights Act of 1964, arguably one of the most important pieces of legislation in our country's history. The result of this act ensured that legal barriers be torn down; they, theoretically, forbid discrimination against African Americans, along with other groups in our society, and level the playing field in American society. Vice President Hubert Humphrey once remarked that the passage of the Civil Rights Act of 1964 was America's greatest act of foreign policy, letting the rest of the world know that our commitment toward peace, equality, and justice for African Americans and other minority communities will be the cornerstone of America and our fledgling democracy. Despite this success and other gains, civil rights remain the pinnacle of debates; protecting rights regardless of color and defending rights against discrimination have long been important issues in America.

The election of the nation's first African American president led to the increased expectation that America will put our ugly racial past behind and move forward into a more racially sensitive and tolerant society, which has enlightened all of us. Yet we see that in the twenty-first century, the African American experience is still being define by race, color, and ignorance. I can conclude that integration of the races has led to a blind eye toward many of the disparities that the Civil Rights movement vowed to dismantle; education, poverty, racial profiling, police brutality, and others such problems continue to be an eyesore in a country that promises so much yet guarantees nothing. Despite African American and civil rights achievements, the twenty-first century is still plagued by many facets of oppression that are prevalent in American society. Silent and not overt racism still exists and is evident in our schools, employment, poverty, healthcare, prison system, immigrant communities, and other sectors of society. Continued racial exclusion permeates our society in ways we do not even realize and takes away the best of who we are and what we can become as Americans.

America is only as strong as its people. Until we understand the African American experience, we remain vulnerable toward committing the same mistakes we did in the past. The African American experience is an American experience. Only conversations about the truth, the need for reconciliation, and America's acknowledgment of its wrongdoing can lead to a more racially tolerant country, where the American dream can be enjoyed by all despite the concept of race or color.

—Stephen Balkaran

PART I

Introduction to the African American Experience

READING 1

The Continuing Significance of Race
An American Dilemma

Stephen Balkaran

> Stephen Balkaran is currently an instructor of political science at Quinnipiac University. He has, in the past, had professorial appointments at Central Connecticut State University, where he was an instructor of African American studies, and he also initiated, developed, and coordinated a Civil Rights Project. He has served on the faculty of the University of Connecticut-Waterbury, Post University, and Capital Community College. He has also served as research fellow for the Human Rights Research Fund at Yale University, working under Black Panther, civil rights activist, and Yale professor of African American studies, Kathleen Cleaver.

ABSTRACT

The idea of America becoming a melting pot, of moving beyond the issue of race and toward a society free of racism and discrimination where all are guaranteed the benefits of this great nation, has always been a myth rather than a reality. The election of President Barack Obama in 2008 has generated more debates on race and the future of race relations in America than in any other time in our country's great history. The increased optimism that America would transcend beyond race, that both White and Black racial attitudes would undergo a fundamental shift, and that race will no longer be part of American society has almost vanished in postracial America in the age of Obama. Despite this expectation, it is apparent that race still matters in America. As we continue to grapple with the issue of race and its impact on society, it is quite clear that race will continue to play an important role in defining who we are as Americans. In the twenty-first century, many facets of oppression still exist and are pervasive throughout American society. Silent, rather than overt, racism exists in our school systems, places of employment, health care systems, prison systems, immigrant communities, and other sectors of societies. Race permeates our society in ways we don't even realize and has taken away the best of who we are and what we can become as a nation.

Stephen Balkaran, "The Continuing Significance of Race: An American Dilemma," *The Harvard Journal of African American Policy*, pp. 57-60. Copyright © 2015 by President and Fellows of Harvard College. Reprinted with permission.

> I wish I could say that racism and prejudice were only distant memories. ... We must dissent from the indifference. We must dissent from the apathy. We must dissent from the fear, the hatred and the mistrust. ... We must dissent because America can do better, because America has no choice but to do better.[1]
>
> —Thurgood Marshall, 1992

The proclivity for many Americans to avoid race-related conversations while promoting the idea of a postracial society voids what would be one of the most debatable topics to emerge in the twenty-first century: postracial America in the age of President Barack Obama. The idea of a postracial America continues to be lost in transition; race and racism continue to be significant factors as we delve into the deep waters of race in America. As we end the second phase of the Obama presidency, several important debates continue to haunt our society, which have taken away the best of who we are as Americans. First and foremost, race and politics are alive and well in America, and second, postracial America continues to be a major disappointment, as we have yet to leave our racist attitudes and mindset behind us.

Because of the visible and widespread contributions of African American civil rights leaders, educators, architects, inventors, scientists, sports heroes, and others, many have wrongly assumed that these racial disparities have already been dismantled. However, the disparities in educational systems, poverty rates, the criminal justice system, and other sectors of society continue to plague a country that promises so much yet guarantees so little.

Why has race continued to play such a large role in America even fifty years after the enactment of the Civil Rights Act in 1964? Since America's inception, its brand of democracy has been plagued with racial and gender discrimination. We have made few attempts to amend these democratic shortcomings during the last three hundred years, and as a result, we have struggled with a defective foundation. Therein lies the answer for why race still matters in America: many Americans refuse to come to terms with the history of African Americans, dismissing the continual struggle against racism and oppression in a country that refuses to either acknowledge or apologize for its harsh treatment and wrongdoing.

Our increased expectation that America would transcend race and that both White and Black racial attitudes would undergo a fundamental change has not come to fruition. Some fifty years after the monumental Civil Rights Act of 1964, America continues to grapple with the issue of race, and it continues to divide us as a nation.

> *... in the twenty-first century, silent, not overt, racism exists in our school systems, places of employment, health care systems, prison systems, immigrant communities, and other sectors of societies.*

Gone are the days of former Alabama Governor George C. Wallace, who famously preached, "Segregation now, segregation tomorrow, segregation forever!" to resounding applause in 1963.[2] Gone are the days when signs reading, "Whites only" and "Colored" hung prominently over water fountains, bathrooms, and restaurant counters. However, in the twenty-first century, silent, not overt, racism exists in our school systems, places of employment, health care systems, prison systems, immigrant communities, and other sectors of societies. It also permeates our society in ways we don't even realize and takes away the best of who we are and what we can become as a nation.

Race relations have always been an important issue in the struggle for equality and reconciliation in America. A July 2013 Gallup poll of over 4,000 Americans asked whether they thought "race relations between Blacks and Whites [would] always be a problem for the United States"; 40 percent answered in the affirmative. In 1964, Gallup posed the same question, with 42 percent of respondents answering in the affirmative.[3] Despite the election of our first African American president, the research shows that little, if any, progress has occurred in the last fifty years when it comes to optimism toward race relations.

Now, more than sixty years since the Supreme Court's decision in *Brown v. Board of Education*, we continue to fight implicit and explicit biases, discriminatory practices, and questionable policies that orchestrated the laws of the past. While the *Brown* decision dismantled state laws that created separate public schools based on race and ruled that such segregation was unconstitutional, the Civil Rights Project at the University of California, Los Angeles, reports that schools today are more segregated than they were in the past. Particularly, segregation for Black students is the highest in the Northeast, schools are substantially more segregated now than they were in 1970 across the South, and both Black and Latino students attend schools with a substantial majority of poor children (while White and Asian students attend middle-class schools).[4]

The Africana Studies and Research Center at Cornell University reported that in 1960, only 20 percent of the Black population finished high school, compared with 43 percent of the White population. Furthermore, only 3 percent of African Americans graduated from college, less than half the White graduation rate of 8 percent.[5] Some fifty years later, a 2013 report by the *Journal of Blacks in Higher Education* indicated that 54 percent of young African Americans were graduating from high school, and 42 percent of African American students were graduating from college—still less than half the rate of White graduates. The report indicates that the vast majority of our nation's highest-ranked colleges and universities have shown significant improvement over the past quarter-century, but at the same time, there is a 20 percent gap in the graduation rate between White and Black students.[6] Schools are becoming more segregated at a time when we hail public policies like No Child Left Behind, Race to the Top, and Common Core, which promised quality and access to education for all, when in reality many Black and Brown kids are Left Behind.

The failure to talk about race and racism, and the failure to acknowledge that racism exists in the present day, is what best defines one of the most contentious subjects in America.

Educational disparities have become the new civil rights issue of the twenty-first century. These disparities are both directly linked to and implicated by policies that seek to eradicate poverty and increase social mobility.

In 1964, President Lyndon B. Johnson declared a "war on poverty," making poverty in America one of his top priorities during his presidency. This not only raised awareness of poverty throughout American communities, but also ensured that early education, food stamps, and other government economic assistance programs would be extended to America's poor. Yet despite this and the initiation of the Poor People's Campaign by Dr. Martin Luther King, Jr., in 1967, poverty continues to be the cancer that threatens our society and remains a significant inhibiting factor in many African American households. According to the US Census Bureau's report on income and poverty in the United States, the poverty rate for African Americans in 2013 was 27.2 percent, as compared to 9.6 percent for non-Hispanic Whites.[7] The report indicated that the poverty rate increased between 2005 and 2013 for every socioeconomic group within African American families.

Further, the Pew Research Center indicated that the wealth gaps between Caucasians and African Americans are at an all-time high. In 2013, the wealth of White households was thirteen times the median of Black households. This is the highest gap since 1989, when White households had seventeen times the wealth of African Americans households.[8] There are a number of factors that contribute to many of the economic disparities between African American and Caucasian households, including access to economic opportunities, educational opportunities, and systematic discrimination in employment, which are still prevalent in society. Economic empowerment of the races has always been a cornerstone of American democracy, African Americans economically continue to lag far behind other races, and a significant section of their community continues to struggle beyond the poverty threshold.

Recent events in Ferguson, Missouri, and New York City as well as other race-related incidents throughout the country have left many issues that continue to haunt our society: the lost community policing, trust in law enforcement, and treatment of young Black males, but more so the continuing significance of race in America. The recent riots that surrounded the deaths of both Michael Brown and Eric Garner have continued to open the debates on race, criminal justice, and America's commitment to a postracial society. These riots have brought many lingering racial issues to the surface, which can only be resolved by having more open dialogue on race and discussion of diversity in America.

With the election of our first African American president, the United States has made great strides toward a more racially harmonious society, one in which all contributions to our great country—despite the color of one's skin—are respected. Despite this optimism, race continues to play a defining role in who we are as Americans in the twenty-first century, just as it did in the past. The failure to talk about race and racism, and the failure to acknowledge that racism exists in the present day, is what best defines one of the most contentious subjects in America. In the twenty-first century, many facets of oppression still exist and are prevalent in American society. Some fifty years after one of the greatest social movements in American history, African Americans and other minority groups are still some of the most underrepresented groups in education, employment, criminal justice, and other sectors in American society. Postracial America has not come to fruition, and the continuous disparities among the races, racial attitudes, stereotypes, racial profiling, and other elements in society have in many ways reinforced the significance of race in the twenty-first century.

ENDNOTES

1. Thurgood Marshall, Liberty Medal acceptance speech (Independence Hall, Philadelphia, Pennsylvania, 4 July 1992).
2. George C. Wallace, inaugural address (Montgomery, Alabama, January 1963).
3. Jeffrey M. Jones, "Americans Rate Racial and Ethnic Relations in US Positively," Gallup, 17 July 2013.
4. Gary Orfield et al., Brown at 60: Great Progress, a Long Retreat and an Uncertain Future, The Civil Rights Project, University of California, 15 May 2014.
5. Michael E. Ross, "Brown v. Board: The Education of a Nation," NBCNews, 15 February 2005.
6. "Black Student College Graduation Rates Remain Low, But Modest Progress Begins to Show," Journal of Blacks in Higher Education, Winter 2005/2006.
7. Carmen DeNavas-Walt and Bernadette D. Proctor, Income and Poverty in the United States: 2013, US Census Bureau, September 2014, 12.
8. Rakesh Kochhar and Richard Fry, "Wealth Inequality Has Widened Along Racial, Ethnic Lines Since End of Great Recession," Pew Research Center, 12 December 2014.

READING 2

A Blueprint for Africana Studies
An Overview of African/African American/African Caribbean Studies[1]

Marquita Pellerin

ABSTRACT

In the 1960s and 1970s several historical phenomenon contributed to the emergence of the study of people of African descent inside of universities and colleges. As a response to the constant demand for a more inclusive curriculum, faculty, and students, universities and colleges across America launched the development of the discipline of Black Studies (Afro-American, Africana, and African American Studies). The aim of this blueprint for Africana Studies is to interrogate previous blueprints, to establish a foundation and create a universal framework for the future of the discipline. The purpose of this blueprint is to (1) formulate a functional model and definition; (2) create a universal program structure; (3) develop a core curriculum model; (4) determine faculty appointment; (5) establish criteria for scholarship; (6) establish a research agenda; and (7) determine community responsibility.

INTRODUCTION

In the 1960s and 1970s several historical phenomenon contributed to the emergence of the study of people of African descent inside of universities and colleges. As a response to the constant demand for a more inclusive curriculum, faculty, and students, universities and colleges across America launched the development of the discipline of Black Studies (Afro-American, Africana, and African American Studies).[2] Ironically, however, no two programs developed along the same structural or organizational lines. According to Darlene Clark Hine in *Black Studies: An Overview*, "today it seems that no two Black Studies programs are alike. Their diversity is evidenced in faculty size and composition, relations with university administrators and more traditional departments, curriculum, degrees offered, budgets, spatial resources, range of special programs, and the nature of their community outreach" (Hine, 7). In effect, the lack of universality across the field has lead to continued questions and debate over the legitimacy and future of the discipline. Such questions are: Is it a discipline or field of study? What nomenclature is most appropriate? Is it interdisciplinary or multidisciplinary? Should it focus solely on African Americans or include the experiences of the continent of Africa and the African Diaspora? What ideology, methodology, and

Marquita Pellerin, "A Blueprint for Africana Studies: An Overview of African/African American/African Caribbean Studies," *The Journal of Pan African Studies*, vol. 2, no. 10, pp. 42-63. Copyright © 2009 by Itibari Zulu. Reprinted with permission. Provided by ProQuest LLC. All rights reserved.

theoretical construct(s) should inform and dictate the content and structure of African American Studies? Has the mandate of community responsibility been followed and/or efficiently maintained? The goal of this blueprint is to formulate a coherent criterion by which Africana Studies departments across the nation can structure their programs.

The aim of this blueprint for Africana Studies is to establish a foundation and create a universal framework for the discipline. The purpose of this blueprint is to (1) formulate a functional model and definition; (2) create a universal structure; (3) develop a core curriculum model; (4) institute faculty appointment; (5) establish criteria for scholarship; (6) establish a research agenda; and (7) institute community responsibility.

RATIONALE FOR BLUEPRINT

At the dawn of the Twenty-First Century, we embark on the twentieth-year anniversary of the first doctoral degree-granting program in African American Studies. It is at this time that the discipline evaluates how far it has come and where it is going. A new generation of scholars has joined to build on a great legacy of 'scholar activism,' and thus a new and united mission for the future of Black Studies must be formulated.

Seeing the need for Black scholars to create our own discipline and produce new knowledge about ourselves, Black scholars joined together and brought about a forced entry into academia; as a consequence, came the emergence of Black Studies departments and programs throughout America.

Upon this victory, scholars sought to draft proposals for the development and function of the discipline. Some of these works include theory building, paradigm structure, curriculum development, the establishment of the master's and doctoral degree, guiding principles and frameworks, and introductory texts. In 1995 Manning Marable in *Beyond Black and White: Transforming African American Politics*, dedicates a chapter to the development of a blueprint for the discipline entitled *Blueprint for Black Studies*. Here Marable outlines a brief historical overview of the discipline and charges it with a new mission for the 21st Century, and the centuries to come. In *Blueprint for Black Studies*, Marable declares that "African American Studies is at the cutting side of a second Renaissance, a just discovered level of growth, institutionalization and theoretical advancement" (109). In essence, he advocates a framework for African American Studies with a decisive role in debate surrounding multiculturalism; however, he does not offer a comprehensive framework for the total discipline. In fact, no comprehensive blueprint has been developed nor implemented on a universal level for Black Studies across the world. It is therefore the aim of this blueprint to create a universal model and foundation for the future of Africana Studies.

Accordingly, the rationale for developing this blueprint is to promote excellence in education, research, and service. Since Africana Studies is concerned with the study of the experiences of African peoples, through the study of such subject areas as history, politics, economics, culture, literature, sociology, and psychology, the aim is to engender an appreciation of oneself and culture and emphasize the ways in which people of African descent have constructed and interpreted their own lives and cultures. In turn, this blueprint provides students with a multidisciplinary understanding of the Black experience in Africa, the United States, and other areas of the Diaspora. As Karenga states in *Afrocentricity and Multicultural Education*, "thus the inclusive approach of Black Studies commits it to a multidisciplinary educational process" (81).

Creating this blueprint also fosters research on Africans and African-Americans and provides conceptual frameworks to address the causes and effects of Africana people's struggle for liberation. In addition, it equips students for critical thinking and creatively. Fourth, a critical component is the creation of new knowledge and research paradigms. Utilizing different paradigms and disciplinary modifications in the discipline of Africana Studies, provides a framework for observations and understandings, which in turn shapes both what we observe and how we understand those observations. In this regard, paradigms serve as a structuring of concepts, theories, and methodologies. In effect, constructing paradigms play a vital role in Africana Studies; and those paradigms should orient the study of people of African decent from a location of African centeredness. Thus, it is Afrocentric in its nature. According to Molefi Asante, Afrocentricity establishes,

> A frame of reference wherein phenomena are viewed from the perspective of the African person ... It centers on placing people of African origin in control of their lives and attitudes about the world. This means that we examine every aspect of the dislocation of African people; culture, economics, psychology, health and religion ... As an intellectual theory, Afrocentricity is the study of the ideas and events from the standpoint of Africans as the key players rather than victims. This theory becomes, by virtue of an authentic relationship to the centrality of our own reality, a fundamentally empirical project ... it is Africa asserting itself intellectually and psychologically, breaking the bonds of Western domination in the mind as an analogue for breaking those bonds in every other field. (1991, 171)

In turn, by centering the African at the core of his/her own reality, enables the Afrocentric study of African peoples. Conversely, an Afrocentric orientation is rooted in self-conscious action. In *Afrocentricity*, Asante states that there are two aspects of consciousness: 1) toward oppression: where one is able to verbalize the conditions of oppression; 2) toward victory: where a victorious historical will is emphasizes. Through consciousness, agency is enacted and liberation can be brought about (217).

Thus, the direction of Afrocentric consciousness is liberation, and thus a key concept of Africana Studies. In creating this blueprint, Afrocentricity will serve as a central component to the development and reconstruction of the discipline.

Another reason for developing this blueprint is to encourage a functional relationship between faculty, students and the community, which entails maintaining a community commitment/responsibility component that promotes collaborative work; and contributes to educational and cultural enrichment which in turn supports the implementation of academic and practical knowledge into the Africana community. Fundamentally, we must keep the Africana community's needs present and the discipline's obligation in aiding to liberate the masses of Africana people. Finally, Africana Studies is imperative in order to reinforce the study of Africana cultural ideals. For these reasons Africana Studies is distinguished from all other disciplines, and this blueprint serves as a critical framework for the future of Africana Studies.

NOMENCLATURE, DEFINITION AND THE ORGANIZATION OF KNOWLEDGE

One of the most pressing issues, that affect the uniformity of Africana Studies, is the issue of nomenclature. It is argued that nomenclature is insignificant, but the fact that a consensus has not been reached about what to entitle the discipline exhibits what Adams argues is the "youthfulness" of the discipline (33). We understand that in its original form, Africana Studies, termed 'Black Studies' was a reflection of the historical, political, and cultural struggle of a people; however, the discipline cannot end there.

It must resurrect the full history and culture of people of African descent while at the same time venerating our historical struggles. In his article *Africana Studies: A Decade of Change, Challenge, and Conflict*, John Henrik Clarke gives reasoning for the departure from the concept of "Black" stating:

> "Black, or Blackness, tells you how you look without telling you who you are, whereas Africa, or Africana, relates you to land, history, and culture" (Clarke 1984, 292).

To accurately study Africana people, researchers must understand the essential interconnectedness of Africana people and thereby locate them under the nomenclature of "Africana." This connection to Africa is very important to a discipline which is supposed to approach scholarship from an Afrocentric perspective (Nelson 1997). It is also important because it more accurately describes what and whom the scholars explore. Darlene Clark Hine states, "Africana Studies encompasses a broader geographical, if not disciplinary, reach spanning the North and South America, the Caribbean, and the African continent—in short, the African Diaspora ..." (Hine 1990, 8). Since these areas are all explored by the discipline, it is imperative that the name of the discipline account for these geographical locations. James E. Turner sums it up when he states, "Africana Studies is a teaching and research enterprise that is committed to the interpretation and explication of the total phenomenon called the Black experience" (Turner 1984, 74–75). When Turner says "total phenomenon called the

Black experience" he alludes to the inclusiveness of Africana as compared to the narrowness of Black or African-American Studies.

In order to build a sense of African community globally, the best appropriate name for discipline is Africana Studies. Under the nomenclature of "Black Studies" Vivian Gordon argues that the discipline is "an analysis of the factors and conditions which have affected the economic, psychological, legal, and moral status of the African in America as well as the African in the Diaspora" (231). While I agree with Gordon's definition of the discipline, I however disagree with the nomenclature used to classify the discipline, and in addition advocate for adding additional dimensions to the overall definition of the discipline. In effect, Africana Studies additionally should locate Africa at the center and ideologically focus on improving the global conditions of the African community.[3] African Studies "seeks not simply to offer information, but also to teach critical thinking and knowledge from an African-centered standpoint. It is at this point that Afrocentricy becomes an indispensable aspect of the Africana Studies project and contributes to the enrichment and expansion of education discourse and practice" (Karenga 2002, 76). In this sense, Africana Studies should remove the Eurocentric worldview and produce corrective truth reflecting the experiences of Africans and an African worldviews; thus liberating and redefining their existence and experiences.

Still, the most effective Africana Studies department must be disciplinary with multi-disciplinary structure; in the sense that multidisciplinary encompasses approaches across all disciplinary lines within its own discipline (i.e. the inclusion of Black psychology, Black economics, etc). In turn, a fully functional multidisciplinary Africana Studies department should be broken up into areas of concentration which would include; Africa, North America, South America, the Caribbean, Europe, and Asia. These areas contain large populations of African descendent people and therefore are valid areas of study. Most departments today deal with almost exclusively African-Americans, with a trivial reference here and there about Africa and other African people in the Diaspora. To truly become a discipline dedicated to the total African experience, it is imperative that more focus be put on the interconnectedness of all African people and also on these areas specific contributions and problems. Thus, functioning first as an independent discipline, Africana Studies must embody a multifaceted structure.

Subsequently, the definition that is most appropriate to define Africana Studies is to conceive of Africana Studies as an instrument whereby knowledge, consciousness and liberation of the global Africana community can transform and decolonize the Africana mind and liberate the Africana community. Within the academic community, the purpose is to serve as an avenue where new methodologies and new technologies relevant to the proper study of people of African descent can develop socially, politically and intellectually, after which the transformation of new knowledge into practical social application is administered to and by the community. In effect, as a critical component of Africana Studies the mandate of community responsibility and empowerment of the Black community "there is a need for African American Studies to fulfill its original mission to liberate African American people and to commit itself to the communities' needs. In this connection, African American Studies must once again become committed to addressing the consciousness, realities, and urgencies of the life situations of African Americans" (Norment, 839). Moreover, the original mandate of community responsibility and empowerment have not been effectively maintained, and there still remains a need for Africana Studies to provide sources of liberation to the Black community outside of the academic walls, and create agency whereby the current political, economic and social issues can be addressed. To accomplish this goal, departments would have to set out to hire scholars with broad research foci (which is exhibited in those who hold Africana Studies degrees). Each department should hire faculty so that each of these areas could be covered to some degree until this system is fully developed; yet, at the same time not forming a strict 'model' department or duplicate departments. In this sense, departments will still maintain some autonomy while at the same time adhering to a broader disciplinary structure. Once it has been settled that Africana Studies should be multidisciplinary, in a department structure and with specific areas of concentration, the next issue becomes the methodology.

In terms of ideology, methodology, and theoretical constructs, it is imperative to address the role of the researcher and the purpose of an Africana Studies method. Accordingly, James E. Turner in *Africana Studies and Epistemology: A Discourse in the Sociology of Knowledge*, correctly states, "as a methodology, history, in Black Studies, constitutes the foundation for the construction of an analysis of the fundamental relationship between the political economy of societal developments and the racial divisions of labor and privilege, and the common patterns of life chances peculiar to the social conditions of Black people" (77). In this regard, the evaluation of people of African descent from a historical background serves as informative force dictating the content and structure of African American Studies. In addition, Abdul Alkalimat and Associates in *Toward a Paradigm of Unity in Black Studies*, defines an ideology as "a set of beliefs that serve to define physical, social, mental, and spiritual reality" i.e. when constructing the content of Africana Studies, the discipline must incorporate the beliefs systems and social and mental patterns from an Afrocentric standpoint (493). Furthermore, the proper study of Africana people entails an Afrocentric approach in the creation of knowledge and methodologies based in a historical context.

The discipline of Africana Studies must give Africana scholars a venue through which we can properly analyze the dynamics surrounding Africana people's history and its link to their everyday experiences. It must provide us with the capacity to ask and answer thought provoking questions based on the phenomenon which people of African descent experience. In order to achieve this goal, the discipline must be cognizant of the historical, empirical, and analytical subject matter of African descended people. Under this umbrella, the scope includes the study of all people of African descent as well as subjects relevant to these people (i.e. history, art, literature, mathematics, philosophy, etc.); while at the same time allowing for the inter-sectionality of the subject areas to emerge for a more inclusive study. As William E. Nelson correctly cites "according to Professor Maulana Karenga, a discipline is by definition a self-conscious, organized system of research and communication in a defined area of inquiry and knowledge" (Nelson 1997, 60). Subsequently, the content of the discipline of Africana Studies is understood as the conscious Afrocentric investigation of Africana phenomena, whereby the interrogation of issues affecting people of African descent are explored/examined using an Afrocentric framework, which allows studies to develop from an Afrocentric perspective. In this regard, Africana Studies also encompasses the exploration of current issues affecting people of African descent and offering solutions to those problems. In addition, the discipline must also create an academic environment which nourishes the intellectual growth and development of both undergraduate and graduate students, which will in turn equip them with the proper knowledge and skills to critically assess the study of people of African descent. Finally, Africana Studies is the analysis and dissemination of knowledge about African people, the creation of Afrocentric methodologies, and the instituting of consciousness 'toward oppression' and 'toward victory' throughout the Africana community (Asante 1988).

The mission of Africana Studies is the liberation of both the mind and the community. While the mind receives it freedom through intellectual work, the community is liberated through a conscious effort to decolonize the minds and to tackle the everyday realities of the Africana community, thereby transmitting knowledge into practical social/cultural application. Thus, allowing studies to occur from an Afrocentric perspective which provides the opportunity to combine the mission, course content, methodology, pedagogy, and research in the development of undergraduate and graduate curricula in Africana Studies. Subsequently, the construction of a curriculum guide for the discipline of Africana Studies must be ordered and arranged according to the principles of Maat, "the central moral and spiritual concept in Kemetic society. Maat means many things, including truth, order, justice, propriety, harmony, balance, reciprocity, and order—in a word, rightness in the divine, natural and social realms" (Karenga 2002, 95). In this regard, Africana Studies must emphasize its focus on justice and truth—while at the same time intellectually stimulating the minds of Africana people and liberating the Africana community. Accordingly, as Darlene Clark Hine articulates, "the curriculum should reflect an ordered and arrangement of courses progressing from the introductory through the intermediate to advanced levels. In terms of content, a sound Black Studies curriculum must include courses in Afro-American history, and Afro-American literature, sound literal science, psychology, and economics. A cluster of courses in art, music, and language or linguistics should be made available to the student" (10). The fusion of the mission, course content, methodology, pedagogy, and research in the development of undergraduate and graduate curricula will produce a functional model for the design and implementation of a curriculum which will provide both a theoretical and methodological foundation while at the same time offering the practical application of the courses into society for the advancement and liberation of people of African descent. For example, offering a course in religion will entail historical context such as African religions, along with the role of the Black church and Islam; it would also encompass the presence of religion in the lives of people of African descent today: i.e. the past, present, and future. Furthermore, developing a curriculum that encompassing the historical, theoretical, and analytical dynamics of the subject area provides Africana Studies with the opportunity to critically assess the current knowledge base, develop methodologies, and apply those skills and knowledge to the Africana community.

FOUNDATIONS AND STRUCTURE

The most practical structure of Africana Studies would be a department in a College of Arts and Sciences—and possibly in the future a College of Africana Studies or University of Africana—utilizing a multidisciplinary approach of study. Departmental status will allow for full time resident Afrocentric scholar/faculty from different disciplines to receive tenure and build careers for their contributions to Africana Studies, thus increasing stability in the discipline and training of graduate students.

The foundation of Africana Studies lies within the structure of the discipline and the practical application of the research statistics to the Africana Diaspora. In this sense, the framework provided by James E. Turner in *Africana Studies and Epistemology: A Discipline in the Sociology of Knowledge*, provides the foundation to formulate the structure of the discipline. According to Turner there are four basic tenants:

1. To defend (legitimize) against racism and intellectual chauvinism the fundamental right and necessity of Africana studies;
2. To disseminate (teach and publish) Black studies social theory and analysis, criticism, and historiography and to reference the work of pioneering Black scholars;
3. To generate (new) knowledge (research) and codify existing information and predicate contemporary study upon the truths formulated by our mentors;
4. To preserve the acknowledged value of rare and classical texts in the field, and maintain the scholarly tradition and rich heritage of African peoples and their descendants (Turner 1984, 75).

In addition to these four basic tenants four additional tenants must be included: (1) To apply and implement community based programs for the revitalization of the Africana community; (2) To facilitate the development of education programs and curriculum for all-grade levels; (3) Provide conceptual frameworks to illuminate the causes and effects of Africana people's struggle for liberation in the global community; and (4) theory building. At this point, focus will be shifted to detail the necessity of theory building in Africana Studies. Theory is defined as a systematic explanation of phenomena as it relates to specific facets of life. Theories decipher human patterns which lead to the investigations of human subject matters; they also shape and direct or reshape and redirect research approaches.

In Africana Studies, in order to combat the domination of outside theories, internal theories emerge which seek to shape the scholarly discourse and provide some parameters for the broad undertaking. To differentiate between Africana Studies and the studying of Black people, Azibo comments that Black Studies departs from the assumptions of Eurocentric universalism and "at the heart of Afrocentric analysis of any phenomena lies the African worldview [which] ... comprises the natural/indigenous/authentic conceptual framework of African people growing out of their history, culture and philosophy" (Azibo 1992, 64). As one of the foremost advancer of African centered theory, Molefi Asante calls the "metatheory" of Afrocentricity, "a theoretical instrument for the examination of phenomena," which seeks to view "African people as subjects of historical and social experiences rather objects in the margins of European experiences" as in traditional Eurocentric disciplines (Asante 1992, 98). Placing African people and their social and historical experiences at the center of the discipline allows for the discipline to grow and unlock the chains of bondage of European knowledge and become the purveyors of the Africana way and an Africana theory of knowledge production.

Continued development and redevelopment of Afrocentric theories and methodologies will move closer to what Outlaw calls Africana Studies' "normative theory," rules that "mark off the field of its operation, set its boundary conditions, and steer the practices executed in its name"; thus moving the field towards standardization and meters of relevance (1996, 10)). Outlaw believes the two pillars for theory in Africana Studies are "knowledge development or consciousness raising" and "the liberation of black peoples," which set forth the directions of applying the academic exercise of Africana Studies to the praxis of serving and improving the African community (Outlaw 1996, 113). Although the extant to which theoretical work needs advancement, it provides a foundation, which if built upon will wean Africana Studies from its intellectual dependence on traditional social and human science theories.

According to McWhorter and Bailey as summarized in *The African American Studies Reader*, there are three basis of theory in Africana Studies, first, to maintain scholarship; second, to produce radical critiques; and finally, to analyze Black intellectual history. The first function of theory building in Africana Studies is that theory serves as an opportunity to provide a general orientation to the important concepts central to the discipline. In this regard, the notions and ideas that shape the development of theories in Africana Studies can be understood at the macro and micro levels. Take for instance the concept of Africology, Lucius Outlaw in *Africology: Normative Theory*, asserts that "Africology can be taken to mean theoretical discourse about norms in general—what they are, their basis, etc.—but discourse steered by partisan foreconceptions about 'Africans.' On the other hand, it can be understood as referring to the specifications of particular norms for Africology as a disciplinary complex" (Outlaw 1996, 97). Moreover, allowing the opportunity for a general orientation to Africology at both the macro and micro level affords theory building in Africana Studies the opportunity to create essential definitions of important concepts that are central to the discipline.

Second, establishing parameters regarding form and content serves as a venue through which Africana Studies can establish a direction and boundaries that will encompass the shaping of the structure and substance of theories within the discipline. Observe Terry Kershaw's (1989) development of a methodology in Africana Studies, he states that "the purpose is to identify the fundamental contradictions between theory and practice, to help develop tools to bring harmony between theory and praxis, and to help in the scholarly study of Black life experiences. The oppression of Black people is not a prerequisite of a Black Studies discipline although oppression led to it" (50). The parameters that Kershaw outlined for the creation of methods in Black Studies illustrates how the establishment of boundaries regarding form and content in theory building serve a functional role in the development of theories in Africana Studies.

Third, formulating empirical generalizations by fusing qualitative and quantitative methodologies allows for both numerical and non-numerical examinations and interpretations of observations, for the purpose of discovering underlying meanings and patterns of relationships in order to build theory in Africana Studies.

The combination of both these methodologies aid in the formulization of empirical generalizations, which in turn support the role of theory building in Africana Studies. Thus, since the discipline of Africana Studies is unlike any other discipline, it must fuse both qualitative and quantitative methodologies from an Afrocentric framework in order to build effective theories in Africana Studies.

Utilizing different paradigms and disciplinary modifications in the interaction of theory and practice, is the fourth and final function of theory building in Africana Studies. Paradigms are the framework for observations and understandings, which in turn shape both what we observe and how we understand those observations. In this regard, paradigms serve as a structuring of concepts, theories, and methodologies. According to Kershaw (1989), "paradigms in Black studies will determine the proper subject matter as well as the appropriate methodology" (46). Thus, when Africana Studies uses various disciplinary modifications in the interplay of theory and practice it should revolve around the understanding of Afrocentricity and utilizing an Afrocentric approach in creating theories for the study Black people. Moreover, Afrocentricity refers to the lived experiences of people of African descent as the center of analysis from an African standpoint. It emphasizes an analysis rooted in the historical reality of Black people. Constructing Afrocentric paradigms plays a vital role in the function of theory building in Africana Studies, in that they orient the researcher to approach the study of people of African decent from an African perspective.

Furthermore, the four above mentioned tenants combined with these four tenants foster the groundwork whereby the structure of Africana Studies can be laid (See the structure below).

TABLE 2.1 Africana Studies Structure-Sample Framework

AFRICANA STUDIES STRUCTURE (SAMPLE FRAMEWORK)

	SOCIOLOGICAL STUDIES	CULTURAL STUDIES	PSYCHOLOGICAL STUDIES	HISTORICAL STUDIES
Africa	African Sociological Studies	African Cultural Studies	African Psychological Studies	African Historical Studies
Asia	Asian Sociological Studies	Asian Cultural Studies	Asian Psychological Studies	Asian Historical Studies
Caribbean	Caribbean Sociological Studies	Caribbean Cultural Studies	Caribbean Psychological Studies	Caribbean Historical Studies
Europe	European Sociological Studies	European Cultural Studies	European Psychological Studies	European Historical Studies
France/Spain	French/Spanish Sociological Studies	French/Spanish Cultural Studies	French/Spanish Psychological Studies	French/Spanish Historical Studies
Latin America	Latin American Sociological Studies	Latin American Cultural Studies	Latin American Psychological Studies	Latin American Historical Studies
North America	North American Sociological Studies	North American Cultural Studies	North American Psychological Studies	North American Historical Studies
Russia	Russian Sociological Studies	Russian Cultural Studies	Russian Psychological Studies	Russian Historical Studies

Under the umbrella of Africana Studies fall three fields: African Studies, African American Studies, and African Caribbean Studies, this allows for a comparative analysis of African people around the globe. In addition to these three major fields, Africans in Asia and Europe will also be studied. The inter-sectionality of these three fields encompasses the study of the Africana family, the Africana male/female, and the Africna community. In terms of major areas of study, students will be afforded the opportunity to chose an area of concentration-such as Cultural Studies-along with a geographic location-such as one of the countries in Africa, say Nigeria-and combine the two within their major area of study. Take for example, a student in Africana Studies department who seeks to study Music in Nigeria. If that student chooses to focus on popular music such as Hip Life, he/she would be classified as a student in the department of Africana Studies majoring in Music with a concentration in African Cultural Studies (See sample outline above).

TABLE 2.2   Africana Studies Sample Student Profiles

AFRICANA STUDIES
STUDENT PROFILES BASED ON MAJORS AREAS OF STUDY AND CONCENTRATIONS

	STUDENT A/B	STUDENT C/D	STUDENT E/F	
Africa	African Musical Art forms	African Dance	African Religious Practices	Cultural Studies
North America	African American Political Practices	African American Social Movements	African American Educational Developments	Sociological Studies

CORE CURRICULUM (GRADUATE AND UNDERGRADUATE)

In 1981 the National Council for Black Studies (NCBS) published what was to be the standardized version of an Africana Studies core curriculum, unfortunately this has been loosely followed at best (Adams, 38). What follows is a synthesis of the curriculum at Temple University, Cornell University, Ohio State University and San Diego State University in an attempt to outline a core curriculum for Africana Studies.[4] For the discipline of Africana Studies, the core curriculum must be formalized to a periodically updated curriculum set forth by the National Council for Black Studies, because Africana Studies encompasses a vast group of scholars, foci should geographically as well as sectioned off by related subject matters. However, it should be noted that the curriculum outlined by NCBS should serve as a guide and should be more in tune with the nomenclature outlined above. For these reasons, undergraduate and graduate curricula should be grounded historically by the courses: Ancient Africa Civilization, Africana Research Methods, Introduction to General Africana Studies, and introductory courses in the student's subject focus and geographic area specialty. The suggested subject focuses currently presented by NCBS are Social Behavioral, Historical, and Cultural Studies (Adams 36). Additionally, undergraduate and graduate students will specialize further in an area of expertise, one of the geographic differentiations and one of the subject areas.

The following is a suggested core curriculum guide for Africana Studies:

CORE CURRICULUM

1. African Civilization: An exploration of the origins of Africana people.
2. African Religion: Examining indigenous African religions as well as Africana peoples participation in Christianity and Islam, etc.
3. African Aesthetics: An exploration of Africana aesthetics (dance, music, totems, etc).

4. Pro-Seminar in Africana Studies: Historical formation of Black Studies. In addition, for undergraduate students at least one of the following:
    i. Introduction to African Studies
    ii. Introduction to African American Studies
    iii. Introduction to African Caribbean Studies
5. African Literature: An exploration of written and oral forms of Africana people.
6. African Language Requirement: (Ibo, Kiswahili, Yoruba, etc.) Two Semesters.
7. The Africana Experience: Explores the shared historical and lived experiences of Africana people.
8. Applied Africana Studies: The implementation of Africana Studies into the community.
9. Africana Philosophical Thought: Examining Africana philosophical and political thought.
10. Research Methods: Studying and applying of Africana research methods (at minimum one year).
11. The Slavery Experience: Examines the enslavement of Africana people's historiographical experiences.
12. Race Theory and Social Thought: Systematic examination of the theories of non-Africana social thinkers.

It is important to note that there are no gender specific courses in this curriculum. It is imperative that Africana Studies scholars get away from the Eurocentric construct of gender and marry Africana Womanism to Africana Studies (Aldridge 1992). As Aldridge correctly states, "integrating Africana women into Africana Studies should not need to be a topic for dialogue. For the incorporation of Africana women should be as natural to the field as breathing is to living" (153). Therefore it is vital in each one of these courses that instructors take close care to deal with all aspects, perspectives and viewpoints and make sure to include the vast contributions of African children, women and men.

The completion of these lower division courses would constitute 36 credit hours (including two semesters for Research Methods and one language requirement). At the upper division level, students would be required to take an additional 10 courses in their area of concentration. Therefore a student would complete 60 credit hours and the general requirements of the university to receive a B.A. in Africana Studies.

The construction of a core curriculum for the discipline of Africana Studies must be ordered and arranged according to the principles of Maat: order, balance, harmony, justice, righteousness, truth, and reciprocity. In this sense the curriculum must start with introductory courses to the discipline and the fields within the discipline, then advance to intermediate and advanced levels. It must include courses in history, literature, science, math, psychology, sociology, political science, and economics; along with art, language, and Africana biology. A cluster of minor areas of study for both undergraduate and graduate students are as follows:

AREAS OF STUDY CONCENTRATION

- Africana Psychology
- Africana Political Science
- Africana Literature
- African Arts
- African Dance
- Africana Philosophy (sample courses below)
  - Introduction to Black Philosophy
  - Ancient Black Philosophy
  - Studies of Alain Locke
  - Studies of Angela Davis
  - Studies of W.E.B. Dubois
  - Contemporary Black Philosophers
  - Comparative Black Philosophers
- Topics in Africana Biology (sample courses next)
  - Ancient Black Biology
  - Race and Biology
  - Re-evaluation of the Racial Myths in Biology
  - Addressing Health in the Black Community
  - Africana Applied Biology
  - Exploring Biological Studies of People of African Descent
  - Africana Medicine
- Topics in Africana Mathematics
- Africana Economics
- Africana aspects in Anthropology
- Africana Humanities
- Africana Social Science
- Africana Linguistics
- Pan-Africanism
- Afrocentricity
- Africana Education
- Africana Public Health
- Africana Public Policy

FACULTY

Faculty formally or informally trained in Africana Studies must show scholarly expertise in some component of the multidisciplinary nature of Africana Studies and be Afrocentric in their approach. In reference to versatility Henderson suggests:

> The Department of African American [Africana] Studies must be truly interdisciplinary and its members must be meta-disciplinarians. They must be academically and intellectually able to range across a variety of traditional areas with facility and sophistication. (Henderson 1971, 16–17)

In this sense, professors in the discipline must be capable and willing to teach in a multidisciplinary capacity in that they must be intellectually equipped with the knowledge and skills to properly teach in their area of expertise. Such qualifications for faculty are present in those who have earned degrees in the discipline; therefore, faculty search committees should first seek the scholars who have graduated from the discipline since they have been trained in the discipline's multidisciplinary structure thereby making those graduates most qualified to govern the future of our discipline. Moreover, faculty should be informed scholars, thus insuring production of competent future scholars for the discipline.

Not only must the discipline of Africana Studies adhere to the principles of Maat, the faculty and staff must also adhere to these principles in order to properly administer course offerings. Accordingly, Dr. Nathaniel Norment Jr., in "Needed Research and Related Projects in African American Studies," "scholars must adhere to the highest possible ethical and technical standards that are reasonable and responsible in research, teaching and service.

They must rely on scientifically, professionally and culturally derived knowledge; act with honesty and integrity; and avoid untrue, deceptive or undocumented statements in under taking disciplinary-related functions or activities" (835). Furthermore, faculty members who adhere to these Afrocentric principles are qualified to teach and research within the discipline of Africana Studies.

CRITERIA FOR SCHOLARSHIP

Africana Studies is systematic and works within the discipline must use a systematic approach to derive conclusions about Africana phenomena. As such, NCBS should define and regulate the standards, thus creating a system of checks and balances for the disciplinary range and codes of the discourse. Also, as stated above, scholarship within Africana Studies must adhere to the principles of Maat. Upon review of scholars' works, their scholarship shall be permitted to be published in journals, and they will also be afforded the opportunity to publish introductory textbooks, as well as other texts. After meeting the criteria outlined throughout this blueprint scholars' research will receive the official seal of approval for Africana Studies. This seal will serve as a symbol to the global community that only the works that are branded with this seal truly embody that which is the proper study of people of African descent—and since NCBS will be defining and upholding the standards, and be mandated with the authority to grant the official seal of approval.

Additionally, in terms of funding, Africana Studies scholars shall be offered scholarships based on their level of education, their academic history, their work with the Africana community, and their overall growth and performance. Also, all scholars accepted into Ph.D. programs will be fully funded; and a select number of Masters students should also receive full funding.

RESEARCH AGENDA

With the nomenclature, department structure and core curriculum now set up the question of research agenda now comes to the forefront. As Adams has argued core curriculum alone does not constitute a fully developed discipline, teaching and research further reinforce it goals (Adams 1993, 38). Over time most scholars hired into Africana Studies departments should have a Ph.D. in the actual field. Understanding that the field is relatively new, the hiring and continued mentorship of our founders and elders is also critical. It is also crucial that the faculty in the discipline in general and specifically at individual universities be guided by the best interests of Africana people and do not allow individual differences to interfere with the duty to their students and community. The research agenda itself should be fully geared towards the accurate documentation of the Africana world experience, the destruction of white racism and to solving the problems of the Africana community (Hare 1969, 167). Again it is imperative that Africana Studies not just be corrective, but innovative and strongly tied to the Africana world community.

In order to expand and authenticate Africana Studies, research centers must be developed as a priority of the discipline. In these institutes and policy centers, scholars will produce "reliable knowledge that can guide and support our discipline" and "should link the academic and social communities" (Norment 837). Research in Africana Studies should be concerned with producing knowledge to transform the community as well as address the biases and inaccuracies in traditional Eurocentric paradigms. In addition, more Introductions to Africana Studies text should be produced through collective efforts on the part of Africana Studies scholars.

The discipline of Africana Studies is a multidisdiplinary field of study that allows for a wide range of research to be conducted in order to fully analyze knowledge about Africana people—this range would include historical, cultural, socio-behavioral, and political aspects of the global Africana community—create new Afrocentric methodologies and epistemologies, and stimulate consciousness throughout the Africana community. Consequently, this research must adhere to the previously mentioned Maatian principles.

COMMUNITY RESPONSIBILITY

Fundamentally, African Studies must keep the Africana community's needs present and the discipline's obligation to join in the liberation of the masses of Africana people. As Dr. Ama Mazama notes in *The Afrocentric Paradigm*, "Afrocentrism, as an ideology committed to the liberation of African people from the destructive grips of the West, involves the displacement of the European mode of thinking and being, and its replacement by concepts, attitudes, and behaviors in tune with African values and the ultimate interest of African people" (201). Thus, "Afrocentrism places Africa at the center of African people's world, while stressing all people's entitlement to practice and celebrate their own culture, as long as it does not interfere with the collective wellbeing" (Mazama, 6). In effect, Mazama is arguing that this paradigmatic approach does not seek to apply itself to world, but instead is the centrality of Africa for the African and therefore applied to the African for the total liberation of African peoples. In this regard, there should be no separation of the community as explained in the definition of Africana Studies; this allows for the foundational connectedness of the Africana academy and the global community. Specialist in every area of the field must play an essential role in the community of scholars and in the larger Africana community. To truly reflect the mission of the discipline, the Africana professional answers "the call to be the scholar/activist" that Gordon mentions (Gordon 1981, 232). Instead of seeking validation in the academy, the discipline should assert its pertinence and validity through work uplifting and positively shaping the Africana experience, and creating solutions, policies, and research focused on the Africana masses.

Hence, the academic realm is only one portion of the discipline of Africana Studies. The application of knowledge into practical social function is the other section of the discipline. The mission of Africana Studies is the liberation of both the mind and the community. As mentioned above, the mind receives it freedom through intellectual work, and the community is liberated through a conscious effort to decolonize the minds and to tackle the everyday realities of the Africana community.

CONCLUSION

The future of Africana Studies depends on the scholars in the discipline today. If stringent boundaries are not set, the discipline runs the risk of becoming integrated into some form of "multi-cultural" studies entity where the African experience cannot be accurately explored (Adams 1993, 49). The focus should be primarily on the global Africana experience and the similarities between Africans worldwide. Although it is important for all departments to adhere to a set core curriculum, there should definitely be room for individuality in the areas of concentration that the department decides upon. It is also significant that the community connection be upheld and that the research is conducted on the basis of improving the state of Africans in the world. If the discipline develops along these lines it should have a very prosperous future.

Uniting the discipline around Afrocentric perspectives will allow for more efficient intellectual exchange and thus increased results for the community. Additionally, an established blueprint, such as this, will leave the next generation of scholars a solid foundation from which to expand and shape Africana Studies to address future issues. With growing affronts to social sciences in academia, specifically ethnocentric fields, Africana Studies must solidify its place and purpose or face an eminent devaluation and relegation to novelty. Furthermore, the widespread crises in the Africana world require solutions from within; and indeed, the production of these solutions should be the primary objective of those who claim to be an Africana activist/scholar. Forming a unified community of well-educated and liberation-driven scholars remains a vital part of hope for the Africana world.

In short, I hope this blueprint serves a model and guide for the future of the discipline of Africana Studies, and for the total liberation of the global Africana community.

ENDNOTES

1. This article is an outgrowth of a class-AAS 8001 Proseminar-group project at Temple University in the Department of African American Studies. I would like to thank Richard Turner and Alhaji Conteh-group members, the entire Proseminar class, and Ibram Rogers and Karanja Keita Carroll for their support and critical feedback.
2. Here after Black, Afro-American, African American Studies and Pan African Studies will be referred to as Africana Studies.
3. Please see section on "Community Responsibility."
4. Note that these schools were chosen for their close compliance with NCBS standards, but due to the fact that the author chose to alter the NCBS standard of area of specialization, it may not meet NCBS standards.

REFERENCES

Abdul Alkalimat and Associates. "Toward a Paradigm of Unity in Black Studies." In Nathaniel Norment Jr. *The African American Studies Reader* 2nd ed. Carolina Academic Press; Durham, NC, 2007.

Adams, Russell L. "African-American Studies and the State of the Art." In Mario Azavedo (ed.), *Africana Studies: A Survey of Africa and the African Diaspora.* Durham, NC: Carolina Academic Press, 1993, pp. 25–49.

Aldridge, Delores P. "Womanist Issues in Black Studies: Towards Integrating Africana Womanism into Africana Studies" 1992. In *Africana Studies: A Disciplinary Quest for both Theory and Meth.* Ed. James L. Conyers, Jr. McFarland and Company, Inc., North Carolina, 1997, pp. 143-154.

Asante, Molefi Kete. "The Afrocentric Idea in Education." *The Journal of Negro Education.* 60 (1991). 170–179.

—*Afrocentricity*. Africa World Press, Inc. Trenton, NJ: 1988.

—"The Afrocentric Metatheory and Disciplinary Implications." *Afrocentric Scholar*: 1.1 (May 1992): 98–117.

Azibo, Daudi Ajani Ya. "Articulating the Distinction Between Black Studies and the Study of Blacks: The Fundamental Role of Culture and the African-Centered Worldview". *Afrocentric Scholar* 1.1 (May 1992) pp 64ff.

Clarke, John Henrik. "Africana Studies: A Decade of Change, Challenge, and Conflict." In Nathaniel Norment Jr. *The African American Studies Reader* 2nd ed. Carolina Academic Press; Durham, NC, 2007.

Daniel, Philip T.K. "Black Studies: Discipline or Field of Study?" *Western Journal of Black Studies*, v4 n3 pp. 195–200: Fall 1980.

Gordon, Vivian V. "The Coming of Age of Black Studies," *The Western Journal of Black Studies* 5:3 (1981): 231–236.

Hare, Nathan. "Questions and Answers About Black Studies." (1969). *In Modern Black Nationalism: From Marcus Garvey to Louis Farrakhan.* Ed William L. Van Deburg. New York University Press, NY 1997: 160–171.

Henderson, Donald. "What Direction Black Studies?" In *Topics in Afro-American Studies*, Henry J. Richards, ed. Buffalo: Black Academy Press, 1971.

Hine, Darlene Clark. "Black Studies: An Overview." In *Africana Studies: A Disciplinary Quest for Both Theory and Method.* McFarland and Company, Inc., North Carolina, 1997:7–75.

Karenga, Maulana. "Afrocentricity and Multicultural Education: Concept, Challenge, and Contribution." In Ama Mazama *The Afrocentric Paradigm*. Africa World Press, Inc., Trenton, 2003: 73-94.

Karenga, Maulana. *Introduction to Black Studies*. 3rd Ed. University of Sankore Press, Los Angeles: 2002.

Kershaw, Terry. "The Emerging Paradigm in Black Studies." *Western Journal of Black Studies*, v13 n1 pp.45-51: Spring 1989.

Marable, Manning. "Blueprint for Black Studies". In *Manning Marable Beyond Blacka and White: Transforming African American Politics*. Verso, 1995: 109-114.

Mazama, Ama. "An Afrocentric Approach to Language Planning." In *The Afrocentric Paradigm*. Africa World Press, Inc. Trenton, New Jersey: 2003. Pp. 201-214.

Outlaw, Lucius. "Africology: Normative Theory." In Outlaw, Lucius T. Jr. *On Race and Philosophy*. Routledge, New York 1996, pp. 97.

Nelson, William E. "Africology: Building an Academic Discipline" (1997). In James L. Conyers, Jr. (ed.), *Africana Studies: A Disciplinary Quest for Both Theory and Method*. McFarland and Company, Inc., North Carolina: 1997: 60-66.

Norment, Nathaniel Jr. "Needed Research and Related Projects in African American Studies." In *The African American Studies Reader* 2nd ed. Carolina Academic Press; Durham, NC, 2007.

Ray Jr., Leroi R. "Black Studies: A Discussion of Evaluation." *The Journal of Negro Education*, Vol. 45, No. 4 (Autumn, 1976), pp. 383-396.

Stewart, James B. "The Field and Function of Black Studies." In *The African American Studies Reader* 2nd ed. Carolina Academic Press; Durham, NC, 2007.

Turner, James E. "Africana Studies and Epistemology: A Discourse in the Sociology of Knowledge." In *The African American Studies Reader* 2nd ed. Carolina Academic Press; Durham, NC, 2007.

PART II

African Americans in America, 1619–1800

READING 3

Africans in the Americas

Anthony B. Pinn

IN THIS CHAPTER

With a definition of African American religion in place, this chapter discusses the slave trade and the establishment of the African presence in North America. It does so through a general presentation of what is commonly called the "Middle Passage," or the mass transportation by force of enslaved Africans into the Americas. It also presents information concerning the early formation of African American communities in the North American colonies and in the subsequent United States. Attention is given, as well, to the religious sensibilities brought by enslaved Africans to the Americas as a consequence of this forced movement. The chapter also addresses the ways these sensibilities were brought into contact with practices already present in North America.

MAIN TOPICS COVERED

- The context and reasons for the African slave trade
- The way the slave trade was conducted and the locations for it in the Americas
- The religious practices and beliefs Africans brought with them to the Americas

WHY AND HOW THE AFRICAN SLAVE TRADE BEGAN

There is some debate over when Africans made contact with the "New World" of the Americas—by "Americas" we mean North America, Central America, South America, and the Caribbean. Some scholars argue that long before Columbus (1492) and the development of the slave trade during the sixteenth century (and lasting for roughly 350 years), Africans had already made themselves known in the Americas—with evidence for this coming from artifacts like sculptures available in locations such as Mexico. While findings to support this claim are noteworthy, most agree that the largest movement of Africans into the Americas is the result of the slave trade that forced upward of 10 million Africans into locations such as North America, Brazil and the Caribbean to serve as labor for Europeans seeking wealth

Anthony B. Pinn, "Africans in the Americas," *Introducing African American Religion*, pp. 15-29. Copyright © 2013 by Taylor & Francis Group. Reprinted with permission.

through agriculture and natural resources. Although there are written records that note the presence of "black" slaves in Europe, as early as the 1300s, it is in 1444 that we find Africans transported by a Portuguese sea captain for the purpose of servitude to Portugal. Spain allowed the transporting of small numbers of enslaved Africans to colonies in the 1500s. Initially the movement of enslaved Africans during this early modern period was small. This would change as European countries recognized the great wealth that could be secured in the "New World." One thing was clear: they needed laborers to work the land and aid in the production of items such as cotton, sugar and the mining of gold in the Americas. Some attention was given to the use of Native Americans as slaves and indentured European workers who labored for a set number of years in exchange for land. Early in the development of the colonies, it was actually less expensive to use indentured servants than to purchase slaves. However, neither of these two sources of labor—Native Americans and Europeans—proved sufficient. For instance, Native Americans knew the land well and controlling them and keeping them on plantations was difficult. Furthermore, periodic wars between colonists and Native Americans only added to the difficulties. There was also a growing interest in religious work amongst them and those interested in saving their souls questioned use of them as slaves. (Africans in North America would come to have a complex relationship with Native Americans in that they at times provided aid, but it was not uncommon for Native Americans to also own slaves.) Indentured Europeans servants couldn't be physically distinguished from landowners, and this could make maintaining them as servants difficult. In addition, and more importantly, European servants did not come to the colonies in sufficient numbers to meet the labor need, and they only worked for a fixed (and often legally arranged) period of time. However, as the number of Africans brought to the Americas increased, the cost of securing them became more easily absorbed. Africans seemed a plentiful source of laborers—ones who had agricultural skills and could easily adapt to the environmental conditions found in South America, North America and the Caribbean. Nonetheless, it is important to note that not all of the first small groupings of Africans brought to North America were slaves for life. This arrangement changed as the need for and benefits associated with their labor became increasingly apparent. They were made slaves for life.

Religion provided an important rationale for this development. Readers should keep in mind that many Europeans who came to the colonies left their homes in search of religious freedom, believing that God has something special for them in the "New World." In this way, religious language and commitment provided a rationale for leaving their homeland, and for assuming the geography of the Americas was theirs to do with as they pleased. Religion, however, performed another task in that it also provided a rationale for their treatment of Native Americans and Africans. Europeans made selective use of the Bible and theological ideas about the nature of humanity to provide religious grounding for the socio-political and economic need for free labor. That is to say, religious ideas about original sin, the curse of Ham's son, and so on, provided talking points for justifying the enslavement of Africans.

The largest numbers of enslaved Africans were brought to places like Brazil and the Caribbean, but North America also received many shipments from West Africa. According to many historians, the first Africans brought to North America arrived in Virginia in roughly 1619. And although most of the enslaved Africans brought to North America worked on plantations in the Southern colonies, growing rice and tobacco, the Northern colonies in New England also received so many slaves that, by 1775, they accounted for something like 10 percent of the total population in the region. However, on most plantations the number of Africans remained relatively small, but the total number of enslaved Africans brought to North America would with time reach roughly 500,000. Those who did not secure enslaved Africans directly from slave traders tried to increase their labor force through the birth of babies by slaves.

ENSLAVED AFRICANS

- Enslaved Africans from West Africa were brought to the Americas as early as the 1500s.
- The first Africans brought to the North America colonies arrived around 1619.
- The total number of enslaved Africans brought to North America during the period of slavery was roughly 500,000.
- The slave trade lasted in the Americas for roughly 350 years.

There was a great deal of money to be made in the capture and transportation of enslaved Africans to labor markets in the Americas. It was a dangerous journey, but the financial rewards for those willing to undertake this travel were substantial. The trip involved equipped ships leaving Europe. Those Africans brought to the Americas were at times sold to slave traders as prisoners of tribal wars but traders, who moved into West Africa, stole the vast majority of Africans forced into the slave trade. These traders worked their way inland as far as they could and used their firepower to subdue and control Africans who were then made to travel by foot from where they were to the coast of countries like the Gold Coast. Those that did not die along the way were placed in dungeons in coastal fortresses until they could be loaded onto ships. There could be a substantial amount of time before a ship arrived, and so due to poor conditions, some Africans who survived the walk to the dungeons would die while awaiting transport. The men, women, and children who survived this ordeal were loaded onto ships and taken away. They resisted as best they could, and some jumped out of the smaller boats that took them to the ships.

> When our slaves were come to the seaside, our canoes were ready to carry them off to the longboat ... if the sea permitted, and she convey'd them aboard ship, where the men were all put in irons, two and two shackled together, to prevent their mutiny or swimming ashore. The negroes are so willful and loth to leave their own country, that they have often leap'd out of canoes, boat and ship, into the sea, and kept underwater till they were drowned, to avoid being taken up ...
>
> (Captain Thomas Phillips as quoted in Hugh Thomas,
> *The Slave Trade: The History of the Atlantic Slave Trade, 1440–1870*.
> New York: Simon & Schuster, 1997, 404)

Still others struggled in different ways once loaded on the ships and once the ships were away from land, but subduing their captors was difficult at best.

Abroad these vessels one typically found a captain in charge of the journey; a doctor to care for the crew and the enslaved Africans; a small group of people responsible for the business records; a crew to work the ship as well as weapons to protect the boat from attack. Ship crews experienced harsh conditions and physical challenges, but this is nothing in comparison to what Africans on the ships encountered. While we do not have direct records from enslaved Africans concerning the journey, we do have historical documents from Europeans that give us some sense of what was involved. The boats were neither designed nor arranged for the comfort of enslaved Africans in that the captain's financial profit was based on the number of slaves transported. The more loaded on each ship, the greater the chance for a big payday. Male slaves were loaded below deck and typically secured to prevent them from harming the crew, or destroying the ship in order to secure their freedom. Males were positioned head to foot in order to get as many on board as possible. Women and children posed less of a threat and so they had a greater range of motion. It was assumed women and children could be overpowered should they attempt anything, and they could be controlled using whips and other tools of punishment.

The air below deck quickly became hot and the floors became littered as Africans experienced seasickness, and developed other illnesses. Their clothes would be taken away to help lessen sickness and to make cleaning them easier. Periodically, men were brought above deck for exercise in order to make certain the captain could make good money through the arrival of somewhat healthy slaves. Those who did not voluntarily dance and move around when above deck would be beaten to get them "dancing," as the crew labeled it. And those who refused to eat were forced to eat in order to maintain their strength, size, and financial potential. This forced feeding was not without damage in that the devices used to hold open their mouths could easily break teeth and cause other problems. The crew kept a careful eye on the slaves to make certain healthy slaves did not jump overboard or throw their small

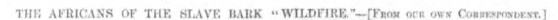

FIGURE 3.1 Africans on the deck of the slave bark Wildfire, brought into Key West on April 30, 1860. Courtesy of the Library of Congress, Prints and Photographs Division [LC-USZ62-41678].

children overboard in order to end their pain and free them from the pain and terror of the "Middle Passage." Those who became ill without perceived possibility of improvement or those who died on the ship would be thrown off the ship.

The journey could take a good deal of time. But, the enslaved Africans who survived the voyage were oiled down, dressed and prepared for the slave market where they would be sold to the highest bidder and transported to plantations to begin their slave labor. On plantations and other locations of slave labor, treatment varied. However, what remained consistent was the fact that enslaved Africans were not free like European colonists. The labor they provided was too important to have slaves questioning the justification of their enslavement, and planters certainly couldn't afford to have slaves seeking freedom. One way to avoid this was to deny them the Christian faith that might spark disruptions to the colonists' way of life.

SELLING SLAVES

The slaves are put in stalls like the pens used for cattle—a man and his wife with a child on each arm. And there's curtain, sometimes just a sheet over the front of the stall, so the bidders can't see the "stock" too soon ... Then, they pulls up the curtain, and the bidders is crowdin' around. Them in back can't see, so the overseer drives the slaves out to the platform ...

(Quoted in James Mellon, ed. *Bullwhip Days: The Slaves Remember*, New York: Weifenfeld & Nicholson, 1988, 291)

During these early years, the vast majority of colonists had limited access to religious communities; however, this was extended to enslaved Africans in that supporters of slavery assumed they did not have the intellectual ability—and perhaps not a soul—necessary to appreciate and accept the gospel message. It was recognized that part of what God wanted accomplished in the "New World" was the conversion of sinners to the Christian faith, but

FIGURE 3.2 Slave sale in Charleston, South Carolina. From a sketch by Eyre Crowe c.1856. Courtesy of the Library of Congress, Prints and Photographs Division [LC-USZ62-49867].

they weren't convinced this included their African slaves. Embedded in this thinking was a fear that efforts to convert Africans once they were in North America might also cause slaves to question their status and seek freedom.

ATTENTION TO THE SOULS OF AFRICANS

While some Africans in North America were free because they had either escaped slavery, purchased their freedom, or had been granted their freedom, the vast majority of Africans in North America were enslaved. Regarding those enslaved, there is a tension in the argument concerning religion: if enslaved Africans were actually meant for slavery based on the scriptures, how could efforts to address their spiritual needs alter this status? Other colonists believed that Africans might be inferior, but this did not rule out their ability to understand and embrace the Christian faith. In fact, they reasoned, colonists had an obligation to bring enslaved Africans into the Christian community. This work, however, had to take place based on an agreement that spiritual salvation did not alter the physical condition of enslaved Africans. They were to remain slaves. It was even hoped embrace of the Christian faith would make enslaved Africans better slaves because they would understand their servitude as part of God's will for their lives and the lives of their descendants.

Christians concerned with the spiritual health of enslaved Africans were not simply Protestants, but Roman Catholics as well. In fact, Roman Catholicism had a presence in the Americas as early as the 1500s, and this included Southern portions of North America where Catholic missionaries worked. More to the point, the first reported African Catholic in North America was Esteban in 1536.

> Catholic masters of course are taught that it is their duty to furnish their slaves with opportunities for being well instructed, and for practicing their religion.
>
> (Quoting William Henry Elder in Cyprian Davis, *The History of Black Catholics in the United States*, New York: Crossroads, 1991, 44)

The willingness of slaveholding Catholics to baptize slaves made their involvement in the Catholic Church more feasible, and this was particularly true in Florida. Even though this did not affect their legal status in most cases and did not involve complete involvement in the church, there is evidence of an African presence in Roman Catholicism. For example, before 1800 there was a reported 100 African Catholics in Pensacola, Florida, alone. The Catholic Church was also present in the middle colonies, in locations such as Maryland. However, travel was difficult and a limited number of priests to conduct missionary work made mass conversion of whites and Africans unthinkable. This, one might imagine, was not a situation only affecting the Catholic Church.

Although ministers were in short supply, some Protestant Christian churches put resources into the development of organizations with the purpose of taking the gospel to slaves—while mindful of the restrictions imposed by slave owners. Beginning with limited conversions in the 1660s, some effort was made to take Christianity to slaves throughout the colonies with enslaved Africans being told that a redeemed soul was worth the price of perpetual servitude. There, however, were limitations to the success of early efforts. For example, in the Northern colonies the emphasis on the Bible and reading the Bible made attention to slaves difficult in that slaves, by law, couldn't be taught to read or write. But Protestantism in those colonies assumed access to the written word. Generally speaking, the results of missionary efforts were only minimally successful because the need to safeguard slavery hampered the work of ministers.

Questions arose: how do preachers avoid harming the slave-based economy and still bring the gospel of salvation to slaves? Did the first concern contradict the second concern? In the South, efforts were also made on a limited scale to convert enslaved Africans, but these activities took place under the watchful eye of plantation owners and their staff who made certain the preachers and missionaries didn't say anything that might result in rebellion on the part of slaves. The intimate relationship between Christian churches and the system of slavery was often portrayed in graphic ways through the presence of Christian ministers who were also slaveholders. Some slave owners were willing to open their plantations to missionaries as long as their activities did not challenge their authority and the religious instruction did not involve teaching slaves to read or write. And all efforts to Christianize the slaves had to take place on the only day they weren't in the fields—Sunday. However, the fact that Sunday was their only day to take care of their own needs often made religious services that simply celebrated their enslavement less than appealing to the enslaved.

Efforts to convert slaves simply limped along without much success until there was a general change in the attitude of colonists toward their own spiritual needs. This came in the 1730s when services highlighted fiery preaching and energetically expressed concern for the saving of souls. This period, called the Great Awakening, brought people back to a strong sense of the need for personal salvation. Through the preaching of ministers such as George Whitefield (1714–1770) there was expressed an equal excitement for converting whites and Africans, and the churches felt that God could make use of anyone in this ministry who was willing to serve God. As a consequence, Baptist and Methodist churches allowed enslaved Africans (and free Africans) to preach, and on some occasions they preached to mixed audiences of whites and Africans. Sermons were passionate and straightforward in their message as black and white preachers told audiences that salvation was answer to all human problems. Whitefield and those like him captured the imagination of huge crowds—preaching the importance of salvation and the joy it provided. This was matched by warnings to those rejecting the Christian faith that they would experience the pain of hell. The passion and energy of these preachers, typically called evangelists because of their effort to convert people to Christ through energetic preaching about personal salvation, was matched by an emotional response from their listeners. The numbers of Africans in Christian churches was once small, but it exploded during the Great Awakening, with tens of thousands joining Methodist and Baptist churches. While slavery continued, within these churches there was shared worship.

The success of the Great Awakening sparked a second Great Awakening in the early 1800s, in the middle of the country, marked by large revival services. These services, led by preachers such as Charles G. Finney (1792–1875), took place over the course of days and drew those seeking salvation. The second awakening had the same energy, the same demand for surrender to God, and access to pulpits for enslaved Africans who felt called to preach. This only served to further increase the number of enslaved and free Africans involved in Christian ministry as well as the number who made their home the churches offering these services. The Great Awakenings brought enslaved Africans and free Africans (those who were not slaves) into churches but conversion did not mean social or political equality. Africans remained subject to abuse and discrimination in that they remained a necessary source of free labor.

CONVERTING ENSLAVED AFRICANS

- The First Great Awakening, beginning in the 1730s, brought large numbers of enslaved Africans into the Methodist and Baptist churches.
- The Second Great Awakening was also composed of revivals and energetic camp meetings that brought colonists and Africans to the Christian faith, but this one in the 1800s took place further south.

These two Great Awakenings worked so well because the camp meetings and revivals allowed missionaries and evangelists to travel with fewer restrictions than pastors would have. It is also believed by many scholars that Methodist and Baptist practices appealed to enslaved Africans because they served as a reminder of practices going back to Africa. For example, many African religious practices involved the importance of water and water spirits. And baptism within Baptist and Methodist churches placed a similar importance on water and spiritual change resulting from being in the water. In addition, being filled with the Holy Spirit within these churches may have reminded some Africans of spirit possession they had encountered in Africa. These are just two of the reasons for the appeal of Baptist and Methodist forms of Christianity in particular. However, this argument also points to the presence of other religious traditions within the newly forming African communities in the North American colonies and later within the growing United States. It is reasonable to believe some Africans, rather than embrace practices and a religious faith offered by colonists, simply continued to practice their original religious traditions as best they could under the conditions of life in North America. Put another way, to the extent Christianity helped Africans in North America make sense of their new world, and develop meaningful life that provided answers to the major questions of life, they embraced the tradition. But this was not the case for all, and those Africans for whom Christianity did not address their concerns embraced other practices and beliefs.

WHAT AFRICANS BROUGHT WITH THEM

By the time Africans embraced Christianity in significant numbers during the first Great Awakening, they had been in North America for almost 100 years. We should not believe that Africans were simply waiting around for their captors to provide them with religious rituals and beliefs. These were people who had come from areas with rich and longstanding religious systems and practices, and they did not forget all they knew of these systems just because they were no longer in Africa. Memory and even limited opportunities to practice based on these memories kept traditions beyond Christianity alive.

The Middle Passage was harsh, and no real attention was given to making certain that Africans from particular cultural groups were kept together, and the ability to maintain their religious practices developed in Africa was hard. However, there is no reason to believe that the trauma of being transported to a new land, where the language is unknown and the social arrangements are foreign, was enough to wipe out *all* practices and beliefs associated with their homes in Africa. Certain things were maintained—words from their languages, artistic practices, social norms, and some elements of their religious traditions. Some religious practices and beliefs were maintained during the period of slavery because they continued to be useful and the elements necessary to keep them in place were available around plantations. For instance, in the French Quarter of New Orleans in what was known as Congo Square, Africans both free and enslaved were allowed to gather, dance, and sing. During these gatherings it was not uncommon for voodoo practices to take place as the centerpiece of the community activities, with whites present. Drumming and songs spoke to the presence of African gods. In the bayous and swamps even more of these activities took place, organized rituals conducted by voodoo priestess and priests. A creative blending of their African religious heritage and the Catholicism encountered in the colonies allowed for the growth of a rich and complex religious landscape composed of a growing African Christian presence as well as the continuation of African traditional practices from West Africa. In addition to ceremonies, small bags of dirt from the cemetery called gris-gris were believed to have particular powers for protection and good luck, and would be carried by Africans for such purposes. These bags and other charms are signs of the existence in North America of West African religious practices. Furthermore, the practice of voodoo in the United States—as attested to by these bags and ceremonies—only intensified when the revolution in Haiti freeing the island from French rule brought

> By means of song, news of the meeting of a voodoo society would be carried from one end of the city [New Orleans] to another and upon the appointed night Negro men and women would slip from their beds before midnight and would assemble for their ceremonies.
>
> (Quoted in Robert Tallant. *Voodoo In New Orleans*, New York: Collier Books, 1946; Macmillan, 1971, 35)

slaveholders and their slaves to the United States. Of course, they brought with them their religious practices and blended with those already in place.

Even efforts to end the practice of voodoo served only to force Africans to hide their practices, but attention to voodoo gods and spirits continued. In addition, with time, some of the particular elements of voodoo were lost, but specialists with recognized abilities would still be sought out by Africans in North America to provide rituals or powerful items that could be used to change their circumstances or secure something they really wanted—such as avoidance of harm by slave holders or the overseers who controlled the plantations on a day-to-day basis.

Outside Louisiana in other Southern locations such as North and South Carolina and Georgia, Africans maintained traditional practices in a somewhat looser manner through systems of magic and conjure that we often call hoodoo, root work, or simply conjure. The signs of these practices could be detected in conversation, and were also represented in items found in the possession of Africans. At times, however, practices could be maintained without a great deal of interference. In particular, the islands off the coast of the Carolinas were the home to slaves but there was a limited white presence that made them ideal locations for the preservation of African practices. Africans were able to conduct themselves in accordance with the beliefs and rituals that had marked life in Africa and they could do this

SIGNS OF MORE THAN JUST CHRISTIANITY

- Similar rituals involving water and possession by God were similar to activities in Africa and this made Methodist and Baptist churches somewhat appealing, but this also pointed to the continued presence of African religious practices despite efforts to destroy them.
- Practices similar to Vodou in West Africa are present in North America in the form of voodoo, hoodoo, conjure and root work
- Roman Catholicism's attention to saints provided a way for Africans to maintain traditions brought from Africa without slaveholders being fully aware of what they were doing.

without interference from whites that might find these African retentions a threat to the slave system and the dominance of white slave owners.

The African gods survived the Middle Passage and found new homes in the Americas, including North America, where Africans continued their devotion, rituals, and requests to the cosmic forces they knew in Africa. But in addition to this, some enslaved and free Africans maintained another tradition brought with them from Africa. Islam had been an important religious tradition on the continent of Africa, moving from East Africa to West Africa long before the slave trade began. By the time ships loaded Africans to take them to the Americas, Islam was firmly established and it was the tradition of many on those ships. While not all of these African Muslims would have landed in North America, there is evidence that some of them did and they maintained as best they could the elements of their faith. The evidence of their presence isn't as readily available as it is for Christianity within African communities in North America, but there are signs nonetheless. For example, there were advertisements for the capture of runaway slaves that described them using Islamic names. Muslims we do know about, such as Umar Ibn Said (1770–1864) from North Carolina provided a sense of the religious practices maintained in North America.

> When I came to the Christian country, my religion was the religion of Mohammed, the Apostle of God—may God have mercy upon him and give him peace.
>
> Quoted from Umar Ibn Said's autobiography

There are five fundamental elements of Islam, referred to as the five pillars of Islam— (1) affirmation that there is only one God, Allah; (2) prayer five times each day; (3) giving of alms; (4) fasting during Ramadan; (5) pilgrimage to Mecca. Clearly, some of these could not be done because of the restrictions of slavery, but others including prayer, feast days associated with the religion, and dietary restrictions were observed.

Other Africans found all forms of theism—Christianity, Islam and African traditions— problematic. For them only attention to their own humanity without reliance on God or gods would work. Evidence for this type of thinking is found in the cultural production of the early period of slavery in things such as work songs, folktales, and the blues that critique reliance on the supernatural and instead celebrate human creativity and ingenuity. This approach to life represents the early signs of what we have come to call African American humanism.

> I prayed for twenty years but received no answer until I prayed with my legs.
>
> Frederick Douglass, abolitionist, political leader, and writer

THE RELIGIOUS LANDSCAPE

Prior to the nineteenth century, Africans both free and enslaved developed a rich and complex religious life. It was composed of humanism, Christianity, Islam, and a host of African-based traditions all meant to provide life meaning within a troubled and troubling world. Africans brought many of these traditions with them to North America and they were exposed to others once enslaved. In both cases, they made these traditions work for them; they made these practices their own and blended them in ways meant to meet their particular needs and address their concerns. It was easier for African-born slaves, who did not know English but communicated in indigenous African languages, to maintain African practices and pass elements of these traditions to their children. However, North American-born slaves, who spoke English and were familiar with the North American context, were further removed from African practices. When they maintained them, they did so in ways that reflected their new location. In all cases, however, they thought about religion in light of their needs and tried to shape practices and beliefs so as to fit their circumstances. Some of this involved holding onto what they could remember and maintain of their African home, but it also involved a creative manipulation of what they discovered in their new land. We see some of this developing during the 1600s and 1700s, but it is within the 1800s—the nineteenth century—that the practice of these traditions really grows amongst Africans and takes on unique and creative aspects and dimensions. Efforts to control how, where, and when Africans practiced their various faiths failed. And they failed in large part as Africans shaped their own versions of religion and used it as an increasingly visible tool for struggle against oppression. In the next chapter, we explore some of the major episodes in this on-going development of what it means to be African American and religious in North America, and we do so through attention to the more secret activities of Africans within the context of what we call hush arbor meetings and the Invisible Institution.

KEY POINTS YOU NEED TO KNOW

- Both Catholics and Protestants participated in efforts to Christianize enslaved Africans.
- Successful Christianizing of Africans takes place in large part because of two religious Great Awakenings.
- African gods were brought to the Americas, and there are reports concerning voodoo in North America that date back to the 1700s.
- Africans brought Islam to North America, and there are clear indicators of its presence.

- Religious conversion did not affect the status of Africans because they remained slaves.
- Some Africans rejected theism altogether and instead relied on an approach to life centered on human creativity and ingenuity.
- Diversity defines the religious landscape of African life prior to the nineteenth century.

DISCUSSION QUESTIONS

1. Why did some slaveholders oppose efforts to convert Africans to Christianity?
2. What were the reasons provided by those who were interested in missionary work amongst enslaved Africans?
3. Why did Methodist and Baptist churches appeal to Africans?
4. What are some of the signs of Islam's presence in North America?
5. What were some of the early practices in North America related to African gods?

FURTHER READING

Allen, Norm Jr. *African American Humanism: An Anthology*. Buffalo, NY: Prometheus Books, 1991.

Austin, Allan D. *African Muslims in Antebellum America: Transatlantic Stories and Spiritual Struggles*. New York: Routledge, 1997.

Balmer, Randall and Lauren Winner. *Protestantism in America*. New York: Columbia University Press, 2002.

Davis, Cyprian. *The History of Black Catholics in the United States*. New York: Crossroads, 1991.

Holloway, Joseph E., ed. *Africanisms in American Culture*. Bloomington, IN: Indiana University Press, 1990.

Pitts, Walter F. *Old Ship of Zion: The Afro-Baptist Ritual in the African Diaspora*. New York: Oxford University Press, 1993.

Tallant, Robert. *Voodoo in New Orleans*. New York: Collier Books, 1946; Macmillan, 1971.

Turner, Richard. *Islam in the African-American Experience*. Bloomington, IN: Indiana University Press, 1997.

READING 4

Why an Atlantic Slave Trade?

Claudius Fergus

ABSTRACT

The origin of transatlantic trafficking in African peoples has its antecedents in the Eastern Atlantic, and its tie-ins with the older, trans-Saharan trade and sugar industries in the Mediterranean and Southern Iberia. The Middle Passage and the so-called triangular trade were simply continuations of this earlier and continuing traffic and its related commercial activities. The discourse raises issues relating to developments in the Western Atlantic prior to the traditional date (1441) for the commencement of this human trafficking. Several key issues are addressed relating to the origin of the trade, including the role of the Catholic Church, the targeting of Africans south of the Sahara, the capitalist ethic, and the extent that the sugar industry featured in the evolution of the traffic and its extension the New World.

INTRODUCTION

The Atlantic trade in enslaved Africans remains a sensitive subject for several reasons, including issues of race, morality, ethics, identity, underdevelopment and reparations. Europeans defended the trade mainly for its role in providing renewable plantation labour and stimulating economic growth, best manifested in the phenomenal expansion of the mercantile marine. By the eighteenth century, the trade had become the "most advantageous and most abundant source of wealth" to participating European nations;[1] its defenders also purported that the trade was indispensable as a nursery for seamen in imperial navies. These considerations do not explain the origins of the trade, but they do help to account for its longevity and resilience against the forces of abolition.

The Atlantic trade in enslaved Africans was not always a Middle-Passage affair. What became the transatlantic trade was a later expression of a slowly evolving commercial and colonizing enterprise within the Eastern Atlantic, the embryo of an Atlantic world order

Claudius Fergus, "Why an Atlantic Slave Trade?" *The Journal of Caribbean History*, vol. 42, no. 1, pp. 1-21. Copyright © 2008 by The University of the West Indies Press. Reprinted with permission. Provided by ProQuest LLC. All rights reserved.

in which slave trading became one of the defining features. The question "Why an Atlantic Slave Trade?" speaks to the entire period of the trade, not its transatlantic dimension alone. In order to account for the origins and persistence of the trade, it is necessary first to account for its Eastern Atlantic expression. The discourse explores the critical role of slavery in this early commercial system as well as the geo-political and ideological underpinnings that made Africa the ideal source of slave labour for four centuries.

For the first six decades, trafficking in enslaved Africans was restricted to a north-south axis, serving the economies of Southern Iberia, the Canary Islands, Madeira, the Cape Verde Islands, Príncipe, São Tomé and the Gold Coast (modern Ghana). Captives were also sent as diplomatic gifts from African rulers to potentates in Europe. The trade in enslaved Africans had already extended through 4,000 miles of coastline by the end of the fifteenth century, encompassing peoples from Senegambia to Angola and increasingly extending its reach into the heartland of the continent. The vast majority of Africans sold into the Atlantic trade originated in lands bordering the coasts and up to some 800 miles inland; a trickle zone extended another 200 miles deeper into the heartland of the continent, with a small percentage originating in Eastern Africa. The four hundred years of slaving activities contributed the largest forced inter-continental labour migration in history.[2] Arguably, the region was less systematically disrupted by the trans-Saharan and Indian Ocean slave trades which, nonetheless, added considerably to the loss of human capital from the recruitment zone.

Explanations for the origins of the trade are seldom satisfactory. According to Patrick Manning, "Slavery caused the slave trade; just as relentlessly as the slave trade brought new slavery."[3] To some extent, this tantalizingly simple construction is sound, because it locates colonial slavery in the Americas within a world-slavery system, particularly as it relates to the African-European experience. Although Manning identified the several "pull" factors for African labour in the Americas, he did not actually examine the reasons for slavery. Whatever its rationale in Europe and the Mediterranean, the institution needed a compelling *quid pro quo* to bridge the gap between Old and New Worlds. The dynamic was the immense profits from mining and plantation agriculture, especially sugar, its signature expression.

Europeans were first introduced to the sugar-slavery nexus during their "Crusades" in Palestine (1095–1291 CE) whence the industry spread to Cyprus, Iberia and the Eastern Atlantic colonies extending from the Azores in the north to São Tomé in the south, and on to the Caribbean and Brazil soon after first European contacts. Inexorably, slavery followed the migration of the industry. In explaining the fateful ties that bound slavery to sugar, Philip Curtin argued that slavery gave early plantation owners control over labour that was "rare for medieval agriculture'; accordingly, "No ordinary agricultural population was dense enough to provide such a concentration of manpower, which meant that massive labor migration was always called for whenever the sugar industry was introduced. In the Mediterranean, the institution for forced labor migration in the Middle Ages was slavery."[4]

To simplify and extend Curtin's analogy, it was sugar that ultimately caused the slave trade. However, Mediterranean plantation slavery did not always involve Africans, or

Africans alone; or, for that matter, sugar alone. Therefore, any meaningful explanation for the Atlantic slave trade must include an explanation for the almost complete exclusivity of African enslavement in the Eastern Atlantic, the Caribbean and continental America, especially against a rising capitalist, Atlantic world order. The onset of European maritime imperialism in the fifteenth century marked the formal end of feudalism and the dawn of modern capitalism. Labour in Europe was still being brutalized but not enslaved. Slavery was an anachronism of capitalist economy, as Baron de Montesquieu and Adam Smith cogently argued. Anachronism or not, the persistence with African enslavement demanded the continuance of slave trading. It is in this context that Manning is correct; his interpretation brings us to the crux of the abolition theme of which the present discourse is a part: "An Outrage to Humanity". Europe had to invent myriad justifications for African enslavement, including the enslavement of African Christians from Spain and the kingdom of Kongo, the earliest victims of the Middle Passage. The church also invented new doctrines to keep Christian Africans in slavery, contrary to principles applied to Christians in the rest of the Old World. These aberrations qualify the slave trade and slavery as crimes against humanity, and an outrage that is still awaiting redress and reparations.

THE EASTERN ATLANTIC

Conventional thinking associates the Portuguese with the launch of the Atlantic slave trade, but this view is somewhat inaccurate. As with most historical phenomena, the Atlantic slave trade from mainland Africa sprang from related antecedents. According to David Birmingham, Castilians were buying enslaved persons from the Canary Islands as early as 1382, thirty-three years before the first Portuguese landed in Ceuta, and almost sixty years prior to the conventional date for the launch of the Atlantic slave trade.[5] The early slave trade was a spin-off from the new mercantile capitalism of the Mediterranean under the sway of Genoese, Venetians and Florentines. As expatriates in Seville, the Genoese wielded considerable influence in the emerging Atlantic economy. They were the principal financiers of Iberian explorers and colonizers; they built the new sugar mills and remained indispensable as the principal technicians for their operations.[6] Not surprisingly, they were key stakeholders in the first *asiento,* or royal permit, that launched the slave trade directly from Africa to the Spanish Caribbean. Thus, they are key players in explaining the emergence of the slave trade into a major branch of Atlantic commerce.

Another antecedent to the Atlantic trade in enslaved Africans was the trans-Saharan gold-and-slave trade. Contrary to conventional scholarship, the Portuguese conquest of Ceuta was not the first phase in a longterm agenda to reach India, but rather the first attempt to cut into the supply of gold and enslaved persons from West Africa. Portuguese occupation of Ceuta was strategic: to establish a bridgehead in North Africa from which to acquire intelligence on West African gold which had long financed Arab-Berber imperialism in the Mediterranean world and beyond. The major towns of the Maghrib (Western North Africa) were also the northern markets for enslaved persons exported from the market towns and cities of the Western Sudan.

In order to meet the cost of occupation, the Ceuta conquerors engaged in slave raiding mainly to supply the growing demand for labour in Southern Portugal. However, the profits from this activity were inadequate to satisfy imperial ambitions or justify continuing occupation. Co-authors James Lockhart and Stuart Schwartz contend that "once the Portuguese discovered that Ceuta did not fulfil their needs, they began to push down the west coast of Africa toward the sources of gold, ivory, and slaves—the traditional staples of the trans-Saharan trade".[7] In refuting the India thesis, they conclude: "Instead, it appears that, even before an interest in spices developed, Africa represented an attraction in itself."[8] Other historians also support this view. It is true that Europe was being drained of bullion to pay for Ottoman and Oriental products, but direct access to tea and spices in the Far East could not provide sufficient political or economic reasons for the vast expenditure necessary to reach India—especially in light of the maritime geography of Atlantic Africa, Access to Africa's gold mines might even the balance of trade between Christian Europe and the Muslim Mediterranean, or even tilt it in favour of the former. Slave raiding and trading in the Atlantic continued as a sideline to finance maritime exploration in search of the African "El Dorado."

It was not by chance that Prince Henry "The Navigator" took on the role of patron of Portuguese exploration. The prince was among the landing party that captured Ceuta, returning, at least on one other occasion, to Morocco. Moreover, Henry originated from the Algarve sugar belt in Southern Portugal, which had a long association with sugar and slavery.[9] Therefore, the Atlantic slave trade must be seen as an expansion of the supply vent for plantation labour in the Algarve and a direct extension of the Western Saharan slave-and-gold trading nexus, the latter predating Portuguese contact by several centuries.

As with most revolutionary transformations in world history, technology played a key role in the development of the Atlantic slave trade. For several decades after the failure of Ceuta, Portuguese expansion down Africa's Atlantic seaboard, most notably beyond Cape Bojador, was circumscribed by maritime geography and primitive technology. Breakthroughs came slowly from new inventions, mainly by Genoese, and Arabs who had long mastered the more dangerous currents of the Indian Ocean. Prior to the adoption of the Arab lateen sail, no Portuguese ship could successfully venture beyond Cape Bojador. This breakthrough in maritime technology virtually launched the Atlantic slave trade, as we know it. In that respect, 1441 was a fateful year for Africa; in retrospect, it was the beginning of a long process leading to European partitioning and colonization.

The first decade of the slave trade on the Atlantic seaboard of mainland Africa was based exclusively on raiding. This was followed by the era of commercial slave trading during which raiding continued. However short it lasted, the raiding phase is important to an understanding of many issues in which the study of the trade is still embroiled, especially the nature of European interests and involvement in it. Another issue is the early endorsement by Christian Europe, which provided the morality and conscience to participants and defenders of the trade and enslavement of Africans. The first slave raiders were Portuguese, Genoese, Florentine and Jewish. The names Antam Gonçalvez and Nuño Tristão are to the Atlantic slave trade what Christopher Columbus and Hernando Cortes are to the colonization of the Americas. Gonçalvez captured the first continentals who were taken into slavery, allegedly as a token of appreciation to Prince Henry; he personally recorded the raid. Gonçalvez and a select member of his crew had ventured inland for some "three leagues" (over twenty-five kilometres). On their way back to the coast they sighted their first prey, a "Moor", who fought until wounded. Shortly afterward, the Portuguese raiders seized their second victim, "a Black Mooress"; she was completely defenceless. Gonçalvez was not alone on the African coast or singular in his mission. He was soon joined by his countryman, "a youthful knight" named Tristão. Without provocation, they ambushed two groups of Africans asleep in their camps, killing some and taking twelve prisoners to be sold in Lisbon.[10] Thus, the Atlantic slave trade was officially launched—the beginning of 400 years of predation, internecine warfare and pillage to provide labour in a growing global capitalist economy.

Both Gonçalvez and Tristão returned to Africa on more slave-raiding ventures. On Gonçalvez's first return, he ransomed two of the original twelve captives for ten others. Tristão pushed further south and captured a group of twenty-nine men and women.[11] These successes sealed the fate of all Africans who would later fall victim to the insatiable European demand for African labour. They also set the pattern for an "Ethiopian" (a pre–slave trade label for "black African") preference and the general devaluation of the humanity of peoples south of the Sahara: the literature on this subject clearly states that one of the ransomed captives referred to above was of "fair" skin, not "Negro", and that an agreement was struck to ransom him for "five or six Black Moors".[12]

Another factor in launching the Atlantic slave trade soon emerged: the cupidity of mercantile capitalists. Slave raiding immediately proved a highly profitable business in its own right. Tristão's second African expedition triggered a wave of speculation in the profitability of kidnapping defenceless Africans. Speculators eagerly financed large expeditions to the continent. In the first of such ventures, six ships were outfitted to engage in what one historian unwittingly describes as a "small-scale war" on the Mauritanian coast, capturing 165 men, women and children, and killing some in the process.[13] The raiders went on to drop anchor at other places, capturing the most vulnerable: women and children. The general pattern of future raiders was disembarkation at night and surprise attacks on sleeping villages of mainly fisher folk along the coastline.[14] By the eighteenth century, the Atlantic slave trade would become one of the most profitable investments in western capitalism.

The single greatest economic factor in the early development of the Atlantic slave trade was sugar. The demand for slave labour grew in direct proportion to the spread of the industry in the Eastern Atlantic islands and the New World. Early success at exploration had led to colonization of Madeira and the establishment of a wheat industry by the 1420s, employing labour from Portugal. From the 1450s, the changeover from wheat to sugar created new demands for labour which could no longer be satisfied from Iberia. In the early stages of the sugar industry, raiding outfits scoured the Canary Islands, lying less than 100 kilometres off the coast of Southern Morocco.[15] As sugar expanded in Madeira, and the Canaries themselves became sugar colonies, it was inevitable that mainland Africa would become the principal target of Portuguese slave raiders.

During the 1450s, new developments emerged to restructure and expand the slave trade. Whereas the coast of Mauritania was arid and sparsely populated, the Senegambian region was more humid and densely populated with centrally governed polities. As Per Hernæs asserts, "The Europeans soon realised that they were up against African polities or local states strong enough to defend themselves."[16] The encounter compelled the Portuguese to adjust to a more orthodox pattern of "trading", more closely approximating the much older networks across the Sahara and actually becoming an appendage of that system. The Portuguese began to supply local merchants with goods traditionally obtained from North Africa, including horses, textiles and other luxury merchandise; these were re-bartered for captives held by chiefs in what became known as Upper Guinea.[17]

Other factors influencing the shift away from Portuguese raiding included the epidemiology and geography of the region beyond Senegambia. The new environment was rife with malaria and yellow fever. Whereas European contact with the New World brought in its wake a demographic disaster for the indigenous peoples, contact with tropical Africa was more likely to lead to European than African fatalities. Traders were safer spending most of their time on board ship than raiding for captives. The geo-politics of the region also demanded change: the hinterland of Upper Guinea was the principal gold-producing region for the trans-Saharan trade. The need to organize labour and defence demanded more complex social structures. However, centralized states with unassimilated tributary appendages or multiple independent polities comprising independent villages and chieftaincies were all vulnerable to divide-and-dominate strategies that would guarantee a steady flow of captives for European merchants.

The gold and slave trades became inextricably intertwined for both Africans and Portuguese even before their arrival in the "Gold Coast". The latter would purchase enslaved Africans on the mainland to grow cotton and to set up and operate African-styled looms in the Cape Verde Islands. These "traditional" African textiles were then bartered for gold and more enslaved persons from local slave traders.[18] A little known fact is that the Portuguese also sold enslaved Africans to other Africans. From the 1470s, the Portuguese transported captives from as far east as Benin City (in modern-day Nigeria) in order to supply Akan-speaking gold miners around the site of the soon-to-be constructed fortress, São Jorge da Mina (Elmina Castle) on the Gold Coast.[19] By the late fifteenth century, Akan miners were buying enslaved persons originating from as far as the kingdom of Kongo, a traffic accounting for as many as one thousand annually in peak years. The Akan were using slave labour for open-pit mining, an operation considered too dangerous for their own people; other enslaved persons were kept for porterage or used as labourers in São Jorge da Mina.[20]

Elmina castle
(http://www.ship-wrecks.co.uk/images/elmina8.jpg)

As the Portuguese crossed the Equator, the movement of enslaved Africans into the East Atlantic economies increased substantially. Again, the most important dynamic was sugar, freshly transplanted in the new colony of São Tomé, some 250 kilometres off the coast of Gabon. The role that Barbados would play in the seventeenth century was the same as that of São Tomé in the sixteenth century: providing an ideal landscape for a sugar revolution and the construction of a model plantation complex based on slavery. The major source of servile labour to São Tomé was the kingdom of Kongo, with a later shift to Angola. In Kongo, the Portuguese used conversion to Christianity as a tool to expand the slave trade. Beginning with Afonso I, the kings of Kongo intensified their conflicts with their neighbours, thus producing a steady supply of captives to Portuguese traders. São Tomé became both a market and *entrepôt* for enslaved Africans to other parts of the Eastern Atlantic, including the Azores, Madeira, the gold-producing states of Ghana, and the Portuguese forts strung along the coasts.

THE EARLY TRANSATLANTIC OR MIDDLE PASSAGE

According to David Brion Davis, slavery was not part of Europe's original plan of colonization in the New World.[21] However, the historical signposts planted in the Mediterranean, Iberia and the Atlantic islands definitely indicated that such would be the status of labour and the fate of Africans. The progression in slave trading from Eastern Atlantic to Western Atlantic coincided with the voyages of Christopher Columbus under the patronage of the Spanish Crown. Columbus was a product of the Eastern Atlantic slave trade, sugar

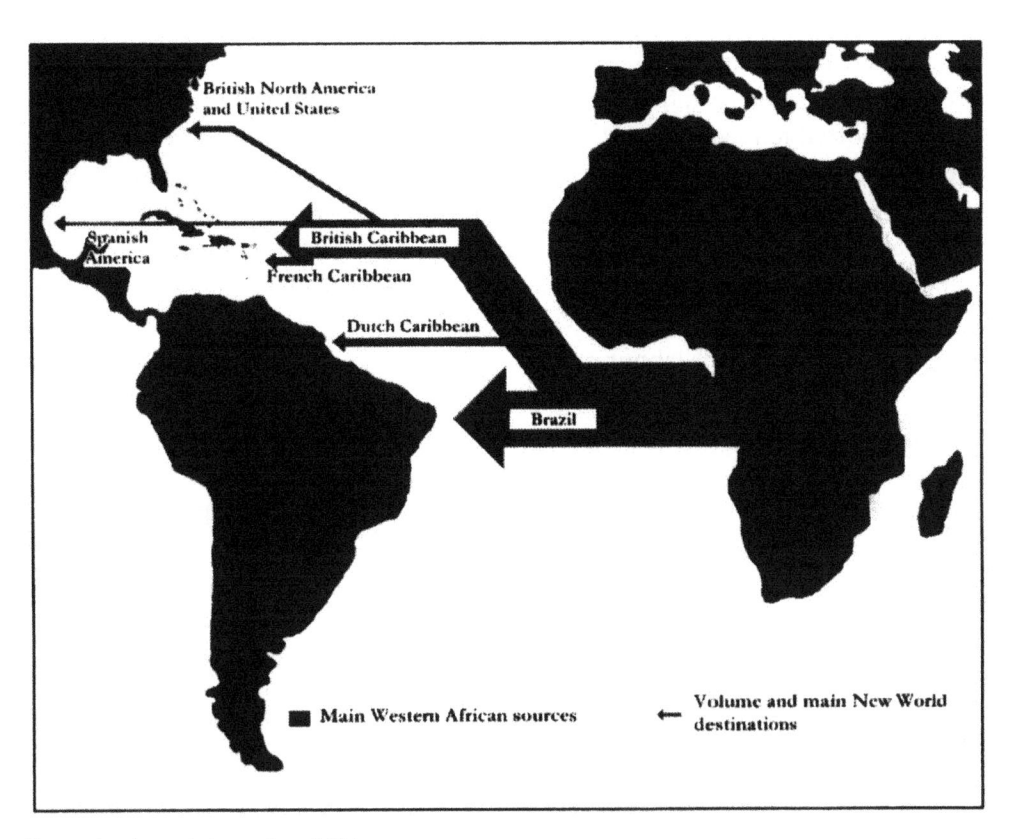

Transatlantic trade in enslaved Africans

and slavery. Some historians have emphasized his Genoese background and connections. Between 1476 and 1486 he lived in Madeira, close to his father-in-law, and participated in the early sugar trade. He made several voyages to the Azores, the Canaries and the African continent, reaching as far as Elmina Castle.[22] It was he who introduced the sugar cane to the Caribbean. Although the first sugar mill or *trapiche* was installed only in 1516, Columbus had boasted of the economic possibilities of sugar since his second voyage.[23] Cultivation spread rapidly from its cradle in Hispaniola to Jamaica, Puerto Rico and Cuba. Just as in the Eastern Atlantic, wherever the sugar industry took root the spectre of slavery loomed large. The establishment of the *trapiche* was the first milestone in the commercialization of the Caribbean sugar industry and the opening up of a new era in the Atlantic slave trade.

It may be useful to note *en passant* that not all Africans in the era of exploration came in chains; African sailors had accompanied Columbus on his first voyage in key positions. Furthermore, Ivan van Sertima has provided empirical evidence of an African presence in Mexico, some Caribbean islands, the Darien region of the Panama peninsula, and several other locations in the Americas prior to the Spanish arrival. The probability of such extensive distribution also links back to Mande oral tradition and Arabic scholarship. Free Africans were also among the *conquistadores* who overran Central America.[24]

Be that as it may, the earliest date for a transatlantic shipment of enslaved Africans to the New World was the year 1501; their immediate origin was Spain, not Africa. The initiative was quickly aborted following reports of runaways teaming up with Tainos of Hispaniola against the Spaniards. In order to pre-empt future insurgencies, the Spanish Crown decreed that only Christian Africans be transported to the New World for enslavement. These precautions were soon to be set aside for purely economic reasons. Notwithstanding the early experiments in transatlantic transfers, we should consider the official launch of the Middle Passage as the issuing of the *asiento* in 1518 to supply African labour direct from Africa and satisfy the new demands for labour created by the commercialization of the Caribbean sugar industry.

Soon after the Portuguese launched their full-scale colonial enterprise in Brazil in 1530, sugar became the most successful business, with São Tomé as the major trans-shipment point. The island was also the principal model for the Brazilian sugar-plantation complex and the organization of slave labour. Although Amerindians provided the bulk of the labour in the early years of the Brazilian sugar industry, African captives still provided critical support as mill workers. By the 1560s, the floodgate of African migration began to open partly because of difficulties in capturing adequate numbers of Amerindians and partly due to the lowering of duties on enslaved Africans.[25]

THE MATURE TRANSATLANTIC

Williams argued that, for several decades of the sixteenth century, the transatlantic slave trade included "white slaves" from Europe, transported under royal authority.[26] Although most scholars prefer the softer label "white indentures", as late as 1780, English press-ganged sailors were still considered in English law as "really slaves".[27] The Spanish hacienda, to which this white bonded labour was destined, operated a feudal mode of production. Although Curtin's earlier-cited frame of reference is feudalism, the sugar industry that flourished in the Caribbean under the impetus of the seventeenth-century Sugar Revolution was anything but feudal. In many ways, a Barbadian sugar plantation was more capitalistic than any industry in the Atlantic World. Sugar colonies were proto-industrial estates; in that sense, Barbados was more industrially advanced than England during the latter seventeenth century. P.C. Emmer succinctly refers to the plantation system as a *"capitalisms sauvage"*.[28] Capitalism and sugar demanded chattel slavery rather than temporary bondage. In explaining the longevity of the slave trade, it is important to see the sugar colonies as capitalist enterprises in relentless pursuit of profit at the total expense of the labouring class.

Unrestrained exploitation saw Africans literally being worked to death. In 1764, the governor of Martinique expressed his astonishment over the failure of the French colonies to reach sustainability in the labouring population. Edward Long, his contemporary, documented this phenomenon in the English colonies.[29] According to contemporary estimates, one-third of newly arrived Africans in the West Indies died within three years, while life expectancy was reduced to less than fifteen years. The absolute inhumanity under which enslaved Africans existed guaranteed the permanence of the Atlantic slave trade.

With the onset of the Sugar Revolution, European indentureship gave way to African enslavement, not only because of the laws of supply and demand, but also because no law protected the latter from the savagery of the enslaver, whether in the fields, the manufactories or the domestic "yards". The testimony of Bartolomé de Las Casas is revealing of the cruelty that enslaved Africans suffered in the Caribbean from earliest times. Las Casas claimed (perhaps not entirely seriously) that prior to the introduction of sugar, only hanging could kill an enslaved African. "But after they were put to work in the ingenios, on account of the excessive labour they had to endure ... death and pestilence were the result, and many of them died."[30] Although separated by centuries, the testimony of Reverend James Ramsay demonstrated that, if anything had changed, it was for the worse. Writing from personal experience as a slave master in St. Kitts, he acknowledged that the interests of enslaved and enslavers were so diametrically opposite that "it is impossible to infuse any other principle than fear into the mind of a slave".[31] Richard Dunn summed up the situation by stating that, even on the most paternalistic plantations, slavery was "one of the most brutally dehumanizing systems ever devised".[32] Thus, although plantation slavery was self-perpetuating—children inheriting the status of their enslaved mothers—the slave trade would continue long after providing adequate numbers for the labour requirements of new plantations and colonies. Between 1700 and 1787 Jamaica imported some 610,000 Africans; but by 1787 the total enslaved population was a mere 250,000. In the colony of St. Domingue, now Haiti, 800,000 Africans were imported in the 100 years ending in 1776, but the enslaved African population then was under 300,000.[33] Similarly, of the 387,000 Africans imported into Barbados between 1640 and 1807, the enslaved population at abolition of the slave trade stood at approximately 75,000.[34]

WHY AFRICA?

Availability of large labour pools and the relative proximity of Africa to America, although a significant factor, cannot alone provide a satisfactory answer to the question, "Why an Atlantic slave trade?" Nor can the trade be explained by the tradition of "domestic slavery" within the African continent. Many scholars have emphasized that the preference for Africans over Amerindians had mainly to do with the superior physical attributes of the former, the need to save the local peoples from extinction or to fill the void caused by their extermination. It is true that by the time the first sugar mill was built in the Caribbean, the local populations in several colonies were already facing extinction. However, whether Las Casas had intervened or not, the fate of Africans would have been sealed: the slave trade was definitely poised for take-off. The demographic disaster of the Amerindians served only to expand and perpetuate the transatlantic dimension of the slave trade, not to initiate it.

The economics of transferring skilled labour from the Eastern Atlantic outweighed the cost of training Amerindians unfamiliar with Old World industrial technology. Other factors may well have been equally or more compelling. Many of the first Africans in the Caribbean were drawn from various industries in Spain and the Eastern Atlantic islands, including gold mining and metallurgy; colonists deployed them in similar industries in the New World. Indeed, the first significant transfers of enslaved Africans in 1510 were specifically to service the gold mines in Hispaniola. African iron-working and cattle-farming were both critical to the operations of sugar mills.[35] All these skills were vital to the emergence of the so-called South Atlantic system.

This brings us to the question: What role, if any, did racism play in the origins and expansion of the Atlantic slave trade? Was the trade solely a response to the demand for labour by European colonizers? According to Williams, "The reason ['for Negro slavery'] was economic, not racial; it had to do not with the color of the laborer, but the cheapness of the labor."[36] We need to consider seriously whether a phenomenon as complex as the Atlantic slave trade could be reasonably reduced to such a simple equation. To subsume racism under the ubiquity of economic necessity is more than a mere scholarly conjecture; it is epistemic. Williams's reference was limited to the New World; it excluded prior enslavement of Africans by Europeans in Sicily, Spain, Portugal and the Eastern Atlantic islands. Indeed, Moses Finley's comment on Williams is that "it is a comforting doctrine, but it is too incompatible with the evidence to survive dispassionate examination".[37] We also need to question David Brion Davis's assertion that it was only in North America that the "concept of the Negro took on the stigma of slave heritage".[38] The truth is that from the very onset of the trade, the guardians and fabricators of European conscience had invoked racist theology and philosophy to moralize the trade by equating the "Negro" or "Ethiopian" with sin and slavery.

The early construction of the "Negro" stereotype in Judeo-Christianity helps to explain the African problematic in slave colonies. In order to enslave African peoples, it was first necessary to dehumanize and demonize them. Although anti-black African prejudices were widely intellectualized by Greco-Roman writers of the pre-Christian era, as Alvin Thompson and other scholars have demonstrated, the devaluation of African humanity began in earnest between the second and sixth centuries CE as a two-pronged assault by Christians and Jews. In 540 CE Byzantine Emperor Justinian sent an army up the Nile River to the island of Philae to destroy the shrine of Isis, the last remaining Egyptian centre for the worship of the black goddess once venerated around the Mediterranean world.[39] The destruction of Philae climaxed the growing trend in the early Christian era to dehumanize, denigrate and demote black Africans to a servile category. Two influential theologians, Origen and Saint Augustine—both born and nurtured on African soil—were among the foremost architects of Christian demonology. Both shared the newly engineered Judaic association of blackness with sin and wickedness, as evidenced in Origen's *The Songs of Sons,* Augustine's *City of God* and the Babylonian *Talmud* (commentaries on the *Torah*). Augustine was particularly important for redeploying the doctrine of slavery as "the desert of sin",[40] which, in time, would be deployed as a yoke round the necks of African peoples.

Mesopotamian Jews of the second to sixth centuries CE set about to reconstruct the mythical "Curse of Canaan" into the "Curse of Ham" with attendant, clearly racialized stereotypes of the "Ethiopian", which were to serve Christians and Muslims alike. This period, according to St. Augustine, saw the widespread ravaging of the hinterland of Hippo in the former land of Carthage, coincidently, a colony founded by Phoenicians (the original "accursed" Canaanites).[41] The association of slavery with dark-hued Africans deepened under Muslim-Arab slave traders operating the trans-Saharan network. Arab preference for enslaved Africans from south of the Sahara—the regions of the so-called Western Ethiopians—institutionalized the connection between black Africans and chattel slavery.

Pope Eugene IV's (1431–1447) earliest edicts on African enslavement are revealing of a Catholic Church that was becoming irrelevant to the new commercial capitalist dispensation; they also betray the syndrome among European intellectuals that Brion Davis calls "dualisms in thought" in matters relating to slavery. Driven into exile in Florence within two years of his incumbency, Eugene vainly sought to prohibit slave trading in, and enslavement of, local Christian Canarians. In 1435 he issued the Bull *Sicut Dudum* ordering that the Canarians must have their freedom restored and remain "totally and perpetually free … without the exaction or reception of money". The Bull also threatened to impose a "sentence of excommunication" on those who disobeyed his edict.[42] Perhaps as a payback to King Alfonso V of Aragon for his role in helping him to return to the Vatican, the beleaguered Eugene made the first major papal compromise with European Atlantic slave traders and, by extension, reconciled the papacy to the new commercial capitalism. Five years after papal prohibition, the Portuguese made their first raids on mainland Africa. Without rescinding his prohibition edict, Eugene proceeded to vindicate the very traders involved in the slave trade from the Canary Islands. The literature tells us that Prince Henry immediately informed the pope of the success of Captain Gonçalvez's first slave raids on African soil. The pontiff welcomed the news and unhesitatingly invoked Talmudic-Augustinian theology, granting "to all of those who shall be engaged in the said war, complete forgiveness of all their sins".[43] Successive popes applied a New Testament spin to the Curse of Ham. Clearly, the purpose of papal intervention was to liberate the conscience of Christian traders from any guilt or doubts concerning the morality of their undertaking. This is clearly demonstrated in the naming of slave ships after the most esteemed icons in Christianity, such as the *Jesus of Lubeck,* the *Madre de Dios,* the *Solomon,* the *Ave Maria* and *The Lord,* to name a few. Similar appellations were given to slave plantations, especially in colonies with strong Catholic connections.

The tenure of Pope Nicholas V (1447–1455), Eugene's successor, coincided with both the transformation of the economy of Madeira from wheat to sugar and the arrival of the Portuguese in Upper Guinea. Eugene's edict had a crusading ring to it; Nicholas was much more cognizant of the economics of slavery. He borrowed or reconstructed the Talmudic

Jesus of Lubeck
(www. histarmar.com. art... /LigaHanseaticabase.htm)

Pope Nicholas V
(http: //commons, wikimedia.org/
wiki/Image: Nicholas_V.jpg)

"curse"—recasting "Ethiopians" as a "children of Satan". His draconian decree, *Romanus Pontiflex,* issued in the last year of his papacy, authorized the Portuguese "to attack, subject and reduce to perpetual slavery ... the enemies of Christ".[44] By that time, the application of the curse would fall squarely on the peoples of the Upper Guinea coast.

Thus, long before the Atlantic trade in enslaved Africans expanded into its transatlantic expression, the trade and the slavery it sustained had already deepened the racism that defined African-European relations. Papal complicity was not restricted to the issuing of edicts and blessings. In 1488, the king of Spain sent a present to Pope Innocent VIII comprising 100 "Moors" whom the latter distributed to his favourite Cardinals and other Italian nobility.[45] During the sixteenth and seventeenth centuries, lesser ecclesiastics added a national flavour to the imperial church. One such individual was French Cardinal Bossouet, who defended the trade and slavery, contending

54 | Introduction to African American Studies

that to abolish slavery would be "to condemn the Holy Spirit who by the mouth of St. Paul orders slaves to remain in their state".[46]

China and India are relevant to this discourse, because they provided the bulk of new labour in the post-slave-trade Caribbean. The Chinese were the first Asian immigrants to arrive in the Caribbean. The earliest immigration scheme was formulated in 1802, before any modification to the systems of slave trading and plantation slavery. However, the new immigrants were to be free settlers, receiving generous grants of land on which to become "independent cultivators of rice and even sugar". They were also to be guaranteed the preservation of their family traditions and religious culture.[47] A related proposal in 1815 for Indians to settle in Trinidad with their families and pundits was also made prior to any alteration in the slave system or the large-scale agitation for emancipation by abolitionists.[48] The different attitudes to Asians related not just to changing values in the Western world, but also to the fact that Asian enslavement was not easily defended by Western philosophy or religion. We should note that even though the East India Company practised slavery in India, English abolitionists strenuously denied this fact as late as the 1830s, reluctantly conceding it only after African emancipation in the colonies.

Prior to the 1830s, only a few voices within the Catholic Church hierarchy were ever raised in defence of the right to freedom for Africans. An outstanding exception was Cardinal Ximenes in 1516. As Spanish Regent, Ximenes invoked the "Law of Nations" to veto the new proposals for a regular transatlantic trade in Africans on the grounds that it was unlawful to consign innocent people to a state of slavery.[49] Ximenes's veto challenged the Bull of Pope Nicholas V. However, like Las Casas, the Cardinal was not representing the church's official position on this issue. Ultimately, he proved to be too insignificant to prevent the entrenchment of the trade *via* the prized *asiento*. From that time, the fate of sub-Saharan Africans became inextricably linked to changing demands for labour in the principal colonial economies of the New World.

Some scholars soften the indictment on the church by citing cases of intervention by the Papacy to prohibit or blunt the trade in enslaved Africans. In 1462, Pius II called for an end to the practice of enslaving African Christians. However, like Eugene, he was not against slavery in general and said nothing about the slave trade of non-Christian Africans. The strongest reaction against the slave trade came form Pope Urban VIII (1623–1644): in 1639 he issued a Bull prohibiting it. Interestingly, the edict came just two years after the Dutch had captured Elmina Castle.[50] At that time, the Dutch were the most powerful Protestant state in Europe, while Elmina was a symbol of Roman Catholic power on Africa's Atlantic seaboard. According to Brion Davis, Urban's prohibition was a response to the growing power of the Dutch rather than concern for African liberty. As a tool of economic and ideological warfare, papal abolition would have been counter-productive, since it would have weakened the Catholic powers more than their enemies. Consequently, the Bull was just as "futile" as earlier interventions by Popes John XXII (1316–1334) and Martin V (1417–1431), all of which were merely intended to use prohibition to strike against the rising power of Ottoman Muslims in the Mediterranean.[51]

From the mid eighteenth century, science began to displace religion as the foundation of knowledge in general. However, for Africans, scientific racism only reinforced the myth of African intellectual inferiority, while emphasizing their superior physical endurance and alleged immunity to pain, thus providing new "empirical" justification for slavery and the slave trade. Enlightenment philosophers complemented racist scientists with a retreat into medieval irrationality on the question of slavery and Africans' right to freedom. Baron de Montesquieu, the renowned French thinker, was typical of this reactionary ambivalence. In attempting to reconcile the irreconcilable, he declared, "But as all men are born equal, slavery must be accounted unnatural, though in some countries it is to be founded on natural reason." He concluded: "Natural slavery, then, is to be limited to some particular parts of the world."[52] Everyone understood him to mean the Americas. After British abolition, scientific racism continued to immunize the conscience of slave traders, including the British, with their continuing vested interest in both the trade and colonial slavery.[53]

In conclusion, the reasons for the launch and duration of the Atlantic slave trade are many and are often inter-connected. However, the principal reason was the difficulty in acquiring vast numbers of coerced labourers from Europe to satisfy the demands of pre-industrialized, tropical and semi-tropical plantation agriculture, especially sugar, rice, cotton and tobacco. Other supporting but indispensable factors include expediency in transferring Africa's technological skills and expertise to New World industries, the ethics of capitalism, the geo-politics of sub-Saharan Africa, the complicity of Christians and the bankruptcy of European moral philosophy.

NOTES

1. Philip Curtin et al., *African History* (Boston: Little, Brown, 1978), 213; Basil Davidson, *Africa in History: Themes and Outlines* (New York: Collier Books, 1974), 180; Eric Williams, *Capitalism and Slavery* (1944; repr., London: Andre Deutsch, 1981), see ch. 3 for an overview of several industries linked to the slave trade.
2. Stephen D. Behrendt, *The Transatlantic Slave Trade: A History,* rev. ed. (1981; repr., Lincoln: University of Nebraska Press, 2005), 20; David Eltis and David Richardson, *Routes to Slavery: Directions, Ethnicity and Mortality in the Atlantic Slave Trade* (London: Frank Cass, 1977), 16. Before the transatlantic dimension of the trade opened up, some 80,000 victims had already been sold into slavery (see Paul Lovejoy, *Transformation in Slavery: A History of Slavery in Africa, Second Edition* [New York: Cambridge University Press, 2000], 36–37). Manning refers to the trade as "mankind's second largest transoceanic migration" (see his "Migration of Africans, Africa and the New World", in *Slave Trades, 1500–1800: Globalisation of Forced Labor,* ed. Patrick Manning [Vermont: Variorum, 1996], 65).
3. Manning, *Slave Trades,* xv. For 'pull' factors in colonial America, see Manning, "Migration of Africans", 70.
4. Curtin et al., *African History,* 216.
5. David Birmingham, *Trade and Empire in the Atlantic, 1400–1600* (New York: Routledge, 2000), 15. The vibrancy of the trade is also evidenced in the intervention of Pope Eugene IV to excommunicate slave owners and traders in his Bull, *Sicut Didum.*
6. Birmingham, *Trade and Empire,* 17; Robin Blackburn, *The Making of New World Slavery: From the Baroque to the Modern, 1492–1800* (London: Verso, 1997), 109.

7   James Lockhart and Stuart Schwartz, *Early Latin America: A History of Colonial Spanish America and Brazil* (New York: Cambridge University Press, 1983), 25.
8   Ibid., 25; see also Joseph E. Inikori, "Africa and the Globalization Process: Western Africa, 1450-1850", *Journal of Global History* 2, no. 1 (2007): 72.
9   Birmingham, *Trade and Empire*, 28-29; Michael Craton, *Sinews of Empire: A Short History of British Slavery* (New York: Anchor Books, 1974), 3.
10 Birmingham, *Trade and Empire*, 10, 40; Basil Davidson, *The African Slave Trade*, rev. ed. (1961; repr., Boston: Little, Brown, 1980), 54-56; Blackburn, *Making of New World Slavery*, 102; Hugh Thomas, *The Slave Trade: The History of the Atlantic Slave Trade 1440-1870* (London: Papermac, 1998), 55-58.
11 Davidson, *African Slave Trade*, 55-56.
12 Quoted ibid., 55.
13 Ibid., 56.
14 Ibid., 55-57; Thomas, *Slave Trade*, 55-56.
15 Birmingham, *Trade and Empire*, 8-10.
16 Per Hernæs, "A Symbol of Power: Christianborg Castle in Ghanian History", *Transactions of the Historical Society of Ghana*, n.s., no. 9 (2005): 141-61; see also Blackburn, *Making of New World Slavery*, 102.
17 Birmingham, *Trade and Empire*, 34-38; Thomas, *Slave Trade*, 60-63,
18 Birmingham, *TYade and Empire*, 36.
19 Manning, "Migration of Africans", 99; Blackburn, *Making of New World Slavery*, 106; Akosua Adoma Perbi, *A History of Indigenous Slavery in Ghana from the Fifteenth to the Nineteenth Century* (Accra: Sub-Saharan Publishers, 2004), 23-24; Birmingham, *TYade and Empire*, 44.
20 Birmingham, *Trade and Empire*, 40.
21 David Brion Davis and Steven Mintz, eds., *The Boisterous Sea of Liberty: A Documentary History of America from Discovery through the Civil War* [Oxford: Oxford University Press, 1998), 4.
22 Lockhart and Schwartz, *Early Latin America*, 29-30; Thomas, *Slave Trade*, 88; Davis and Mintz, *Boisterous Sea*, 33-34.
23 Eric Williams, *From Columbus to Castro: The History of the Caribbean 1492-1969* (1970; repr., London: Andre Deutsch, 1983), 25; Craton, *Sinews of Empire*, 5-6.
24 Ivan van Sertima, *They Came before Columbus* (New York: Random House, 1976); Ivan van Sertima, *Early America Revisited* (London: Transaction, 1998). Evidence from Arabic scholars, Ibn Kaldun and Al-Umari support Atlantic voyages undertaken by 'Mandingoes" during the reign of Abu Bakr II in the early fourteenth century see J. Spencer Trimingham, *A History of Islam in West Africa* (London: Oxford University Press, 1962), 67; George Reid Andrews, *Afro-Latin America, 1800-2000* (New York: Oxford University Press, 2004), 13.
25 Lockhart and Schwartz, *Early Latin America*, 199.
26 Williams, *Columbus to Castro*, 38; Williams, *Capitalism and Slavery*. The closest reference to slavery was the term "unfree labor" (ibid., 7).
27 David Eltis, *The Rise of African Slavery in the Americas* (New York: Cambridge University Press, 2000), 16.
28 P.C. Emmer, "The Dutch and the Making of the Second Atlantic System", in *Slavery and the Rise of the Atlantic System*, ed. Barbara L. Solow (New York: Cambridge University Press, 1993), 78.
29 Edward Long, *History of Jamaica* (London: Frank Cass, 1970; orig. 1774), 2:432-42.
30 Williams, *Columbus to Castro*, 43. The earliest mills were animal-driven *trapiches*, but they were soon replaced by water-powered *ingenios*.
31 James Ramsay, *An Essay on the Treatment and Conversion of African Slaves in the British Sugar Colonies* (London: 1784), 173.
32 Richard Dunn, "A tale of Two Plantations: Slave Life at Mesopotamia in Jamaica and Mount Airy in Jamaica, 1799-1828", in *The Black Diaspora: African and their Descendants in the Wider World 1800 to the Present*, ed. the Black Diaspora Committee of Howard University (Washington: Gin Press, 1990), 151.
33 British Library, *Parliamentary History of England from the Earliest Period to the Year 1803*, vol. 36, *1801-1803*, cols. 863-64.

34 Not all sources agree on labour demographics, sometimes even within the same source See B.W. Higman, *Slave Populations of the British Caribbean, 1807-1834* (Baltimore: Johns Hopkins University Press, 1984). For the year 1810, tables 3.8 and 4.2 of this work contain figures of 82,000 and 93,040 respectively.

35 Basil Davidson tells us that in many respects these Africans "were far superior ... to the Europeans as well" (See his *Africa in History*, 183).

36 Williams, *Capitalism and Slavery*, 19.

37 Moses I. Finley, *Ancient Slavery and Modern Ideology*, expanded ed. by Brent D. Shaw (New Jersey: Marcus Weiner, 1998), 289.

38 Lewis Fried, "David Brion Davis: Challenging the Boundaries of Slavery", in *African American Review* 38, no. 3 (2004|, 530 (accessed on Questia online library: http://www.questia.com/PM).

39 St. Clair Drake, *Black Folk Here and There: An Essay in History and Anthropology* (Los Angeles: Center for Afro-American Studies, 1990), 1:275; Alvin O. Thompson, "Race and Colour Prejudices and the Origin of the Trans-Atlantic Slave Trade", *Caribbean Studies* 16, nos. 3-4 (1976-77): 33-37.

40 Stephen R. Haynes, *Noah's Curse: Biblical Justification of American Slavery* (New York: Oxford University Press, 2002), 7; R.V.G. Thsker, ed., *The City of God* (John Healey trans. London: Dent, 1962), 1:xviii; see also Thompson, "Race and Colour Prejudices", 37-38.

41 See Finley, *Ancient Slavery*, 22. According to Finley, the information comes to us from letters written by Augustine but first published only in 1980,

42 Joel S. Panzer, "The Popes and Slavery" (The Church in History Information Centre, http://www.churchinhistory.org [last accessed on 26 February 2008], 3. Panzer hailed the Bull as a major milestone in the church's position on slavery but was silent on his subsequent Bull sanctioning the slave trade from mainland Africa. For the full text of the Bull, see http://www.fisheaters.com/sicutdudum.html; or http://www.papalencyclicals.net/Eugene04/eugene04sicut.htm (last accessed on 26 February 2008).

43 Davidson, *African Slave Trade*, 55.

44 David Brion Davis, *The Problem of Slavery in Western Culture* (New York: Cornell University Press, 1966), 100; Eugene H. Korth, *Spanish Policy in Colonial Chile; The Struggle for Social Justice, 1535-1700* (Stanford: Stanford University Press, 1968), 106. Blackburn, *Making of New World Slavery*, 103-4.

45 Davis, *Problem of Slavery*, 100-101.

46 John T. Noonan Jr., 'Development in Moral Doctrine", *Theological Studies*, 54, no. 4 (1993).

47 British National Archives, CO 296/4, Hobart to Commissioners, 16 October 1802, enclosure no. 20, folio 72d.

48 British National Archives, CO 295/33, Woodford to Bathurst, 3 October 1814, folio 24.

49 C.H. Haring, *The Spanish Empire in America* (1947; repr., San Diego: Jovanovich, 1975), 52-53.

50 Davis, *Problem of Slavery*, 100nl8.

51 Ibid.

52 See F.T.H. Fletcher, *Montesquieu and English Politics, 1750-1800* (London: Arnold, 1939), 44-48.

53 See Warren S. Howard, *American Slavers and the Federal Law, 1837-1862* (Chapel Hill: University of Carolina Press, 1963), 7-11.

READING 5

Slavery and States' Rights in the Early Republic

Jeffrey Rogers Hummel

THE AMERICAN REVOLUTION'S ASSAULT ON HUMAN BONDAGE

Slavery had not always divided the South from the North. Prior to the American Revolution, all British colonies in the New World legally sanctioned the practice. Nearly every colony counted enslaved blacks among its population. And most colonists accepted this as normal and inevitable. A full 42 percent of New York City households possessed slaves at the end of the seventeenth century. As late as 1770, nearly twice as many blacks were in bondage throughout the colony of New York as within Georgia, even though blacks were a much larger proportion of less populous Georgia.

John Jay, a prominent New Yorker who coauthored the famous *Federalist* papers and was first Chief Justice of the Supreme Court, remembered the widespread acceptance of slavery among both Northerners and Southerners: "Prior to the great revolution … the great body of our people had been so long accustomed to the practice and convenience of having slaves, that very few among them even doubted the propriety and rectitude of it. Some liberal and conscientious men had … drawn the lawfulness of slavery into question, and they made converts to that opinion;" Jay conceded, "but the number of those converts compared with the people at large was then very inconsiderable."[1]

The Revolution, however, dislocated slavery both directly and indirectly. Virginia's royal governor ushered in the direct dislocation on November 7, 1775, when he proclaimed free any slave who would bear arms against the rebellious colonists. At least eighteen thousand freed blacks accompanied British forces as they evacuated Savannah, Charleston, New York City, and other places at the end of the war. South Carolina, the only colony with a slave majority when independence was declared, lost as much as one-third of its black population to flight or migration.

The indirect impact was still more profound, as the Revolution's liberating spirit induced many white Americans to challenge slavery. Quakers organized the world's first antislavery society in Philadelphia in 1775, and soon similar organizations dotted the colonies. Some states offered freedom to blacks who enlisted in the military. Vermont in its constitution of 1777 became the first to abolish the institution. The Pennsylvania legislature enacted gradual emancipation in 1780, while the Massachusetts courts pronounced slavery inconsistent with

Jeffrey Rogers Hummel, "Slavery and States' Rights in the Early Republic," *Emancipating Slaves Enslaving Free Men: A History of the American Civil War*, pp. 9-29, 367-368. Copyright © 2013 by Cricket Media. Reprinted with permission.

the state's declaration of rights in 1783. State after state followed with either outright abolition or gradual emancipation. The Continental Congress meanwhile passed the Ordinance of 1787, prohibiting slavery in the western territories north of the Ohio river. New Jersey in 1804 became the last remaining state above the Mason-Dixon line to put chattel slavery on the road to extinction.

Slavery was more economically entrenched in the former southern colonies, where 90 percent of British America's 460,000 blacks had resided. But even there, the Revolution's ideological assault upon any form of human bondage made significant inroads. Many southern states banned the importation of slaves; southern societies encouraging masters to free their human chattel flourished; and several states relaxed legal obstacles to such voluntary manumissions. These actions spawned the first substantial communities of free blacks, concentrated in the upper South. Delaware saw the process furthest; three-quarters of the state's blacks were out of bondage by 1810.

Enlightened southern statesmen, such as Thomas Jefferson, a slaveholder himself, condemned slavery as evil and endorsed steps towards its ultimate extinction. "Nothing is more certainly written in the book of fate than that these people are to be free," pronounced Jefferson, yet like so many of his neighbors, he also had strong reservations about the two races living side by side after emancipation. "Nor is it less certain that the two races, equally free, cannot live in the same government. Nature, habit, opinion have drawn indelible lines of distinction between them." Sending former slaves out of the country seemed the only solution. "It is still in our power to direct the process of emancipation and deportation, peaceably, and in such slow degree that the evil will wear off insensibly, and their place be, *pari passu,* filled up by free white laborers."[2]

The first cooling of antislavery fervor became evident in the drafting of the Constitution in 1787. On the one hand, the Constitution never acknowledged slavery's existence by using the term, and it contained a clause permitting Congress to outlaw the Atlantic slave trade after twenty years. On the other hand, this gave the states of the lower South plenty of time to replenish their diminished slave populations, and during this time imports would exceed those in any other two decades in American history.

The Constitution also made two other key concessions to slaveholders. First, Article IV, Section 2, compelled the return of fugitive slaves even if they escaped to states that had abolished the institution: "No person held to Service or Labour in one State, under the Laws thereof, escaping into another, shall, in Consequence of any Law or Regulation therein, be discharged from such Service or Labour, but shall be delivered up on Claim of the Party to whom such Service or Labour may be due." This in effect required the national government to subsidize the enforcement of the slave system with resources from slaveholders and non-slaveholders alike. Second, the Constitution counted three-fifths of a state's enslaved population to determine its representation in the House of Representatives. This "federal ratio," although applied to direct taxes as well, principally increased the political power of slaveholders in proportion to the number of enslaved blacks.

Congress's final abolition of the slave trade with other countries took effect in 1808, during Jefferson's presidency and just after the British Parliament enacted a similar prohibition. This was the last triumph within the United States for the Revolutionary surge against slavery. Southerners had begun to draw back from any commitment to the institution's eventual demise. This reversal ironically owed much to the international spread of Revolutionary ideals. Embraced in the French Revolution of 1789, these radical ideals soon helped spark a bloody slave insurrection in the French West Indies. By New Year's Day, 1804, the successful black rebels had established the Republic of Haiti, the second independent nation in the New World. Southerners looked on in horror as surviving white refugees fled to American shores. They suddenly felt more uneasy about the racial consequences of too strict an adherence to the principles of the American Revolution.

At the same time that the apparition of slave revolts was haunting Southerners, American slavery enjoyed an economic resurgence. Prior to the Revolution, it had been mainly viable along the seaboard South, in areas suitable for tobacco and rice cultivation. But Eli Whitney's invention of the cotton gin in 1793 helped slavery transcend these geographical limits. A cotton boom enticed settlers into the rich lands of the Gulf, converting the formerly slave-free southern frontier to plantation agriculture. In 1820 the United States slave population was three times what it had been at the outset of the Revolution. Thus, while slavery was disappearing throughout the rest of the world, it was expanding in the American South.

MISSOURI—"A FIRE BELL IN THE NIGHT"

Not until the decade following the War of 1812 did slavery fully divide the South from the North. The northern states still contained some 3,000 slaves as late as 1830, but these blacks would shortly join the 125,000 of their race in those states who were free. Opponents beat back last efforts to legalize the institution in Indiana and Illinois. Simultaneously, the free states were beginning to overwhelm the slave states in total population. Already in 1819, the North outvoted the South in the lower house of Congress, 105 to 81. Only the Senate maintained a balance between the country's two sections: eleven free states to eleven slave states.

At this point, Missouri petitioned Congress for admission to the Union. One-sixth of its 60,000 inhabitants were slaves. Representative James Tallmadge, Jr., of New York proposed several conditions on Missouri's statehood: additional slaves would be prohibited from entering Missouri, and the children of those slaves already there would be freed when they reached the age of twenty-five. Tallmadge's amendment did not touch any of the blacks already in bondage within Missouri. His plan of gradual emancipation would have taken half a century to complete. Still it provoked a fierce debate that kept Congress hopelessly deadlocked for a year. The House, with its free-state majority, approved Tallmadge's amendment.

But the Senate rejected it. The elderly Thomas Jefferson best expressed the ominous dread for the future of the Union that this deadlock evoked. "This momentous question, like a fire bell in the night, awakened and filled me with terror. I considered it at once as the knell of the Union."[3]

Many northern politicians, however, were more worried about the additional political influence southern interests would receive through the federal ratio if new slave states were admitted. "The disproportionate power and influence allowed to the slave-holding states, was a necessary sacrifice to the establishment of the constitution," admitted the aging Senator Rufus King of New York, a veteran of the Constitutional Convention. "But the extension of this disproportionate power to the new states would be unjust and odious. The states whose power would be abridged, and whose burdens would be increased by the measure, cannot be expected to consent to it."[4]

Eventually Henry Clay, a Kentucky slaveowner serving as Speaker of the House, used the immense powers of his office to push through a compromise in February 1820. Missouri was admitted as a slave state. Maine, which had been a district of Massachusetts, was admitted as a free state. This maintained the sectional balance. The remainder of the national government's Louisiana Territory was divided along a line that ran parallel to Missouri's southern border. South of the line was open to slavery. The territory north of the line, except for the new state of Missouri, was closed to slavery.

Clay was hailed as the "Great Pacificator." This convivial, hard-drinking late-night gambler had saved the Union. But the Missouri crisis revealed fundamental shifts in the terms of Union. Southerners were now wholeheartedly committed to the expansion of their peculiar institution. Only expansion into new territories could mitigate the South's minority status. But because of that status, Southerners still needed the votes of some northern representatives. Called "doughfaces" by John Randolph of Roanoke, a Virginia Congressman, these northern men with southern principles made passage of the Missouri Compromise possible. Whereas Southerners had united behind slavery's spread, Northerners were not yet united behind restrictions upon it.

Southerners furthermore became advocates of inviolate states' rights. What particularly disturbed them was that Tallmadge's amendment would have imposed antislavery upon a full-fledged state, and not just a territory. Previously states' rights had been an ideological issue with support and opposition in all parts of the country. But once the Missouri controversy exposed the South's vulnerability as a minority, states' rights increasingly turned into a sectional issue. Southerners came to realize that only strict limits upon national authority could protect their existing slave system from hostile interference.

No one understood the reinforcing relationship between states' rights and slavery better than John Randolph of Roanoke. Although nearly all the influential speeches that he made during the House debates on Missouri were never recorded, he reiterated the same theme very soon thereafter when opposing nationally financed roads, canals, and other internal improvements. "If Congress possesses the power to do what is proposed in this bill,"

Randolph lashed out in his shrill, piercing soprano, "they may emancipate every slave in the United States—and with stronger color of reason than they can exercise the power now contended for." His warning to fellow Southerners about emancipation under the cover of the Constitution's war powers was prophetic. "I ask gentlemen, who stand in the same predicament as I do, to look well to what they are doing—to the colossal power with which they are now arming this Government. The power to do what I allude to is, I aver, more honestly inferrible [sic] from the war-making power, than the power we are now about to exercise. Let them look forward to the time when such a question shall arise, and tremble with me at the thought that the question is to be decided by a majority of the votes of this House."[5]

SOUTH CAROLINA NULLIFIES THE TARIFF

Clay's compromise quieted the controversy over slavery in the territories for nearly a quarter of a century but not the controversy over states' rights. No southern state was more locked into slavery than South Carolina. It had the densest concentration of slaves, with blacks well outnumbering whites. A small planter aristocracy monopolized political power. Even during the American Revolution, South Carolina had stoutly resisted any efforts to weaken the peculiar institution. Within less than a decade after the Missouri crisis, the state was militantly defying national power.

The issue that brought forth this defiance was not slavery but the tariff. Even though the Constitution authorized a tariff for revenue purposes, that did not mean, according to those who wished to interpret the document strictly, that it also authorized a tariff to protect domestic producers from foreign competitors. Southerners generally had come to oppose the steady rise in protectionist duties after the War of 1812; they correctly recognized that any restraints on free trade economically exploited an exporting region such as the South. When Congress passed in 1828 what came to be known as the Tariff of Abominations, raising duties to their highest level prior to the Civil War, the South's minority status received further confirmation. The legislature of South Carolina denounced the tariff as "unconstitutional, oppressive, and unjust," and printed up a lengthy essay on the subject of states' rights entitled *The South Carolina Exposition and Protest*.[6]

Vice-President John C. Calhoun had secretly authored the *Exposition and Protest*. Nothing better illustrates the way states' rights was being transformed into a sectional issue than the political swings of this South Carolina statesman. The Scots-Irish, Yale-educated, upcountry Southerner had started his political career as an extreme nationalist, supporting the War of 1812 and an expansive central government. Initially he favored a large standing army, a strong navy, a national bank, federally funded internal improvements, and a protective tariff. But by the time he wrote the *Exposition and Protest,* Calhoun had abandoned all these earlier positions.

Calhoun's *Exposition and Protest* defended what has become known as the compact theory of the Constitution. This theory contends that the Constitution was a compact, or contract, among sovereign states. The states had established the central government as their agent to perform specific delegated powers, such as national defense. "The general Government," explained Calhoun in a later public address, "emanated from the people of the several States, forming distinct political communities, and acting in their separate and sovereign capacity, and not from all of the people forming one aggregate political community."

Not only was the central government strictly limited, but if any dispute arose over the extent of these powers, it was the creators of the compact, the states—not their agent, the central government—that should be the final arbiter. "The Constitution of the United States is in fact a compact, to which each State is a party," and "the several States or parties, have a right to judge of its infractions."[7]

The compact theory had a long history running back to the Philadelphia Convention of 1787. To ease the Constitution's ratification among an American populace decidedly unfriendly to a consolidated government, the framers had been deliberately vague about the document's exact nature. The Virginia and Kentucky Resolutions of 1798, written by James Madison and Thomas Jefferson, had enunciated the compact theory, as had representatives of the New England states at the Hartford Convention during the War of 1812. But the *Exposition and Protest* added an additional twist: the doctrine of nullification. Calhoun argued that state conventions, the bodies that had first ratified the Constitution, could also nullify within individual states any federal law they thought unconstitutional.

The only way the central government could override such state nullifications was through a new constitutional amendment approved by three-fourths of the states. Although this cumbersome doctrine may appear to take states' rights to a logical extreme, the South Carolina political theorist actually intended nullification as a moderate compromise. Rather than promoting disunion, he saw it as the best way to preserve the Union. According to the compact theory, each state still retained the sovereign right to secede. Nullification gave the southern states an alternate way of protecting themselves from majority tyranny while remaining within the Union. Calhoun believed that only recognition of this "fundamental principle of our system, resting on facts historically as certain, as our Revolution itself, and deductions as simple and demonstrative, as that of any political or moral truth whatever" could ensure "the stability and safety of our political institutions."[8]

South Carolina did not immediately test the doctrine of nullification. But the doctrine received a full hearing in one of the most famous debates on the Senate floor. South Carolina's Robert Hayne faced off against Bostonian Daniel Webster in 1830. Vice-President Calhoun silently presided over the debate. The Senate galleries were filled with spectators, and so many Congressmen attended the debate that the House lacked a quorum to conduct business.

Webster's ideological career had been almost a mirror image of Calhoun's, demonstrating again the steady ascent of sectionalism. A staunch opponent of national power during the War of 1812, the New England orator now contemptuously disparaged states' rights. He argued that the Constitution was *not* a compact establishing a voluntary federation among sovereign states. The American people, not the states, had ratified the Constitution and thereby created a consolidated government. Hence the states had no right to nullify a national law or secede from the Union.

Webster, massive, craggy, with jutting brows, pounded home the chaos that would follow from frequent nullification at every state's whim. "The doctrine for which the honorable gentleman contends leads him to the necessity of maintaining ... that this General Government ... is the servant of four and twenty masters, of different wills and different purposes, and yet bound to obey all. This absurdity (for it seems no less) arises from a misconception as to the origin of this Government in its true character. It is, sir, the people's constitution, the people's Government, made for the people; made by the people; and answerable to the people."[9]

Webster closed his arguments with a spread-eagled appeal to American nationalism. "When my eyes shall be turned to behold, for the last time, the sun in heaven, may I not see him shining on the broken and dishonored fragments of a once glorious Union; on States dissevered, discordant, belligerent; on a land rent with civil feuds, or drenched, it may be, in fraternal blood! Let their last feeble and lingering glance, rather, behold the gorgeous ensign of the republic, ... not a stripe erased or polluted, nor a single star obscured; bearing for its motto no such miserable interrogatory as, What is all this worth? Nor those other words of delusion and folly, Liberty first, and Union afterwards: but every where, spread all over in characters of living light, blazing on all its ample folds, as they float over the sea and over the land, and in every wind under the whole heavens, that other sentiment, dear to every true American heart,—Liberty *and* Union, now and forever, one and inseparable!"[10]

The cry of "Liberty *and* Union" has since reverberated down through the history books, and to be sure, Webster's assertion of national supremacy possessed some historical validity. A permanent consolidated government had been what many of the Constitution's framers had hoped for. But the remarkable fact remains that Webster's theory did not have a venerable tradition to match that of the compact theory. Prior to the challenge of nullification, American nationalists had never systematically defended perpetual Union.

The nullification controversy reached a climax two years after the Webster-Hayne debate. Congress passed a new tariff lowering duties slightly. But the tariff was still protectionist and not low enough to suit South Carolina. The state's legislature called a convention, which promptly nullified both the Tariff of Abominations and the new Tariff of 1832. State and federal officials were prohibited from collecting duties within South Carolina after February 1, 1833. The state vowed to secede if the national government tried to coerce it.

The hot-tempered Andrew Jackson was President. A Tennessee slaveholder himself, he favored strict construction of the Constitution and sympathized with South Carolina on the tariff. But he drew the line at nullification and dismemberment of the Union. He issued a proclamation accusing South Carolina of treason, while he privately threatened to lead an invasion and hang Calhoun, who had finally revealed his authorship of *The South Carolina Exposition and Protest*. A force bill, permitting the President to use the army and navy to enforce the laws, began making its way through Congress. In response, South Carolina's government started raising a military force of its own.

An armed clash was averted when the Great Pacificator wielded his persuasive charm again. Clay put together a tariff that would reduce duties by 20 percent over nine years. It passed Congress at the same time as the Force Act. South Carolina accepted the Compromise Tariff of 1833 yet, conceding nothing in principle, nullified the Force Act. Helping to prevent the state's plunge toward disunion was its temporary isolation from the other southern states. South Carolina stood alone against the national government in 1833.

THE IDEOLOGICAL RIFT OVER SLAVERY

Although South Carolina challenged the national government over the tariff, protection of slavery was the hidden agenda. "I consider the Tariff act as the occasion, rather than the real cause of the present unhappy state of things," Calhoun himself admitted in a letter. "The truth can no longer be disguised, that the peculiar domestick *institution* of the Southern States, and the consequent direction, which that and her soil and climate have given to her industry, has placed them in regard to taxation and appropriations in opposite relation to the majority of the Union." Without the protection of states' rights, Calhoun warned, Southerners "must *in the end* be forced to rebel, or submit it to have their paramount interests sacraficed [sic], their domestick institutions subordinated by Colonization and other schemes, and themselves & children reduced *to* wretchedness."[11]

The "Colonization scheme" that disturbed Calhoun was the last expression of Revolutionary antislavery. Entailing the removal of freed blacks to Africa, it remained the panacea of those opponents of slavery such as Jefferson who believed that a biracial American society was untenable. Prominent national leaders, many from the upper South, Henry Clay and John Randolph of Roanoke among them, had founded the American Colonization Society after the War of 1812. With endorsements from five slave-state legislatures and some financial aid from the national government, the society established the nation of Liberia on the west African coast in 1822. By 1860 it had transported over six thousand blacks.

Extreme Southerners such as Calhoun were not the only ones who opposed colonization. Free blacks themselves were generally unenthusiastic about voluntary deportation. But no one attacked colonization with greater vehemence than a group of young, radical abolitionists who burst upon the national scene in the 1830s. Exasperated at the betrayal of the Revolutionary promise that American slavery would wither away, and marshaling all the evangelical fervor of the religious revivals then sweeping the country, they demanded immediate emancipation.

The most vitriolic of these abolitionists was William Lloyd Garrison. The son of a drunken sailor who had abandoned his family, Garrison grew up in a poor but piously Baptist household in Newburyport, Massachusetts. He served as a printer's apprentice and then made his first notable mark on antislavery activism when he went to jail rather than pay a fine for libeling as a "highway robber and murderer" a New England merchant who shipped slaves between Baltimore and New Orleans. From Boston on January 1, 1831, the near-sighted, prematurely balding, twenty-five-year-old editor brought out the first issue of a new weekly paper, *The Liberator*. Garrison left no doubt about his refusal to compromise with the sin of slavery:

"I *will be* as harsh as truth, and as uncompromising as justice. On this subject, I do not wish to think, or speak, or write with moderation. No! No! Tell a man whose house is on fire, to give a moderate alarm: tell him to moderately rescue his wife from the hands of the ravisher; tell the mother to gradually extricate her babe from the fire into which it has fallen;—but urge me not to use moderation in a cause like the present. I am in earnest—I will not equivocate—I will not excuse—I will not retreat a single inch—AND I WILL BE HEARD."[12] Garrison conceded that the elimination of slavery would take time in practice. But that should not inhibit forthright condemnation of moral evil. "Urge immediate abolition as earnestly as we may, it will alas! be gradual abolition in the end. We have never said that slavery would be overthrown by a single blow; that it ought to be we shall always contend."[13]

The crusading editor called not only for immediate emancipation of all slaves, without any compensation to slaveholders, but also for immediate and full political rights for all blacks. Colonization was to him a blatantly racist sop that would only strengthen slavery. Garrison, however, did not look to direct political action to eradicate slavery. Moral suasion and non-violent resistance were his strategies. By agitation, he hoped to shame slaveholders into repentance. Indeed, he went so far as to denounce the Constitution for its proslavery clauses as "a covenant with death and an agreement with hell." During one 4th of July celebration, he publicly burned a copy, proclaiming: "So perish all compromises with tyranny!" He believed that if anything the North should secede. That way it could become a haven for runaway slaves. The slogan "No Union with Slave-Holders" appeared on the masthead of Garrison's *Liberator* for years.

Garrison helped organize the American Anti-Slavery Society in 1833. Two thousand local societies with 200,000 members had sprung into existence by 1840. Supporting this network was the northern community of free blacks. Frederick Douglass, a former slave who had escaped from Maryland in 1838, became their preeminent spokesman. Over six feet tall, broad-shouldered, with long hair and a majestic face, he was a striking and popular draw at abolitionist meetings throughout the North. His melodious and rich voice boldly informed white audiences that slavery "brands your republicanism as a sham, your humanity as a base pretense, and your Christianity as a lie."[14]

Although abolitionists were only a tiny minority in the North, they definitely were heard—especially in the South. Southern slaveholders viewed American abolitionists as part of an international movement steadily encircling them. Most of the new nations of Central and South America abolished slavery when they gained their independence from Spain. British abolitionists, who were intimately linked with their American counterparts, pressed Parliament into implementing compensated emancipation in its West Indian colonies in 1833; France and Denmark followed in 1844. By 1850, slavery persisted only in the

United States, Puerto Rico, Cuba, and Brazil, although the total slave population in the Western Hemisphere was larger than it had been half a century earlier.

Slaveholders were even a minority within the southern states. Only one-fourth of white households owned slaves, and about half of those owned fewer than five. The typical Southerner was a yeoman farmer or herdsman. Yet political power was concentrated in the hands of large planters, who held the allegiance of other southern whites by relying on the issue of race. "We have but little interest in the value of slaves," a North Carolina mountaineer subsequently wrote to his Civil War governor, "but there is one matter in this connection about which we feel a very deep interest. We are opposed to negro equality. To prevent this we are willing to spare the last man."[15]

Confronted with mounting moral condemnation, Southerners ceased apologizing for their peculiar institution as a "necessary evil." They instead began boldly to defend it as a "positive good," to use Calhoun's very words. The hierarchical premises of the proslavery defense ironically had originated after the Revolution among New England conservatives of the Federalist Party and been carried south by clergymen of the so-called Benevolent Empire, a loose association of philanthropists and reformers determined to impose Yankee culture on the rest of the country—the same Benevolent Empire within which many young abolitionists had gotten their start. Not until the 1830s did Southerners take this proslavery argument to heart.

The Virginia legislature during the winter of 1831–32 became the last official body within the slave states to debate gradual, compensated emancipation—coupling it with expulsion of all freed blacks. Calhoun could therefore announce in 1838 that most Southerners, goaded by abolitionist propaganda, had now adopted the new attitude toward slavery. "This agitation has produced one happy effect at least; it has compelled us to the South to look into the nature and character of this great institution, and to correct many false impressions that even we had entertained in relation to it. Many in the South once believed that it was a moral and political evil; that folly and delusion are gone; we see it now in its true light, and regard it as the most safe and stable basis for free institutions in the world."[16]

The proslavery defense was built upon a belief in Negro inferiority. "In all social systems, there must be a class to do the menial duties, to perform the drudgery of life," stated Senator James Henry Hammond, another South Carolinian. "It constitutes the very mud-sills of society and of political government." This class requires "but a low order of intellect and but little skill," yet "fortunately for the South, has found a race adapted to that purpose to her hand."[17]

Southerners did not stop with an open defense of slavery. They went on to attack northern society for its "wage slavery" and "exploitation of workers," using arguments repeated by socialist critics of capitalism. The southern writer who developed these arguments most extensively was George Fitzhugh, a Virginia planter and lawyer. His two books were provocatively entitled *Sociology for the South: Or the Failure of Free Society* and *Cannibals All! Or Slaves Without Masters*. In them, Fitzhugh defended slavery as a practical form of socialism that provided contented slaves with paternalistic masters, thereby eliminating harsh conflicts between employers and allegedly free workers. Liberty, he believed, places classes in a position of antagonism and war, whereas slavery identifies the interest of rich and poor, master and slave, begetting domestic affection on the one side, and loyalty and respect on the other. "A Southern farm is the beau ideal of Communism; it is a joint concern, in which the slave consumes more than the master, of the coarse products, and is far happier, because although the concern may fail, he is always sure of support."[18]

The Virginia author's enthusiasm for slavery led him explicitly to reject the radical principles behind the American Revolution. "The best governed countries, and those which have prospered the most, have always been distinguished for the number and stringency of their laws," he wrote; "liberty is an evil which government is intended to correct." Denying that men are "born entitled to equal rights," Fitzhugh turned around a metaphor employed in Jefferson's last letter before his death: "It would be far nearer the truth to say, 'that some were born with saddles on their backs, and others booted and spurred to ride them'—and the riding does them good. They need the reins, the bit and the spur."[19]

If slavery were justified, it followed that there could be nothing wrong with the African slave trade. Since the Missouri controversy, American law had made slavers subject to hanging as pirates, although the U.S. navy was never as assiduous in hunting them down as the much larger British navy. Slave traders smuggled their cargoes mainly into Cuba and Brazil, but most of them hid behind the American flag, because the United States was one country that would not permit British patrols to search its vessels. By the 1850s the most provocative proslavery agitators were clamoring to reopen this traffic into the ports of the South. "If it is right," asked William Lowndes Yancey, an Alabama fire-eater, "to buy slaves in Virginia and carry them to New Orleans, why is it not right to buy them in Cuba, Brazil, or Africa, and carry them there?"[20] The primary forum for this agitation was a series of commercial conventions held annually at varied locations throughout the southern states, and finally the 1859 convention in Vicksburg demanded the repeal of all prohibitions on the Atlantic slave trade. Already southern juries were refusing to convict participants in this illicit commerce whom federal officials had apprehended.

Many Southerners held back from this proslavery extreme, especially in the northern tier of slave states, where the peculiar institution was less entrenched and the "positive good" argument never won universal acceptance. Nevertheless, as more and more embraced the morality of slavery at the very time that abolitionists became more and more confrontational, religion in America could not bear the strain. Until the second decade of the nineteenth century, most Protestant churches had cautiously conceded the contradiction between slavery and Christianity. But the Methodists, after futile attempts to paper over increasingly acrimonious controversy within the ranks, split into northern and southern branches in 1844. The next year the Baptists divided, leaving the country's two largest denominations broken in halves. The Presbyterians already had a theological schism only tangentially related to slavery between Old School and New School, and each school was able therefore to maintain a semblance of sectional unity well into the next decade. The trend however was unmistakable. Slavery was dissolving ideological and institutional bonds between North and South.

ABOLITIONISTS—FROM UNPOPULARITY TO POLITICS

Moral condemnation was not what alarmed Southerners most about the small number of radical abolitionists in the North. Far more unsettling was the growing southern conviction that any antislavery activity inevitably fanned the ubiquitous fires of servile insurrection. Back in 1800 a black bondsman named Gabriel, having imbibed Jeffersonian rhetoric, had carefully planned an attack on Richmond involving thousands of his compatriots, only to be betrayed by an informer. In 1822 South Carolinians had uncovered Denmark Vesey's plot among some of Charleston's most trusted house servants and hanged thirty-five blacks. Nine years later Nat Turner led about seventy slaves on a bloody rampage through Southhampton County, Virginia.

To squelch any further resistance, Southerners extended many of slavery's totalitarian controls to the free blacks and eventually to whites. Virginia required any slave, upon receiving freedom, to leave the state within twelve months, while South Carolina put all black sailors who landed at Charleston into jail until their ships departed. If no one paid the costs of detention, the authorities would sell such foreign sailors into slavery for reimbursement. Nearly every slave state reintroduced or tightened restrictions upon whites privately emancipating their chattels. Seven simply outlawed manumission unless the legislature granted specific permission, and courts increasingly overturned wills that freed slaves upon the owner's death. Throughout the South, free blacks had their movements watched and regulated, their right to testify against whites denied, and the types of jobs they could do limited. Sometimes they were literally forced to work, being re-enslaved in all but name.

The South's siege mentality turned it into a closed society. Advocating abolition became a felony in Virginia in 1836. The Georgia legislature offered a reward of $5,000 for anyone who would kidnap Garrison and bring him south for trial and punishment. Louisiana established a penalty ranging from twenty-one years hard labor to death for speeches and writings "having a TENDENCY to promote discontent among free colored people, or insubordination among slaves."[21] All slave-state legislatures except Kentucky's passed similar laws censoring free speech. The surveillance and violence of private vigilance committees made the region unsafe for even the most restrained critic of the peculiar institution. A theology student from the Lane Seminary in Cincinnati who carried abolitionist literature into Tennessee in 1835 was lucky to escape with a public whipping of twenty lashes, while one Virginia newspaper editor was gunned down in a duel in 1846 because of his alleged antislavery sympathies.

When northern abolitionists employed new and cheaper printing technologies to flood the South with antislavery tracts, mobs seized and burned much of this mail. Southerners even appealed to northern officials to cooperate in the suppression of abolitionist agitation. In this case, President Jackson shared the concern of his fellow slaveholders. He asked Congress in 1835 for a law barring abolitionist propaganda from the mail. Although the House of Representatives failed to heed Jackson's request by a narrow margin, his postmaster general acquiesced in the illegal refusal of local postmasters to deliver antislavery literature. Moreover, Congress did bow to southern outrage over the antislavery petitions now pouring in, most commonly demanding an end to slavery in the District of Columbia. It instituted a "Gag Rule" that automatically tabled such petitions.

Both measures were possible because abolitionists were unpopular in the North too. Although slavery had passed out of existence there, racism, already prevalent, was on the rise among northern workers. Alexis de Tocqueville, the perceptive French commentator on 1830s America, observed that "race prejudice seems stronger in those states that have abolished slavery than in those where it still exists, and nowhere is it more intolerant than in those states where slavery was never known."[22] Only five New England states allowed blacks to vote on an equal footing with whites, and New York allowed them to vote only if they could meet a special property qualification. Several western states emulated the common southern prohibition upon free blacks entering the state. Most northern locales had legally mandated discrimination of some sort. One infamous incident involved a Quaker schoolmistress named Prudence Crandall, who decided in 1833 to racially integrate her private academy for girls in Canterbury, Connecticut. The state legislature passed a special act that threw her behind bars. Nowhere could blacks serve on juries before 1860. The abolitionist championing of racial equality therefore received a cool reception.

The abolitionist disrespect for the Union did not sit well in the North either. Even when abolitionists did not share Garrison's explicit repudiation of the Constitution, their stridency still seemed to be provoking southern sectionalism. The abolitionists thus incurred the animosity of those Northerners who put their American nationalism above any opposition to slavery. One northern Congressman gave vent to both anti-abolitionist sentiments. "When gentlemen pretending to love their country would place the consideration of the nominal liberation of a handful of degraded Africans in the one scale, and this Union in the other, and make the latter kick the beam, [I] would not give a fig for their patriotism."[23]

Within the hostile atmosphere of the 1830s, abolitionist lecturers, presses, and property were frequent targets of northern violence, often instigated and directed by gentlemen of prominence and high rank. A Boston mob dragged Garrison through the streets and almost lynched him. One anti-abolitionist riot in New York City went on for half a week, during which crowds of day laborers damaged several churches, invaded black neighborhoods, and sacked the home of Lewis Tappan, a wealthy silk importer who generously financed anti-slavery organizations. These assaults finally reached a fateful culmination in 1837. Elijah Lovejoy, an abolitionist editor, was killed while defending his press from an Illinois mob. The Lovejoy murder marked a turning point, however, "a shock as of an earthquake throughout the continent," remarked former President John Quincy Adams.[24] An increasing number of Northerners began to sympathize with the abolitionists as courageous defenders of civil liberties, and they began to fear that slaveholders harbored contempt for the freedom of white as well as black Americans.

Hope for greater public sympathy helped splinter the abolitionist crusade into doctrinal factions. One source of discord was the role of women. Many remarkable female abolitionists, such as the Grimke sisters, Angelina and Sarah, Quaker converts from a wealthy

South Carolina family who had fled north, made major contributions as speakers and organizers, but only Garrison and his followers were willing to flout prevailing mores by permitting women to participate on equal terms with men. Similarly, many abolitionists in their quest for respectability turned away from Garrison's pacifism and anarchism to take up political activity. Delegates from six states organized the Liberty Party in 1839 and, for their presidential candidate, choose James G. Birney, a former slaveholder from Alabama who had moved north after converting to abolitionism.

Rather than viewing the Constitution as a proslavery document, the Liberty Party viewed it as antislavery in spirit. The party's leaders accused the South of betraying an implicit constitutional understanding that slavery should disappear within the United States. Their 1844 platform, written by Salmon Portland Chase, a Cincinnati lawyer, expounded this new interpretation. One of the platform's most important planks resolved that "it was understood in the time of the Declaration and the Constitution, that the existence of slavery in some of the States, was in derogation of the principles of American Liberty, and a deep stain upon the character of the country, and the implied faith of the States and the Nation was pledged, that slavery should never be extended beyond its then existing limits; but should be gradually, and yet at no distant day, wholly abolished by State authority."[25]

As Libertymen hammered out this interpretation's concrete implications, very few would go along with Boston freethinker Lysander Spooner, who insisted that the national government directly abolish slavery in the southern states. Spooner contended that, whatever the intention of the framers, the inherent language of the Constitution—when properly interpreted within a natural-law framework—made slavery automatically unconstitutional throughout the Union. Most members of the new party instead settled for policies designed by Chase to bring about "the absolute and unqualified divorce of the General Government from slavery."[26] This involved abolition of slavery in the territories, in the District of Columbia, and in interstate and coastal commerce. No new slave states would be admitted, no slaveholder would be appointed to federal office, and no slaves would be employed in federal construction projects. The Liberty Party believed that if the national government cordoned off slavery in this rigid fashion, abolition by the South would have to follow.

Birney received a negligible number of votes in the 1840 presidential election and not many more in 1844. Most political abolitionists preferred to support antislavery candidates from the two major parties. During the 1830s, John Quincy Adams, or "Old Man Eloquent" to his admirers, had led a lonely fight against the Gag Rule on the House floor, where the ex-Chief Executive modestly sat as a Massachusetts Whig for the last seventeen years of his life. But with the arrival of the 1840s, several newly-elected members of both the Whig and Democratic Parties centered their political careers around antislavery stands right out of the Liberty Party's program. By the end of 1844, the House had lifted the Gag Rule. The Liberty Party was thus a harbinger of the future direction of antislavery. The resort to the ballot box would bring both a broadened appeal and a dilution of purity.

NOTES

1. Jay to the English Anti-Slavery Society, [1788], Henry P. Johnston, ed., *The Correspondence and Public Papers of John Jay* (New York: G. P. Putnam's Sons, 1890-93), v. 3, p. 342.
2. Jefferson, "Autobiography," in Merrill D. Peterson, ed., *Thomas Jefferson: Writings* (New York: Library of America, 1984), p. 44.
3. Jefferson to John Holmes, 22 April 1820, *ibid.,* pp. 1433-35.
4. Charles R. King, ed., *The Life and Correspondence of Rufus King: Comprising His Letters, Private and Official, His Public Documents, and His Speeches* (New York: G. P. Putnam's Sons, 1894-1900), v. 6, pp. 699-700.
5. *Annals of Congress,* 18th Cong., 1st sess. (30 January 1824), p. 1308.
6. Resolution of 19 December 1828, reprinted in Henry Steele Commager and Milton Cantor, eds., *Documents of American History,* 10th edn. (Englewood Cliffs, NJ: Prentice-Hall, 1988), v. 1, p. 251.
7. Fort Hill address, 26 July 1831, Robert L. Meriwether, *et. al.,* eds., *The Papers of John C. Calhoun* (Columbia: University of South Carolina Press, 1959-), v. 11, p. 415.
8. *Ibid.*
9. *Congressional Register,* 21st Cong., 1st sess. (27 January 1830), v. 1, p. 74.
10. *Ibid.,* p. 80.
11. Calhoun to Virgil Maxey, 11 September 1830, Meriwether, *The Papers of John C. Calhoun,* v. 11, p. 229.
12. *The Liberator,* 1 (1 January 1831), p. 1.
13. *The Liberator,* 1 (13 August 1831), p. 129.
14. Speech delivered at Rochester, New York, 5 July 1852, John W. Blassingame, ed., *The Frederick Douglass Papers; Series One: Speeches, Debates and Interviews* (New Haven: Yale University Press, 1979-1992), v. 2, p. 383.
15. D. W. Siler to Governor Z. B. Vance, 3 November 1862, U.S. War Department, *The War of the Rebellion: A Compilation of the Official Records of the Union and Confederate Armies* (Washington: Government Printing Office, 1880-1901), ser. 1, v. 18, pp. 772-73.
16. *Congressional Globe,* 25th Cong., 2nd sess. (10 January 1838) appendix, pp. 61-62.
17. *Ibid.,* 35th Cong., 1st sess. (4 March 1858), p. 962.
18. George Fitzhugh, *Sociology for the South: Or the Failure of Free Society* (Richmond: A. Morris, 1854), p. 245. Incidentally, this was one of the first books in English to employ the term "sociology."
19. *Ibid.,* pp. 30, 170, 179. Jefferson's original statement, "the mass of mankind has not been born with saddles on their backs, nor a favored few booted and spurred, ready to ride them legitimately," appears in his letter to Roger C. Weightman, 24 June 1826, Peterson, *Thomas Jefferson,* p. 1517.
20. As quoted in "Late Southern Convention at Montgomery," *De Bow's Review,* new ser., 24 (June 1858), p. 585.
21. As quoted in William Goodell, *The American Slave Code in Theory and Practice: Its Distinctive Features Shown by its Statutes, Judicial Decisions, and Illustrative Facts* (New York: American & Foreign Anti-Slavery Society, 1853), p. 384.
22. Alexis de Tocqueville, *Democracy in America,* trans, by George Lawrence (New York: Harper & Row, 1969), v. 1, p. 342.
23. Congressman John S. Chipman of Michigan, *Congressional Globe,* 29th Cong., 2nd sess. (8 February 1847), appendix, p. 322.
24. Introduction to Owen and Joseph C. Lovejoy, *Memoir of the Reverend Elijah P. Lovejoy* (New York: John S. Taylor, 1838), p. 12.
25. Liberty Party Platform of 1844, in Donald Bruce Johnson, ed., *National Party Platforms,* rev. edn. (Urbana: University of Illinois Press, 1978), v. 1, p. 5.
26. *Ibid.,* p. 4.

READING 6

Slavery and the Problem of Democracy in Jeffersonian America

Padraig Riley

From the American Revolution to the Civil War, antislavery critics of the United States converged on a stock image of American hypocrisy: the slave-holding republican who yelped for freedom while he drove his Negroes, declaimed in the legislature by day and abused his human chattels by night. From Samuel Johnson to Frances Trollope and beyond, the slaveholding republican was a damning metaphor, capturing in one instant the contradictory reality of early American political culture. Yet it was also fundamentally inaccurate. For many enslaved African Americans, masters who spoke of liberty while they raised the lash were an all-too-frequent reality. The large majority of white Americans, however, confronted slavery far less directly: they were neither slaves nor masters, but members of a nation in which slavery was both extremely powerful and yet not always so ominously present. All white Americans remained connected to slavery, because it was such a powerful institution in the Southern and national economies and because slaveholders held considerable power in national politics. Yet for many non-slaveholders, slavery remained both geographically and ideologically distant. Even those who confronted slavery struggled to explain their complex ties to the power and oppression at the heart of the institution.

This was especially the case in the post-Revolutionary North after 1790, as the Democratic-Republican and Federalist Parties became consumed by an intense conflict over freedom and power in representative government. During the heyday of what came to be called "Jeffersonian democracy," Northern Republicans fought to obtain the basic institutional conditions of a democratic political order: they removed suffrage restrictions and qualifications for political office based on wealth; they elected lesser men to positions of power; they fought against nativism and religious establishments; and they built an impressive political coalition that brought Thomas Jefferson to the presidency in 1800.[1] Yet as Federalists observed in 1800, and as more and more historians have come to argue in recent years, Jefferson's election was marked not by the triumph of democracy but by the triumph of slavery. Jefferson's base was in the Southern states, and the Democratic-Republican Party would remain strongest there throughout its history. While post-Revolutionary Northerners acted to bring slavery to an end, gradually but decisively, Southern Republicans were the

Padraig Riley, "Slavery and the Problem of Democracy in Jeffersonian America," *Contesting Slavery: The Politics of Bondage and Freedom in the New American Nation*, ed. John Craig Hammond and Matthew Mason, pp. 227-246. Copyright © 2011 by University of Virginia Press. Reprinted with permission.

political face of an expanding and powerful slave society. They often restrained democratic practices for white men in their own states, while fighting to protect and expand slavery in the new American nation.[2]

These two conflicting visions of Jeffersonian politics—one based on democracy, one based on slavery—dominate current historiography, but historians have been hesitant to integrate them. Doing so requires moving beyond the metaphor of the republican slaveholder and looking more closely at how non-slaveholding Americans encountered the power of slavery in the early nation. We especially need to know more about how Northern Democratic-Republicans, the vanguard of democratization in the 1790s and 1800s, came to terms with their supposed antithesis—the powerful slaveholders who were their comrades and leaders in the Jeffersonian coalition.

Some historians see racism as the primary explanation for these Northern Jeffersonians: by emphasizing the grievances of white men, excluding free blacks from political and social life, and embracing slaveholders' fears of emancipation, Northern Republicans formed a powerful racial bond to the slaveholding South.[3] Others historians seem to believe that ignorance of slavery was possible, to some degree. In their view, Northern politics were primarily local, while Southern slavery was a distant problem that most Northerners overlooked in favor of political struggles closer to home.[4] More recently, historians have begun to dissent from both of these arguments, by claiming that Northern Republicans frequently opposed slavery at the national level. While Northern Federalists made the boldest attacks against slavery, Northern Republicans routinely fought against proslavery legislation in Congress and maligned slaveholders (much as they maligned Federalist elites) as an anti-democratic force.[5]

Together, these three conceptions of the Northern Jeffersonian relationship to slavery seem inconsistent, yet all can claim equal validity, depending on who one is looking at and when. The infamous Jeffersonian printer, William Duane, for example, opposed slavery in 1796; reconciled himself to the institution after 1800; attacked slavery again after the War of 1812; and then ended his political career by reaffirming the commitments that had suppressed his antislavery convictions in the first place. Such variation allows for endless conflict between those who see democratic promise in the Jeffersonian tradition and those who see the origins of a white man's republic. Neither position lacks evidence, but both lack perspective. Interpretation should begin by recognizing that the Jeffersonian Republicans, North and South, were tightly bound to both slavery and democracy.

William Duane's ideological itinerary reflects a wider pattern. In the 1790s, many leading Northern Republicans opposed slavery in public. But their hostility did not prevent an alliance to Southern Republicans, in large part because all Republicans, slaveholders and non-slaveholders alike, were focused on their domestic battle against Federalism and the international crisis that followed the French Revolution. Yet slavery could not be fully ignored, and many Northern Jeffersonians therefore began to either suppress or transform their antislavery convictions after 1800. Had slavery remained a static institution, this state of affairs might have persisted for some time. But Southern Republicans ensured that slavery would remain a central issue in national politics, by facilitating the expansion of slavery to the West and by advocating for slaveholders in the federal government. They effectively forced Northerners to either relinquish their antislavery principles altogether or engage in sectional conflict.

Southern hubris on the slavery question frequently provoked Northern dissidence, but such dissidence had limited outlets in the Jeffersonian period: no political coalition openly opposed to slavery (other than, at times, the expiring Federalists) ever took hold in the early republic. This was due to the power of slaveholders, the persistent cupidity and racism of many Northerners, and the weaknesses of organized abolitionism. But it was mostly due to the multiple ways in which democracy had become entangled with slavery since the 1790s.[6] After building an egalitarian political culture in alliance with slaveholders, Northern dissidents found it difficult to salvage a democratic antislavery argument. In the end, they were undone by the resiliency of the Jeffersonian coalition, which continued to bring slaveholders to power while making Northerners free.

FROM ANTI-SLAVERY TO PRO-JEFFERSON

Before 1800, many Northerners who would later become prominent Republicans directly attacked slavery in the United States. William Duane, soon to become an infamous Jeffersonian printer from Philadelphia, closed a 1796 assault on George Washington by decrying the fact that Washington held "FIVE HUNDRED of the HUMAN SPECIES IN SLAVERY." In 1791, Abraham Bishop, later an important Jeffersonian in Connecticut, defended the Haitian Revolution in terms which would have appalled most Southern slaveholders. Other Northern Jeffersonians were less radical, but no less opposed to slavery. Back in 1781, Levi Lincoln of Worcester, Massachusetts, who served as Jefferson's first Attorney General, argued on behalf of Quock Walker in a case that helped to end slavery in that state. The lesser-known John Leland, originally a Baptist from Massachusetts, spent many years as a missionary in Virginia, and left the state in 1790 as an open opponent of slavery. In the federal government, the Northern Jeffersonians Albert Gallatin and Matthew Lyon defended the right of antislavery petitioners to have a hearing in Congress.[7]

The antislavery words and actions of these men were tied to a wider post-Revolutionary political argument about the nature and character of the American government, an argument that would come to define the Democratic-Republican Party in the North. That argument had multiple sources, and it varied in emphasis from moderates like Lincoln to radicals like Duane and Lyon. But it had some obvious common themes: a powerful critique of aristocracy that Northern Republicans applied to local Federalist elites as well as European states; a generic belief in human equality and a specific argument for the political equality of all male citizens of the new American republic; a strong commitment to religious liberty; and an enthusiasm for self-government that led to the open advocacy of "democracy," a word that remained something of an epithet for many early American political leaders. In

1781, Levi Lincoln had claimed that "the air in America is too pure for a slave to breathe in" and that all men were equal before "the law of God"; Leland's 1790 attack on slavery followed a long fight to bring religious freedom to Virginia; Duane's critique of Washington was part of a vehement diatribe against Federalist Anglophilia and conservatism; Bishop praised the rebels of Saint-Domingue soon after his alienation from the Federalist leadership in Connecticut; and Matthew Lyon's defense of the right of petition but a few months before he infamously spat in the face of Connecticut Federalist Roger Griswold, precipitating a brawl on the floor of Congress.

All of these men supported Jefferson in 1800, and all helped to build the Democratic-Republican Party in the Northern states. Given their antislavery convictions, such an alliance appeared contradictory, since Jefferson's party was clearly dominated by the slaveholding South. In 1800, Jefferson won only 27 percent of the Northern electoral vote, but 82 percent of the Southern vote. The House races in 1800 told a somewhat different story, since Democratic-Republicans ran well throughout the country. Still, Southerners had a clear edge in the new Republican majority that came to the House in 1801, and Virginia, the largest slaveholding state in the Union, held over one-quarter of all Republican seats, twice as many as any other state.[8] These Virginian congressmen tended to be slaveholders, and as a class they were the closest thing to a European aristocracy in American political life. But in the national politics of the 1790s, they had become outspoken critics of Federalism and John Adams, allying themselves with a broad coalition of Northerners to undermine what Jefferson termed "kingly" government—by which he meant the Federalist-sponsored Alien and Sedition Acts, Federalist partiality for Britain, and the Federalists' unconcealed disdain for political upstarts like William Duane and Matthew Lyon.

The alliance between Virginia and Northern Democratic-Republicans paid obvious dividends when it came to defeating Federalism, but it created an ideological problem for Northerners who had spoken so militantly against slavery. Some of those Northern Jeffersonians who had once expressed strong antislavery views simply forgot or neglected them over time. Levi Lincoln, for example, never spoke publicly on slavery in his Jeffersonian years. Others, however, clearly attempted to reassess their feelings on slavery, now that they were allied to the most prominent slaveholders in the nation. Duane, for example, tried to argue that slavery was on a path to extinction, led by Thomas Jefferson, whose "whole life has been marked by measures calculated to procure the emancipation of the blacks." His newspaper, the *Aurora General Advertiser,* also echoed Jeffersonian rhetoric about the expansion of slavery, explaining that the growth of cotton production would lead to "the happy diffusion" of slaves "over a greater extent of country, so as to be mixed with and checked by the white people."[9]

Such racial considerations were not part of Duane's criticism of Washington as a slaveholder, but they became commonplace in his commentaries on slavery in the Jeffersonian years. Unlike Bishop in the 1790s, Duane saw the Haitian Revolution less as an expression of universal liberty, than as a racial catastrophe with dire lessons for America. Like many other Northern Republicans, he supported Jefferson's embargo of the island in 1805. Both Duane and Thomas Branagan, a militant Northern critic of slavery, fantasized about the horrors of American slave revolt, in which a local Dessalines would slaughter the white population of Philadelphia, while Branagan added crude details about the dangers of interracial mixture as well. These Northern fears of black rebellion made little practical sense, given the demography of Philadelphia compared to Virginia, let alone Saint-Domingue, but they made profound ideological sense. Racist paranoia about liberated blacks provided Northern whites with a compelling psychological reason to support Southerners and to discard their earlier opposition to slavery. By 1814, Duane would tell Thomas Jefferson that slavery was the appropriate condition for African Americans.[10]

Abraham Bishop did not overhaul his own heroic story about the slave rebellion in Saint-Domingue, but he too began to develop a powerful investment in whiteness. Rather than adopt the racist fears of Southern masters, Bishop glorified the struggles of Republicans in Connecticut. Such men were, he claimed, also slaves, to Federalists and Congregational ministers, and it was "high time that societies for the emancipation of white slaves were established in New England." John Leland, back in western Massachusetts, followed suit on behalf of the slaves of his state—the dissenting Christians who were slaves of conscience to the established Congregational church. Matthew Lyon had actually been the closest thing to a white slave among all of these men—he had come to the United States as an indentured servant from Ireland, a fact which Federalists often cited to his discredit. But Lyon's experience of bondage made him no convinced enemy of slavery: by 1803, he had become a slaveholder in Kentucky, and explained to Congress that he found blacks more useful as slaves than as free men.[11]

The Jeffersonian tendency to aggrandize the oppression of Northern whites, in addition to a growing Northern racism, helped bind Northern Republicans to their Southern colleagues. But there were also good instrumental reasons for Northern Jeffersonians to suppress or at least modify their antislavery convictions. Joining the Democratic-Republican cause paid obvious dividends, and blunt attacks on slavery at the national level were not likely to perpetuate party unity. Many Northern Jeffersonians benefited, or hoped to benefit, from political patronage: Levi Lincoln became the Attorney General, and a paper he founded in Worcester, the *National Aegis,* received federal printing contracts. Duane never received the patronage he thought he was due (and which he requested in letter after self-righteous letter), but he did obtain some federal business. Abraham Bishop fared far better—his father was appointed the customs collector at New Haven, Connecticut, and Bishop took the post on his death, and became fairly well-off.[12]

But while the combination of race, patronage, and self-aggrandizement may account for a lot, one still struggles to fully explain the bizarre story of John Leland and the giant cheese, recently retold by Jeffrey Pasley. In 1801, Leland and his fellow Baptists in Cheshire, Massachusetts, decided to produce what came to be called "The Mammoth Cheese," to celebrate President Jefferson's victory over Federalism. In December, Leland trucked this massive,

1,235-pound cheese by sled, ship, and wagon from the Berkshires to Washington, D.C., arriving in early January. What motivated such an endeavor? Leland was not obviously looking for patronage or racial pride, though he certainly hoped to make a public spectacle—to demonstrate, one might say, on behalf of the oppressed Baptists of New England. More generally, though, Leland was simply inspired by a powerful democratic enthusiasm. "We believe the supreme Ruler of the Universe," Leland said, as he presented the cheese to his president, "has raised up a Jefferson at this critical day, to defend *Republicanism* and to baffle the arts of *Aristocracy*."[13]

Such language may appear bombastic, but it was heard everywhere in Jeffersonian orations. Jeffersonian rhetoric had a distinct nationalist tone, but Northerners usually had local referents in mind when they decried aristocrats. To most Northern Jeffersonians, the Federalist Party, which continued to hold regional power in New England after 1800, remained the chief impediment to expanding democracy in the United States. New England Republicans like Lincoln, Bishop, and Leland constantly assaulted the Federalists, who still dominated their states, while Duane spent the late 1790s in a bitter newspaper war with rival Federalist papers. Federalism died out fairly quickly in Pennsylvania after 1800, but Duane soon became involved in a factional fight against the more elite members of the Pennsylvania Democratic-Republican Party. Consumed by local struggles, Duane and the New Englanders had plenty of aristocrats to attack without paying much attention to slaveholders.

These Northern conflicts were overdramatized by their protagonists, but they were also unambiguous fights for democratization. Lincoln and John Leland hoped to undermine the power of the Congregational church in Massachusetts and expand religious liberty, while Duane helped elaborate one of the most radical theories of democracy in the early nation. Northerners contributed most of the actual "democracy" to Jeffersonian democracy, and helped elevate their president, the Declaration of Independence, and the Republican cause to an almost sacrosanct political status. Jefferson arguably deserved such affirmation—not because he was such a wonderful thinker and person, but because he proved, for most of his presidency, to be an excellent political leader for his Northern allies. While Federalists scoffed, Jefferson received Leland and his cheese with fanfare at the White House, and acknowledged Duane as a party leader. Most important, Jefferson's election paid huge political dividends to his Northern partisans. Before the congressional elections of 1800, Democratic-Republicans held only 34 percent of the Northern seats in the House. Afterwards, they held 54 percent, and that majority grew over time. Combined with their Southern colleagues, they had an unshakeable majority in the Congress, and they overturned hated Federalist legislation of the 1790s.

But if that congressional success helped bind Northerners to Jefferson, it also created new sources of discord. Once in Congress, Northern Republicans had to confront slavery, because it was such a powerful institution in the national economy and because slaveholders dominated the Southern contingent in Congress. While president, Jefferson never took a strong public stance against slavery, for fear of alienating his Southern base, but neither did he publicly defend the institution. This was not true, however, of most Southern Republicans, as Northerners who came to Washington learned fairly quickly. Even moderate antislavery arguments were subject to unremitting attack on the House floor, as Southerners unified around protecting the inviolable rights of masters. Southern defiance helped catalyze a new antislavery passion among Northern Republicans, who began to see the power of slavery not only as morally illegitimate, but as a malignant force within their own political coalition. As they confronted version after version of the republican slaveholder, most of whom were far less palatable than Thomas Jefferson, some Northern Republicans began to question the ideological convictions that had brought them to Congress and brought the Democratic-Republican party to power.

SOUTHERN POWER AND NORTHERN DISSIDENCE

In Republican rhetoric, the Federalist Party was the most aristocratic force in the United States, bent on subverting liberty and democracy. But such pronouncements were easier to make in Massachusetts and Philadelphia than in Washington, D.C., after 1800. After Jefferson's first election, the Federalists were palpably weak at the national level: they were a minority in both houses of Congress and they never again proposed a serious contender for the presidency. Except for brief and minor revivals during the embargo of 1807 and the War of 1812, their limited numbers only waned during the Virginia dynasty. Yet Federalists proved a troublesome minority. On the subject of slavery, they consistently challenged Southern Republicans: they opposed the expansion of slavery into the new territory of Louisiana; the Jeffersonian embargo of Haiti; and the linchpin of Southern political power, the three-fifths clause of the Constitution. On all of these questions, the majority of Northern Democratic-Republicans were either indifferent or publicly hostile to Federalist criticism of the South.

The most significant Jeffersonian debates over slavery, however, focused on the international slave trade, which South Carolina had reopened in 1803, per the twenty-year exception allowed by the Constitution. Here, the Northern Jeffersonians would play a very different role, attacking first South Carolina and then the Southern Republican contingent as a whole. In doing so, they came to blows with the most obviously powerful group in early Washington: the slaveholders who dominated Congress, the presidency, and their own party. Northern Jeffersonians in the House caused major sectional fights over a proposed tax on the international trade in 1804 and 1806, and by 1807, when the House debated legislation to close the international trade altogether, sectional lines were firmly drawn. Most Northerners supported abolition of the trade on antislavery terms, while Southerners unified around the protection of domestic slavery within the United States. In the end, almost every member of Congress voted to abolish the international slave trade, misleading some historians to see a consensual antislavery intent in the legislation. The full record of debate and the larger history of American slavery indicate an opposite conclusion: that the slave trade debates marked the genesis of a full-fledged and ambitious defense of Southern slavery.

Outside of Washington, planters and merchants were laying the major foundations for antebellum slavery: aggressive Western expansion; the production of cotton; and an internal slave trade that grew substantially after 1810, tying the Chesapeake to the Deep South. Almost in tandem, Southerners began to articulate the major points of the proslavery argument during the debates over closing the international trade. They claimed that slaves were better off in America than in Africa; that slavery was not inherently evil; that free blacks could never be tolerated in a slave society; that the property rights of slaveholders were inviolable before federal law; and that slaveholders should have the exclusive right to frame any and all legislation affecting slavery. In response, Northern Republicans and Federalists gave notice that they wanted federal law to reflect the values and constitutions of their own states, which were, many claimed, hostile to slavery as an institution. Some Northerners argued that ending the international slave trade would be the first step in the abolition of domestic slavery. But Southern representatives won the major legislative conflicts in 1807, imposing critical weaknesses on the American ban of the international slave trade. This pro-slavery victory set the tone for a miserable American record in curtailing slave trafficking for years to come.[14]

Southern political unity gave slaveholders considerable power in setting national policy toward slavery. The 1807 debates recalled previous fights where the South, by acting with greater unanimity when it came to slavery, was able to prevail against a divided North. Sectional alignment in the House also anticipated things to come: as long as a relatively solid South could carry a crucial minority of Northern votes, it could win majority-rule contests on questions relating to slavery. Later termed "doughfaces" by the raving John Randolph, those Northerners willing to back the South came predominantly from the Jeffersonian camp.[15] But exertion of Southern power was a double-edged sword, since defiance on slavery repeatedly incited Northern dissidence. The Jeffersonian alliance, like the Jacksonian alliance which succeeded it, effectively suppressed debate on slavery, so long as proslavery voices were as marginal as antislavery advocates. But when men like Randolph and Peter Early of Georgia assaulted the Congress with their defenses of mastership, Northerners found it hard to maintain their Jeffersonian idylls, and some turned to open criticism of the South.

James Sloan, member of Congress from New Jersey, was a case in point. Sloan was an almost prototypical Northern Jeffersonian: he came from a middling background (before serving in Congress, he had been, among other things, a butcher) and rose to prominence during the electoral contest of 1800. Jefferson did not win New Jersey in 1800, but his partisans did extremely well in congressional races, winning all five House seats. They likewise swept the House races in 1802, and sent James Sloan to Washington.[16] Though he was one of the more active members in Congress, Sloan has not gone down in history as a very auspicious character. Many historians know him only through Henry Adams, who described Sloan at one point as "a sort of butt in the party," and at another as simply "the butt of the house." Federalists frequently singled out Sloan as a sign of democratic degradation. He "is emphatically the small end of small things," wrote Massachusetts Federalist Samuel Taggart, indicative of the "scum" on the boiling pot of democracy. He was described as "the honourable James Sloan, member of Congress, *and butcher*"; a man who "has been so often seen with his apron, his steel, and his cleaver, in the Philadelphia shambles, grease and blood to the eyes." A butcher in the Congress—to Federalists, this was democracy run amok.[17]

Given the barrage of Federalist insults hurled in his direction, one might expect Sloan's Washington years to reinforce the central narrative of Northern Jeffersonian politics, where aristocratic Federalists suppressed the democratic aspirations of virtuous Republicans. But Sloan moved in the opposite direction. Writing retrospectively in 1812, he complained that members of the "middle and eastern states" had joined with the Southern Republicans "under the specious pretex[t] of unity to prevent the Federalists from obtaining their former power." And yet the Southerners, since at least Jefferson's embargo, had proven far more oppressive than John Adams's Federalists had ever been. This was only to be expected, Sloan claimed, because their "education and local situation hath had a tendency to bias the mind in favour of that anti-christian, tyrannical, and inhuman principle of slavery of the human species."[18]

Sloan confronted slaveholders in almost every congressional session. He supported the call to tax the international slave trade in 1804, he moved to gradually emancipate all of the slaves in Washington, D.C., in 1805, and he introduced the tax again in 1806. He played a major role in the debates over the abolition of the trade, and, in 1808, he moved that the national capital should be removed to Philadelphia, causing a bitter sectional division in the House. He joined the Republican caucus to nominate James Madison for the presidency in January of 1808, but by April he had broken with the party and declared his support for George Clinton of New York, who ran a stunted campaign to challenge Madison. Alienated from the Republican leadership, Sloan only became bolder. In a floor fight over the embargo, he assaulted the Republican heartland in Virginia, where "*three hundred forty-six thousand nine hundred and sixty eight* HUMAN SOULS are kept in a state of *perpetual bondage,* and used as an article of *traffic,*" and where even free whites were denied full political power. "I will never hold up as an example," said Sloan, "any government, where the choicest of all earthly blessings, '*liberty,*' is extended only to a chosen few, and withheld from the many."[19]

Sloan had clearly crossed the Potomac, but his antislavery speeches led only to relative obscurity. He never returned to Congress, having lost the support of Republicans in New Jersey and at the federal level. As a final testament to his inauspicious character, a number of newspapers reported his death in the fall of 1811, a date that continues to stand in official records. Yet Sloan does not seem to have died in 1811. A few papers ran a notice claiming that Sloan was still alive; he published a pamphlet in 1812; and he was reported as a bank director in Trenton the same year. His actual death, meanwhile, received far less official notice, and he survives more or less in minor infamy, as the butt of the House.[20]

While I may not be able to redeem him from that reputation, it is important to recognize that Sloan, like other Northern Jeffersonians in Congress, did not make his peace with slavery. The course of Jeffersonian politics catalyzed a new antislavery argument among

Northerners that was quite different from the sentiments of Republicans before 1800. Men like Sloan now viewed slavery not simply as an abstract political evil, but as a powerful institution in the American political economy with equally powerful ambassadors in the federal government. Northern Federalists had made similar arguments since Jefferson's first election, but they did so while maligning impetuous Democrats like Sloan. This in turn only reinforced the North-South ideological alliance that brought Jefferson to power. But when Northern Republicans turned toward a politically driven, sectional critique of slavery, they threatened to undermine the Republican alliance altogether. This was most obvious in 1812, when DeWitt Clinton, George Clinton's nephew, renewed an internal Republican challenge to "Virginia Supremacy" by running against James Madison. In what proved to be the most competitive contest for the presidency since 1800, DeWitt Clinton came close to victory, taking every Northern state except Pennsylvania and Vermont.[21]

The Clinton campaign drew on sectional feelings that were more pro-Northern than anti-slavery in nature. Many Northern Republicans were simply tired of being ruled by Virginians, and many remained angry on account of Jefferson's embargo of foreign commerce in 1807. Such dissidents believed that they would never obtain beneficial economic policies until a Northern man occupied the presidency. Slavery was at best a marginal issue in these sectional complaints, but its absence did not render them benign. Sectionalism was dangerous in and of itself, insofar as it worked to undermine the ideological bonds that had sustained the Republican alliance since 1800. When Clintonian Republicans did attack slavery, moreover, it was far more difficult to simply malign them as jealous regional elites. Had Clinton succeeded, he would have given Northern sectionalism greater legitimacy in national politics, and he would have made Northerners far more powerful in Congress, especially once the new House, reapportioned based on the 1810 census, sat in 1813. At that date, the Northerners held a 105 to 81 majority over Southerners, one that would only rise over time.

But the Clintonian threat did not persist long after the election of 1812, in large part because of the war with Britain that began earlier that same year. Initially, the War of 1812 maintained the possibility for a sectional rift in the Republican Party, but the progress of the conflict helped reinforce a nationalist ideology that brought Republican adherents closer together and destroyed Federalist opposition at the national level. Even as Federalists in New England bitterly resisted Madisonian war aims and objectives, Republicans in that region grew more attached to the national administration. Joseph Story of Massachusetts, for example, who had shown signs of Republican dissidence over Jefferson's embargo, vilified Federalist critics of the war as traitors. The same spirit of nationalism spread throughout the North: young Pennsylvania Republicans Richard Rush and Charles J. Ingersoll viewed the war as a glorious national cause, while freshman congressman (and Clinton supporter) John W. Taylor, from upstate New York, received letter after letter demanding a more powerful federal commitment to the war. By 1815, Republican nationalism was at high tide: Andrew Jackson's victory at New Orleans became a cause for celebration throughout the country, while the Federalist representatives from the Hartford Convention, arriving in Washington with a list of regional grievances, were slandered throughout the Republican press.[22]

Northern Republicans like Story and Taylor left the war convinced that the United States was on the verge of realizing a new political destiny: Story dreamt of "great national interests which shall bind us in an indissoluble chain"; Taylor was a strong supporter of a new national bank, a high tariff, and a more powerful (and well-paid) federal legislature. Both men envisioned a national political future that would transcend partisanship and sectional feelings, but their dreams would be short-lived. During the Missouri Crisis of 1819–20, both became outspoken critics of the South. That legislative fight remains the traditional starting point for serious consideration of the sectional politics of slavery, but the sectional passions of 1819 would have been no surprise to a man like James Sloan, or to many of the Jeffersonians involved in the bitter slave trade debates of 1807.[23]

For Joseph Story, the conflict over Missouri "let out the great secrets of Virginia, and blabbed that policy by which she has hitherto bullied us, and led us, and wheedled us, and governed us." By sowing political divisions in the North, Virginia Republicans insured that they would consistently claim national power. Sloan had already learned that lesson, but after the War of 1812, his dissent was replicated on a wider scale. William Duane, for example, echoed Sloan's attacks on Virginia as early as 1816, providing Republican dissidence with a national venue in his newspaper. During the Missouri Crisis he defined a radical Northern position, and the Virginian James Garnett considered him "designedly cooperating with the Abolitionists."[24] In the House of Representatives, John W. Taylor was equally blunt, exposing the underlying structure of Southern politics. "When have we seen a Representative on this floor," he wondered, "from that section of our Union, who was not a slaveholder?" Should a "laboring man" arrive in Washington as a representative of the South, Taylor claimed, it would be "an extraordinary event."[25]

Like Sloan before them, Northern Republicans during the Missouri Crisis began to insist that slavery had no place in democratic political culture. But now their voices were both louder and more widespread. To think that "FREEDOM and SLAVERY can exist long in the same country" was certainly absurd, claimed "Hancock" in William Duane's *Aurora.* The Southern argument on Missouri, especially from Virginians in Congress, was no less defiant, and only served to spur Northerners along the path of sectional self-consciousness. Joseph Story was aghast at the antics of the crazed John Randolph: "He said, 'the land is *ours,* (meaning Virginia's,) and we will have it, and hold and use it as we (Virginians) please.' He abused all the Eastern States in the most bitter style; and intimated, in the most direct manner, that he would have nothing to do with them." But again, anyone who had seen Randolph during the debates on the international slave trade could hardly have been surprised at his support for slavery in Missouri. Back in 1807 he had promised to personally violate any law that threatened a master's property rights in slaves.[26]

The eventual Missouri Compromise only briefly stemmed the tide of sectional passion. It was arguably less a compromise than a stalemate: many Northerners saw the compromise as a victory for slavery, while a key Southern contingent, dominated by Virginia, saw the 36°30″ restriction as an invasion of property rights. John W. Taylor at first greeted the compromise as the best possible outcome under the circumstances. In late 1820, he was elected Speaker of the House of Representatives, which many Northerners took as a sign that sectional disputes might be suppressed in favor of "national interests," and that Northerners, rather than Virginians, might lead a new nationalist coalition. Republicans like Taylor and Joseph Story pursued such a coalition throughout the 1820s, and the breakdown of the Democratic-Republican Party in 1824 offered a clear moment of possibility, bringing John Quincy Adams to the presidency. He was the first Northerner to hold that office since his father, back in the 1790s. After 1828, however, both Story and Taylor grew pessimistic. Andrew Jackson became president in a landslide, and the old alliance between Northern democracy and Southern slavery was revived in a new form.[27]

For Taylor and Story, the rise of Jackson was a travesty, but for Jeffersonians like Martin Van Buren and William Duane, who helped build the Jackson movement, 1828 represented the rebirth of democracy in America. For Van Buren, Jackson meant a chance for institutional power; for Duane, he meant the chance to relive the ideological passions of his youth. For both, Jackson meant the return of "nothing more nor less than OLD FASHIONED JEFFERSONIAN DEMOCRACY," as Duane put it. Back in 1819, the *Aurora* had considered the coexistence of freedom and slavery downright absurd, but that statement was more than naive, considering William Duane's previous and subsequent history. He had helped bring Northern democratic freedom and Southern slavery together in his early Jeffersonian years, and after flirting with antislavery dissidence, he became one of Jackson's strongest supporters. Late in his life, he once again demonstrated the power of Northern democracy not to oppose slavery, but to accept it—an object lesson that would be repeated throughout the Jacksonian era.[28]

So was there ever a Jeffersonian antislavery tradition? Clearly, there were many Northern Democratic-Republicans who opposed slavery. But for Duane, Bishop, Leland, and Lincoln, opposition to slavery diminished in proportion to one's commitment to the Jeffersonian cause. Sloan's story, on the other hand, suggests that persistent opposition to slavery led only to dissidence: one could not be both Jeffersonian and antislavery at the same time. By the time of the Missouri Crisis, Northern Republicans like Taylor and Story seemed prepared to break with the South altogether. They chose nationalism over sectionalism, only to learn the hard way, as Sloan had before them, how thoroughly the combined force of Northern democracy and the Southern slavery could control national politics.

Jeffersonian and Jacksonian democracy recast national politics in terms which frequently made "slavery" more relevant as an abstract metaphor for the political and economic oppression of white men (and especially Northern white men) than as an extremely powerful institution in the national political economy. Focusing Northern attention on local elites allowed Southern slaveholders to appear as democratic icons rather than anti-democratic masters; aggrandizing the oppression of whites helped to build a racist democracy on which slaves had no claim and in which free blacks had no place. Finally, Jeffersonian and Jacksonian ideology helped preserve the political ties that produced "doughface" votes during sectional crises. The democratic passions of Northern Jeffersonians became a crucial part of a political system that protected slavery for decades.

The Jeffersonian and Jacksonian coalitions also contained the seeds of their undoing: defiant slaveholders and an egalitarian faith that refused to tolerate the claims of mastership. Yet dissident Jeffersonians, trapped by their own history, struggled to find a political coalition and a political language in which to press their claims. American democracy had never inherently opposed slavery, no matter how many protestations to the contrary. The very experience of democratic freedom in the North had sanctioned slavery from the outset, and overcoming that legacy proved difficult, if not impossible. Even the most antislavery Northern Jeffersonians became subject to the growing power of racism and proved unable to maintain the radical humanism of the 1790s. The Jeffersonian and then the Jacksonian alliance became vehicles not only for the political power of slaveholders, but for a racist social and political order in the North. From the perspective of Northern African Americans, "the slavery-pole of democracy" had triumphed.[29]

The rising virulence of Northern racism provides reason enough for scholars to remain skeptical of the egalitarian promises of Jeffersonian democracy. Yet it seems important not to lose sight of the lesson that Sloan learned so well: that slavery in the United States persisted because of the anti-democratic power of slaveholders. How and why men like Sloan first sanctioned that power and then attempted, but failed, to restrain it remain fundamental problems for the early republic. They are problems not of the republican slaveholder but of the confused democrat, struggling to define who is included in an egalitarian polity, what types of power are excluded, why oppression can or cannot be tolerated. Many Northerners in the early nation took the path of least resistance and answered these questions with racism and the elevation of white men. But, at heart, these are questions not about race but about the conflict between democratic ethics and arbitrary power, between individual freedom and the distant suffering of others. They continue to be hard ones to answer.

NOTES

1. Paul Goodman, *The Democratic-Republicans of Massachusetts* (Cambridge, Mass.: Harvard University Press, 1964); Alfred Young, *The Democratic-Republicans of New York* (Chapel Hill: University of North Carolina Press, 1967); Noble E. Cunningham, *The Jeffersonian Republicans: The Formation of Party Operations* (Chapel Hill: University of North Carolina Press, 1957); idem, *The Jeffersonian Republicans in Power: Party Operations, 1801–1809* (Chapel Hill: University of North Carolina Press, 1963); Joyce Appleby, *Capitalism and a New Social Order: The Republican Vision of the 1790s* (New York: New York University Press, 1984); Gordon S. Wood, *The Radicalism of the American Revolution* (New York: Vintage, 1993); David Waldstreicher, *In the Midst of Perpetual Fetes: The Making of American Nationalism, 1776–1820* (Chapel Hill: University of North Carolina Press, 1997); Jeffrey Pasley, *"The Tyranny of Printers": Newspaper Politics in the Early American Republic* (Charlottesville: University Press of Virginia, 2001); Andrew Shankman, *The Crucible of Democracy: The Struggle to Fuse Egalitarianism and Capitalism in Jeffersonian Pennsylvania* (Lawrence: University Press of Kansas, 2004); Sean Wilentz, *The Rise of American Democracy: Jefferson*

to Lincoln (New York: Norton, 2005); Gordon S. Wood, *Empire of Liberty: A History of the Early Republic, 1789–1815* (New York: Oxford University Press, 2009).

2. Leonard Richards, *The Slave Power: The Free North and Southern Domination, 1780–1860* (Baton Rouge: Louisiana State University Press, 2000); Peter Onuf and Leonard Sadosky, *Jeffersonian America* (Malden, Mass.: Blackwell, 2002); William Cooper, *Liberty and Slavery: Southern Politics to 1860* (New York: Knopf, 1983); Robin L. Einhorn, "Institutional Reality in the Age of Slavery: Taxation and Democracy in the States," *Journal of Policy History* 18, no. 1 (2006): 21–43; Einhorn, *American Taxation, American Slavery* (Chicago: University of Chicago Press, 2006).

3. For Northern racism in the Jeffersonian era, see Leon Litwack, *North of Slavery: The Negro in the Free States, 1790–1860* (Chicago: University of Chicago Press, 1961); Gary Nash, *Forging Freedom: The Formation of Philadelphia's Black Community, 1720–1840* (Cambridge, Mass.: Harvard University Press, 1988); *Race and Revolution* (Madison, Wis.: Madison House, 1990); idem, *The Forgotten Fifth: African-Americans in the Age of Revolution* (Cambridge, Mass.: Harvard University Press, 2006); Joanne Pope Melish, *Disowning Slavery: Gradual Emancipation and "Race" in New England, 1780–1860* (Ithaca, N.Y.: Cornell University Press, 1998); Paul Finkelman, "The Problem of Slavery in the Age of Federalism," *Federalists Reconsidered,* ed. Doron Ben-Atar and Barbara Oberg (Charlottesville: University Press of Virginia, 1998); and Rogers Smith, *Civic Ideals: Conflicting Visions of Citizenship in U.S. History* (New Haven, Conn.: Yale University Press, 1997).

4. See Appleby, *Capitalism and a New Social Order,* 102. This view is an implicit, if never fully acknowledged, assumption of much of the work in the democratization tradition, especially that of Wood.

5. For the strong version of this argument, see Sean Wilentz, "Jeffersonian Democracy and the Origins of Political Antislavery in the United States: The Missouri Crisis Revisited," *Journal of the Historical Society* 4 (September 2004): 375–401; and idem, *The Rise of American Democracy.* For more balanced accounts, see Matthew Mason, *Slavery and Politics in the Early American Republic* (Chapel Hill: University of North Carolina Press, 2006); and John Craig Hammond, *Slavery, Freedom, and Expansion in the Early American West* (Charlottesville: University of Virginia Press, 2007). For the extension of this argument to the Jacksonian period, see Wilentz, "Slavery, Antislavery, and Jacksonian Democracy," in *The Market Revolution in America: Social, Political, and Religious Expressions, 1800–1880,* ed. Melvyn Stokes and Stephen Conway (Charlottesville: University Press of Virginia, 1996), 202–23; and especially Jonathan Earle, *Jacksonian Antislavery and the Politics of Free Soil* (Chapel Hill: University of North Carolina Press, 2004).

6. In emphasizing political rather than racial ties to slavery, I follow François Furstenberg's suggestive analysis of how early national concepts of political freedom helped justify slavery. In contrast to his emphasis on "autonomy," however, my analysis here focuses on the idea and practice of democracy (see Furstenberg, "Beyond Freedom and Slavery: Autonomy, Virtue, and Resistance in Early American Political Discourse," *Journal of American History* 89 [March 2003]: 1295–1330; and idem, *In the Name of the Father: Washington's Legacy, Slavery, and the Making of a Nation* [New York: Penguin, 2007]).

7. Jasper Dwight [William Duane], "A Letter to George Washington, President of the United States ..." (Philadelphia, 1796), 46–48; Tim Matthewson, "Abraham Bishop, 'The Rights of Black Men,' and the American Reaction to the Haitian Revolution," *Journal of Negro History* 67 (Summer 1982): 148–54; "Brief of Levi Lincoln in the Slave Case Tried 1781," *Massachusetts Historical Society Collections,* 5th ser., vol. 3 (1877), 438–42; John Leland, "The Virginia Chronicle," in *The Writings of John Leland,* ed. L. F. Greene (1845; repr., New York: Arno Press, 1969), 96–97, 105–7; *Annals of Congress,* 5th Cong., 2nd sess., 656–70.

8. The electoral vote in 1800 was not an exact index of the popular vote, since many states chose electors in the state legislature. Congressional numbers in this essay are based on Kenneth C. Martis, *The Historical Atlas of Political Parties in the United States Congress, 1789–1989* (New York: Macmillan, 1989).

9. *Aurora General Advertiser* (Philadelphia), 24 September 1800, 18 February 1803.

10. William Duane to Joel Barlow and Fulwar Skipwith, 2 January 1801, William Duane Correspondence, Library of Congress; *Aurora General Advertiser* (Philadelphia), 23 January 1806; Duane to Jefferson, 11 August 1814, "Letters of William Duane," ed. Worthington C. Ford, in *Proceedings of the Massachusetts Historical Society,* vol. 20, *May 1906,* 373–75. For comment on Branagan, see Nash, *Forging Freedom;* and idem, *The Forgotten Fifth.* On the American reaction to the rebellion in Saint-Domingue, see, among many accounts, Robin Blackburn, "Haiti, Slavery, and the Age of Democratic Revolution," *William and Mary Quarterly,* 3rd ser., 63 (October 2006): 643–74; and Michael Zuckerman, "The Power of Blackness: Thomas Jefferson and the Revolution in St. Domingue," in *Almost Chosen People: Oblique Biographies in the American Grain* (Berkeley: University of California Press, 1993).

11. Abraham Bishop, *Oration Delivered in Wallingford, on the 11th of March 1801, ...* (New Haven, 1801), iii–iv; John Leland, "An Oration Delivered at Cheshire ...," in *The Writings of John Leland,* 268–69; Aleine Austin, *Matthew*

Lyon, "New Man" of the Democratic Revolution (University Park: Penn State University Press, 1981), 131–33; *Annals of Congress,* 8th Cong., 1st sess., 543–44.

12. Pasley, *"The Tyranny of Printers,"* 203–19. See also the Lincoln-Jefferson correspondence in the Jefferson Papers, Library of Congress. On Duane, see Pasley, *"The Tyranny of Printers";* and especially Kim Phillips, *William Duane: Radical Journalist in the Age of Jefferson* (New York: Garland, 1989). For Bishop, David Waldstreicher and Stephen R. Grossbart, "Abraham Bishop's Vocation; or, The Mediation of Jeffersonian Politics," *Journal of the Early Republic* 18 (Winter 1998): 617–57.

13. Jeffrey Pasley, "The Cheese and the Words: Popular Political Culture and Participatory Democracy in the Early American Republic," in *Beyond the Founders: New Approaches to the Political History of the Early American Republic,* ed. Jeffrey L. Pasley, Andrew Robertson, and David Waldstreicher (Chapel Hill: University of North Carolina Press, 2004); Lyman Butterfield, "Elder John Leland, Jeffersonian Itinerant," in *Proceedings of the American Antiquarian Society,* vol. 62, pt. 2, *1952,* 155–242 (Leland's address to Jefferson is reprinted at p. 224).

14. *Annals of Congress,* 9th Cong., 2nd sess., 167–90, 200–204, 220–44, 264–74, 373–74, 477–87, 527–28, 626–27, 636–38; Matthew Mason, "Slavery Overshadowed: Congress Debates Prohibiting the Atlantic Slavetrade to the United States, 1806–1807," *Journal of the Early Republic* 20 (Spring 2000): 59–81; Robin Einhorn, "The Early Impact of Slavery," in *The American Congress: The Building of Democracy,* ed. Julian E. Zelizer (New York: Houghton Mifflin, 2004), 77–92; Adam Rothman, *Slave Country: American Expansion and the Origins of the Deep South* (Cambridge, Mass.: Harvard University Press, 2005); W. E. B. Du Bois, *Suppression of the African Slave Trade to the United States of America* (New York: Longmans, Green, 1896); Fehrenbacher, *The Slaveholding Republic,* 149–204; Walter Johnson, "White Lies: Human Property and Domestic Slavery Aboard the Slave Ship *Creole,*" *Atlantic Studies* 5 (August 2008): 237–63.

15. See Richards, *The Slave Power.*

16. James Sloan, *An Address, Delivered at a Meeting of the Democratic Association* (Trenton: Mann and Wilson, 1801); *An Oration, Delivered at a Meeting of the Democratic Association ...* (Trenton: Wilson and Blackwell, 1802); Carl Prince, *New Jersey's Jeffersonian Republicans: The Genesis of an Early Party Machine, 1789–1817* (Chapel Hill: University of North Carolina Press, 1967).

17. Henry Adams, *History of the United States during the Administration of Thomas Jefferson,* 723, 855; Samuel Taggart to John Taylor, 17 November 1804, in "Letters of Samuel Taggart ... Part One," in *Proceedings of the American Antiquarian Society* 33, pt. 1, *April 1923,* 133; *Newburyport (Mass.) Herald,* 18 April 1806.

18. James Sloan, *An Address to the Citizens of the United States, but More Particularly to Those of the Middle and Eastern States* (Philadelphia: James Maxwell, 1812), 12–14.

19. James Sloan, *Politics for Farmers* (Salem, N.J.: Cushing and Appleton, 1809), 13; *Annals of Congress,* 10th Cong., 2nd sess., 915–30.

20. For reports of Sloan's death, see, among other papers, the *Trenton Federalist,* 11 November 1811; the *New York Evening Post,* 12 November 1811; and the *National Aegis* (Worcester, Mass.), 20 November 1811. For counterreports that he still lived, see the *New York Evening Post,* 15 November 1811; and the *New-York Spectator,* 20 November 1811. Sloan was noted as a bank director in the *New England Palladium,* 17 November 1812, and in the *Tickler* (Philadelphia), 8 December 1812, and a pamphlet under his name was published in that year as well. A recent study of Sloan establishes a birth date of 10 October 1748 and a death date of 7 September 1831. See Bruce Bendler, "James Sloan: Renegade or True Republican?" *New Jersey History* 125, no. 1 (2010): 1–19. For 1831 obituaries, see the *Daily National Intelligencer,* 19 September 1831, and the *Philadelphia Inquirer,* 19 September 1831.

21. For an overview, see Steven E. Siry, "The Sectional Politics of 'Practical Republicanism': De Witt Clinton's Presidential Bid, 1810–1812," *Journal of the Early Republic* 5 (Winter 1985): 441–62; and Steven E. Siry, *De Witt Clinton and the American Political Economy: Sectionalism, Politics, and Republican Ideology, 1787–1828* (New York: P. Lang, 1989).

22. Joseph Story to Nathaniel Williams, 24 August 1812, in *The Life and Letters of Joseph Story,* ed. William Wetmore Story (Boston: Little and Brown, 1851), 1:228–29. In the John Taylor Papers at the New-York Historical Society, see: Barry Fenton to John Taylor, 13 January 1814 and 15 January 1815; Isaac Pierson to John Taylor, 15 January 1814; George and Thomas Palmer to John Taylor, multiple letters; and John Taylor to James Hawkins et al., 7 February 1814. See also Richard Rush to Charles J. Ingersoll, multiple letters, in the Charles J. Ingersoll Papers, Historical Society of Pennsylvania, Philadelphia.

23. Joseph Story to Nathaniel Williams, 22 February 1815, in *The Life and Letters of Joseph Story,* 1:254; John Taylor to Jane P. Taylor, 26 March 1816, John Taylor Papers, New-York Historical Society; Edward K. Spann, "John W. Taylor, The Reluctant Partisan, 1784–1854," Ph.D. diss., New York University, 1957.

24 For Duane's later hostility, see Matthew Mason, *Slavery and Politics in the Early American Republic,* 78–80, 101, 136, 144, 189–90, 194; Phillips, *William Duane,* 537–38; and Garnett to John Randolph, 22 February 1820, Randolph-Garnett Letterbook, Library of Congress.

25 Joseph Story to Stephen White, 27 February 1820, in *The Life and Letters of Joseph Story,* 1:362–63; *Annals of Congress,* 15th Cong., 2nd sess., 1170–79.

26 Phillips, *William Duane,* 537; Randolph in *Annals of Congress,* 9th Cong. 2nd sess., 528.

27 Robert Forbes, *The Missouri Compromise and Its Aftermath: Slavery and the Meaning of America* (Chapel Hill: University of North Carolina Press, 2007); Glover Moore, *The Missouri Controversy, 1819–1821* (Lexington: University of Kentucky Press, 1953); John Taylor to Jane Taylor, 1 March 1820, Taylor Papers, New-York Historical Society; Harlow Sheidley, *Sectional Nationalism: Massachusetts Conservative Leaders and the Transformation of America, 1815–1836* (Boston: Northeastern University Press, 1998); Richards, *The Slave Power;* Daniel Walker Howe, *What God Hath Wrought: The Transformation of America, 1815–1848* (New York: Oxford, 2007); Richard Brown "The Missouri Crisis, Slavery, and the Politics of Jacksonianism," *South Atlantic Quarterly* 61 (Winter 1966): 55–72.

28 For Duane and Jackson, see Phillips, *William Duane,* 638.

29 To borrow a phrase from Joseph Sidney (see "An Oration Commemorative of the Abolition of the Slave Trade in the United States ..." [New York, 1809]), in which he argues that free blacks should back the Federalist Party. See also David Gellman, *Emancipating New York: The Politics of Slavery and Freedom, 1777–1827* (Baton Rouge: Louisiana State University Press, 2006); David Gellman and David Quigley, *Jim Crow New York: A Documentary History of Race and Citizenship* (New York: New York University Press, 2004); and Dixon Ryan Fox, "The Negro Vote in Old New York," *Political Science Quarterly* 32 (June 1917): 252–75.

PART III

African Americans and the Meaning of Freedom, 1865–1900

READING 7

Jim Crow

Kenneth T. Walsh

ULYSSES GRANT

Ulysses S. Grant, who followed Johnson into the presidency after winning the election of 1868, had been the commander of all the Union armies in the Civil War. As president, he is generally regarded by historians as a failure because of corruption in his administration and because he allowed many abuses by greedy businessmen. But in recent years, Grant has been credited with a more enlightened view on racial issues than had been earlier realized.

Grant's father, Jesse, was strongly anti-slavery, and refused to attend his son's wedding to a woman from a slave-owning family, but this did not seem to shape the son's attitudes one way or the other.[1] Grant seemed ambivalent about slavery until the Civil War actually began, when he turned against it.

His wife, Julia Dent of St. Louis, Missouri, had as childhood playmates the daughters of slaves who tended her father's crops and worked in her family's house.[2] But she was not in the least troubled that her family owned human beings, and there is evidence that she believed blacks were an inferior race.

When he was working his farm in rural Missouri during 1858, Grant endured hard times and scraped by as best he could. He never succeeded at farming and named his self-built house Hardscrabble. Grant worked the farm with two slaves he hired from their owners and one, William Jones, whom he borrowed from his father-in-law.[3] Grant later bought Jones outright but freed him on March 29, 1859. Julia owned four slaves: Eliza, Julia, John, and Dan. When the family later moved to Galena in the free state of Illinois, all of their slaves became free, but the future first lady kept the former slave Julia as her personal maid.

Like so many others in the North, Grant held views similar to Lincoln's at the start of the Civil War: His main goal was saving the Union, with slavery or without it. He wrote in August 1863, "I never was an abolitionist, not even what could be called anti-slavery."[4] However, after the bloody battle of Shiloh in 1862, he concluded that the North had to crush the rebels totally, and that meant destroying slavery, a pillar of the Southern economy.

Grant also supported using blacks in combat, and after he saw them fight, was more convinced than ever that they would make good soldiers. His trips into the South during the war gave him important insights into the anti-black culture there.[5] This helped to persuade

Kenneth T. Walsh, "Jim Crow," *Family of Freedom: Presidents and African Americans in the White House*, pp. 61-78, 231-232. Copyright © 2014 by Taylor & Francis Group. Reprinted with permission.

him that the federal government was needed to protect blacks in the South. One outcome was enactment of the Ku Klux Klan Act of 1871.

As president, he tried to enforce the civil rights laws vigorously and favored granting African Americans universal suffrage and equality under the law. Grant also appointed blacks to federal office for the first time. The abolitionist Frederick Douglass said Grant never showed "vulgar prejudices of any color."[6]

"For Grant," writes historian Sean Wilentz, "Reconstruction always remained of paramount importance, and he remained steadfast, even when members of his own party turned their backs on the former slaves. After white supremacists slaughtered blacks and Republicans in Louisiana in 1873 and attempted a coup the following year, Grant took swift and forceful action to restore order and legitimate government. With the political tide running heavily against him, Grant still managed to see through to enactment of the Civil Rights Act of 1875, which prohibited discrimination according to race in all public accommodations. [This law was declared unconstitutional by the Supreme Court in 1883.] … That he accomplished as much for freed slaves as he did within the constitutional limits of the presidency was remarkable. Without question, his was the most impressive record on civil rights and equality of any president from Lincoln to Lyndon B. Johnson."[7]

Grant won ratification of the Fifteenth Amendment to the Constitution, which guaranteed every citizen the right to vote. "He sent federal troops into the South to support state militias that policed elections," Felzenberg notes. "He took action against the Ku Klux Klan, formed in 1866, which tried to intimidate and bully blacks into not voting. His administration's anti-KKK efforts led to the prosecution and jailing of hundreds of violent racists in the South."[8] Grant felt that the resistance to suffrage and to any semblance of equal rights for blacks in the South was based on the worst of motives. He said bitterly that when white Southerners spoke of having their rights "respected," what they really wanted was "the right to kill Negroes and Republicans without fear of punishment and without loss of caste or reputation."[9]

As a way to provide blacks with a safe harbor, Grant favored annexation of the island republic of Santo Domingo in the Caribbean, partly as a naval base and partly to allow blacks to relocate there as a new part of the United States.[10] Grant believed that such an option would give blacks a way to persuade their employers to raise their wages and improve their living conditions in order to retain their labor. And while some key black leaders, including Frederick Douglass, endorsed the plan, Grant was unable to get much support for the idea in Congress.

Responding to critics who said they were tired of his brand of racial politics, Grant said, "Treat the Negro as a citizen and a voter, as he is and must remain, and soon parties will be divided not on the color line, but on principle. Then we shall have no complaint of sectional interference."[11]

Although Grant disavowed social equality between the races, he also began appointing blacks to important federal positions, including Ebenezer D. Bassett, principal of the

Institute for Colored Youth in Philadelphia, as U.S. minister to Haiti, the first black man to hold such a diplomatic job, and Frederick Douglass as marshal of the District of Columbia and, later, minister to Haiti.[12] Yet in his personal life, he apparently had little contact with African Americans except for a few personal assistants such as Jeremiah Smith, a former slave who was one of Grant's valets, and a black cook. He also had an orderly, James Young, during the Civil War and he kept Young on as a valet in the White House and during his post-presidency until Grant died in 1885.[13]

At the end of his administration, Grant offered an apology to the country in his farewell message to Congress. "It was my fortune, or misfortune, to be called to the office of Chief Executive without any previous training," Grant said.[14] "Under such circumstances it is but reasonable to suppose that errors of judgment must have occurred." He admitted there were serious problems gaining support from Congress for his Reconstruction policies but explained that his goal was to decide "whether the control of the Government should be immediately thrown into the hands of those who had so recently and so persistently tried to destroy it or whether the victors should continue to have an equal voice with them in this control. Reconstruction, as finally agreed upon means this and only this, except that the late slave was enfranchised, giving an increase, as was supposed, to the Union-loving and Union supporting votes. If free in the full sense of the word, they would not disappoint this expectation."

RUTHERFORD B. HAYES

After Grant, the trend was clear: The North backed away from attempts to force black equality on the South, and Southern states passed laws and imposed rules designed to keep blacks in an inferior status, suppress voting, and impose segregation in schools, businesses, and other public places. Meanwhile, the nation focused on other tasks, such as taming the frontier, constructing a vast industrial economy, and dealing with immigration.

During the 1876 campaign, Alfonso Taft, Grant's last attorney general, wrote Republican nominee Rutherford B. Hayes with a warning. "It is a fixed and desperate purpose of the Democratic Party in the south that the Negroes shall not vote, and murder is a common means of intimidation to prevent them," Taft observed.[15] Under Hayes, little was done to keep this from happening, even though Hayes during the campaign claimed to be a friend of the freed slaves.

At first Democrat Samuel J. Tilden, the governor of New York, seemed to have won the presidential election of 1876, after eight years of Republican rule under Grant. But the electoral votes of Florida, Louisiana, and South Carolina were in doubt. Without them, Tilden had only 184 electoral votes, one short of a majority. If Hayes carried those three states, he would have 185 electoral votes and would win the presidency.

Each of the states sent two sets of electoral voters to Washington to be counted, one set for Tilden and one for Hayes. Congress responded by creating a fifteen-member electoral commission with eight Republicans and seven Democrats, to figure out who won.[16] At this point, the Compromise of 1877 was struck: In return for congressional Democrats' acceptance of Hayes's election, the Republicans promised to remove occupying troops from the South. So on March 2, 1877, the electoral commission rejected the Democratic returns from the uncertain states and declared Hayes the winner by a margin of one electoral vote. This was accepted by the House of Representatives, and President Hayes then removed federal troops from the South, ending virtually all attempts to enforce the Fourteenth Amendment's guarantee of civil rights to every citizen, including former slaves. It also meant an end to efforts to enforce the Fifteenth Amendment, which since 1870 had affirmed the right of citizens to vote, regardless of race, color, or previous condition of servitude.

Hayes had the naïve view that Southerners would do the right thing in dealing with blacks.[17] But after he removed federal troops from the region, the Democrats in whom he entrusted the future of the freedmen did all they could to keep the blacks in second-class citizenship or worse. Democrat-controlled state legislatures, for example, enacted impossibly arcane literacy tests in order to restrict black voter registration—a technique that remained in use for many years. After Hayes left office, white supremacy was stronger in the South than before he became president.

After Hayes, there followed several decades when most presidents displayed little interest in the problems of race. White public opinion was indifferent or hostile to the African American quest for freedom, and American presidents, whatever their personal attitudes, were content to follow public opinion rather than lead it.[18]

THEODORE ROOSEVELT

President Theodore Roosevelt did things differently. He redefined the presidency as an activist institution that aimed to take the side of everyday people against the financial barons and corporate giants. Unfortunately, except for some personal gestures toward blacks, the progress he presided over on racial issues was very limited.

Roosevelt developed his theories about white supremacy from studying history and science. He believed that whites from Europe had proven themselves as the dominant race on Earth through their successes in war, in science, and in the arts, from 1492 to the early 1900s. He wrote that "peoples of European blood [held] dominion over all America and Australia and the Islands of the sea, over most of Africa and the major half of Asia."[19] And he attributed "substantially all of the world's achievements worth remembering [since 1492] ... to the people of European descent," especially the white, English-speaking people of the United States and Great Britain, although he did credit the Japanese for developing an advanced and successful civilization, too.[20] He thought that, over many generations, other races could improve themselves, but that it would not happen any time soon.

As a corollary, Roosevelt believed that it was the duty of the white race to propagate as much as possible, and he advocated that every white married couple have no fewer than four children.[21] To do otherwise would be to commit "race suicide," he argued.

And Roosevelt believed in the inferiority of blacks. "I entirely agree with you that as a race, and in the mass, the [blacks] are altogether inferior to the whites," he wrote to author Owen Wister in 1901.[22] He added: "I do not believe that the average Negro in the United States is as yet in any way fit to take care of himself and others as the average white man—for if he were, there would be no Negro race problem."[23] He wrote to another friend, Grenville Dodge: "I wish to emphasize that we are not fighting for social equality, and that we do not believe in miscegenation; but that we do believe in equality of opportunity, in equality before the law."[24]

Roosevelt had told black educator Booker T. Washington that he "would help not only the Negro, but the whole South, should he ever become president," writes historian Lewis L. Gould.[25] At the time the South was generally poor but African Americans were at the very bottom of the economic ladder. They were segregated and endured rampant poverty, illiteracy, and powerlessness. Life expectancy in 1901 for white men and women was almost 49.5 years. For non-whites it was 33.7 years. There were about 100 lynchings of blacks annually as a means of terrorizing them.

Throughout his public life, Roosevelt was troubled and puzzled by what to do about the divisions between blacks and whites. He never found the answer, but some historians believe that Roosevelt had more meetings and conferences at the White House on what he called "the question of the colored race" than any president until Lyndon Johnson in the heyday of the civil rights movement in the 1960s.[26] There is no reliable count of such meetings, but among those he met with were educators, politicians, religious leaders, journalists, social philosophers, and activists, both black and white. Among them was Booker T. Washington, whom Roosevelt respected for his prudence and restraint. Roosevelt said this black adviser "was not led away, as the educated Negro so often is led away, into the pursuit of fantastic visions."[27] Roosevelt also held meetings on race with Ed-ward A. Alderman, president of the University of Virginia; Judge Thomas Jones of Alabama; Silas McBee, editor of the *Churchman*; Lyman Abbott, editor of the *Outlook*; and many others.

Roosevelt was distressed about the virulence of Southern opposition to equality for blacks and the South's determination to resist advances for the African American, and privately he castigated Southern country gentlemen as "grown-up and often vicious children" on the question of race.[28] Even though he opposed special government programs to assist blacks, Roosevelt said he judged every individual on his or her merits, and his rhetoric was uplifting. "A man who is good enough to shed his blood for the country is good enough to be given a 'square deal' afterward," he told black soldiers standing guard at Lincoln's tomb, in an apparently spontaneous moment early in his presidency.[29] "More than that no man was entitled to, and less than that, no man shall have."

In November 1901, having been president for less than a year, he said, "I have not been able to think out any solution of the terrible problem offered by the presence of the Negro in this continent, but of one thing I am sure, and that is that in as much as he is here and can neither be killed nor driven away, the only wise and honorable and Christian thing to do is to treat each black man and each white man strictly on his merits as a man. … Of course I know that we see through a glass dimly, and, after all, it may be that I am wrong; but if I am, then all my thoughts and beliefs are wrong, and my whole way of looking at life is wrong. At any rate, while I am in public life, however short a time it may be, I am in honor bound to act up to my beliefs and convictions."[30]

He condemned lynching as fundamentally immoral and corrupting. After Governor Winfield T. Durbin of Indiana supported the right of a black man accused of murder to a fair trial, Roosevelt sent Durbin a public letter on August 9, 1903: "My dear Governor Durbin, permit me to thank you as an American citizen for the admirable way in which you have vindicated the majesty of the law by your recent action in reference to lynching. ... All thoughtful men must feel the gravest alarm over the growth of lynching in this country, and especially over the peculiarly hideous forms so often taken by mob violence when colored men are the victims—on which occasions the mob seems to lay most weight, not on the crime, but on the color of the criminal."[31] Roosevelt continued: "Whoever in any part of our country has ever taken part in lawlessly putting to death a criminal by the dreadful torture of fire must forever after have the awful spectacle of his own handiwork seared into his brain and soul. He can never again be the same man."

But Roosevelt quickly concluded that this condemnation was sufficient. He didn't want to risk his presidency in the election of 1904 by turning the South completely against him, and he pivoted away from the issue of lynching, on which he took no action, and race, and focused on other policy areas. During the 1904 presidential campaign, he wrote a friend, "I have nothing to gain and everything to lose by any agitation of the race question."[32] As with so many of his predecessors, Roosevelt showed little sustained moral courage on race because he feared a political backlash. And he wasn't proud of his decision. At another point in the 1904 campaign, he said, "If I am to be blamed by anyone for any failure in my duty, active or passive, toward the South, it must be for failure to take action as regards the nullification of the Fourteenth and Fifteenth Amendments in the South." He also felt constrained because he claimed that blacks had failed to demonstrate "both intelligence and moral vigor" in confronting the white power structure in the South.[33] Finally, there was little or no support in the North for reopening the old racial wounds of the past. Roosevelt complained in 1904 about "the indifference of the great masses of people [in the North] to whom the wrongdoing in the South is a matter afar off and of little immediate consequence, and who are impatient of any attempt to make things better in any way."

After his election victory that year, he told associates that he wanted to improve the racial climate but wasn't sure how to proceed. He felt that one huge obstacle was a "partially successful movement to bring back slavery."[34]

In the end, however, Roosevelt retreated from his racial goals and ideals. He simply decided that the issue of race was intractable, and he couldn't do much about it. He told friends that a president led best by avoiding unpopular social causes and seeking goals he could actually achieve. And racial justice was not one of them.

* * *

Yet in personal terms, Roosevelt apparently had no problem associating with blacks. He had a black valet, James E. Amos, who accompanied him on many trips around the United States. Amos remained as his personal assistant after he left the presidency and returned to the family estate at Sagamore Hill, New York.[35]

In particular, Roosevelt reached out to educator Booker T. Washington. Washington, who lived in Tuskegee, Alabama, was a leader of black Republicans in the South, a region that Roosevelt believed would be an important force at the Republican National Convention in 1904. And he reasoned that Southern delegates could be pivotal to ensuring him the presidential nomination. Some even thought that Washington was the dominant black political figure in the country. He was considered so important that Roosevelt, on the day he took office after William McKinley's death in 1901, asked Washington to visit the White House for a meeting "as soon as possible." His goal was to discuss and coordinate government appointments in the new administration. The two men met on October 4, 1901.

On October 16, 1901, Roosevelt went further by hosting Washington for dinner at the White House, the first time a president had brought in an African American leader to share a meal there on purely social terms. The president considered it quite routine, he said later. He told a friend that it seemed natural to "show some respect to a man whom I cordially esteem as a good citizen and a good American." During their discussion, Roosevelt focused on politics in the South and he treated his black guest with respect. In fact, Roosevelt considered the dignified, erudite Washington a proof of his theory that some blacks could achieve great success on an individual basis. He told friends that blacks were subject to "natural limitations" and that in nine cases out of ten, disenfranchisement was justified.[36] But he also said that a black man who managed to advance should be respected and rewarded by society. He believed that over many years, blacks could lift themselves up on the social ladder if they emulated whites, but it would take a long time.

Word of the dinner quickly spread in the newspapers, and it received favorable reaction in African American communities and in the North. But in the South, it was an entirely different story. This pleasant social encounter prompted condemnations of the most vile sort, including the comment by Senator Benjamin "Pitchfork" Tillman of South Carolina that, "The action of President Roosevelt in entertaining that nigger will necessitate our killing a thousand niggers in the South before they will learn their place again."[37]

Southern newspapers attacked Roosevelt for dining with "a darkey," said he was a "coon-flavored president," noted that "Roosevelt proposes to coddle the sons of Ham," and said he was promoting "mingling and mongrelization" of the white race.[38]

The *Memphis Scimitar* wrote:

> The most damnable outrage which has ever been perpetrated by any citizen of the United States was committed yesterday by the president, when he invited a nigger to dine with him at the White House. It would not be worth more than a passing notice if Theodore Roosevelt had sat down to dinner in his own

> home with a Pullman car porter, but Roosevelt the individual and Roosevelt the
> president are not to be viewed in the same light.
>
> It is only very recently that President Roosevelt boasted that his mother was a Southern woman, and that he is half Southern by reason of that fact. By inviting a nigger to his table he pays his mother small duty. ... No Southern woman with a proper self-respect would now accept an invitation to the White House, nor would President Roosevelt be welcomed today in Southern homes. He has not inflamed the anger of the Southern people; he has excited their disgust.[39]

The outrage was so intense that Roosevelt and Washington agreed not to discuss their dinner in public, lest it generate more ill will, and Roosevelt never received African Americans in such a social setting again, only in business meetings. He continued to privately seek the advice of Washington on racial issues but the next time Washington visited the White House it was at 10 a.m., during official business hours.[40] No black person apparently received a social invitation to the White House for many years afterward, according to White House historian William Seale.[41]

Another blemish on Roosevelt's record was his handling of a violent racial incident at Brownsville, Texas. On August 13, 1906, about twenty to thirty black soldiers from the Twenty-fifth United States Infantry, a black unit commanded by white officers, left their garrison in Brownsville, walked into town, and began firing their rifles "directly into dwellings, offices, stores, and at police and citizens," the mayor reported in a telegram to President Roosevelt on August 16.[42] One citizen was killed in his yard, and a police lieutenant was shot through the right arm, which was amputated at the elbow, the telegram reported, adding: "After firing about 200 shots, the soldiers retired to their quarters. We find that threats have been made by them that they will repeat this outrage. We do not believe their officers can restrain them. ... Our condition, Mr. President, is this: our women and children are terrorized and our men are practically under constant alarm and watchfulness. No community can stand this strain for more than a few days. We look to you for relief; we ask you to have the troops at once removed from Fort Brown and replaced by white soldiers."

It was an urgent appeal that no president could ignore, least of all the action-oriented Roosevelt. He ordered a full and immediate report from the War Department, and learned from the military and from initial accounts in the press that the black battalion had arrived in Brownsville about three weeks before, and racial tension with the white community had been growing ever since.[43] The black soldiers were banned from local bars, pushed off sidewalks, beaten, and threatened with murder. On the day before the incident, a white woman reported that a black man had made unwanted advances on her. The press reports said about fifteen of the men had violated a curfew imposed by their white commander, Major Charles W. Penrose, and went on a vengeful shooting spree.

There were contradictions in the accounts almost from the start, such as the fact that a head count during the incident found all the soldiers present and accounted for on the base.[44] But other evidence seemed to support the original accusations, including more than seventy casings from Army rifle ammunition and a soldier's cap found at the scene.

Roosevelt sprang into action on August 20, four days after receiving the telegram and after a follow-up request from a Brownsville citizens' committee that Fort Brown be temporarily abandoned.[45] Roosevelt ordered the battalion to redeploy to Fort Ringgold nearby until a full military investigation could be completed. After a preliminary report from the military arrived, Roosevelt moved the battalion away so as to avoid mob attacks from the local community. Roosevelt proceeded to send most of the battalion to Fort Reno, Oklahoma, while twelve suspects were held in the guardhouse at San Antonio. Military authorities eventually concluded that some black soldiers had indeed conducted the violent raid and that there was a conspiracy within the unit and among the prime suspects to obstruct justice because none of the black soldiers would identify the shooters.

Roosevelt clearly sided with the whites of Brownsville. He didn't want to alienate white Southern voters in that fall's mid-term congressional elections.[46] He said, "The colored man who fails to condemn crime in another colored man ... is the worst enemy of his own people, as well as an enemy to all the people." The final military report recommended that if no soldier confessed or provided information on the perpetrators, all of the black enlisted men should be judged guilty and held responsible and all should be dishonorably discharged.[47] Booker T. Washington met with Roosevelt privately at the White House, at the president's request, and recommended that members of the Twenty-fifth Infantry receive their day in court. But Roosevelt was in no mood to compromise and he "discharged without honor"—and without trial—167 black soldiers. As a result, many of America's blacks turned against him.

WOODROW WILSON

Woodrow Wilson, former president of Princeton University and governor of New Jersey, was raised in the segregated South. He is widely known for his high-minded ideals about promoting peace around the world after World War I and his unsuccessful effort to have the Senate approve the creation of a League of Nations to promote peace. But on racial matters, Wilson was retrograde.

Wilson was a self-styled Virginia gentleman, steeped in the idea that educated, upper-class whites were the superior class and blacks were inferior and needed constant guidance and supervision. While president of Princeton University, Wilson had discouraged African Americans from seeking admission and none were admitted while he was in charge. He believed the violent and racist Ku Klux Klan in the 1860s through the 1870s properly preserved the right of Southern whites to run their states for their own benefit and keep blacks in subservient positions.[48]

His presidency was very damaging to racial progress. "Through a combination of his own racial attitudes, his willingness to act on them, and the influence southern Democrats exerted over his administration, Wilson set back the aspirations and hopes of African Americans by more than a generation," Felzenberg writes.[49]

Black leaders had high hopes for Wilson early on. As he campaigned for the presidency in 1912, Oswald Garrison Villard, editor of the *New York Evening Post* and grandson of abolitionist William Lloyd Garrison, talked to Wilson about ways to expand black support for him and the Democratic party. W. E. B. Du Bois, editor of *The Crisis,* the magazine of the National Association for the Advancement of Colored People (NAACP), endorsed Wilson in August and wrote: "He will not advance the cause of the oligarchy in the South, he will not seek further means of 'Jim Crow' insult, he will not dismiss black men from office, and he will remember that the Negro in the United States has a right to be heard."[50]

On October 21, as the election approached, Wilson sent a letter assuring African American leaders of "my earnest wish to see justice done them in every matter, and not mere grudging justice, but justice executed with liberality and cordial good feeling. ... My sympathy with them is of long standing and I want to assure them through you that should I become President of the United States they may count upon me for absolute fair dealing and for everything by which I could assist in advancing the interest of their race in the United States."[51]

And he seemed to have an easygoing relationship with individual blacks. The black press reported that as governor of New Jersey in 1911, as he prepared to run for president the following year, Wilson met former slave Joseph Ford, a railroad employee at Union Station in Grand Rapids, Michigan. As Ford reached for Wilson's three suitcases, Wilson protested that they were too heavy for one person to carry.[52] But the porter, aware of Wilson's admiration for the author Rudyard Kipling, said, "Oh, no, governor, I am used to carrying the white man's burden." Wilson smiled broadly in appreciation of the literary reference. In 1917, when Wilson was president, he was again introduced to Ford, then active in political circles, and Wilson joked, "I remember him. He carries the white man's burden."

* * *

But during his first year in office, in 1913, Wilson's racial prejudices showed through.[53] He didn't object when in early April Postmaster General Albert S. Burleson of Texas, whose father had been a military officer in the Confederacy, sided with Southern whites who were angry that the races were mingling in federal offices and that black supervisors were overseeing white clerks. Burleson and Treasury Secretary William McAdoo went about systematically segregating blacks and whites at the offices, restrooms, and eating facilities of the government, starting with the Post Office, Treasury Department, and Bureau of Printing and Engraving.

This was a big setback. After the Civil War, Washington, DC, didn't have the Jim Crow laws legalizing segregation that existed in the Deep South. In fact, when the city of Washington had home rule after the Civil War, laws gave blacks equal rights in public places. Over time, these laws were ignored and segregation became the rule in most public places, such as hotels and restaurants, which would not serve blacks at all or would keep them apart from whites. But it wasn't until the Wilson administration that segregation of federal offices, restrooms, and cafeterias became widespread.[54] In some post offices, partitions were installed to separate black workers from whites.

The NAACP quickly objected. Villard, a founder of the NAACP, wrote Wilson that, "I cannot exaggerate the effect this has had upon colored people at large." Villard said African Americans had assumed that Wilson's commitment to democracy, much ballyhooed during the campaign, "was not limited by race or color." Wilson was defensive when he wrote back. "It is as far as possible from being a movement *against* Negroes," the president said.[55] Wilson told his aides that he had made no promises to blacks during the campaign except to "do them justice," and while he didn't want them fired from their jobs, he felt that segregation reduced racial friction and he wanted the matter settled in the least contentious way possible.

In November 1913, Wilson met in the Oval Office with critics of his racial policies. Their spokesman, the fiery Boston editor William Monroe Trotter, an African American and a leader of the National Equal Rights League, delivered a lengthy indictment and challenged the president. "Not since Frederick Douglass came to Washington to lobby President Johnson for black suffrage in 1866 had such a bold and demanding black figure stood in the White House face-to-face with a president," writes historian Nicholas Patler.[56] "Now, almost fifty years later, Trotter wasted no time getting to the crux of the problem."

Trotter said segregation was an "indignity" and an "insult" that suggested that "African Americans are unclean, diseased, or indecent as to their persons, or inferior beings of a lower order."[57] He went on to say that denying equality was in "violation of the Constitution." Throughout the meeting, Wilson was polite and seemed sympathetic, although he claimed not to know all of the steps toward widespread segregation in the federal government that were being taken in his administration.

At one point, Wilson lamely responded, "I am not familiar with it all," and admitted, "Now, mistakes have probably been made, but those mistakes can be corrected."[58] The meeting ended with the African American representatives mildly hopeful that Wilson would look into the matter and do something to stop the abuses.

A year later, in November 1914, Wilson again met with Trotter and other anti-segregation leaders.[59] Little had improved, and Trotter was confrontational from the start, even more so than the first time. "Only two years ago," Trotter said, "you were heralded as perhaps the second Lincoln, and now the Afro-American leaders who supported you are hounded as false leaders and traitors to their race. What a change segregation has wrought!" Wilson didn't address the charges directly, noting that "it takes the world generations to outlive all its prejudices" and no one could be "cocksure about what should be done." But Trotter didn't back off. "We are not here as wards," he replied. "We are not here as dependents. We are here as full-fledged American citizens."

Trotter said the government's backing for segregation was based on prejudice and he reminded Wilson of the black support he had received in the 1912 election. But Wilson, in a rare lapse in his self-discipline, couldn't control his anger and fumed, "Please leave me out. Let me say this, if you will, that if this organization wishes to approach me again, it must choose another spokesman. ... You are an American citizen, as fully an American citizen as I am, but you are the only American citizen that has ever come into this office who has talked to me with a tone with a background of passion that was evident." Trotter came back, "I am from a part of the people, Mr. President." And Wilson retorted, "You have spoiled the whole cause for which you came."

Wilson was ill disposed to accept their confrontational attitude, partly because he was dispirited and embittered by the recent death of his wife, Ellen. But an angry Trotter refused to back down and was defiant.[60]

"Mr. President," he said, "we are here to renew our protest against the segregation of the colored employees in the departments of our national government." He said segregation had been spreading through the government in the year since they last met, including the use of separate offices and "toilet rooms," and urged Wilson to reverse course and "abolish segregation of Afro-Americans in the executive department."[61]

Wilson responded hotly that the segregation was designed to minimize the friction that inevitably arises "when the two races are mixed." Besides, he said, he was assured by his staff that blacks were receiving separate but equal treatment, and that the arrangement really wasn't harmful or degrading to blacks. Trotter replied that this was false, and he went on to declare that black voters were very disappointed with Wilson, and his Democratic party would suffer for lack of black support in the future.

Wilson later told an adviser he regretted losing his temper and should have simply listened to Trotter's heated remarks and moved on.[62] But the incident was revealing because Wilson was much more upset over the perceived lack of respect for his office than the substance of what his visitor was saying about the poor state of race relations and the evils of segregation. Overall, the number of black-held positions in government was reduced during the Wilson administration.

The meeting, in the end, had no effect on policy. Segregation worsened, and civil rights activist Oswald Villard wrote in his memoirs that "the colored people were left much worse off than when Wilson took office, for the precedent had been set" of official sanction for segregation in federal facilities.[63]

The relationship between Wilson and black leaders deteriorated. At the start of 1915, the NAACP was protesting against showings of *Birth of a Nation,* a new film by D. W. Griffith that took a racist view of blacks and glorified the Ku Klux Klan in the post–Civil War period, even though it was considered a breakthrough in cinematography. Thomas Dixon, who wrote *The Clansman,* a novel on which the film was based, had been a student of Wilson's at Johnson Hopkins years earlier, so the president had a personal connection to the producers of the film. Wilson agreed to see the movie at the White House on February 18 with his family, aides, and their wives.

This incensed black leaders, and many African American voters took it as Wilson's endorsement of the movie.[64] The president explained to aides that he was unaware of the movie's content in advance and never expressed approval for it, and that his attendance was a courtesy for an old acquaintance. These feelings were conveyed by an adviser to political allies. But Wilson failed to condemn the racism conveyed in the film, and the damage to his reputation among blacks was irreparable.

As the migration of African Americans from the South to the North grew amid increased demand for workers in war-related industries, racial tensions grew in the North. In July 1917, a riot erupted in East St. Louis, Illinois; thirty-nine blacks and nine whites were killed and several black neighborhoods were badly burned.[65] Wilson asked Attorney General Thomas W. Gregory if the federal government could "check these disgraceful outrages" but Gregory replied that no federal action was warranted. Wilson made no public statement deploring the violence, but on August 14 he met with four black leaders and allowed them to say publicly that he condemned the violence and wanted to punish the offenders.

But on August 23, a confrontation occurred between black troops and a crowd of whites in Houston, Texas; fifteen whites and three blacks died before white troops and local police restored order.[66] The next day, an aide took shorthand of Wilson's reaction at a cabinet meeting: "Race prejudice. Fight in Houston, Texas. Negro in uniform wants the whole sidewalk." The Army quickly hanged thirteen black soldiers and sentenced forty-one to life in prison. Courts martial later resulted in sixteen more death sentences, and although Wilson commuted some of them, his partial leniency did little to strengthen African Americans' trust in him.

Lynchings were also a continuing problem. The NAACP reported that nearly 100 blacks were lynched in both 1917 and 1918, and black and white leaders pressured Wilson to speak out. On July 26, 1918, Wilson issued a statement "on a subject which so vitally affects the honor of the nation and the very character and integrity of our institutions."[67] He condemned the "mob spirit" of lynching and added: "I say plainly that every American who takes part in the action of a mob or gives it any sort of countenance is no true son of this great Democracy but its betrayer, and does more to discredit her by that single disloyalty to her standards of law and of rights than the words of her statesmen or the sacrifices of her heroic boys in the trenches can do to make suffering people believe her to be their savior." He urged governors and law-enforcement officers to end "this disgraceful evil."

But he did little at the federal level to back up his rhetoric. And Wilson showed no interest in an anti-lynching bill that made the practice a federal crime and that was pending before the Democrat-controlled Congress, where it died.

The irony is that while all these injustices were going on, Wilson committed the United States to what he called a war to "make the world safe for democracy." Just as disgraceful, America's armed forces—in which 350,000 African Americans served, as laborers and cooks, as well as in other jobs at the bottom of the social hierarchy—were racially segregated.[68]

*＊＊

Meanwhile, the black household staff saw a private and troubling version of President Wilson and his second wife Edith that few others did, especially after Wilson suffered a series of strokes in 1919 and became partially paralyzed. "As the president hovered between life and death, no one dared tell him how grave his condition was, for fear he would lose his will to live," recounts African American maid Lillian Rogers Parks.[69] "Even as he lay at death's door, word came that the Senate had rejected the Versailles Peace Treaty, because the League participation was part of it. Mrs. Wilson was in continual consultation with the doctor over whether or not the President should resign."

"As the crisis passed," Parks adds, "the word got around the White House that the first lady could still not even suggest to the president that he resign, because if he could not work toward the eventual American acceptance of the League of Nations, he would quite possibly lose any hope or will to live. The League was his magnificent obsession, even in his sickbed ramblings. From then on, the White House saw Mrs. Wilson become more and more involved in the actual workings of the government. Documents were delivered directly to her. … In the kitchens and back halls of the White House, the regulars were shaking their heads. They were glad that the President had weathered the storm and was improving, but most of them thought he should resign and allow a competent man to take over the reins of government."[70]

The first lady was strongly criticized in the newspapers for amassing too much power and acting as the unofficial president. There were also reports that Wilson had gone insane. All this bothered Mrs. Wilson profoundly. She insisted that her husband was mentally sound, and she was just helping him and conveying his wishes to other staffers. "I just don't know how much more criticism I can take," she told Lillian Rogers Parks's mother, also a maid at the White House, as she pointed to a stack of newspapers.[71]

NOTES

1 Meyer, Howard N. 1966. *Let Us Have Peace: The Story of Ulysses S. Grant.* New York: The MacMillan Company, p. 32.
2 McFeely, William S. 1982. *Grant: A Biography.* New York: W.W. Norton and Company, pp. 71–72.
3 Ibid., p. 62. See also Sinkler, George. 1972. *The Racial Attitudes of American Presidents from Abraham Lincoln to Theodore Roosevelt.* Garden City, NY: Anchor Books, p. 146.
4 Sinkler. *The Racial Attitudes of American Presidents from Abraham Lincoln to Theodore Roosevelt,* p. 147.
5 Ibid., p. 156.
6 Walton, Hanes Jr. and Robert C. Smith. 2008. *American Politics and the African American Quest for Universal Freedom.* New York: Pearson Longman, p. 199.
7 Wilentz, Sean. 2010. "Who's buried in the history books?" *The New York Times Week in Review* (March 14), p. 9.
8 Felzenberg, Alvin Stephen. 2008. *The Leaders We Deserved (And a Few We Didn't): Rethinking the Presidential Rating Game.* New York: Basic Books, pp. 282–284.
9 Ibid., p. 285.
10 Ibid., p. 282.
11 Ibid., pp. 283–284.
12 *Baltimore Afro-American.* 1922. "First colored man given a federal job." August 11, p. 7.
13 *Atlanta Daily World.* 1935. "Orderly, 102, dead." January 22, p. 1.
14 Felzenberg. *The Leaders We Deserved (And a Few We Didn't),* pp. 285–286.

15. Ibid., p. 286.
16. Ibid., pp. 286-288. See also Milkis, Sidney M. and Michael Nelson. 1999. *The American Presidency: Origins and Development, 1776-1998*. Washington, DC: Congressional Quarterly (CQ) Press.
17. Felzenberg. *The Leaders We Deserved (And a Few We Didn't)*, p. 288.
18. Walton and Smith. *American Politics and the African American Quest for Universal Freedom*, p. 199.
19. Sinkler. *The Racial Attitudes of American Presidents from Abraham Lincoln to Theodore Roosevelt*, p. 381.
20. Ibid., pp. 381-382.
21. Ibid., p. 408.
22. Ibid., p. 387.
23. Ibid., p. 388.
24. Ibid., p. 400.
25. Gould, Lewis L. 1991. *The Presidency of Theodore Roosevelt*. Lawrence: University Press of Kansas, p. 23.
26. Sinkler. *The Racial Attitudes of American Presidents from Abraham Lincoln to Theodore Roosevelt*, p. 418.
27. Ibid., p. 428.
28. Ibid., p. 418.
29. Felzenberg. *The Leaders We Deserved (And a Few We Didn't)*, p. 290.
30. Morris, Edmund. 2001. *Theodore Rex*. New York: Random House, p. 58.
31. Quoted in Morris, *Theodore Rex*, pp. 261-262.
32. Sinkler. *The Racial Attitudes of American Presidents from Abraham Lincoln to Theodore Roosevelt*, p. 423.
33. Ibid., p. 424.
34. Ibid., p. 419.
35. *Pittsburgh Courier*. 1927. "Intimate impressions of Rooseveltian personality recorded by former secretary." (April 23), p. A2.
36. Morris. *Theodore Rex*, pp. 52-53.
37. Ibid., p. 55. See also Felzenberg. *The Leaders We Deserved (And a Few We Didn't)*, p. 291.
38. Morris. *Theodore Rex*, pp. 54-55.
39. Quoted in Morris, *Theodore Rex*, pp. 54-55.
40. Morris. *Theodore Rex*, p. 58.
41. Seale, William. 1986. *The President's House: A History*. Washington, DC: The White House Historical Association in cooperation with the National Geographic Society, p. 653.
42. Morris. *Theodore Rex*, p. 453.
43. Ibid.
44. Ibid., p. 454.
45. Ibid., pp. 454-455.
46. Ibid., p. 455.
47. Ibid., pp. 465, 467.
48. Felzenberg. *The Leaders We Deserved (And a Few We Didn't)*, pp. 294-295.
49. Ibid., p. 294.
50. Cooper, John Milton Jr. 2009. *Woodrow Wilson, A Biography*. New York: Alfred A. Knopf, pp. 170-171.
51. Ibid.
52. *Norfolk Journal and Guide*. 1931. "Native Virginian, ex-slave, was mentioned for presidential nomination, married 50 years." (October 10), p. A11.
53. Cooper. *Woodrow Wilson*, p. 205.
54. Lightman, David. 2009. "Racial barriers fell slowly in capital." McClatchy News Service (January 16).
55. Cooper. *Woodrow Wilson*, p. 25.
56. Patler, Nicholas. 2004. *Jim Crow and the Wilson Administration: Protesting Federal Segregation in the Early Twentieth Century*. Boulder: The University Press of Colorado, p. 137.
57. Ibid.

58 Cooper. *Woodrow Wilson,* pp. 205-206.
59 Ibid., pp. 270-271.
60 Patler. *Jim Crow and the Wilson Administration,* p. 177.
61 Ibid., p. 178.
62 Cooper. *Woodrow Wilson,* p. 205.
63 Patler. *Jim Crow and the Wilson Administration,* p. 206.
64 Cooper. *Woodrow Wilson,* p. 273.
65 Ibid., p. 407.
66 Ibid., pp. 407-408.
67 Ibid., pp. 409-410.
68 Felzenberg. *The Leaders We Deserved (And a Few We Didn't),* p. 298.
69 Parks, Lillian Rogers, with Frances Spatz Leighton. 1961. *My Thirty Years Backstairs at the White House.* New York: Fleet Publishing Corporation, pp. 154-155.
70 Ibid.
71 Ibid., p. 155.

READING 8

Public Rights, Social Equality, and the Conceptual Roots of the *Plessy* Challenge

Rebecca J. Scott

> The citizens of this State ... shall enjoy the same civil, political, and public rights and privileges, and be subject to the same pains and penalties.
>
> Louisiana Constitution of 1868[1]

> Slavery not only introduced the rule of caste but prescribed its conditions, in the interests of that institution. The trace of color raised the presumption of bondage and was a bar to citizenship. The law in question [the Separate Car Law] is an attempt to apply this rule to the establishment of legalized caste-distinction among citizens.
>
> Brief of the plaintiff in error,
> filed April 6, 1893, *Plessy v. Ferguson*[2]

INTRODUCTION

In 1892, the Louisiana Supreme Court ruled that when Homer Plessy refused to give up his seat in a whites-only, first-class train carriage he was displaying an "unreasonable insistence upon thrusting the company of one race upon the other, with no adequate motive."[3] In 1896, the U.S. Supreme Court agreed that the citizenship granted by the Fourteenth Amendment contained no grounds on which to assert a right to the "social equality" that they claimed Homer Plessy's refusal of legally mandated segregation implied. Indeed, Justice Henry Billings Brown declared that "in the nature of things" the Amendment could not have been intended to "enforce" social equality.[4] The Court therefore ruled that the legislature of the State of Louisiana had not violated the U.S. Constitution when it passed a statute that obliged railroad companies to provide "equal but separate" railway cars and to have their agents assign passengers to one or another car based on race.[5] Homer Plessy's contrasting

Rebecca J. Scott, "Public Rights, Social Equality, and the Conceptual Roots of the Plessy Challenge," *Michigan Law Review*, vol. 106, no. 5, pp. 777-804. Copyright © 2008 by Michigan Law Review Association. Reprinted with permission. Provided by ProQuest LLC. All rights reserved.

claim that the statute in question established "an insidious distinction and discrimination between citizens of the United States, based on race, which is obnoxious to the fundamental principles of national citizenship" thus failed.[6]

Precisely because the *Plessy* decision appears, in retrospect, to have been both repellent and consequential, it often seems to tempt constitutional analysts to shift a portion of the burden for its most repellent aspects onto what is imagined to be "the historical context." In turning to the historical record to illuminate the *Plessy* case, legal scholars have characteristically asked a set of broad questions derived from the language of the decision: Did the drafters of the Fourteenth Amendment indeed mean to include "social equality," or racial integration, as a component of citizenship? Was racial segregation perhaps already a well-established norm, rendering the decision a mere formality? And most importantly, could one have expected any other outcome from within a society so pervaded with racism of various kinds?

While deploring the decision in *Plessy*, analysts often come up with answers that hew rather closely to the framing proposed in the majority opinion. After examining the complexity of the debates and maneuvering surrounding the drafting of the Fourteenth Amendment, William Nelson concludes that the Reconstruction Congress had not resolved "the question whether the Fourteenth Amendment permits or prohibits segregation."[7] In Nelson's view, the judges in *Plessy* should not be charged with racism for having chosen to interpret an indeterminate doctrine in a way that conformed to the pressures of the time.[8] Michael Klarman argues that the decision in *Plessy* "simply mirrored the preferences of most white Americans" and that a contrary decision could hardly be expected unless a strong social movement had existed that could support a campaign against segregation.[9] Owen Fiss views the outcome of the case as doctrinally "a foregone conclusion," and characterizes Homer Plessy's attorney as a visionary and a legal Don Quixote whose "conception of citizenship" was "shaky." Charles Lofgren views the decision as in keeping with "the spirit of the age."[10]

In these formulations, "historical context" takes on an almost fatalistic explanatory value. Michael Klarman thus writes, "Justices in the *Plessy* era were too immersed in their historical context to spot the oppression that historical hindsight can readily see in racial practices at the turn of the twentieth century."[11] This is, I will argue, an unnecessarily impoverished way of thinking about the relationship of law and historical inquiry. For one thing, the bog of determinism versus contingency is a famously deep one, generally better skirted than plunged into.[12] After a certain point, most things "have to" turn out more or less the way they turned out—but this hardly means that we are bound from the outset to accept the terms of the actual decision as defining the parameters of the possible in a given society. Moreover, invoking the larger "historical context" to argue that rights-denying court decisions were largely epiphenomenal seems oddly ahistorical: as those who fought over the legislation were well aware, law was an absolutely crucial component of formal segregation, and formal segregation was a linchpin of the conscious political project of white supremacy. This is why the *Plessy* challenge drew the energies of equal-rights activists for many years, even as they recognized the high probability of losing the case.[13]

The dialogue between historians and legal scholars is productive precisely because historical context is *not* simply a backdrop, a stage setting, or an external force pressing judicial events in one direction or another. A full historical context incorporates wide networks of social interaction and situates legal and other initiatives within shared and competing structures of discourse in order to illuminate the origins of a case as well as its meanings for different actors.[14] Knowing that the 1890s were marked by pervasive racism, or that the Republican Party was becoming more conservative, or that "public opinion" did not endorse "social equality" does not really tell us how the challenge was seen by Homer Plessy, his allies, and his enemies. Such generalities do not capture the dynamics of their activism and the historical constraints upon it. The New Orleans Citizens' Committee for the Annulment of the Separate Car Law set out to *create* a context, drawing upon public practices, shared values, and social networks that now require considerable digging to reconstruct. Tracing these ideas and practices, one can see how a group of men and women built on their own understandings of the past and deployed vernacular as well as formal concepts of equality. Some among them may have been Quixotes, but more in the sense of citizens insisting on honorable conduct than in the sense of men and women tilting at windmills.[15]

In this Article I will argue that Homer Plessy's supporters—and his opponents, though they were only later to acknowledge it—envisioned his legal challenge to a large extent as a claim to what the 1868 Louisiana Constitution had defined as *public rights*. That constitution, in force until 1879, had assured all of the state's citizens access to the same "civil, political, and public rights and privileges."[16] For Plessy's fellow activists in New Orleans, "public rights and privileges" were essential to the substance and symbolism of the equal dignity of citizens in the public sphere. Moreover, a claim of equal standing in public directly challenged the effort to impose white supremacy; it was not simply an expression of a preference for one rather than another mode of assorting individuals on a train.[17] "Social equality," by contrast, was a label their enemies had long attempted to pin on the proponents of equal public rights in order to associate public rights with private intimacy and thereby to trigger the host of fears connected with the image of black men in physical proximity to white women. To conflate the phrase "social equality" with an imagined taxonomy of civil, political, and social rights is to mistake an insult for an analytic exercise.[18]

The argument of this Article will proceed in three steps. First, I will explore the process by which the concept of "public rights" made its way into the 1868 Louisiana Constitution and the disparate historical traditions on which the delegates to Louisiana's constitutional convention seem to have drawn. Second, I will trace the public rights jurisprudence that emerged in Louisiana in the early 1870s in response to a variety of cases brought by men and women of color. I will also describe some of the ways ordinary citizens of color in Louisiana acted on their claims to public standing after the defeat of Reconstruction, thereby keeping alive in practice an idea that was no longer part of the state's written law. Third, I will argue that in the course of the *Plessy* challenge the idea of equal public rights developed into a broad anticaste principle that sought to change the course of a rapidly narrowing Federal Fourteenth Amendment jurisprudence.

From this perspective, the Louisiana Separate Car Law was not a mere expression of deteriorating "race relations." It was part of a frontal attack by white supremacists on the belief that the citizenship recognized by the Fourteenth Amendment—if not the Amendment itself—prohibited the state from becoming complicit in public acts of disrespect. The anticaste principle expressed by Plessy's supporters encompassed the earlier concept of equal public rights and constituted a reply to that attack. By fusing historical inquiry with doctrinal analysis across the three decades that linked the *Plessy* challenge to the 1868 Constitution, we can thus reframe the interpretation of the *Plessy* decision and situate it somewhat differently with respect to the Fourteenth Amendment.

I. WRITING PUBLIC RIGHTS INTO LAW

Louisiana's state constitutional convention of 1867–68 was a remarkable conclave. Its members were elected in the tense aftermath of a murderous 1866 vigilante attack on white and black Republicans in which the police appeared to be complicit. The behavior of local authorities in turn had helped to discredit President Andrew Johnson's conciliatory policy toward white Southerners and hastened the advent of congressional Reconstruction.[19] Drawn from an electorate that included newly enfranchised male former slaves, the convention comprised nearly equal numbers of men categorized as white and those categorized as black or of color.[20] On the floor of the convention, agrarian reform and women's rights were debated alongside suffrage and the content of citizenship. In Louisiana's "constitutional moment," various delegates revealed a strong form of anticaste thinking that had its roots in the cosmopolitan world of free men and women of color in the Gulf Coast and the Caribbean and that was reinforced by the aspirations of former slaves in Louisiana to a place in the politics and public culture of the state.[21]

The phrase "public rights" was introduced into debate in the early weeks of the convention. An initial draft of a proposed bill of rights, from a committee chaired by the former slaveholder Judge William H. Cooley, proposed a brief text guaranteeing all citizens the "same civil and political rights and privileges." This much even conservative Republicans understood to be essential. A dissenting minority of the committee, including a schoolteacher of color from Ascension Parish named P. F. Valfroit, the shoemaker Charles Leroy, and the former slave James H. Ingraham, immediately counter-proposed a fuller text. In keeping with a longstanding radical Republican belief that the Declaration of Independence was the foundation upon which the U.S. Constitution should rest, the minority report argued that the state constitution should begin by declaring that "all men are born free and equal."[22] It should explicitly guarantee all citizens "the same public, civil, and political rights and privileges."[23]

The origins of the phrase *public rights* are difficult to pin down. At least three lines of thought came together to give meaning to the concept: longstanding conceptions of personal honor, French and Caribbean revolutionary ideas of equality, and nineteenth-century European liberal codifications of rights. Ideas of honor underlay the belief that forced separation on the basis of color constituted what would today be called a dignitary injury. Egalitarian currents from the age of revolution provided a basis for arguing that all citizens had a standing of equality incompatible with the imposition of such dignitary injuries. And formal European political theory could be invoked to argue that the state was obliged to guarantee what were alternatively characterized as "social rights" or "public rights."

An honor-based right to respect in public places can be traced far back in the jurisprudence of *ancien régime* and colonial societies, though it was conferred only on certain members of such societies. In eighteenth-century Spanish America, for example, a white man aggrieved by what he saw as the insolent or importunate public behavior of a black slave could invoke not only his own personal honor but also a public right or interest that was offended when necessary hierarchies were thus publicly affronted.[24] Once colonies became republics, free and freed men could argue that self-dishonoring public displays of deference should be a thing of the past.[25] But as long as slavery existed, states generally continued to require public deference on the part of those with apparent or known slave ancestry, in a mix of class and color subordination thought essential to the maintenance of slavery itself. Free people of color in antebellum Louisiana had been subjected to a particularly exigent set of such required acts of deference, and relief from these humiliations was very much on the minds of many of the members of the 1867–68 convention.[26]

The fundamental idea of differential public standing had been challenged by the 1789 French Declaration of the Rights of Man and of the Citizen, which reflected a conscious assault on the allocation of rights and privileges according to birth, rank, and estate. The Declaration did not directly address the question of equal access to public accommodation or public transport, nor did it speak of color. But it reflected the dignitary dimension of public rights in declaring all citizens eligible for public office, and it located such rights within the essential nature of human beings:

> Article 6. The Law is the expression of the general will. All citizens have the right to take part, personally or through their representatives, in its making. It must be the same for all, whether it protects or punishes. All citizens, being equal in its eyes, are equally eligible for all public honors, positions, and employment [*toutes dignités, places et emplois publics*], according to their ability, and without any distinction other than their virtues and talents.[27]

In late eighteenth-century France, the claim that all men had equal standing in civil society was a powerful statement about the respect that should be accorded to citizens, and a call for the state to protect basic liberties.[28] In practice, however, the legislators of Revolutionary France equivocated on the applicability of the Declaration of the Rights of Man to the colonies, first holding back on the extension of civil equality to free men of color, then conceding such equality and consenting to the abolition of slavery, then reimposing slavery during the reign of Napoleon Bonaparte.[29]

The most explicit assertion of the dignitary component of the claim to equal rights came not from Paris, but from the colonies themselves. At the end of the eighteenth century, free men of color Vincent Ogé and Julien Raimond from Saint-Domingue had allied with French abolitionists to advance the case for equal political rights for free men of color, and Raimond became highly influential in the French National Assembly. Free men of color had also carried their struggle to the battlefield, particularly in the western part of Saint-Domingue. At Mirebalais in 1791, for example, "citizens of color" signed a "Concordat" with white colonists that obliged the latter to recognize their "violated and misunderstood rights" and repudiated "the progress of a ridiculous form of prejudice." These struggles overlapped and sometimes conflicted with the struggle against slavery itself that culminated in Haitian independence in 1804.[30]

In France, the rise of the Empire under Napoleon Bonaparte and the subsequent restoration of monarchical rule eclipsed many of the egalitarian claims of the Declaration of the Rights of Man. By the time of the 1830 Revolution, however, some of the key ideas of the Declaration had been adjusted to fit France's constitutional monarchy, and the first formal use of the precise phrase *public rights* seems to have come from a jurist writing in Paris in the 1830s. Pellegrino Rossi, an exiled Italian federalist, had been named by Minister François Guizot to a chair of constitutional law at the Collège de France in the 1820s. Rossi developed a detailed theory that divided the rights of people living in a state of law into three categories: private rights, public rights, and political rights.[31] While *political* rights, in Rossi's view, should be limited based on the different presumed capacities of certain groups (hence, for example, denied to women, children, and the insane), *public* rights should be open to all.[32] He judged privileges for private persons in the public domain to be impermissible.[33]

In 1846, the French jurist Denis Serrigny enumerated a set of "public rights" that were absolute and belonged to all citizens. These rights were constitutive of "social equality," including "the absence of castes which place one portion of the members of the State into orders or classes from which they cannot exit."[34] By 1848, with the revolution that brought the Second Republic, the previous reluctance to advocate full political equality gave way to a more egalitarian picture of rights, yielding a final abolition of slavery in the French colonies and an accompanying text that endorsed the dignity of all citizens. Minister François Arago declared that law in the colonies should henceforth make no distinctions that would violate the principle of "*égalité sociale*" [social equality].[35] In this context, the phrase "social equality" had both a formal legal meaning and a positive, anti-aristocratic resonance.

These European and colonial strands of public rights thinking were intellectually and socially available to the legislators of the 1867–68 Louisiana constitutional convention. Louisiana had lived under Spanish rule for the latter part of the eighteenth century, and everyone knew that how one was treated in public constituted a measure—indeed, it was often *the* measure—of one's honor. The transfer of the colony to France and then to the United States brought a formal guarantee of the rights of U.S. citizenship, a guarantee quickly invoked by men of color who had served in the militia under Spain. President Jefferson's refusal to honor this portion of the treaty did not diminish the militia members' perception of themselves as honorable citizens.[36]

Both the French Revolution and the ideology of the revolutionary *gens de couleur* of Saint-Domingue in the 1790s were thoroughly familiar to the immigrant free people of color in New Orleans and to their descendants—including convention delegate Edouard Tinchant, whose mother, a Saint-Domingue émigrée, had settled in New Orleans and later migrated to France.[37] The French revolution of 1848 was also part of the lived experience of European radicals like the New Orleans newspaper editor Jean-Charles Houzeau, a Belgian, and Edouard Tinchant, who had attended school in the French town of Pau during 1848.[38] Tinchant made the connection quite clear, explaining that his father had left antebellum Louisiana for France in order to raise his six sons "in a country where no infamous laws or stupid prejudices could prevent them from becoming MEN."[39]

In Reconstruction New Orleans, the claim to equal "public rights," with its strong implication of equal access to public accommodations and public transport, brought the Louisiana legislators into bitterly disputed territory. Rossi, writing in France in the 1830s, had treated the terms "public rights" and "social rights" as interchangeable. But by the 1860s, the phrase "social rights" had become associated with a claim to "social equality"—an expression of positive aspiration in 1848 France, but generally employed as a term of opprobrium in the nineteenth-century United States.[40]

As recent residents of a slave society, many of the delegates retained a keen understanding of the ways in which one's treatment in public was decisive for one's honor. By framing their claims to equal access to public transportation and public accommodation within the rubric of public rights rather than social rights, Louisiana activists of the 1860s could both assert their status as honorable citizens and try to avoid the charge that they were claiming "social equality" in matters of intimate or private life. Although any scheme that divides rights into fixed categories is to some extent artificially neat, a great deal was at stake in these distinctions.[41] To use the phrase "public rights" was to emphasize those forms of equality manifested in the public sphere. This might amount to the same thing as what others called "social rights," but it distanced the claim from the overtones of enforced intimacy and intrusion into private space that the term "social equality" had come to connote.[42]

The language of public rights could appeal to bilingual Creole men of color, to English-speaking former slaves, and to white Republicans, giving a name to the dignitary dimension of public life that they knew quite well. Denials of access to public transportation in Union-occupied New Orleans in 1863, for example, had been much more than the perpetuation of "custom." A man of color in Union uniform shoved off a streetcar knew the meaning of the gesture, whether the perpetrator was an ex-Confederate or a white Union soldier. Edouard Tinchant had been thus treated, and he later reasserted his affronted honor in a detailed letter to the editor of the New Orleans *Tribune*. In that letter Tinchant invoked his personal integrity, his military service, and a recent opinion on citizenship issued by U.S. Attorney General Edward Bates.[43]

English-speaking conservatives, by contrast, professed to find the concept of public rights utterly incoherent. They argued that in the proposed language for the state constitution, "social equality is attempted to be enforced, and the right of citizens to control their own property is attempted to be taken from them for the benefit of the colored race."[44] William H. Cooley, a judge and conservative Republican, furiously opposed the language and insisted that individuals could not be the carriers of such rights: "Because, I never heard the term 'public rights' mentioned as a private one, and because I cannot understand the idea of a private individual exercising public rights."[45]

In a sense, Judge Cooley's bafflement was warranted. "Public rights" as individual rights were undoubtedly absent from the curriculum when he studied law, even in the famously mixed civil law–common law jurisdiction of Louisiana.[46] The words "public" and "rights" were indeed used together in the Anglo-American tradition, in particular by the English jurist Sir William Blackstone, for whom "public rights" referred to the broad interest of the public at large in being protected against criminal acts. But for Blackstone, *individual* rights of citizens or subjects varied depending on status and office.[47] The activists of Reconstruction Louisiana, by contrast, used the phrase "public rights" to invoke, on the basis of individual dignity, a whole range of rights including what we would now characterize as equal access to public accommodations and common carriers. Cooley, for his part, was opposed not only to the concept but also to the evident egalitarian purpose of the invocation of "public rights." By renaming and denouncing this notion of public respect, calling it "social equality," Cooley and his allies sought to deny that any judicially cognizable claim could be attached to it.

As even the irascible Judge Cooley would have known, however, at least some elements of the public rights concept did have a counterpart in Anglo-American common law, namely the "duty to serve" that a tradesman or corporation incurred when offering a service to the public.[48] Prior to 1865, some courts had viewed forced separation of passengers on common carriers on the basis of color as a violation of this common law duty; many others had let it stand as a "reasonable regulation."[49] The Union victory now opened the question back up, and Judge Cooley and his allies hoped that by invoking the rights of private property and the danger of "social equality" they could fend off legislation guaranteeing equal access.

After long wrangling over the language, the time for decision on the new state bill of rights arrived. On December 26, 1867, the twenty-fourth day of the convention, schoolteacher Edouard Tinchant moved to endorse attorney Simeon Belden's proposal that article I should read, "all men are created free and equal." The proposal passed, 57 to 11. Then Thomas H. Isabelle, a Union veteran and man of color, proposed to add the term "public" after the word "political" in the list of rights guaranteed in article II. His amendment passed by a vote of 59 to 16.[50] In their constitutional moment, the delegates showed conceptual flexibility and linguistic ingenuity. The overlap between Anglo-American common law and continental concepts of equality, including the language used by Pellegrino Rossi, meant that the phrase "public rights" was both intelligible and coherent to members of the Francophone-Anglophone coalition in the state convention. At a purely practical level, the new Louisiana Constitution aimed to wipe out the invidious distinctions based on color that had pervaded the Louisiana Civil Code and subsequent legislation; the bill of rights was one tool toward that end.[51] At the same time, this bill of rights asserted a key portion of the "emancipationist" legacy of the Civil War and filled out the idea of equal rights as part of *state* citizenship, all the more important in light of the ambiguous and incomplete definition of the rights attached to national citizenship in the Fourteenth Amendment.[52]

The 1868 constitution left undefined the full scope of the guarantee to all citizens of the same "public rights and privileges." But article XIII of the bill of rights stated that all persons "shall enjoy equal rights and privileges upon any conveyance of a public character."[53] It went on to specify that

> all places of business, or of public resort, or for which a license is required by either State, parish or municipal authority, shall be deemed places of a public character, and shall be opened to the accommodation and patronage of all persons, without distinction or discrimination on account of race or color.[54]

In effect, the guarantee that all citizens would enjoy the same public rights had a double meaning. It invoked specific rights to equal treatment in public places and equal access to public services, and it implied that whatever other rights or privileges might subsequently be deemed "public" would apply equally to all citizens.[55] This formula had no precise equivalent in the constitutions of the other reconstructed states, though a few came close. Virginia's 1868 bill of rights, for example, held that "all citizens in the State are hereby declared to possess equal civil and political rights and public privileges."[56] Louisiana stood at the forefront in making public rights explicit, but the concept was not a Creole idiosyncrasy. Its core components would be reformulated in federal legislation, and the phrase itself would appear four years later in the Republican Party's national platform.[57]

II. LITIGATING IN DEFENSE OF EQUAL "PUBLIC RIGHTS"

By the time that the new Louisiana Constitution went into effect in 1868, the idea of equal public rights had become tightly linked to a broad and inclusive concept of United States citizenship. Like many radical Republicans in other states, Louisiana activists viewed the Fourteenth Amendment as recognition of a set of claims to citizenship that had always been legitimate, not simply as the conferring of citizenship on men and women of color at the moment of ratification.[58] The argument for an inclusive national citizenship had a long pedigree in Louisiana, dating back to the era of the Founders, when article III of the 1803 Louisiana Purchase Treaty guaranteed those who had been under French rule access to all the rights and privileges of citizens of the United States. President Jefferson had tried to ignore this promise and maneuvered adroitly to defeat the citizenship claims of the men of color serving in the militia, but the Treaty would none-theless be invoked in the rhetoric of men of color throughout the ensuing decades.[59]

These claims had been reinforced by the wartime opinion of U.S. Attorney General Bates, who in 1862 issued a far-reaching ruling that people of color should be understood to be citizens of the United States.[60] Creole activists in New Orleans quickly seized upon this decision and published it on the front page of their newspaper, *l'Union*, to strengthen their claims to both public and political rights. The future delegate to the 1867–68 convention Edouard Tinchant publicly quoted the Bates ruling in 1864 in a vigorous defense of a deep set of citizenship rights that transcended not only the errors of the *Dred Scott* decision but also the hesitations of many federal officials and Union officers. Tinchant himself had been born in France, but he believed himself to have achieved the equivalent of "letters of naturalization" in the United States through his service in the Union army in defense of New Orleans against a potential Confederate attack.[61] In the heady atmosphere of wartime Louisiana, the content of citizenship could be seen to be expanding, along with eligibility for it.

Once the 1868 Louisiana Constitution was drafted and ratified under the terms of congressional Reconstruction, the Louisiana Supreme Court made earlier precedents explicit by ruling that "[b]y the treaty whereby Louisiana was acquired, the free colored inhabitants of Louisiana were admitted to citizenship of the United States."[62] At stake in this 1872 case was the "private right" of an antebellum free man of color to hold land, not his "public rights." But the ruling reflected the longstanding belief of free Creoles of color that they held a promise of citizenship rights from the very moment of Louisiana's acquisition.[63] Present at the creation, as it were, people of color could claim a right to be seen as full members of civil society and the public sphere. The historical argument for national citizenship had been articulated by free people of color in the state long before the Fourteenth Amendment was drafted. Its ratification vindicated their sense of rights; it did not create it.[64]

Louisiana's 1868 organic law, in turn, had given precise content to the longstanding ideals of equal citizenship. The attribution to all citizens of "the same civil, political and public rights and privileges" provided the basic framework, while article XIII spelled out the details of the right to equal treatment.[65] Thus, when Mrs. Josephine Decuir found herself denied access to the ladies' stateroom on the steamer *Governor Allen* in July of 1872, she had a basis on which to bring suit under the state constitution and subsequent state statutes.[66]

Josephine Decuir's experience on the steamboat encapsulated the humiliation of "customary" racial segregation and exposed the fiction of consent on which it rested. John Cedilot, the steward on the *Governor Allen*, was by his own account a Frenchman raised in Louisiana. He viewed the separation of white and "colored" passengers to be a reasonable response to the preferences of white passengers. But when it fell to him to enforce the rules against Mrs. Decuir by denying her a ladies' cabin, the situation became awkward. His job was to provide passengers with supper and a berth on this overnight journey from New Orleans to Pointe Coupée. He struggled to persuade Mrs. Decuir to accept a berth in the windowless "colored bureau" or, failing that, in the "saloon" located below the "recess," a thoroughfare used by nursemaids and their charges. She refused. He offered to bring her supper in her chair. She refused. The otherwise deferential steward seems to have been no match for this well-dressed widow stubbornly defending her own dignity. Try as he might, he could not persuade her to consent to her own humiliation—even in return for a plate of fried oysters and warm rolls.[67]

Mrs. Decuir was on a journey to deal with legal matters in the case of her late husband's inheritance and thus happened to be accompanied by an attorney, who could later testify that the employees of the steamer had told him that their refusal of a stateroom was based on her perceived color. Mrs. Decuir's invocation of her class standing (her husband had been a planter, and her brother was now state treasurer), as well as her performance of feminine delicacy, give the case a quaint tone compared to the egalitarianism of twentieth-century sit-ins. But the underlying point was much the same: by refusing to accept forced segregation presented as custom, Mrs. Decuir framed her claim within article XIII of the Louisiana Constitution and state statutes protecting the right of *any* well-behaved female citizen to pay for and receive a stateroom in the ladies' cabin.[68]

Under the Louisiana Constitution, Mrs. Decuir was in the right, and the state Supreme Court awarded her $1,000 and court costs. Like the male plaintiffs in similar Louisiana cases involving admission to a coffee house and to a theater, she obtained redress under state law. The heirs of the owners of the steamboat, however, appealed the case to the U.S. Supreme Court. In a somewhat forced interpretation of the Commerce Clause, the Supreme Court ruled that even though her journey had been entirely within the State of Louisiana, the state constitution's prohibition of segregation on a steamboat constituted an undue interference with interstate commerce, thereby violating the Federal Constitution. The Court thus awarded victory to the captain's heirs and undermined the capacity of Louisiana to enforce its own antidiscrimination statutes.[69]

Louisiana's 1868 constitutional framework provided a particularly explicit basis for legal challenges to forced segregation, but citizens of other states had framed their claims in similar language, drawing on both common law and state and federal statutes. In 1872, the national Republican Party had called for legislation to establish "complete liberty and exact equality in the enjoyment of all civil, political, and public rights" and sought to remind Congress and the courts that the "recent amendments to the national Constitution should be cordially sustained because they are right, not merely tolerated because they are laws."[70] During discussion of the proposed 1875 Federal Civil Rights Act, one man from Ohio wrote that "[s]ocial equality seems to be the bugbear at which American justice is frightened, and the colored man denied many public privileges accorded to other American citizens."[71] The 1875 Act is now remembered mainly for having been overturned by the Supreme Court in the 1883 *Civil Rights Cases*, but while it was in effect, it provided a lever with which men and women in states like Maryland could attack segregation on the railroads.[72] The Republican

Party platform in 1876 again called for "complete liberty and exact equality in the exercise of all civil, political and public rights."[73]

With the federal government's retreat from Reconstruction in 1877, however, Louisiana's self-avowed white supremacists took control of the state through the Democratic Party. In 1878–79, the new state legislature drafted and promulgated a constitution in which the phrase "civil, political, and public rights" no longer appeared. The principle of racial separation in the schools also made a discreet appearance through the funding of an all-black university.[74]

In practice, the affronts to men and women of color in public spaces multiplied, and a statutory basis for appeals for damages or redress no longer existed. The struggle for public voice continued, however, both in the city and the countryside. Defending the Reconstruction-era conception of public rights after the defeat of Reconstruction itself was not merely the province of urban activists; it was a matter of importance to thousands of Louisianans of African descent, for whom the ability to travel freely and to gather in public were the bedrock for claims-making of various forms. Local activists like the blacksmith Pierre Carmouche in Donaldsonville and the schoolteacher Junius Bailey in Thibodaux turned their skills toward organizing for the Knights of Labor and drafting collective communications to the sugar planters' organization. In late November of 1887, a huge strike swept through the sugar fields. The strike was crushed when the governor deployed the now all-white militia to force strikers out of their homes on the plantation, and vigilantes organized to confront the workers when they took refuge in the towns.[75]

The withdrawal of federal support for Louisiana's Republicans and for its citizens of color did not mean that they ceased entirely to be heard. Moreover, the courts' refusal to support their public rights did not prevent these citizens from acting in public as bearers of such rights. Indeed, such public displays of a claim to equality were precisely the target at which the Louisiana legislature aimed the 1890 Separate Car Law.[76]

III. ORGANIZING THE *PLESSY* CHALLENGE

In a post-slavery society in which large numbers of former slaves and their descendants did not possess the skills of reading and writing, it might seem difficult to nurture an oppositional movement centered on formal rights and legal claims-making. But through what Armando Petrucci has referred to as the "delegation of writing," the oral claims of many people of color of modest birth were routinely transformed into legal language by skilled members of the community.[77] The legal systems of both France and Spain had long attributed a central role in private law to the legal practitioner known as a *notaire* (*escribano* in Spanish), and the State of Louisiana had retained the public notary as an essential actor in the legal system. Charged with formalizing and recording consensual understandings, the notary conferred enforceability at law on a multitude of transactions. He was a key figure in the branch of private law designated "non-contentious," giving authenticity to texts and conferring "executory force" on their stipulations, without the necessity of court action. Notarial acts could also be drawn upon in court proceedings if the matter at hand moved into the realm of the "contentious."[78] Under Louisiana law, the notary, with his duty to serve all who sought him out, brought formal writing within the reach of ordinary people and was legally obliged to transcribe and retain for future reference the full text of most of the documents that he notarized.[79]

In New Orleans, at the nexus between these everyday practices of writing and the larger campaign for public rights, was an intriguing individual: Louis A. Martinet, notary public. Martinet's mother was a Louisiana-born woman of color and his father was apparently a Belgian immigrant. After the Civil War, Martinet attended Straight University Law School, obtained admission to the bar, and, a decade later, acquired certification as a notary.[80]

It was in the tense post-Reconstruction environment of 1888 that Louis Martinet opened his office as a notary public on Exchange Alley, in the commercial district of New Orleans. The pluralism and public character of the office of the notary gave it a particular importance. The ratification of the Thirteenth and Fourteenth Amendments to the U.S. Constitution had made it clear that former slaves, their descendants, and others of African ancestry would now unequivocally have juridical personality, becoming subjects of law, not the objects of property transactions. But by the 1880s, the restoration of white supremacy in Louisiana was well underway. If the juridical capacity of persons of color was in theory equal to that of other citizens, as a practical matter they often faced severe hostility in the courts. The notary's office, however, remained a place where some of the benefits of law could be invoked outside of the gaze of juries and the judiciary. Martinet's reach, moreover, extended from downtown New Orleans outward to the lively multiracial community of Faubourg Tremé, where his colleagues Homer Plessy, shoemaker, and Rodolphe Desdunes, schoolteacher and cigar-seller, lived.[81]

As Kathryn Burns has phrased it, the function of the notary was to pour meaning into the molds provided by law, precedent, and handbooks, producing texts to serve the needs of his clients.[82] Among Louis Martinet's clients, these needs included the preparation of documents making property transactions official, establishing and cancelling mortgages and other loans, and providing for inheritance by will. The notary also formalized families' decisions on the care of an infirm relative and issued powers of attorney. As a result, the volumes of documents transcribed by Martinet reveal a web of interactions among people of differing degrees of literacy and prosperity, Catholic and Protestant, former slave and long-free. Although many of his clients were men and women who could have been categorized as "colored," Martinet rarely employed color terms of any kind, except when those coming before him explicitly chose to invoke African ancestry.[83]

Martinet routinely documented the establishment of mutual aid societies, giving legal recognition to various forms of social solidarity.[84] On October 3, 1890, for example, three months after the Louisiana legislature passed the Separate Car Law, a group of eight women appeared before Martinet. They wished to incorporate legally as a mutual aid society under the name La Dignité, or Dignity. They committed themselves to providing medical assistance to their members and, when necessary, a funeral and burial, and they set procedures for the calling of meetings and the elections of officers. Most striking is the provision that all of their subsequent documents were to be stamped using a copper emblem bearing the word "Dignité." These women were explicitly asserting their dignified public presence, in life as in death.[85]

These expressions of dignity and equal public standing in the office of Louis Martinet, public notary, provide us with an appropriate vantage point from which to view the *Plessy* challenge itself. In July of 1890 the Louisiana legislature passed Act No. 111, designated, "An act to promote the comfort of passengers on railway trains; requiring all railway companies carrying passengers on their trains, in this State, to provide equal but separate accommodations for the white and colored races." It held that "the officers of such passenger trains shall have power and are hereby required to assign each passenger to the coach or compartment used for the race to which such passenger belongs." Entry into a coach other than the one assigned by the officer was a criminal offense, punishable by a fine of twenty-five dollars or not more than twenty days in the parish prison.[86]

In response to this blow to equal public rights, Louis Martinet, Paul Bonseigneur, Rodolphe Desdunes, and others founded the Citizens' Committee for the Annulment of Act No. 111, commonly known as the Separate Car Law, and expanded their newspaper the *Crusader* to raise money and publicize their campaign. Some of those joining with the Committee, including teachers, traders, and artisans, had come of age in the era of Louisiana's radical 1868 constitution with its ringing claim of equal public rights. Others were younger, but recalled that constitution as a moment of principled triumph in the generation of their parents.[87]

The networks and solidarities registered in Martinet's notarial records would underlie and reinforce the Committee's litigation. Many of these organizations and their counterparts in the countryside contributed to what was called "Mr. Desdunes' stocking," the fund to support the *Crusader* and the lawsuits. The schoolteacher Alice E. Hampton, who taught at the Donaldsonville Academy upriver in Ascension Parish, put in her fifty cents in July of 1895, along with dimes and quarters collected from dozens of young women, despite its being "so hot going to and coming from school every day" that she had found it hard to do her "whole duty." Her neighbor Pierre Carmouche, the blacksmith and former Knights of Labor organizer, gathered funds from his colleagues in a mutual-aid society called the True Friends.[88]

In claiming the right to equal treatment on public transportation, the organizers of the *Plessy* challenge were well aware of the power of "customary" forms of racism to continue to inhibit their public practices, with or without a Separate Car Law. But they were determined to try to prevent the central tenet of white supremacist ideology from being enforced *by* the law. Public rights, with their intimate connection to public standing, were a key component of honorable citizenship. If they fell, civil and political rights were at increased risk as well.

The story of the *Plessy* test case itself has been carefully told by several authors who have reconstructed the process by which first Daniel Desdunes, musician, and then Homer Plessy, shoemaker and Freemason, stepped forward to test the constitutionality of Louisiana's Separate Car Law. Desdunes, who had purchased an interstate ticket, successfully invoked a recent ruling based on the Commerce Clause of the U.S. Constitution that barred Louisiana's legislature from regulating carriers traveling between Louisiana and Alabama. For a moment the Committee of Citizens dared to exult, "Jim Crow is Dead!"; but the ruling in the Desdunes case did not address the broader claims of individual rights. By careful pre-arrangement, Homer Plessy had bought a ticket on the East Louisiana Railroad from New Orleans to Covington, Louisiana, and taken a seat in the "white" car, where he was confronted by the conductor and removed from the train. He had then been arrested, arraigned, and released on bond. The Committee vowed that they would "exhaust all remedies which the laws of our country allow to its citizens for a redress of grievances."[89]

Over the next four years, the case made its way through the courts on a writ of prohibition challenging the constitutionality of the Separate Car Law. When it reached the United States Supreme Court, Plessy was represented by J.C. Walker, a Louisiana attorney, and by Albion Tourgée, the eloquent novelist, Republican activist, Union veteran, and former judge.[90] Their briefs built on both the Thirteenth and the Fourteenth Amendments and made a variety of ingenious arguments about the indeterminacy of race and the "property" value of a reputation of whiteness.[91] Blocked by the weight of precedent from simply claiming a right under the Fourteenth Amendment to freedom from discriminatory treatment, Plessy's attorneys drew attention to the state's action in forcing the railways to discriminate. Key to the whole structure of their claim, however, was the identification of the Separate Car Law with the concept of caste. In language that recalled the 1868 Louisiana Constitution's guarantee of equal access to all enterprises holding a franchise or charter from the state, the brief for Plessy argued as follows:

> It is not consistent with reason that the United States, having granted and bestowed *one equal citizenship* of the United States and prescribed *one equal citizenship in each state*, for all, will permit a State to compel a railway conductor to assort them arbitrarily according to his ideas of race, in the enjoyment of chartered privileges.[92]

By 1896 it was no longer possible to invoke the 1868 Louisiana Constitution's bill of rights, with its guarantee to all citizens of the same "civil, political, and public rights and privileges." That text had been replaced by the state constitution of 1879, and the new Louisiana Supreme Court would not interpret the new constitution as granting any such public rights. The concepts and formulas of the 1868 Constitution nonetheless underlay the spirit of Plessy's brief, echoed in references to "the enjoyment of chartered privileges." The earlier terms were now re-molded to try to fit the language of the Thirteenth and Fourteenth Amendments, and the unifying concept was the impermissibility of caste: "The effect of a law distinguishing between citizens as to race, in the enjoyment of a public franchise is to legalize caste and restore, in part at least, the inequality of right which was an essential incident of slavery."[93]

By "caste," the attorneys for Homer Plessy meant something quite different from the term as employed (for better or for worse) by twentieth-century historians and anthropologists. Early in the period of European colonial expansion, the word *casta* and its variants had been used to designate a pure or separate lineage (such as a "race" of horses or a variety of grapes). After the French Revolution, the word could be used—pejoratively—to designate a system of privileges based on birth and rank.[94] In this latter sense, the term *caste* was easily recognizable to jurists and activists in the United States in the late nineteenth century. To argue that the Separate Car Law imposed and enforced caste was to declare that law unworthy of a nation founded on the proposition that all men are created equal.

A majority of the justices on the U.S. Supreme Court chose to ignore virtually all of this reasoning and to accept instead the argument proffered by the attorneys for the State of Louisiana, who presented the law as a simple exercise of the state's legitimate police power. To them, Plessy's challenge was an illegitimate effort to gain legal backing in the pursuit of "social equality." The language of the majority decision thus incorporated a key tenet of white supremacist ideology—the sleight of hand through which *public rights* were re-characterized as importunate *social claims*. These, in turn, were associated with "social equality," with all the blurring of boundaries between public and private, the phantasms of "miscegenation," and the dangers of social transgression that phrase could evoke.[95] Persuading the Court to participate in the white supremacists' key rhetorical elision was perhaps the most consequential victory for the government of Louisiana in *Plessy*, both in the domain of discourse and in the domain of doctrine.[96]

CONCLUSION

Once we define historical context to include vernacular concepts of rights, it becomes clear that reframing the *Plessy* challenge to emphasize its dignitary dimension is not an anachronism, a mere artifact of our own post–*Brown v. Board of Education* consciousness.[97] When the bill of rights in the 1868 Louisiana Constitution granted state citizenship to residents regardless of race and assured all citizens of the "same civil, political, and public rights and privileges," the choice of language reflected decades of discussion among free persons of color in Louisiana, invigorated by the emancipationist energies of the Civil War.[98]

By the time Homer Plessy took his seat in the first-class railway car in June of 1892, he and his colleagues had been exercising important public rights in multiple spheres of daily life in New Orleans for decades, despite many informally enforced practices of segregation. By their own account, the organizers of the challenge to the Separate Car Law had staked their personal and political identities on a claim of equal public dignity that was incompatible with the legal recognition of caste-like distinctions. They designed the test case to highlight the ways in which the Separate Car Law affronted that dignity. In their view, the Separate Car Law was "intended to nullify the Fourteenth Amendment to the Federal Constitution, and to subordinate the dignity of the citizen to the malice and caprice of a few tyrant[s] and demagogues."[99]

Taking public rights seriously as a concept offers several kinds of insight into the *Plessy* appeal. First, it recognizes a construction of rights that was crucial to the plaintiff and powerfully unacceptable to the defendant. Second, it helps explain the persistence of the plaintiff. To claim public rights at law was, in effect, another way of exercising them in practice. Even as the odds against victory mounted, the members and supporters of the Citizens' Committee continued their campaign to demonstrate that the dignity they asserted was indeed theirs to exercise, whatever the judicial outcome. Third, examining the *Plessy* challenge in this way encourages us to link the formal strategy of litigation with the vernacular practices of writing and legal reasoning in the larger community. Because these practices occurred in places like the local office of the notary public, they are below the radar of most jurisprudential analysis. But they were, in fact, part of the public legal culture in which public rights as a concept made sense.

By restoring the *Plessy* challenge to its precise context, we can go beyond its familiar portrayal as the effort of members of what is often misleadingly referred to as a "light-skinned elite." The case in fact gives evidence of a cosmopolitan activist tradition with its own broad social base and conceptual roots in the city and the countryside of Louisiana. The Citizens' Committee found allies among former union organizers upriver in Donaldsonville and among émigré Cuban revolutionary cigar workers in New Orleans. The money to support the campaign came in from schoolteachers in Ascension Parish as well as from artisans and philanthropists in the city. They knew what they were doing, even though they knew quite well that they might not win.[100]

For the long years of the campaign, Rodolphe Desdunes and Louis Martinet explicated their thinking and exhorted their neighbors and supporters through their writings in the New Orleans *Crusader*. From further north, their attorney Albion Tourgée did the same on a national stage in the Chicago *Inter Ocean*. But even as they were seeking to secure public rights, the next wave of white supremacist legislation was coming up fast behind them. Across the 1890s, one after another southern state moved to deny to black men the political rights that had seemingly been secured by the Fourteenth and Fifteenth Amendments. Many southern states had already undertaken constitutional disfranchisement, and others were accomplishing the same goal through statute.[101] By the time the Court issued its opinion in *Plessy*, the suggestion by the majority that "political equality" was indeed guaranteed under the Fourteenth Amendment rang very hollow.[102]

Rodolphe Desdunes later reflected upon the failed *Plessy* challenge, and addressed those who asserted that it would be better to remain silent than to draw attention to the misfortunes and powerlessness of the population of color. He disagreed: "We believe that it is more noble and worthy to fight nonetheless, rather than to show oneself passive and resigned.

Absolute submission augments the oppressor's power and creates doubts about the sentiment of the oppressed."[103] It has been the goal of this Article not only to reconstruct some of that "sentiment," but also to trace the political philosophy and social network to which Desdunes was heir. The right to respectful treatment in the public sphere was at the core of that philosophy, and Louisiana's constitutional concept of equal "public rights" provided a precedent and a jurisprudence that framed the enterprise. By bundling together "civil, political, and public rights," those who wrote the Constitution of 1868 had been trying to assure both the long-free and the newly freed that they would be treated as equal citizens in the public culture of the post-slavery world. Private matters could, in their view, remain private, but freedom from public disrespect and exclusion as one boarded a train car or took a seat in a café was not a private matter. Honor, to use the ancient term, and dignity, to use the Republican one, depended on that respect.[104]

By contrast, once the Supreme Court Justices accepted white supremacists' claim that what was at stake was a presumption to "social equality," the next step was the easy denial that the Fourteenth Amendment guaranteed such "social equality." It is perhaps unsurprising that powerful and relatively conservative white men of the 1890s took this path. But it *is* surprising that modern legal and historical scholars would adopt without careful scrutiny the "social equality" framing offered by the Democrats of late nineteenth-century Louisiana. For the equal public rights tradition had its own history, one that would have been immediately recognizable not only to Rodolphe Desdunes in Louisiana, but to his predecessors Edouard Tinchant from France and Julien Raimond from Haiti. By 1868, the idea of equal public rights made sense to the Massachusetts-born attorney Simeon Belden, and to the Louisiana-born former slave Thomas Isabelle. It underlay the successful claims of plaintiffs in antidiscrimination cases in Louisiana in the 1870s. And even into the 1880s, it was recognizable to some white men from Louisiana: George Washington Cable evoked the phrase when he wrote that "the day must come when the Negro must share and enjoy in common with the white race the whole scale of *public* rights and advantages provided under American government."[105]

Despite the revisions to the Louisiana Constitution, both the concept and the phrase lived on into the 1890s. Ramón Victor Pagés, the head of the union of Spanish-speaking cigar workers in New Orleans, invoked "public rights" when he spoke to an 1893 mass meeting in support of the Citizens' Committee.[106] And although Justice Harlan's famous dissent in *Plessy* did not use the words "public rights," his claim that the Constitution "neither knows nor tolerates classes among citizens" and thus "[t]here is no caste here" echoes the plaintiff's brief in its underlying logic.[107]

Ironically, the white supremacists would themselves later drop the veil and acknowledge that their own claims in the *Plessy* case had been disingenuous. As the Citizens' Committee had known all along, the Louisiana legislature was explicitly concerned with refusing public respect to citizens of color. In his inaugural address in 1904, Governor Newton Blanchard acknowledged that the real goal of the white supremacist project was to deny to Louisiana's citizens of color the very essence of public dignity and recognition: "No approach towards social equality or social recognition will ever be tolerated in Louisiana. Separate schools, separate churches, separate cars, separate places of entertainment will be enforced. Racial distinction and integrity must be preserved."[108]

There it was: no "social recognition." Segregation was not merely an end in itself; it was a means to an end, that of denying social recognition to people of color. In perceiving the Separate Car Law as an act of intentional humiliation, as a public assertion of a fundamental inequality of standing among the state's citizens, Homer Plessy and his allies were not, as Justice Brown had opined, showing a prickly hypersensitivity, envisioning disrespect where none was intended. They were accurately gauging the intent of those who now ruled them and accurately predicting the consequences of a loss of "public rights." After their defeat in the Supreme Court, there was only one cold comfort for Plessy's supporters, which was to have succeeded in using a branch of the federal government to expose the state's violation of their rights. Like the ordinary men and women of Louisiana who formalized their claims at the office of the notary, they had used law and writing to register their assertion of public standing. The year before their defeat, Rodolphe Desdunes had reflected on the ironies they faced and charted the only remaining path of action: "'It is well for a people to know their rights even if denied them,' and we will add that it is proper and wise for people to exercise those rights as intelligently as possible, even if robbed of their benefits."[109]

NOTES

1. La. Const. tit. 1, art. ll (1868).
2. 163 U.S. 537 (1896).
3. *Ex parte* Plessy, 11 So. 948, 951 (La. 1892). The decision is also excerpted in The Thin Disguise: Turning Point in Negro History 71-74 (Otto H. Olsen ed., 1967).
4. Plessy v. Ferguson, 163 U.S. 537, 544 (1896) ("[I]n the nature of things [the Fourteenth Amendment] could not have been intended to abolish distinctions based upon color, or to enforce social, as distinguished from political equality, or a commingling of the two races upon terms unsatisfactory to either.").
5. *Id.* at 552. "Equal but separate" rather than "separate but equal" is the precise wording of the statute. Act of May 12, 1890, No. 111, 1890 La. Acts 152.
6. *Ex parte Plessy*, 11 So. at 949.
7. William E. Nelson, The Fourteenth Amendment: From Political Principle to Judicial Doctrine 186-87 (1988).
8. *Id.*
9. Michael J. Klarman, From Jim Crow to Civil Rights: The Supreme Court and the Struggle for Racial Equality 22 (2004) [hereinafter Klarman, From Jim Crow to Civil Rights]; *see also* Michael Klarman, *The* Plessy *Era*, 1998 Sup. Ct. Rev. 303.
10. Owen M. Fiss, Troubled Beginnings of the Modern State, 1888-1910, at 354, 357, 362 (1993); Charles A. Lofgren, The *Plessy* Case: A Legal-Historical Interpretation 197 (1987).
11. Klarman, From Jim Crow to Civil Rights, *supra* note 9, at 58. For alternate perspectives, see Matthew D. Lassiter, *Does the Supreme Court Matter?—Civil Rights and the Inherent Politicization of Constitutional Law*, 103 Mich. L. Rev. 1401 (2005), and Kenneth W. Mack, *Rethinking Civil Rights Lawyering and Politics in the Era Before* Brown, 115 Yale L.J. 256 (2005).

12 On the metaphor of the "Serbonian bog," see John Milton, Paradise Lost 46 (Merritt Y. Hughes ed., Bobbs-Merrill Educ. Publ'g. 1983) (1667). For law-related use of the metaphor, see *Landress v. Phoenix Mutual Life Insurance Co.*, 291 U.S. 491, 499 (1934) (Cardozo, J., dissenting), and John Fabian Witt, The Accidental Republic: Crippled Workingmen, Destitute Widows, and the Remaking of American Law 20–21 (2004).

13 For the contrary view, see Klarman, From Jim Crow to Civil Rights, *supra* note 9, at 59, who argues that "[m]ost Jim Crow laws merely described white supremacy; they did not produce it."

14 The term "mutually constitutive" is often invoked to denote this back-and-forth between law and other forms of action, in which the distinction between "law" and "society" is intentionally blurred. The elegant and now classic manifesto for one variant of this approach is Robert W. Gordon, *Critical Legal Histories*, 36 Stan. L. Rev. 57 (1984). See also the discussion in the dossier on history and law in Numéro Spécial, *Histoire et Droit*, 57 Annales: Histoire, Sciences Sociales 1425 (2002), especially Alain Boureau, *Droit naturel et abstraction judiciaire: Hypothèses sur la nature du droit médiéval*, 57 Annales: Histoire, Sciences Sociales 1463 (2002).

15 I thank Roger Chartier for pointing out this alternate reading of the Quixote metaphor.

16 La. Const. tit. I, art. II (1868).

17 For an intriguing discussion of the interplay of public standing and social status in conservative thought in Britain after the French Revolution, see Don Herzog, Poisoning the Minds of the Lower Orders 414–546 (1998). For an explication of the dignitary content of the *Plessy* case from the point of view of normative political philosophy, see Gerald J. Postema, *Introduction: The Sins of Segregation*, 16 L. & Phil. 221 (1997). Postema argues that segregation's core evil is the public denial of the fundamental good of "status or standing as a full and equal member of one's society." *Id.* at 241.

18 The language used in the Reconstruction-era struggle can be followed in the pages of the New Orleans *Tribune* and the New Orleans *Daily Crescent* during late 1867 and early 1868.

19 These events were discussed in the New Orleans *Tribune* in the months surrounding July of 1867, the first anniversary of the massacre at Mechanics' Hall.

20 Eric Foner, Reconstruction: America's Unfinished Revolution, 1863–1877, at 62–67, 262–63 (1988). A close analysis of the composition of the delegates is presented in chapter six of Ted Tunnell, Crucible of Reconstruction: War, Radicalism and Race in Louisiana, 1862–1877, at 111–35 (1984).

21 Portions of the debate appear in Official Journal of the Proceedings of the Convention, for Framing a Constitution for the State of Louisiana (1867-68) [hereinafter Official Journal]. An overview of the legislature is provided in Roger A. Fischer, The Segregation Struggle in Louisiana, 1862–77, at 48–56 (1974).

22 This concept of the Declaration was vividly expressed by both Charles Sumner and Frederick Douglass. *See* John Stauffer, The Black Hearts of Men: Radical Abolitionists and the Transformation of Race 22–26 (2001). Some prewar state constitutions had done the same, though the import of the phrase "free and equal" had been diminished by the decision in *State v. Post*, 20 N.J.L. 368, 373–76, 378–86 (1845). For the successive draft wordings of the bill of rights, see Official Journal, *supra* note 21, at 84–109, 116–117.

23 Official Journal, *supra* note 21, at 96.

24 A case of this kind from colonial Peru is carefully analyzed in Tamara J. Walker, Ladies and Gentlemen, Slaves, and Citizens: Dressing the Part in Lima, 1723–1854, at 142–43 (2007) (unpublished Ph.D. dissertation, University of Michigan) (on file with author). For a discussion of honor, illegitimacy, and constructs of "the public," see Ann Twinam, Public Lives, Private Secrets: Gender, Honor, Sexuality, and Illegitimacy in Colonial Spanish America 25–37 (1999).

25 On the transformations of these concepts in the nineteenth century, see Honor, Status, and Law in Modern Latin America (Sueann Caulfield et al. eds., 2005).

26 *See* Caryn Cossé Bell, Revolution, Romanticism and the Afro-Creole Protest Tradition in Louisiana, 1718–1868, at 222–75 (1997).

27 For the text of the *Déclaration*, see Louis Tripier, Les Constitutions Françaises 10 (1848). The term *dignité* evoked both merit and respect as well as honorableness. 1 Dictionnaire Historique De La Langue Française 1085 (Alain Rey et al. eds., 1998).

28 Within the *droits de l'homme* (rights of man) one finds the complementary concept of *libertés publiques* (public liberties). For a mid-nineteenth-century discussion, see 1 Denis Serrigny, Traité Du Droit Public Des Français, Précédé D'une Introduction Sur Les Fondements Des Sociétés Politiques 287–88 (1846). *See also* Jean-Luc Aubert, Introduction au droit et thèmes fondamentaux du droit civil § 56, at 47–48 (9th ed. 2002). The "rights of man"

can be seen to include the right to "public liberties." These do not translate directly as "public rights," but could be so named in English.

29 *See* Laurent Dubois, Avengers of the New World: The Story of the Haitian Revolution (2004); John D. Garrigus, Before Haiti: Race and Citizenship in French Saint-Domingue (2006).

30 *See* Dubois, *supra* note 29, at 80-88, 119-20; Laurent Dubois, A Colony of Citizens: Revolution and Slave Emancipation in the French Caribbean, 1787-1804 (2004); Garrigus, *supra* note 29. For a synthesis, see Laurent Dubois, *An Enslaved Enlightenment: Rethinking the Intellectual History of the French Atlantic*, 31 Soc. Hist. 1 (2006).

31 1 P. Rossi, Cours de droit constitutionnel professé à la Faculté de Droit de Paris 9 (1866).

32 *Id.* at 11-12.

33 *Id.* This is one of many re-editions of a set of lectures dating originally to 1836. *See* Philippe Braud, La notion de liberté publique en droit français ii, 9-10, 45 (1968). I thank Pasquale Pasquino for discussions of Rossi's history.

34 1 Serrigny, *supra* note 28, at 287-88.

35 *See* Maurice Agulhon, 1848 ou l'apprentissage de la République, 1848-1852 ch. 1 (1973). The 1848 abolition decree spoke of *dignité*. *See* D'une abolition, l'autre: Anthologie raisonnée de textes consacrés à la seconde abolition de l'esclavage dans les colonies françaises 17-19 (Myriam Cottias ed., 1998). Arago's instructions were Portant instructions pour l'exécution du décret du 27 avril 1848, Circulaire Ministérielle No. 358 of May 7, 1848, Bulletin Officiel de la Martinique [Official Bulletin of Martinique], May 7, 1848, p. 594.

36 *See* Bell, *supra* note 26, at 29-34; Ira Berlin, Generations of Captivity: A History of African-American Slaves 51-96 (2003); Kimberly S. Hanger, Bounded Lives, Bounded Places: Free Black Society in Colonial New Orleans, 1769-1803 (1997).

37 Rebecca J. Scott, *Public Rights and Private Commerce: A Nineteenth-Century Atlantic Creole Itinerary*, 48 Current Anthropology 237-49 (2007).

38 Jean-Charles Houzeau, My Passage at the New Orleans Tribune: A memoir of the Civil War Era (David C. Rankin ed., Gerard F. Denault trans., 1984).

39 Scott, *supra* note 37, at 241 (quoting a letter from Tinchant to General Máximo Gómez). For more on Tinchant, see Rebecca J. Scott & Jean M. Hébrard, *Les papiers de la liberté: Une mère africaine et ses enfants à l'époque de la révolution haïtienne*, Genèses, March 2007, at 18-25.

40 On the charge of "social equality" as a label to disqualify proposals to the Louisiana constitutional convention of 1867-68, see Official Journal, *supra* note 21, at 277. A small number of radical antislavery activists in the North did embrace the concept of social equality, along with an aspiration to friendship across the color line. *See* Stauffer, *supra* note 22, at 8-44.

41 On the variability of schemes of rights, see Richard A. Primus, The American Language of Rights 124-26, 127-76 (1999).

42 The battle over the phrase "social equality" emerged in many Reconstruction contexts, and was closely associated with thinking about gender and sexuality. *See* Hannah Rosen, Terror in the Heart of Freedom: Citizenship, Sexual Violence, and the Meaning of Race in the Postemancipation South (forthcoming 2008); Barbara Y. Welke, *When All the Women Were White, and All the Blacks were Men: Gender, Class, Race, and the Road to Plessy, 1855-1914*, 13 L. & Hist. Rev. 261, 261-316. A full analysis of the concept and label "social equality" is beyond the scope of this Article. As specialists in African American history have demonstrated, however, the negative connotations of "social equality" as a framing device led even quite radical thinkers to eschew the term. W.E.B. Du Bois makes this point most vividly in W.E.B. Du Bois, *On Being Crazy*, 26 Crisis 55, 55 (1923).

43 Tinchant's letter appeared in the French-language pages of the New Orleans *Tribune*, July 21, 1864. On the "protectable legal interest" in defense of one's honor under French law, see James Q. Whitman, *Enforcing Civility and Respect: Three Societies*, 109 Yale L.J. 1279, 1279-1398 (2000).

44 Official Journal, *supra* note 21, at 290.

45 *Id.* at 117 (emphasis omitted); *see also id.* at 275-277.

46 On various complexities of this mixture, see Vernon Valentine Palmer, The Louisiana Civilian Experience: Critiques of Codification in a Mixed Jurisdiction (2005).

47 *See* 4 William Blackstone, Commentaries on the Laws of England ch. 1 (Univ. of Chicago Press 1979) (1769); William J. Novak, *The Legal Transformation of Citizenship in Nineteenth-Century America, in* The Democratic Experiment 85, 95 (Meg Jacobs et al. eds., 2003).

48 The classic formulation can be found in 3 Blackstone, *supra* note 47, at 348: "if an inn-keeper, or other victualler, hangs out a sign and opens his house for travellers, it is an implied engagement to entertain all persons who travel that way. ..." *See also* Barbara Young Welke, Recasting American Liberty: Gender, Race, Law, and the Railroad Revolution, 1865-1920, at 323-75 (2001).

49 For an erudite examination of this question, see Joseph William Singer, *No Right to Exclude: Public Accommodations and Private Property*, 90 Nw. U. L. Rev. 1283 (1996). For a sociolegal interpretation of the rise of racial segregation in rail travel, with attention to the construct of "social equality," see Kenneth W. Mack, *Law, Society, Identity, and the Making of the Jim Crow South: Travel and Segregation on Tennessee Railroads, 1875-1905*, 24 Law & Soc. Inquiry 377 (1999).

50 Official Journal, *supra* note 21, at 114-18; *see also* Tunnell, *supra* note 21, at 117-19 (analyzing roll call votes on these questions). On Thomas Isabelle, see Eric Foner, Freedom's Lawmakers: A Directory of Black Officeholders During Reconstruction 115 (2d ed. 1996).

51 On the early Code Noir and the later Civil Code, see Palmer, *supra* note 46, at 23, 62-65, 71, 101-34.

52 For a careful tracing of the "emancipationist" thread in post–Civil War thought, see David Blight, Race And Reunion: The Civil War in American Memory (2001).

53 Offficial Journal, *supra* note 21, at 294.

54 *Id.*

55 In 1872, for example, state delegates to the Republican convention struggled over the nomination of Aristide Mary, a man of color, for the office of governor. As Rodolphe Desdunes later emphasized, at stake here was not the politics of the particular nomination, but the *right* of such a man to be a candidate for public office. Rodolphe L. Desdunes, Nos hommes et notre histoire: Notices biographiques accompagnées de reflexions et de souvenirs personnels 183-84 (1911) ("[J]e dirai que les partisans d'Aristide Mary ont revendiqué *le droit d'aspirer au poste* de gouverneur, mais qu'ils n'ont pas convoité le poste même." ["I would say that the supporters of Aristide Mary were claiming *the right to aspire to the post* of governor, but that they did not seek the post itself."]).

56 Va. Const. art. I, § 20.

57 *See* Kirk H. Porter & Donald Bruce Johnson, National Party Platforms, 1840-1956, at 47 (1956) (describing the 1872 platform); *id.* at 54 (describing the 1876 platform, which called on Congress and the executive branch to secure "to every American citizen complete liberty and exact equality in the exercise of all civil, political, and public rights").

58 For a careful exploration of the competing interpretations of the Fourteenth Amendment as either a new citizenship, or the recognition of an unjustly denied prior citizenship, see Richard A. Primus, *The Riddle of Hiram Revels*, 119 Harv. L. Rev. 1681 (2006).

59 Article III of the Treaty of Cession reads:

> The inhabitants of the ceded territory shall be incorporated in the Union of the United States and admitted as soon as possible according to the principles of the federal Constitution to the enjoyment of all the rights, advantages and immunities of citizens of the United States, and, in the mean time they shall be maintained and protected in the free enjoyment of their liberty, property and the Religion which they profess.

Cession of Louisiana, U.S.-Fr., Apr. 30, 1803, 1803 U.S.T. 10, *reprinted in* Report of the Secretary of State to His Excellency W. W. Heard, Governor of the State of Louisiana 45-48 (1902). Its importance to subsequent generations of activists is discussed in Bell, *supra* note 26, at 29-40.

60 The decision by Bates arose from a dispute over the citizenship claims of ship captains who were men of color. To the Secretary of the Treasury, 10 Op. Att'y Gen. 382, 382-83 (1862).

61 *See Importante Décision*, L'Union, Dec. 25, 1862, at A1; Edouard Tinchant, Letter to the Editor, La Trib., July 21, 1864, at 2 ("[N]é Français, nous avons gagné [le]s lettres de naturalisation américaine sur les [rem]parts de la Nouvelle Orléans, debout, l'arme [au] bras, au pied du drapeau des Etats-Unis pour [le]quel nous étions prêts à verser la dernière goutte de notre sang; quelle est donc la puissance [h]umaine qui peut nous nier notre titre de citoyen américain." [[B]orn French, I earned my naturalization papers on the ramparts of New Orleans, upright, with my weapon in my hand, at the foot of the flag of the United States, prepared to spill the last drop of my blood; what then is the human power that could deny my title to American citizenship?]). The available microfilm edition is made from a torn copy; material in square brackets is inferred. I thank Diana Williams for alerting me to the existence of this letter.

62 Walsh v. Lallande, 25 La. Ann. 188, 189 (1873).

63 The Louisiana Supreme Court was ruling on the retrospective citizenship claim of Charles Lallande, who had lost claim to a piece of property in 1860 when a land office commissioner judged that as a "free negro" he had no right to hold property under the pre-emption laws of 1841. *See id.* at 188-89. The language of the case is, among other things, a nice technical rebuttal of Chief Justice Taney's argument in the *Dred Scott* decision that people of color had never held national citizenship in the era of the founders. *Id.* at 189-90.

64 *See* Bell, *supra* note 26, at 41-64. On the educational institutions that helped to nurture these claims of right, see Mary Niall Mitchell, *"A Good and Delicious Country": Free Children of Color and How They Learned to Imagine the Atlantic World in Nineteenth-Century Louisiana*, Hist. Educ. Q., Summer 2000, at 123.

65 La. Const. tit. I, arts. II, XIII (1868).

66 The testimony from this case at the state level is transcribed in Transcript of Record, Hall v. Decuir, 95 U.S. 485 (1877) (No. 294). The manuscript originals of the state case are in the Supreme Court of Louisiana Collection, Department of Archives and Manuscripts, Earl K. Long Library, University of New Orleans.

67 *Id.* at 51. On the question of women's particular claims to respect and respectability, see Welke, *supra* note 42.

68 Mrs. Decuir, who had lived twelve years in France, was a strong-minded woman. On an earlier journey, she had planted herself firmly in a rocking chair in the ladies' cabin. The distressed captain had a "note" conveyed to her telling her to leave. She responded by "summoning" the captain and trying to shame him into letting her remain. Transcript of Record, *Decuir*, 95 U.S. 485 (No. 294).

69 *Decuir*, 95 U.S. at 488-91, *rev'g*, Decuir v. Benson, 27 La. Ann. 1 (1875). For other challenges brought under the 1868 Constitution and the subsequent Civil Rights Act of 1869, see *Sauvinet v. Walker*, 27 La. Ann. 14 (1875) (upholding a district court grant of damages to the civil sheriff of the parish of Orleans, who had been refused service at a coffeehouse), and *Joseph v. Bidwell*, 28 La. Ann. 382 (1876) (upholding ruling granting damages to a man refused entrance to a theater). *See also* Roger A. Fischer, The Segregation Struggle in Louisiana, 1862-77, at 80-87 (1974).

70 Francis H. Smith, Proceedings of the National Union Republican Convention Held at Philadelphia, June 5 and 6, 1872, at 51 (1872).

71 Patrick O. Gudridge, *Privileges and Permissions: The Civil Rights Act of 1875*, 8 Law & Phil. 83, 125 (1989).

72 On Maryland test cases under the federal Act, see Libby Benton, Claims to Rights Under the Civil Rights Act of 1875 (Apr. 24, 2006) (unpublished manuscript, on file with author). On Tennessee, where common law claims were the preferred strategy, see Mack, *supra* note 49.

73 M.A. Clancy, Proceedings of the Republican National Convention Held at Cincinnati, Ohio June 14, 15, and 16, 1876, at 56 (1876).

74 *See* La. Const. art. CCXXXI (1879). Rodolphe Desdunes was furious that the few remaining black legislators had accepted the offer of a separate university: "C'était la fin. L'homme de couleur avait accepté la subordination légale, c'est-à-dire l'idée d'être traité *conventionellement* et non *constitutionellement*." ["It was the end. Men of color had accepted legal subordination, that is, the idea of being treated according to *custom* rather than according to the *constitution*."] Desdunes, *supra* note 55, at 181.

75 *See* Rebecca J. Scott, Degrees of Freedom: Louisiana and Cuba after Slavery 61-94 (2005); Rebecca J. Scott, *"Stubborn and Disposed to Stand their Ground": Black Militia, Sugar Workers, and the Dynamics of Collective Action in the Louisiana Sugar Bowl, 1863-1887*, Slavery & Abolition, April 1999, at 103, 104.

76 On the political context in which the legislation was passed, see Keith Weldon Medley, We as Freemen: *Plessy v. Ferguson* (2003).

77 *See* Armando Petrucci, *Escribir para otros, in* Petrucci, Alfabetismo, escritura, sociedad 105-16 (1999).

78 *See* Aubert, *supra* note 28, § 179, at 180-81 (discussing the notary as a public officer).

79 For the general regulations governing notaries and their records, see Civil Code of Louisiana: Revision of 1870 with Amendments to 1947, arts. 2234, 2251-66 (Joseph Dainow ed., 1947).

80 For biographical information on Martinet, see Medley, *supra* note 76, at 150-58.

81 *See id.* at 33-34, 159 (discussing the residences of Plessy and Desdunes).

82 *See* Kathryn Burns, *Notaries, Truth, and Consequences*, Am. Hist. Rev., Apr. 2005, at 110.

83 These characterizations are based on a review of the indices and many of the acts recorded in Martinet's notarial records, which are in the New Orleans Notarial Archives Research Center ("NONARC"). For a detailed analysis, see Rebecca J. Scott, *Se Battre Pour Ses Droits: Écritures, Litiges et Discrimination Raciale en Louisiane (1888-1899)*, 53/54 Cahiers du Brésil Contemporain 182-209 (2003), and Scott, *supra* note 75, at 75, 88, 161, 172, 200.

84 Under Louisiana law, a notary recorded the formation of societies and transcribed their bylaws. Formal recognition came by depositing these texts with state officials. For examples, see the notations to 1 Notarial Acts of Louis Martinet (1890) in NONARC.

85 Act No. 6, Chartre "La Dignité" Société d'Assistance Mutuelle (Oct. 3, 1890), *in* 1 Notarial Acts of Louis Martinet (1890) *in* NONARC. Each of the women signed in her own hand. "Dignité" had been a key term in the lexicon of France's 1848 republican revolution. One didactic text emphasized that "une République est l'état qui concilie le mieux les intérêts et la dignité de chacun avec les intérêts et la dignité de tout le monde." ["A Republic is the state that best reconciles the interests and the dignity of each with the interests and dignity of all."] Charles Renouvier, Manuel Républicain de i'homme et du citoyen 93 (Garnier Frères ed., 1981) (1848).

86 Act of July 10, 1980, No. 111, 1890 La. Acts 152, 152–53, *reprinted in* Record of Case at 6–7, Plessy v. Ferguson, 163 U.S. 537 (1896) (No. 15,248).

87 See Desdunes, *supra* note 55, at 165–67, on the "generation of 1860." On support in the countryside, see Scott, *supra* note 75, at 90–91. *See also* Joseph Logsdon & Lawrence Powell, *Rodolphe Lucien Desdunes: Forgotten Organizer of the* Plessy *Protest, in* Sunbelt Revolution: The Historical Progression of the Civil Rights Struggle in the Gulf South, 1866–2000, at 42, 56 (Samuel C. Hyde, Jr. ed., 2003); and the Crusader, June 1895 (on file with Archives, Xavier University of Louisiana Library, New Orleans, La., available in the *Crusader* clippings file in Special Collections).

88 On these fundraising efforts, see the clippings from the Crusader, *supra* note 87, especially June 22, 1895, and July 12–20, 1895. *See also* Medley, *supra* note 76, at 130–31.

89 Crusader, *supra* note 87, *reprinted in* Medley, *supra* note 76, at 165; *see also* Lofgren, *supra* note 10. Excerpts from newspaper reports are in The Thin Disguise, *supra* note 3, and in the Crusader, *supra* note 87. The initial report of the detective who arrested Plessy, described him as "being a passenger of the colored race on a train of the East Louisiana Railroad Co." Record of Case at 4, *Plessy*, 163 U.S. 537 (No. 15,248).

90 Mark Elliott, Color-Blind Justice: Albion Tourgée and the Quest for Racial Equality from the Civil War to *Plessy v. Ferguson* (2006).

91 The argument that the actions of conductors under the law could imperil the property interest that a man or woman might have in the reputation of whiteness is analyzed in Cheryl I. Harris, *Whiteness as Property*, 106 Harv. L. Rev. 1707, 1746–50 (1993).

92 Brief for Plaintiff in Error, *Plessy*, 163 U.S. 537 (1896) (No. 210), 1869 WL 13992, at *11.

93 *Id.* at *14.

94 *See* 1 Dictionnaire historique de la langue française, *supra* note 27, at 646. By a somewhat puzzling linguistic turn, the word also came to be applied in Spanish in the plural to *castas*, those who by virtue of mixed ancestry occupied specified roles in a hierarchy of human types in colonial society. I thank the Portuguese linguist Rita Marquilhas, of the University of Lisbon, for her assistance in tracking the term through various Spanish and Portuguese dictionaries from the eighteenth and nineteenth centuries.

95 One of the few white southern observers who denounced this sleight of hand was New Orleans resident George W. Cable, *The Silent South*, 30 Century Mag. 647 (1885), *reprinted in* George W. Cable, The Negro Question: A Selection of Writings on Civil Rights in the South 83, 92–96 (Arlin Turner ed., 1958).

96 Among works that follow the Court in treating *Plessy* as involving "social rights" are Klarman, *supra* note 9, at 325, which distinguishes civil rights from social rights in the case of school integration, and Plessy v. Ferguson: A Brief History with Documents 13 (Brook Thomas ed., 1997). For convincing demonstrations that the triumvirate of civil, political, and social rights involves a continual shifting of boundaries, see Primus, *supra* note 41, and Mark Tushnet, *The Politics of Equality in Constitutional Law: The Equal Protection Clause, Dr. Du Bois, and Charles Hamilton Houston*, 74 J. Am. Hist. 884 (1987).

97 Klarman treats most critiques of the Plessy decision as falling into anachronism, because, he argues, "it may be fanciful to expect the Justices to have defended black civil rights when racial attitudes and practices were as abysmal as they were at the turn of the century." Klarman, *supra* note 9, at 305. In Michael J. Klarman, *Rethinking the Civil Rights and Civil Liberties Revolutions*, 82 Va. L. Rev. 1, 27–28 (1996), Klarman uses the idea of "dominant racial norms" to similar effect: "The *Plessy* decision was, indeed, so fully congruent with the dominant racial norms of the period that it elicited little more than a collective yawn of indifference from a nation that would have expected precisely that result from its Supreme Court."

98 *See* La. Const. tit. I, art. II (1868).

99 Medley, *supra* note 76, at 167 (quoting Rodolphe Desdunes in the *Crusader*).

100 For a discussion of the participation of Ramón Victor Pagés, a Cuban émigré, see Louis A. Martinet, The Violation of A Constitutional Right 16 (1893), and Scott, *supra* note 75, at 76–77.

101 *See* J. Morgan Kousser, The Shaping of Southern Politics: Suffrage Restriction and the Establishment of the One-Party South, 1880–1910 (1974); Michael Perman, Struggle for Mastery: Disfranchisement in the South, 1888–1908 (2001).

102 Plessy v. Ferguson, 163 U.S. 537, 544 (1896). Justice Brown's phrasing ("[The Fourteenth Amendment] could not have been intended … to enforce social, as distinguished from political equality. …") implied a constitutional guarantee of political equality, a guarantee the Court would walk away from within the next few years, particularly in *Giles v. Harris*, 189 U.S. 475 (1902). *See* Richard H. Pildes, *Democracy, Anti-Democracy and the Canon*, 17 Const. Comment. 295 (2000).

103 Desdunes, *supra* note 55, at 192 ("Nous croyons qu'il est plus noble et plus digne de lutter quand même, que de se montrer passif et résigné. La soumission absolue augmente la puissance de l'oppresseur et fait douter du sentiment de l'opprimé.").

104 Indeed, private matters could be seen as public to the extent that they conferred civil effects. On the floor of the convention, Edouard Tinchant proposed that all women, regardless of color, have the same right to sue for breach of promise (of marriage), and that all women be able to compel to marriage any man with whom they had lived for a year. Louisiana's Creole activists did not shy away from the controversial question of interracial marriage, for in a setting in which women of color had often entered into long-term intimate relationships with men—relationships that had little or no civic protection—the right to marriage had a strong dignitary component. *See* Official Journal, *supra* note 21, at 192.

105 Cable, *supra* note 95, at 9–10.

106 For a discussion regarding Pagés, see Martinet, *supra* note 100, at 16.

107 *Plessy*, 163 U.S. at 559.

108 Sidney J. Romero, My Fellow Citizens: The Inaugural Addresses of Louisiana's Governors 245–46 (1980).

109 Desdunes, *in* Crusader, June 1895, *supra* note 87.

READING 9

The Question of Color-Blind Citizenship
Albion Tourgée, W.E.B. Du Bois and the Principles of the Niagara Movement

Mark Elliott[1]

> The colored man and those white men who believe in liberty and justice—who do not think Christ's teachings a sham—must join hands and hearts ... without both united, there is no hope of success.
> —Albion Tourgée, 1893.

> We believe it is the duty of the Americans of Negro descent, as a body, to maintain their race identity until this mission of the Negro people is accomplished, and the ideal of human brotherhood has become a practical possibility.
> —W.E.B. Du Bois, 1897.

At the founding meeting of the Niagara Movement in 1905, the organization adopted a statement of principles declaring that "any discrimination based simply on race or color is barbarous." It further described racism as an impediment to enlightened reason and humanitarian progress, an unfortunate relic of "unreasoning human savagery of which the world is and ought to be thoroughly ashamed." Calling for "the co-operation of all men of all races" in "persistent manly agitation" against racial discrimination, the Niagara-ites overtly invoked the abolitionist heritage of protest.[2] To honor this tradition, they pledged to hold a memorial meeting every Thanksgiving to honor the "Friends of Freedom" in whose radical steps they hoped to follow. Its first Thanksgiving memorial was dedicated to three men: William Lloyd Garrison, Frederick Douglass, and Albion Tourgée.[3]

The Niagara Movement's selection of heroes was significant. An interracial trio of civil rights leaders—two of them white and one black—Garrison, Douglass and Tourgée had stood not only for a spirit of uncompromising agitation for full equality, but also for the principle that American citizenship should be "color blind." Garrison had argued that American citizenship "knows nothing of white or black men; it makes no invidious distinctions with regard to the color or condition," and he dismissed prejudices based on physical differences by saying "I would as soon deny the existence of my Creator as quarrel with the workmanship of his hands."[4] Douglass too repeatedly expressed his hope for a society of perfectly equal individuals, where race would not matter—a faith manifest in his marriage

Mark Elliott, "The Question of Color-Blind Citizenship: Albion Tourgée, W.E.B. Du Bois and the Principles of the Niagara Movement," *Afro-Americans in New York Life and History*, vol. 32, no. 2, pp. 23-49. Copyright © 2008 by Afro-American Historical Association of the Niagara Frontier. Reprinted with permission. Provided by ProQuest LLC. All rights reserved.

to Helen Pitts, a white feminist radical, in 1884.[5] But, it was Tourgée who brought the phrase "color-blind" citizenship into the legal and political discourse when he argued before the Supreme Court as the lead attorney for Homer Plessy in 1896 that "the Law ought to at least color-blind." Tourgée furthermore launched an interracial national civil rights organization in 1891 that declared as a founding principle that "justice is color-blind."[6] Considering its reverence for these forbearers, it may be regarded as strange—and a surprise to some historians to learn—that the Niagara Movement originally restricted its membership to black men only. What was the relationship between the ideal of "color-blind citizenship" and the Niagara Movement's decision to organize along the color-line? What conflicts existed between this principle in the abstract and the real world of interracial relationships, alliances, and organizing strategies?

This paper examines the concept of color-blind citizenship in the years leading up to the founding of the Niagara movement in 1905. In particular, I probe the conflicts and contradictions of civic "colorblindness" as it influenced both the philosophies and organizational strategies of two civil rights leaders, Albion Tourgée and W.E.B. Du Bois. The attitude of Du Bois and his fellow Niagara-ites to the "colorblind" principle must be understood in light of the prior experience of Tourgée, whose interracial movement of the 1890s foundered partly because of the difficulties he encountered in putting the "color-blind" ideal in practice. The failure of his movement begged the question: *could* American citizenship be color-blind? In light of Tourgée's experience, Du Bois's famous reflections upon black civic identity, and his ambivalence toward American citizenship, can be understood as a response to a specific historical moment—as well as a philosophical position of trans-historical significance.

"He asks nothing as a Negro," Tourgée wrote in 1889, "It is as a citizen merely that we are called on to consider what rights and privileges he is entitled to exercise."[7] This statement was made in a high-profile debate, published in *The Forum,* in which Tourgée answered Alabama Senator John T. Morgan's unapologetic defense of the suppression of black voting rights in the Southern states. At issue in the Tourgée-Morgan debate was a major new legislative initiative, the Federal Elections Bill that proposed to put the ballot box under Federal supervision, with an expressed intention to protect the African American vote in the South—fulfilling a long-time Republican proposal. While Tourgée resolutely defended the Reconstruction Era ideal of color-blind citizenship, Morgan insisted that the immutable fact of race must be taken into account, and pointed to the "horrors of enforced Negro rule" during Reconstruction as evidence of the need for safeguards against black voting majorities.[8]

Tourgée was one of the last figures from the Reconstruction era to defend "color-blind" citizenship in its original Radical Republican formulation. By the time of his debate with Senator Morgan, this principle was in the process of being transformed into something less than radical in its capacity to challenge the privileges of whiteness. For instance, Supreme Court Justice Joseph Bradley in his majority opinion in *Civil Rights Cases* used the rationale of "color-blind citizenship" for purposes diametrically opposed to his, narrowly construing the

Reconstruction Amendments so that they did not prohibit most forms of racial segregation. Declaring the Federal Civil Rights Act of 1875 unconstitutional, Bradley explained: "There must be some stage in the progress of his [the "Negro's"] elevation when he takes the rank of *mere citizen,* and ceases to be the special favorite of the laws, and when his rights as a citizen are protected in the ordinary modes by which other men's rights are protected."[9] The implication that the Civil Rights Act amounted to special government protection for blacks, fit perfectly with the growing myth of Reconstruction. Like Senator Morgan, Justice Bradley's logic depended upon a view of Reconstruction as an attempt to establish "Negro Rule," or "Black Supremacy," or "Black Domination," or any of the above descriptions so commonly used as a euphemism for the Reconstruction era by its opponents—a host of terminology that George Washington Cable memorably called the "hysterics of the race question".[10]

Albion Tourgée understood better than most how the mythologizing of Reconstruction was shaping the public discourse over civil rights. Formerly a Radical Republican "carpetbagger" in Reconstruction North Carolina, he had a long history of promoting aggressive government action against racial oppression in order to make equal citizenship a reality for blacks. Like many other radicals, his enthusiasm for equal citizenship was combined with a fierce nationalism that came out of the experience of the Civil War (he was also a Union veteran) and that inclined him toward a stronger Federal government. After the collapse of the Republican governments in the South, Tourgée spent most of the 1880s attempting to vindicate Reconstruction from the propaganda that had distorted its historical record and derided its purposes. Significantly, each of his major works on the subject had been well-received in the North, which included his two Reconstruction novels *A Fool's Errand* (1879) and *Bricks Without Straw* (1880), and a historical-sociological analysis of the "race problem," *An Appeal to Caesar* (1884). In 1888, Tourgée began publishing a popular weekly newspaper column, "A Bystander's Notes," in the Chicago *Daily Inter Ocean* (the city's leading Republican newspaper) that addressed the on-going issues of racism, North and South. Through these writings he had come to almost personify Radical Republicanism, an association that doubtless stigmatized him as biased and disreputable to believers in the Conservative Reconstruction myths.[11]

Tourgée pressed forward in a crusade for Radical Republican principles in the 1890s where he encountered a sea-change in public attitude towards the "color-blind" ideal. 1890 was the critical year. Despite a Republican majority in both Houses of Congress, and a Republican, Benjamin Harrison, in the White House, the Federal Election Bill failed to pass in the Senate—abandoned after a lengthy filibuster. That same year, the Blair Education Bill that promised massive federal aid especially for Southern black schools that were being starved nearly out of existence in many places, also failed to pass the Senate by six votes. The controversy over both of these measures sparked a fierce national debate on race in which the mythological version of Reconstruction began to take on new life and force. In August of 1890, Mississippi held a Constitutional Convention that pioneered the disenfranchisement of African-American voters by employing the use of literacy tests and poll taxes that were ostensibly "color blind" but purposefully designed to exclude blacks while including poor whites—a practice to be adopted by most Southern states by the end of the decade.[12] Even the Louisiana Separate Car Act, passed in 1890, appropriated the language of equal citizenship, though not "colorblindness," when it required that racially segregated railroad cars be kept "equal" as well as separate (an insincere gesture to be sure). At this transitional moment, a dizzying array of organizations were founded, and conventions were held, to promote various courses of action in respect to the "race problem," each of which touched upon the relation of race to citizenship.

Coinciding with the failure of the proto-Civil Rights legislation in Congress, a national convention was held on the "Negro Question" in June 1890 at Lake Mohonk in upstate New York that seemed to signal a rupture in Southern black-Northern white alliance. Organized at the suggestion of former President Rutherford B. Hayes who would preside over the conference, it brought together a distinguished gathering of white Northerners and Southerners, including former abolitionists and slaveholders. Its purpose was to foster a cross-sectional consensus, in a spirit of reconciliation, on the best method of aiding the cause of Southern blacks. The meeting, however, excluded black people as participants. This was galling to some of the invitees (including Tourgée) who protested this decision. Those who complained were told "a patient is not invited to the consultation of the doctors on his case" and that the exclusion of blacks would help to foster an "uninhibited" conversation.[13]

The conference framed the "Negro Question" so that white oppression of equal citizenship was not the issue, but rather black shortcomings or failure to demonstrate qualities necessary for "citizenship" was. Reverend Amory D. Mayo who spoke on the topic of "The Negro American Citizen" formulated his inquiry precisely in these terms—"The pivotal question on which this vast problem turns," Mayo said, "is 'Has the Negro, in his American experience, demonstrated a capacity for self-developing American citizenship?'"[14] The vast majority of the participants answered this inquiry with an implicit "no" as they voiced support for black self-help and especially "industrial" education to put them on the long road to progress.[15]

Tourgée did his utmost to disrupt the complacent consensus of the meeting. As one of the main speakers, he protested black exclusion by entitling his lecture "The Negro's View of the Race Problem." His lecture actually did not attempt to explain or characterize what "the Negro's View" was, but instead it berated the organizers for failing to seek it out—reminding them "the man who wears the shoe knows better than anybody else where it pinches." Their knowledge of the "Negro," he told them, was based on a mixture of misinformation and false suppositions. "The manner in which they live and the things they do *not* do have been alluded to here as if they were racial qualities, and not fortuitous resulting conditions," he told them.[16] He invoked his own authority as an eyewitness and participant in Reconstruction to proclaim:

> [After] constant study of their conditions since emancipation, I do not hesitate to say that the colored people of the South have accomplished more in twenty-five years, from an industrial point of view, than any people on the face of the earth ever before achieved under anything like such unfavorable conditions.[17]

He did not hide his repulsion at the prevailing arrogance of the attendees who believed they could proscribe solutions without true knowledge of African Americans, remarking, "I am inclined to think that the only education required is that of the *white* race."[18]

Tourgée also challenged the presumption of whites that the Christian obligation to do something could be fulfilled by mere charitable donations. Rather he described his own view of Christ as a redeemer who was no "respecter of persons" and who consorted with those whom society had shunned—something the conference had refused to do. He reminded them that Christ "lived in a cabin not much better than those we have heard so much about at this Conference; that he probably sat upon the floor, ate his food with his fingers, found his friends among the poorest of the poor, and would not be patronized by the rich." In short, Christ chose to live among the oppressed and became one of them—a statement reminiscent of another of his that once scandalized conservative North Carolinians when he claimed that "Jesus Christ himself was a carpetbagger." Suggesting that their own reluctance to follow Christ's example had made their proceedings futile, he offered the Mohonk conferees not a solution, but a method towards discovering a solution: "I have never been so sure as many of our friends what was the very best thing to be done for the colored man; but I have never doubted that the most exact justice and fullest recognition of his equality of right must be the prime elements of successful policy," were his main words of advice.[19] Though Tourgée's speech received a great deal of praise from the participants, it seemed to have little effect. He declined an invitation to the Second Annual Mohonk Conference in 1891 when he learned that it would be still exclusively white.[20]

While blacks were being excluding from a major national conference on their behalf, two groups of black leaders held national conferences of their own. The first national conference of the Afro-American League, held in January 1890, had been organized by leading black newspaper editors, led by T. Thomas Fortune of the New York *Age*. The main idea was to forge a "unity of sentiment and purpose" among African-Americans as a political entity, and to put the interests of the race ahead of party or individual interest. It called for black solidarity to form a political force independent of the major parties, and for agitation for full civil rights.[21] This approach was immediately controversial for two reasons: first, many black leaders remained politically loyal to the Republican Party and could not abide the League's rule that members could not hold positions in any political party.[22] Secondly, some felt that a black organization would only re-enforce the color line.

Louis A. Martinet, editor of the New Orleans *Crusader,* an elected delegate to the Afro-American League convention, urged Fortune to adopt an organizational name that made no reference to race. Prevented from attending at the last moment, Martinet sent a message to be read at the convention signed by several others stating that, in his words, "if the organization were to be on a distinct race or color line that we would have nothing to do with it."[23] Washington *Bee* editor Calvin Chase, who joined in Martinet's appeal, warned against the perception that the League was "discriminating against whites," and he called for "an organization whereby all good Americans can be members" not just blacks.[24] After Fortune did not read their letter at the convention, Martinet and Chase joined with another group of black leaders who founded a second civil rights organization in Washington, DC only a month later.

Although it did not declare itself a rival to the Afro-American League, the American Citizens' Equal Rights Association (ACERA) clearly was meant as an alternative in the mind of Martinet and his allies who ensured that its name made no reference to race. Notably, its leadership was dominated by figures of the Reconstruction Era including John Mercer Langston, Blanche K. Bruce, James M. Townsend, and its President P.B.S. Pinchback, former Louisiana Lieutenant Governor.[25] Pinch back's Presidential address began by expressing his "regret that it is necessary for the colored American citizens to meet in a separate body for consideration of questions National in their character."[26] The Republican Party during Reconstruction, especially in the South, had been an interracial organization whose survival had depended upon integrated civic bodies including legislatures, cabinets, conventions, meetings, rallies, and even fraternal organizations like the loyal Republican Union League. Though some members of ACERA urged a merger with the Afro-American League, it was perhaps for these reasons that the merge never occurred.

Tourgée's attitude toward the Afro-American League was conflicted. He sent a letter of support to the league that was read at its convention in Chicago, but offered advice out of harmony with what the League was attempting to do. He believed that an organization for blacks should operate only as a private fraternal order—not as the public voice of African Americans. While calling it a great step in "self-assertive freedom," his letter proposed that the League should be conceived as a self-defense order designed, he said, "for action—not display," and that it should avoid all public meetings and declarations. "To be effective, the League should be at least semi-secret," he wrote, "it should be organized by word of mouth alone; and be as effective and intangible as the Ku Klux Kian. Indeed, this should be your model."[27] Though he surely did not mean that the League should be a terrorist organization, he had been proposing since 1889 that blacks take the law into their own hands against lynch mobs by exercising their right kill in self-defense. "Every colored man who kills a lyncher ought to have his name inscribed very high up among the race's heroes and benefactors," he would later write in his *Inter Ocean* column.[28]

Tourgée's letter had little influence on the League. While this probably disappointed him, more irksome was the controversy that broke out over the very reading of his letter at the Conference. As one newspaper reported it, before his letter was read some delegates at the Convention proposed that it be returned to him unopened on the grounds that "Judge

Tourgée was not an Afro-American, and that it was time for the Negroes to show they could get along without the help of white men."[29] Newly-elected League President Joseph C. Price helped defeat this motion, and Tourgée's letter was read. Afterwards, Tourgée congratulated Price reaffirmed his support of the League, but expressed concern about the incident. Though he disclaimed any personal bad feelings, he told Price "the colored people of the United States cannot afford to allow its representative men to offer the almost unprecedented insult of returning the letter" of an ally like himself. "The hope of the Colored people depend on their achieving the support and approval of a majority because majorities rule" he went on, "It will not pay to kick a faithful champion because he is white … such conduct won't hearten people up to advocate your rights."[30] Price tried to reassure Tourgée that the incident was merely the ill-considered suggestion of a few cranks, but he also reiterated that the purpose of the League was to foster black "self-reliance" and to make its appeal to "men more than parties" because political parties had shown themselves more responsive to expediency than to justice.[31]

A year later, Tourgée founded a civil rights organization of his own. It began with yet another letter of advice when he wrote to Louis Martinet and his colleagues in the Louisiana chapter of ACERA who had announced their plans to challenge the constitutionality of Louisiana's Separate Car Act of 1890. With his experience as jurist and lawyer, Tourgée gave extensive legal advice on how to challenge the law and soon he became a prime mover, along with Martinet, in launching the test case that would become *Plessy* v. *Ferguson.*[32] At the same time, he suggested that a national citizen's rights organization should be established to replace ACERA (which had fallen apart) and to mobilize public opinion in support of their crusade against segregation. Martinet agreed with enthusiasm: "I heartily approve your suggestion for a national organization without the color or race line, to speak for the oppressed & defend their rights,' Martinet replied to him, "we want no distinct association [for blacks] & no distinct appellation, except when necessary for descriptive purposes."[33] ACERA had failed, Martinet explained, for lack of publicity and because "the proper men were not at the head" (an apparent criticism of ACERA President Pinchback, a longtime antagonist of Martinet's in Louisiana).[34]

Significantly, Martinet was a member of the Creole class of New Orleans who spoke French and took pride in their Catholic French identity. Like others of his class, Martinet was decidedly *not* an assimilationist when it came to his cultural identity—the *Crusader* was published in both French and English. Inspired especially by the French Revolution, he embraced the egalitarian promises in the concept of citizenship. He explained that the "Afro-American League would not take among the best people" in New Orleans because it reinforced the color line. In the *Crusader,* Martinet criticized its moniker "Afro-American" whose hyphen, he said, "keeps the 'Afro' always just so far away from the 'American.'"[35] For Martinet, civic identity was separate from cultural identification—and evidently he felt no conflict between the two.[36]

On October 17, 1891, Tourgée announced the founding of the National Citizen's Rights Association (NCRA) in his weekly column. His call implicitly was aimed at a white, Northern readership "Will the people of the North stand by the colored citizen in his appeal to the law?" he asked.[37] He explicitly challenged the white perception of blacks—promoted at Mohonk and enshrined in the mythology of Reconstruction—as failing in their ability to carry out the duties of citizenship. "It is a wonderful thing," he observed, that "by dimes and half-dimes an oppressed an impoverished race who are asserted to be incapable of self-government or co-operation are raising a fund to bring before the courts of the land the question of their rights as citizens." "Thanks to the civic instinct of an 'inferior' race," he concluded, "we shall see whether justice is still color-blind or National citizenship worth a rag for the defense of right."[38]

Citizenship for Tourgée, like Martinet, simply meant enjoyment of the rights and responsibilities that came as a birthright for all born or naturalized in the United States according to the 14th Amendment. But, as the inclusion of blacks, which had been the work of Reconstruction, had been discredited, the discussion of black equal citizenship itself became a question of black racial character. Whites were presumed citizens, while blacks were called on to prove or demonstrate their worthiness for citizenship. Even in trying to oppose it, Tourgée found himself capitulating to the terms of this discourse. By targeting white readers, Tourgée risked alienating black supporters from the start by taking their support for granted. On the other hand, organizing along racial lines reinforced the perception of blacks as a special category of citizen, whose circumstances and needs needed to be considered separately, or in a different way, from other citizens.

Despite the strategic conundrum it posed, "color-blind citizenship" was not yet dead as a principle. By the summer of 1892, the NCRA appeared to have considerable momentum behind it. Ida B. Wells, George Washington Cable, T. Thomas Fortune, Charles W. Chesnutt, and Florence A. Lewis, all were named to the NCRA executive counsel and the organization claimed over 100,000 members. At the Republican National Convention in June, the NCRA even received acknowledgement from some Presidential contenders, such as Thomas B. Reed, the powerful Republican House Speaker, a show of respect that suggested the organization just might play a role in keeping equal rights on the agenda of the Republican Party.

Yet, Tourgée was very cautious about how to proceed. He feared that a convention or mass meeting would expose the potentially paralyzing conflicts among those whose support he needed. After his experience at Mohonk, he worried that even Northern whites might not tolerate interracial meetings. "Thousands who say they are willing the colored citizen should have equal rights would abandon all idea of it if they had to attend a public meeting," he explained to one white member of the NCRA, "this is very foolish and wrong but true. Even our Mohonk people dare not ask a Negro to consult with them." "I don't care anything about the prejudice," he explained to another, but "I do not think I have any right to endanger good results by trying to compel compliance with my notions … How shall this [interracial meetings] be avoided?"[39]

His answer was to avoid public meetings altogether. There will be "no conventions, no delegates, no speeches, no parades, no eloquence," Tourgée concluded, "I see no use of these instrumentalities now but their employment would kill our work." He decided that it was better to have more supporters than to risk divisiveness. To any whites who needed reassurance, Tourgée would insist, as he wrote to one member:

> [the NCRA] is not a colored movement. They are oppressed because they are colored. But that is not the reason they are entitled to protection, justice, and equal opportunity. That is because they are human beings, citizens of the United States, and people whom we have wronged until our sin has ripened into curses."[40]

The interracial civic ideal, advanced by Radical Republicans during the Reconstruction era, seemed to be foundering on both sides of the color line. Tourgée heard rumors that African Americans "of means and influence ... among them editors of the race papers" were disgruntled "that they had not been 'consulted or invited to cooperate'" with him before he launched the NCRA.[41] He often expressed frustration at the lack of public support the NCRA received from black Northern leaders. "The colored people of the North remain indifferent, unresponsive—doing nothing," he complained to Florence A Lewis: "Most of them seem to wonder at the intensity of my conviction and I'm not sure that many of them do not feel a mild contempt for me on account of it ... The NCRA has for its roll ten white names for every one colored. What does it mean?"[42] Lewis could offer little explanation, except to suggest that the NCRA needed more publicity.

While a lack of evidence makes it difficult to discern the root of the problem, it seems likely that Tourgée had alienated some Northern black leaders because he had aimed his arguments too much at the white public. This dynamic replicated the one that T. Thomas Fortune and the Afro-American League wished to repudiate in the Republican Party—white leadership that represented black interests while asking blacks to understand the concessions that had to be made in the effort to advance those interests. Tourgée needed to find some way to escape this dynamic. The racialized discourse about citizenship inhibited interracial coalitions and facilitated a public sphere divided by race, fostering a separate white press and black press, white organizations and black ones. He found it impossible to cast the problem as one of *citizens'* rights, when both whites and blacks were inclined to see the problem as one of *blacks'* rights.

Tourgée's most promising plan was to establish a major journal to be called *The National Citizen* as the NCRA organ. Tourgée hoped *The National Citizen* would provide tangibility and a consistent public voice for the organization, much as Du Bois's *The Crisis* would later do in the early years of the NAACP. A weekly of twelve to twenty pages, its features would include political and literary contributions from both black and white authors, "a monthly Lesson Leaf on the duties of the citizen, and a monthly record of outrages upon the citizen."[43] Building a community of support through the readership of the journal, Tourgée could create an interracial community of readers that would be a virtual community that need not meet face-to-face—thus avoiding the hazards of an interracial public meeting or an open conversation that may sow discord. What the public needed more than anything, he believed, was to become educated and informed on these issues—and this is what he intended to provide. Fundraising for the NCRA went exclusively toward finding investors and backing for the proposed journal.[44]

Tourgée's missed his best opportunity to see *The National Citizen* become a reality, partly because of the very dilemma that his strategy for promoting "color-blind" citizenship perpetuated. T. Thomas Fortune, who kept up a friendly correspondence with Tourgée throughout this time, made an extraordinary offer in November of 1893. He declared that he could guarantee $5000 of stock if Tourgée agreed to have the proposed *National Citizen* absorb the New York *Age,* and employ Fortune as its managing editor (or perhaps co-editor). Fortune had declared the Afro-American League dead a few months earlier in August. He confessed to Tourgée that he had been thinking of launching a "high class monthly" for some time, realizing that "we can never reach the better class of whites through a race newspaper." He promised Tourgée: "[the *Age*] enjoys the confidence of the colored people and the respect of the leading editors of the country. We have 5,000 subscribers [and] the addition of your prestige and influence would undoubtedly double these figures within a reasonable time."[45] It was an impressive offer that promised to heal past conflicts, real or perceived. "I have become dissatisfied with race journalism," Fortune declared, assuring Tourgée, "We are so fully agreed on so many points."[46]

Without hesitation, Tourgée rejected his offer. In doing so, he defended the importance of "race journals" to Fortune, and insisted that the *Age* and the *National Citizen* each would be more effective as allies working in conjunction. *"The Age* has its own field; and a most necessary one," Tourgée replied, "as long as the colored man is distinguished against in any way, he must keep up his distinctive sentiment, organization, speciality [sic] of interest in sheer self-defense." Moreover, he promised that the *National Citizen* would "make liberal and frequent excerpts from race journals … so [as to] bring them into notice by people who do not now, and would not otherwise see them." Group advocacy and self-assertion by blacks, in his view, should continue independent of the effort to reach a white audience. The *National Citizen* "could not combine with *The Age* without spoiling both," he insisted.[47]

Tourgée offered his rationale as strategic and pragmatic, rather than a matter of principle or personal preference. White readers not already inclined to support black rights would stay away if the journal appeared to be an "organ" established solely for the advancement of blacks. The *National Citizen* "cannot accomplish results … by antagonizing those to whom it must appeal" and "however deplorable, [race prejudice] is still a fact and like all prejudice must be overcome by patience and example as much as by argument." With author and folklorist Charles Chesnutt already enlisted as associate editor, he told Fortune, they will have done enough to "make plain [our] disapproval of race distinctions and thus gradually accustom people to disregard such prejudice." Yet, Tourgée seemed to conclude that only with him, a white man, as general editor could his journal truly be viewed as a journal of "citizenship without regard to color."[48] On this point, he was probably correct in his analysis of the prejudices of his white middle-class audience. One is left to wonder whether it might have been a better strategy to exchange his ambition to reach moderate whites for the chance to unite Northern black leadership behind the NCRA.[49]

In retrospect, Tourgée's decision to spurn Fortune's offer turned out to be a mistake. Plans for the *The National Citizen* would unravel nine months later, when Tourgée's beloved daughter became gravely ill and required extended and expensive treatments. The family crisis caused him to back out of plans for the journal and lose his investors.[50] A year later, he did produce a journal called *The Basis: A Journal of Citizenship* that bore resemblance to his planned *National Citizen,* but it lasted barely one year from 1895-1896, operating on a small budget, with little financial backing. *The Basis* was unable to do what he had intended with *The National Citizen:* its staff was limited to members of Tourgée's own immediate family and its readership never exceeded a few thousand.

Tourgée did press forward with the *Plessy* case, of course. His arguments before the Supreme Court in April of 1896, that reasserted the principle of legal color-blindness among its objections to the law, have been analyzed in detail by this author elsewhere.[51] The Supreme Court upheld "separate but equal" segregation, and Justice Henry Billings Brown argued that civic assortment by race was not inherently discriminatory because "in the nature of things [the 14th Amendment] could not have been intended to abolish distinctions based upon color, or to enforce ... commingling of the two races upon terms unsatisfactory to either."[52] The confidence with which Justice Brown could imply that the "two" races did not prefer to intermingle certainly seemed to be reflected in the tendency of civil rights organizations divided along racial lines.

Just six months before he wrote the opinion, Booker T. Washington made his famous "Atlanta Compromise" speech that captured national headlines. It gave Brown further justification for his conclusions. What made the speech so remarkable to observers was his proposal that blacks ought to accept segregation, and by implication other denials of full citizenship, in exchange for black support for their economic and educational progress. Washington had declared, "the wisest among my race understand that agitation of questions of social equality is the extremist folly."[53] Though Booker T. Washington may have been following a strategy that he believed would lead to full equality, he fully embraced the discourse on citizenship that cast black citizens as "unworthy citizens" until they proved otherwise.

Notably, Washington in the Atlanta speech and elsewhere often ridiculed what he called the "absurd" policies of Reconstruction that had given political power to ignorant field hands whom were utterly unprepared to wield such power. For this, he blamed that "element in the North which wanted to punish Southern white men by forcing the Negro into positions over the heads of the Southern whites," adding that "I felt that the Negro would be the one to suffer for this in the end."[54] Blaming Reconstruction on vengeful whites who had no real interest in aiding blacks, he made these statements, presumably, to achieve peace between the races in the South, and to ingratiate himself to wealthy Northern philanthropists like those at Mohonk from whom he needed contributions to implement his program of "industrial education." In so doing, he sanctioned Northern acquiescence in segregation and encouraged Northerners to salve their consciences with charitable contributions.[55]

Washington's influence was enormous, and not only among whites. T. Thomas Fortune, for one, reprinted Washington's "Atlanta Compromise" speech in the *Age* with glowing commentary that asked whether the "Negro Moses" had been found. By 1896, the *Age* was receiving financial support from Tuskegee and had become an avid supporter of Washington.[56] But, despite their seeming rejection of the ideals of Reconstruction, Washington and Fortune continued to imagine a color-blind future. As Fortune once put it, economic progress for blacks would lead one day to the "promised land" of equality for the "Negro" when "his color will be swallowed up in his reputation, his bank account, and his important money interests."[57] Yet, by having put that day too far off into the future, they may have done more to reify the use of "color-blind" citizenship as a means to argue that blacks were impoverished and politically oppressed according to merit—or rather demerit—because they were unable to perform equally to whites.

W.E.B. Du Bois, on the surface, would seem an unlikely candidate to rally behind the principle "color-blind" citizenship. He addressed this principle directly in his 1897 address to the American Negro Academy, later published as the pamphlet, "the Conservation of the Races." Emphasizing the importance of race as a deep psychological and spiritual difference, and controversially even suggesting that biological differences may be real and important, he declared that, "the history of the world is the history, not of individuals, but of groups, not of nations, but of races." With this in mind, Du Bois framed the critical issue: "He then is the dilemma, and it is a puzzling one, I admit ... Am I an American or am I a Negro? Can I be both? Of is it my duty to cease to be a Negro as soon as possible and be an American? If I strive as a Negro, am I not perpetuating the very cleft that threatens and separates black and white America?"[58] His answer was that racial identity must be embraced, even at the risk of perpetuating the racial divide. Race solidarity should be cultivated "in planning our movements, [and] in guiding our future development," because the race had "its particular message, its particular idea" to contribute to civilization. He concluded: "We believe it is the duty of the Americans of Negro descent, as a body, to maintain their race identity until this mission of the Negro people is accomplished, and ideal of human brotherhood has become a practical possibility."[59] But, in the present, this ideal evidently was not practical.

Yet, like Washington and Fortune, Du Bois dreamed of a colorblind future. Du Bois repeatedly made reference in his work to, in his words, "that far off ... event ... that perfection of human life for which we all long" when the divine purpose of "race" may be exhausted and perfect individual equality may be achieved.[60] Yet, it is critical that his desire to be simply an equal citizen, an individual, existed alongside his desire to see the "Negro" race fulfill its destiny. For Du Bois, equal *citizenship* must not be delayed, even while racial identity remained significant. Indeed, it seemed that racism would not be overcome, in his view, until whites—and the rest of humanity—heard the message of the black race. Thus, Du Bois's emphasis on racial identity, ironically, was intended at least in part to speed the process of abolishing race itself, and making "human brotherhood" a "practical possibility."

The groundwork for the Niagara Movement began with the publication of the *Souls of Black Folk* (1903) that announced Du Bois's arrival as a counterforce to Tuskegee around whom a new movement might be formed. *The Souls of Black Folk* is in large part an extended meditation on the consequences of white racism and the inability of white Americans to see beyond the color of one's skin. In one of its most moving passages, Du Bois described the "color-blind" world he imagined when alone with his books:

> I sit with Shakespeare and he winces not. Across the color line I move arm in arm with Balzac and Dumas, where smiling men and welcoming women glide in gilded halls ... I summon Aristotle and Aurelius and what soul I will, and they come all graciously with no scorn or condescension. So, wed with Truth, I dwell above the Veil. Is this the life you grudge us, O knightly America?[61]

The above passage is a telling reflection on the prospects of "colorblind" citizenship on the eve of the Niagara Movement. Du Bois dreamed of meeting "smiling men" and "welcoming women" across the color line who accepted him with no "condescension," but he experienced this only in his imagination. In the real world, he felt that whites could not penetrate the "veil" of his racial identity and treat him as a fellow, equal citizen.

An overlooked dimension within the Du Bois-Washington debate of great importance on the question of citizenship concerns their conflicting view of Reconstruction. The second chapter of *Souls,* "On the Dawn of Freedom," (less famous than the third chapter, "Of Booker T. Washington and Others") began his project of vindicating Reconstruction from the conservative mythology that was coming to dominate public memory of it. A Ph.D. in History from Harvard University, Du Bois was well positioned to undertake the project, though he would encounter powerful resistance within (and outside) the historical profession. He would later deliver his essay "Reconstruction and Its Benefits" at the 1910 Annual Meeting of the American Historical Association in front of leading academic proponents of the conservative mythology, including Columbia University Professor William Dunning. Booker T. Washington had accepted the conservative rendering of Reconstruction as fact, except that he declared black people could become capable citizens one day, with the proper training and self-discipline. Renouncing this view, Du Bois suggested that ideal of an interracial democracy had been proved eminently possible during Reconstruction.[62]

Tourgée and Du Bois rejected the conservative myth about Reconstruction outright, and they both insisted that blacks and white radicals had acted with courage, honor and self-restraint during both the Civil War and Reconstruction. In AHA paper, Du Bois prominently used a long passage from Tourgée, taken from one of his "Bystander's Notes" columns, as testimony that described the relative honesty of the governments and the long-term beneficial reforms of the Reconstruction governments.[63] Not until 1935 did Du Bois complete his magisterial *Black Reconstruction in America* that depicted the era as a radical experiment in interracial democracy. He describes Tourgée at one point in the text as "the bravest of the carpetbaggers," and at another as "one of the ablest and most honest" of them. He also gives due credit to other white Radical Republicans whom "reached the highest level of self-sacrificing statesmanship ever achieved in America" and whom "laid down their lives on the altar of democracy and were eventually paid ... by the widespread contempt of America."[64] Du Bois showed here an appreciation for white radicals of the Reconstruction era whom Washington had explicitly scorned.

In his political strategizing, Du Bois followed a path that sought to foster black political solidarity and cultural achievement with hope that white acceptance and integration would follow afterward. He embraced equal citizenship but insisted upon an empathetic understanding of the different historical experience of black people. Prophetically, Du Bois believed that higher education would facilitate this understanding. "Herein the longing of black men must have respect," Du Bois wrote of the University curriculum, "the rich and bitter depth of their experience, the unknown treasures of their inner life, the strange renderings of nature they have seen, may give the world new points of view and make their loving, living, and doing precious to all human hearts."[65] Here Du Bois posited a fully realized pluralist, even multicultural, vision of citizenship. Only when black culture and historical experience could be fully understood by whites, and the conservative myths of black shortcomings as citizens repudiated, would the barrier to civic equality be removed. Thus, when the Niagara Movement was first organized, racial integration was a goal but not an immediate expectation.

In the summer of 1905, Du Bois was one of a handful of black activists who decided to launch a new organization to oppose Booker T. Washington's Tuskegee Machine. Their intention was to operate outside the influence of Washington, who had increasingly used his patronage network to censor the black press and silence those who publicly disagreed with his tactics and opinions. Du Bois and his collaborators invited fifty-nine black men of distinguished achievement in the professions and business world, all of whom they considered "unpurchaseable" by the Tuskegee wizard, to their first meeting in Buffalo, New York, in July. No whites were invited to attend or involved in the planning of the meeting, which was surely meant to send a message of black self-assertion. Unlike Washington, who relied heavily on white patronage and financial backing, the new movement would be free of any such influence.[66]

Du Bois's own relationship with white "liberals" had been a vexed one, especially in the months leading up to the Niagara Movement's first meeting. Oswald Garrison Villard, a grandson of William Lloyd Garrison and powerful newspaperman, had vigorously defended Booker T. Washington against Du Bois's allegations of misconduct in early 1905, and the two had engaged in a sharp private exchange. Villard's unswerving support of Washington probably added to Du Bois's caution in bringing whites into the inner circle of the Niagara-ites. But the history of interracial cooperation was not forgotten at the meeting.

The "Declaration of Principles" drawn up at the meeting included a tribute of remembrance of "our fellow men form the abolitionist down to those who today still stand for equal opportunity" while calling on the cooperation of "all men of all races" in supporting their goals. Of course, Du Bois did not fail to name Villard's grandfather, along with Albion Tourgée, as one of the notable "Friends of Freedom" to be honored in a special service of Thanksgiving.[67]

In 1906, the Niagara Movement held its second annual meeting at Harper's Ferry, Virginia to coincide with John Brown Day on August 17. This symbolic gesture, once again, was meant to honor the movement's radical forbearers—in this case, John Brown and his interracial band of raiders—who had advanced the cause of racial equality. It is not surprising that Du Bois chose Harper's Ferry. He had recently begun work on a biography of John Brown, subsequently published in 1909. In that book, Du Bois would praise Brown as the preeminent example of a white American who transcended racial barriers and enacted civic colorblindness. "John Brown worked not simply for Black Men—he worked with them; and he was a companion of their daily life, knew their faults and virtues, and felt, as few white Americans have felt, the bitter tragedy of their lot," Du Bois wrote. "He came to them on a plane of perfect equality—they sat at his table and he at theirs," and it was this that brought him "nearest to touching the real souls of black folk" than any other white American.[68] Du Bois had not given up on the dream of color-blind citizenship.

Du Bois was inclined to move toward integration more slowly and deliberately, than events would ultimately dictate. In 1908, he invited Mary White Ovington, with whom he had forged a strong personal bond, to become the first white member of the Niagara Movement after she gave a talk at its fourth annual conference in Oberlin, Ohio (significantly, the site of America's first integrated institution of higher education). By that time, however, the Niagara Movement began to lose momentum. In 1909, Du Bois took the opportunity presented by a group of white radicals to merge his weakening movement into a new one that would soon adopt the name the National Association for the Advancement of Colored People. The NAACP from the outset would be an interracial organization. But, Du Bois would always remain wary of its white members' tendency to prioritize racial integration over black cultural self-development, believing that the latter must come before the former could be truly realized. In fact, Du Bois's famous break with the NAACP in 1930s would occur because he felt the organization's focus on achieving *de jure* integration was injurious to the work of black cultural institutions.[69]

The complicated stance of W.E.B. Du Bois toward the principle of civic "color-blindness" reflected an alternative solution to the same difficulties Tourgée encountered when he tried to rally the forces of racial equality behind this principle in the 1890s. Tourgée despaired at the distrust between white and black allies in the aftermath of the Republican party's failures to follow through on the promises of Reconstruction. Du Bois despaired at the possibility of achieving a truly integrated, interracial society in the face of widespread presumptions of black civic inferiority—bolstered by misinformation about Reconstruction—shared not only by many white allies, but by some black leaders like Booker T. Washington. These

Reading 9—The Question of Color-Blind Citizenship | 147

presumptions had to be dismantled, he believed, before blacks would ever be accepted into civil society on a truly equal basis as whites. The desire to be viewed, and accepted, by one's fellow citizens according to one's own unique individual attributes—the promise of "color blind" citizenship—was at the heart of both men's antiracist crusades. Fittingly, it was enshrined in the principles of the Niagara Movement. But Du Bois believed that goal would not be achieved until whites fully understood the experience of African Americans, and were able to penetrate the veil of racial distortion. Until then, the "color-blind" society he fantasized about would remain an unrealized dream.

NOTES

1. Mark Elliott is a member of the History faculty at Wagner College. His book, *Color-Blind Justice: Albion Tourgée and the Quest for Racial Equality from the Civil War to Plessy v. Ferguson,* earned the Organization of American Historian's Avery O. Craven Award for 2007.

2. Niagara Statement of Principles, 1905. The Gilder Lehrman Center for the Study of Slavery, Abolition, and Resistance, Yale University. On-line document library: <http://www.yale.edu/glc/archive/1152.htm>. First epigraph, Tourgée to Louis A. Martinet, October 31, 1893, #7438, Albion Winegar Tourgée Papers, Chautauqua County Historical Society, Westfield, NY; second epigraph, W.E.B. Du Bois, "The Conservation of the Races" in David Levering Lewis, ed., *W.E.B. Du Bois, A Reader* (New York: Henry Holt and Company, 1995), 26.

3. "The Growth of the Niagara Movement," *The Voice of the Negro* III (January 1906): 19–20; Otto H. Olsen, *Carpetbagger's Crusade: The Life of Albion Winegar Tourgée* (Baltimore: The Johns Hopkins Press, 1965), 352; Elliott M. Rudwick, "The Niagara Movement," *Journal of Negro History* 42 (July 1957): 177–200.

4. William Lloyd Garrison, *Thoughts on African Colonization: Or an impartial Exhibition of the Doctrines, Principles, and Purposes of the American Colonization Society* (Boston: Garrison and Knapp, 1832), 145; Garrison also quoted in Andrew Kull, *The Color-Blind Constitution* (Cambridge: Harvard University Press, 1992), 10–11.

5. David Blight, *Frederick Douglass' Civil War: Keeping Faith in Jubilee* (Baton Rouge: Louisiana State University Press, 1991), 144; Wilson Jeremiah Moses, *Creative Conflict in African American Thought: Frederick Douglass, Alexander Crummell, Booker T. Washington, W.E.B. Du Bois, and Marcus Garvey* (Cambridge University Press, 2004), 128–129.

6. Albion W. Tourgée, "A Bystander's Notes," Chicago *Daily Inter Ocean,* October 17, 1891, 4.

7. Albion W. Tourgée, "Shall White Minorities Rule?" *The Forum* VII (April 1889): 146–147.

8. John Tyler Morgan, "Shall Negro Majorities Rule?" *The Forum* VI (February 1889): 595.

9. [My emphasis] *The Civil Rights Cases,* 109 U.S. (1883), 25.

10. Cable identified several national politicians who referred to black "supremacy," "black oligarchy," and the "Africanization" of the South having been the political objective of Reconstruction in his "A Simpler Southern Question," *The Forum* VI (December 1888): 396.

11. Albion W. Tourgée, *A Fools Errand By One of the Fools* (New York: Fords, Howard & Hulbert, 1879); *Bricks Without Straw: A Novel* (New York: Fords, Howard & Hulbert, 1880); *An Appeal to Caesar* (New York: Fords, Howard & Hulbert, 1884); George Fredrickson has called Tourgée "the North's leading exponent of racial egalitarianism" and deemed his *An Appeal to Caesar* "the most profound discussion of the American racial situation to appear in the 1880s" in *The Black Image in the White Mind: The Debate on Afro-American Character and Destiny, 1817–1914* (Middletown, Conn.: Wesleyan University Press, 1971), 242–43. See also, Olsen, *Carpetbagger's Crusade;* Richard Nelson Current, *Those Terrible Carpetbaggers: A Reinterpretation* (Oxford: Oxford University Press, 1988); Mark Elliott, *Color-Blind Justice: Albion Tourgée and the Struggle for Racial Equality from the Civil War to* Plessy v. Ferguson (New York: Oxford University Press, 2006).

12. Thomas Adams Upchurch, *Legislating Racism: The Billion Dollar Congress and the Birth of Jim Crow* (Lexington, KY: University Press of Kentucky, 2004), 46–65; Daniel W. Crofts, "The Black Response to the Blair Education Bill," *The Journal of Southern History* 37 (February 1971): 52–53.

13 Leslie H. Fishel, Jr., "The 'Negro Question' at Mohonk: Microcosm, Mirage, and Message," *New York History* (July 1993): 277-314; Albion Tourgée, "The Negro's View of the Race Problem" in *First Mohonk Conference on the Negro Question. Held at Lake Mohonk, Ulster County New York, June 4, 5, 6*, ed. Isabel C. Barrows (Boston: George H. Ellis, Printer, 1890), 7-12; Ralph Luker, *The Social Gospel in Black and White: American Racial Reform, 1885-1912* (Chapel Hill: University of North Carolina Press, 1991), 26-27; Eric Foner, *Reconstruction: America's Unfinished Revolution, 1863-1877* (New York: HarperCollins, 1988), 605-6.

14 A.D. Mayo, "The Negro American Citizen in the New American Life," in Barrows, *Mohonk Conference,* 39; Luker, *Social Gospel,* 26-27.

15 Luker, *Social Gospel,* 26-27.

16 Tourgée, "The Negro's View of the Race Problem," 106, 108.

17 [His emphasis removed] Tourgée's comment recorded in Barrows, *Mohonk Conference,* 25.

18 Tourgée, "The Negro's View of the Race Problem," 108.

19 [Tourgée's emphasis removed]. Ibid., 104-105, 108; "Judge Tourgée's Splendid Speech," *The Republican*, #8251, Tourgée Papers. For his comparison of Jesus Christ to a carpetbagger, see "Horrible Blasphemy," Southern Home, #2428, Tourgée Papers.

20 Luker, *Social Gospel,* 28.

21 In the wake of the Blair Bill's defeat, T. Thomas Fortune who would later ally with Washington urged: "Let the race pull itself together. What others will not do for us we must do for ourselves," Quoted in Crofts, "The Black Response," 59.

22 T. Thomas Fortune, in particular, had rankled loyal Republicans a few years earlier when he broke with the party and campaigned for the Democrat Grover Cleveland in the Presidential election of 1888. His leadership reinforced the impression that the League's main purpose was to encourage blacks to break with the Republican Party. Emma Lou Thombrough, *T. Thomas Fortune: Militant Journalist* (Chicago: University of Chicago Press, 1972), 95-104.

23 Louis Martinet to Albion W. Tourgée, October 5, 1891, #5760, Tourgée Papers. Frederick Douglass too may have been obliquely criticizing the Afro-American League when he denounced separate black organizations in a speech delivered a month prior to their meeting on December 16, 1889. See, Moses, *Creative Conflict,* 128-129.

24 Quoted in Shawn Leigh Alexander, *"We Know Our Rights and have the Courage to Defend Them:" The Spirit of Agitation in the Age of Accommodation, 1883-1909,* Ph.D. Dissertation, University of Massachusetts, 2004,25. Washington *Bee,* November 16, 1889.

25 All were active Republicans and held positions attained through the Harrison Administration (as did Calvin Chase). Thombrough, *T. Thomas Fortune,* 116-117.

26 Pinchback quoted from "Address of the Colored Citizens," Chicago *Tribune,* February 7, 1890.

27 Tourgée quoted in Luker, 72. Original, Tourgée to W.S. Scarborough, November 27, 1889, W.S. Scarborough Papers, Wilberforce University.

28 Albion Tourgée, "A Bystander's Notes," Chicago *Daily Inter Ocean,* November 30, 1894.

29 The incident was reported as follows, "This proposition [to accept Tourgée's letter] was opposed by several delegates on the grounds that Judge Tourgée was not an Afro-American, and that it was time for the Negroes to show they could get along without the help of white men. Prof. J.C. Price of [North Carolina] declared that Tourgée had written for the good of the Negro and knew more about the Negro question than many of the colored men themselves. He favored the adoption of good suggestions, no matter from where they came," "To Relieve the Whites: Afro-Americans Petition Congress," Chicago *Daily Tribune,* January 17, 1890.

30 Tourgée to Joseph C. Price, [1890], #11043, Tourgée Papers; Alexander, *"We Know Our Rights,"* 89-90.

31 J.C. Price to Tourgée, March 18, 1890, #4568, Tourgée Papers.

32 Eli C. Freeman to Tourgée, Aug. 4, 1890, #4872; Eli C. Freeman to Tourgée, August 26, 1890; #4895, Tourgée Papers; Charles A. Lofgren, *The Plessy Case: A Legal-Historical Interpretation* (Oxford and New York: Oxford University Press, 1987), 28-32.

33 Louis A. Martinet to Tourgée, Oct. 5,1891, #5760, Tourgée Papers.

34 Ibid. Martinet blamed Pinchback, who failed to attend its second annual convention despite being the organization's President. It seems likely that Pinchback never intended to do anything with ACERA other than use it to keep blacks out of the Afro-American League and within the Republican Party.

35 *The Daily Crusader,* May 10, 1890, clipping in the Rousseve Papers, Folder 15, The Amistad Research Center, New Orleans; Louis A. Martinet to Tourgée, Oct. 5, 1891, #5760, Tourgée Papers.

36 For more on the civil rights ideology of Martinet and the Louisiana creoles, See Rebecca J. Scott, *Degrees of Freedom: Louisiana and Cuba After Slavery* (Cambridge: Harvard/Belknap Press, 2005), 30-93.

37 Albion W. Tourgée, "A Bystander's Notes," Chicago *Daily Inter Ocean,* October 17, 1891, 4.

38 Ibid.

39 Tourgée to Hon. Phillip C. Garret, [July, 1892?], #6439, Tourgée Papers.

40 Ibid.

41 Thomas W. Griffin to Tourgée, May 1, 1894, #7664, Tourgée Papers.

42 Tourgée to "Madame"[Florence A. Lewis] with letters of June, 1892, #6297, Tourgée Papers.

43 *Headquarters. National Citizen's Rights Association.* Broadside. Included with Tourgée to Flavius Josephus Cook, Oct. 15, 1893, F.J. Cook Papers, William R. Perkins Library, Manuscripts Department, Duke University,

44 Inquiring about the purchasing of stock, T.B. Morton, the President of the Afro-American League to Tourgée, July 7, 1894, #7874, Tourgée Papers.

45 T. Thomas Fortune to Tourgée, Nov. 16, 1893, #7499, Tourgée Papers; Alexander, *"We Know Our Rights,"* 98.

46 T. Thomas Fortune to Tourgée, Nov. 23, 1893, #7533, Tourgée Papers.

47 Tourgée to T. Thomas Fortune, Nov. 20, 1893, #7510, Tourgée Papers.

48 Ibid.

49 Another factor in Tourgée's decision was his distrust and personal animus for Fortune that probably derived from his stint with the Democratic Party. In 1890, Tourgée warned League President Joseph C. Price about him: "Fortune, who is simply a restless, self-seeking, ambitious demagogue, will unquestionably foster [factionalism] … his idea of heaven is to be the focus of attention and he would see his race at the devil if it would make the world talk about him." Tourgée to J.C. Price, January [?], 1890, #11043, Tourgée Papers; Thombrough, *T. Thomas Fortune),* 86-95.

50 Tourgée to unknown, August 1894, #8234, Tourgée Papers.

51 Marie Elliott, "Race, Color Blindness and the Democratic Public: Albion W. Tourgée's Radical Principles in *Plessy v. Ferguson," The Journal of Southern History* LXVII (May 2001): 287-330; Elliott, *Color-Blind Justice,* 262-96; see also Lofgren, *Plessy Case-,* Sidney Kaplan, "Albion W. Tourgée: Attorney for the Segregated." *Journal of Negro History* 49 (1964): 128-133.

52 Justice Henry Billings Brown Majority opinion in *Plessy v. Ferguson,* quoted from Brook Thomas, ed. Plessy v. Ferguson, *A Brief History with Documents* (New York: Bedford Books, 1997), 44.

53 From the "Atlanta Exposition Address" quoted in W. Fitzhugh Brundage, ed. *Up from Slavery By Booker T. Washington with Related Documents* (New York: Bedford/StMartin's, 2003), 142-145. [Original edition, New York: Doubleday, Page and Co., 1901], See his comments in "Chapter V. The Reconstruction Period," 76-82.

54 Washington, *Up From Slavery,* 79.

55 Michael Rudolph West, *The Education of Booker T. Washington: American Democracy and the Idea of Race Relations* (New York: Columbia University Press, 2006), 23-60.

56 Thombrough, *T. Thomas Fortune,* 118-19, 161-71.

57 T. Thomas Fortune, *Black and White: Land, Labor and Politics in the South* (New York: Fords, Howard & Hulbert, 1885), 180-81.

58 Du Bois, "The Conservation of the Races," 24.

59 Ibid, 26.

60 Ibid, 23.

61 W. E. B. Du Bois, *The Souls of Black Folk* (1903; reprint, New York: Bantam Books, 1989), 75-76.

62 W.E.B. du Bois, "Reconstruction and Its Benefits," *American Historical Review XV* (July 1910): 796.

63 Ibid.

64 David Levering Lewis, "Introduction," *Black Reconstruction in America, 1860-1880* (New York: Free Press, 1998, org. 1935), ix, 186, 621.

65 Du Bois, *Souls of Black Folk,* 75-76.

66 David Levering Lewis, W.E.B. Du Bois: Biography of a Race (New York: Henry Holt, 1993), 316–322.
67 Niagara Statement of Principles; Lewis, *Du Bois,* 314–322.
68 W.E.B. Du Bois, *John Brown. New Introduction by Herbert Aptheker* (Millwood, NY: Kraus-Thomson, 1972), 7–8.
69 Rudwick, "The Niagara Movement," 195–198; David Levering Lewis, *W.E.B. Du Bois: The Fight for Equality and the American Century, 1919–1963* (New York: Henry Holt, 2000), 288–340.

PART IV

African American Literature, Arts, and Culture: The Harlem Renaissance, 1927–1940

READING 10

Black Voices
Themes in African-American Literature

Gerald Early

In one of the essays in his 1957 book, *White Man, Listen!,* Richard Wright claims, "The Negro is America's metaphor." By this he meant not only that blacks were the symbolic embodiment of the history of America, an outcast people trying to find a new identity in the New World, but also that they were, through the circumstances of being forced to live in a country "whose laws, customs, and instruments of force were leveled against them," constant reminders of the anguish of being without an identity, constant reminders of human alienation. According to Ralph Ellison, Wright's good friend back in the 1930s, "The white American has charged the Negro American with being without a past or tradition (something which strikes the white man with a nameless horror), just as he himself has been so charged by European and American critics with a nostalgia for the stability once typical of European cultures."

But Wright saw in the African-American's quest for an identity, in his struggle against human alienation, against being a symbol of the abyss of estrangement, a deep political and philosophical resonance that, in fact, gave America both an aesthetic—blues music—and crucial forms of social engagement that blacks, and the political culture of the United States itself, used as forms of dissent against the idea of human alienation: first, abolition, then, Reconstruction, and, finally, the Civil Rights movement. "Is it not clear to you that the American Negro is the only group in our nation that consistently and passionately raises the question of freedom?" asks Wright. "This is a service to America and to the world. More than this: The voice of the American Negro is rapidly becoming the most representative voice of America and of oppressed people anywhere in the world today." In effect, Wright is suggesting that black Americans, within the framework of their isolation, had managed to create community and common cause with other victimized peoples in the world (particularly the "colored" world). Wright suggests that black Americans were to construct a penetrating view of the general human condition through the prism of their own localized experience.

Because the quests for a usable community and for identity have shaped black experience itself in America, Wright argues his essay, these quests ultimately inform all of African-American literature.

Gerald Early, "Black Voices: Themes in African-American Literature," *Upon These Shores: Themes in the African-American Experience 1600 to the Present*, ed. William Randolph Scott and William G. Shade, pp. 270-284. Copyright © 2000 by Taylor & Francis Group. Reprinted with permission.

A QUESTION OF IDENTITY: FROM PHILLIS WHEATLEY TO RICHARD WEIGHT

When one thinks of poet Phillis Wheatley (1753?–1784), the earliest black writer in America to produce an estimable body of work, this observation certainly seems true, not simply about black people generally but about the black writer especially. Wheatley, born in Senegal and brought to America at the age of eight, had to learn both a new language and a new religion, indeed, an entirely new way of life, the same cultural disruption and brutally imposed cognitive dissonance that other Africans experienced as well, except that in some manner, as a child, the adaptation had to be, paradoxically, both easier and harder. Yet she so completely absorbed aspects of her new culture that she was able to write poetry in the leading literary style of the day by the time she was a teenager. Naturally, because of her age, some of her poetry exhibits facility but lacks depth. But the question of identity, while muted in most of her work, still appears here and there, and one must suppose that she thought a great deal about her precarious fate as a favored slave and about the nature of the black community that she was not fully a part of for a good portion of her life in America and which was powerless to support her as a writer. In any case, she never forgot that she was an African. It was hardly likely that she forgot that passage or the circumstances that brought her over to the New World. She wrote in the poem, "To the Right Honorable William Early of Dartmouth, His Majesty's Principal Secretary of State for North America, Etc.":

> Should you, my lord, while you pursue my song,
> Wonder from whence my love of Freedom sprung,
> Whence flow these wishes for the common good,
> By feeling hearts alone best understood,
> I, young in life, by seeming cruel fate
> Was snatch'd from Afric's fancy'd happy seat:
> What pangs excruciating must molest,
> What sorrows labour in my parent's breast?
> Steel'd was the soul and by no misery mov'd
> That from a father seiz'd his babe belov'd
> Such, such my case. And can I then but pray
> Others may never feel tyrannic sway?

In these lines, there is not only a sense of being taken away from the life and culture and from parents who felt concern and cared for their child (concerns seldom attributed to Africans by whites at the time) but also a sense of thwarted justice born from having endured the experience of a disrupted community. Wheatley, who died poverty-stricken, abandoned by both the black and white communities, in some ways both voiced and personified the themes of identity and community that were to be fully developed and elaborated upon by later black writers.

"The radical solitude of human life," wrote José Ortega y Gasset in his 1957 philosophical treatise, *Man and People,* "the being of man, does not, then, consist in there really being nothing except himself. Quite the contrary—there is nothing less than the universe, with all that it contains. There is, then, an infinity of things but—there it is!—amid them Man in his radical reality is alone—alone *with* them." Somehow, this seems to capture Wheatley herself, mastering foreign cultural tools for a self-expression that was never quite her own, a sly and complicated ventriloquism that was both the triumph and the tragedy of her assimilation. By redefining her theft from Africa as a providential plot for placing her in a more transcendent community, she might ultimately find closure for her predicament. Thus, she writes, in "On Being Brought From Africa to America":

> Twas mercy brought me from my Pagan land,
> Taught my benighted soul to understand
> That there's a God, that there's a Saviour too:
> Once I redemption neither sought nor knew.
> Some view our sable race with scornful eye,
> "Their colour is a diabolic die."
> Remember, Christians, Negroes, black as Cain,
> May be refin'd, and join th' angelic train.

In eighteenth-century New England, with the rise of liberalism, Calvinism was forced to retreat before a more humanitarian worldview, before the view that, despite their condition, babies, "idiots," blacks, and others "naturally perverse in their will toward sin" ought not be consigned to hell. This view obviously affected Wheatley in two ways: first, as a product of the new liberalism where her poetry would be appreciated and encouraged as a sign of God's deliverance of the benighted; and second, as a believer in the new liberalism as a way to explain her fate and the form of cultural assimilation that she was experiencing. More important, the idea that blacks could be or had to be, in one way or another, "refin'd" or uplifted as a cure for their alienation or degradation, has been a constant in African-American thought, from the earliest writings in English to the ideas of nationalists like Marcus Garvey (whose organization was called the Universal Negro *Improvement* Association) and Malcolm X. Perhaps one way in which Richard Wright was truly path-breaking was in his reluctance to think in those terms.

Struck deeply by the alienation described by Ortega y Gasset, Wright was one of the major African-American writers of the twentieth century, a figure so monumental that the era from the late Depression when Wright began publishing through 1960, the year of his death, is often referred to as his epoch. Wright was heavily influenced by Marxism, a philosophy he learned during his days as a Communist writer and editor in Chicago and New York in the early and mid-'30s, and by existentialism, a philosophy he felt intuitively from his youth when it provided a substitute for the Christianity that he abhorred. Wright read deeply about existentialism after World War II, existentialism's heyday. In his major works before his self-imposed exile from America after the Second World War, it was not that Wright introduced new themes to African-American writing. Instead, he concentrated, as had others before him, on the quests for identity and for usable community. However, partly because Wright was born and reared, for the most part, in Mississippi, the most backward and brutal state in the Union on the matter of race, no black writer before him achieved either Wright's visceral intensity in describing black-white relations or displayed as deep a passion for seeking broad philosophical implications in black American life. And no black writer before him saw black life in such stark, often cosmically lonely terms. Finally, no black writer until Wright had become as famous, as accepted in this country, and particularly abroad, as a genuine man of letters and a writer of unquestioned stature.

The works for which Wright became known—*Uncle Tom's Children* (1937), a collection of novellas set in the South, *Native Son* (1940), his grand urban novel of crime and punishment set in Chicago, and *Black Boy* (1945), his autobiographical exploration of black adolescence in the American South—emphasize a deep sense of estrangement in characters unable to connect with a larger aggregate of humanity, characters trying heroically to establish their identities but confounded by incredible forces that manipulate and annihilate their sense of place and belonging, by forces that transform anxiety into impotent rage and turn fear into inexhaustible dread. The stories in *Uncle Tom's Children,* all about black rebellion against the violent white power structure, move from heroes who are unconscious of any political significance in their acts, largely buffeted by the tides and whimsies of a cruel, indifferent world, trying desperately to extricate themselves from a seemingly inescapable fate, to more politically aware heroes (the heroine of the last story is a Marxist as well as a deep believer in black solidarity) whose revolts are self-consciously motivated. But even in the most restricted circumstances, Wright gives his black characters choices. Wright was never to abandon his Marxist/existentialist belief that man makes his world, makes his circumstances, and makes his fate.

In *Native Son,* considered by most critics Wright's masterpiece, the reader is given the most vehement critique against the idea of welfare-state liberalism ever written by a black to this time. In this ideologically driven novel, Wright presents welfare-state liberalism, which for the rich, white Dalton family of the novel, represents a mere mask for exploitative power and for maintaining the status quo of keeping black families like that of Wright's protagonist, Bigger Thomas, poor and huddled in ghettos. Bigger's psychotic attempt at liberation is doomed to failure because he has accepted the terms of blackness that white society has imposed upon him. In other words, he has sought his humanity by becoming the very inhuman thing that white society said he was and, in effect, made him. In *Black Boy,* by looking in an exaggerated and not entirely factual way at his family and rearing in the South, Wright explores exclusively the idea of what black community means. It was in this book that Wright made one of his striking, and, for some, disturbing, statements about the meaning of black community:

> After I had outlived the shocks of childhood, after the habit of reflection had been born in me, I used to mull over the strange absence of real kindness in Negroes, how unstable was our tenderness, how lacking in genuine passion we were, how void of great hope, how timid our joy, how bare our traditions, how hollow our memories, how lacking we were in those intangible sentiments that bind man to man, and how shallow was even our despair. After I had learned other ways of life I used to brood upon the unconscious irony of those who felt that Negroes led so passional an existence! I saw that what had been taken for our emotional strength was our negative confusions, our flights, our fears, our frenzy under pressure.
>
> Whenever I thought of the essential bleakness of black life in America, I knew that Negroes had never been allowed to catch the full spirit of Western civilization, that they lived somehow in it but not of it. And when I brooded upon the cultural barrenness of black life, I wondered if clean, positive tenderness, love, honor, loyalty, and the capacity to remember were native with man. I asked myself if these human qualities were not fostered, won, struggled and suffered for, preserved in ritual from one generation to another.

Wright had two aims in writing this passage: first, despite his own love of sociology, he wanted to lift the level of discourse about the black condition from mere sociology to something philosophical, to something which spoke of the problem of human community. Second, hoping to reverse, harshly and shockingly, a tendency he disliked in earlier black writing, particularly in some of the writing of the Harlem Renaissance, he wanted to de-romanticize and de-exoticize black life.

THE FOUNDATION OF AN AFRICAN-AMERICAN LITERARY TRADITION

To understand fully how an author like Wright shaped his work, it is necessary to go back to the slave narrative, the earliest form of black American writing that formed a coherent body of work, that expressed a plain ideological task and purpose and set forth the themes of identity and community that were to characterize all the black writing that came after. While poet Phillis Wheatley's work exhibited these themes, almost as a subtext, the antebellum slave narratives sharpened and strengthened these concerns by making the black writer a presence in American life and letters.

One of the antecedents of the antebellum slave narrative was the Indian captivity narrative of the eighteenth century, usually a tale about a white captured and forced to live for some period of time among Indians. Other captivity narratives tell of persons surprisingly impressed in the navy or unfairly or unfortunately seized by the nation's enemy. The earliest black narratives such as *A Narrative of the Uncommon Sufferings and Surprizing Deliverance of*

Briton Hammon, a Negro Man, published in 1760, and *A Narrative of the Life of John Marrant of New York, in North America: With An Account of the Conversion of the King of the Cherokees and his Daughter,* published in 1785, were precisely in the captivity narrative mode. Indeed, slavery was scarcely the subject of them in any sort of political way. Built on the captivity narrative model, *The Interesting Narrative of the Life of Olaudah Equiano or Gustavus Vassa, the African* (1791), was the first true slave narrative in that it was a self-conscious and explicit protest against slavery. It was the first self-conscious black or African political literature in English in the Western world.

Although there were important black publications of a political or polemical sort published earlier, works such as *A Narrative of the Black People during the Late Awful Calamity in Philadelphia* (1794) by Richard Allen and Absalom Jones, and *David Walker's Appeal in Four Articles; Together with A Preamble, To the Coloured Citizens of the World, but in Particular, and Very Expressly, To Those of the United States of America* (1829), the full development and enrichment of black literature occurred in the antebellum period of 1830 to 1860. From small tracts and pamphlets to major, polished autobiographies, literally hundreds of slave narratives were published. Sponsored largely by white abolitionist societies in the North, where antislavery had become a major political and social movement in the United States, much of this writing suffered from the same problems as early European-American literature, an imitative or dull style and an overwrought Christian piety. Moreover, because they were unable to appear before the public as guarantors of their own stories, without the aid of a vouching white editor or friend, black authors were at a severe disadvantage. Finally, there was the problem of audience—whom did the slave narrator wish to address and why? Obviously, the slave narrator desired to move white readers to act against slavery. This meant that the literature had to present the black narrator as palatable to whites who were, almost exclusively, committed to white supremacist ideals. But the black narrator, and all black writers since this period, also felt the pressure of being representative of his race and wanted to cast no undue aspersions upon it. That is to say, the slave narratives were meant both to be a protest, crossover literature for whites (to help them understand the true nature of slavery or, one might say, the black American experience) and, in some sense, a "race" literature addressing the needs of black self-esteem and racial community.

The idea or ideal of black community during antebellum America was a difficult one to maintain. First, the black community was a complex set of structures: there were various divisions within slavery, fieldhands versus house servants, artisans versus the unskilled, light-skinned versus dark-skinned, more recent African arrivals versus third-, fourth-, or fifth-generation "detainees." In addition there were the free black communities of both the North and South. Because it was the free blacks who could effectively or at least more visibly agitate for freedom, these free communities, although small, were essential to the much larger slave communities. But the free community was a complex mixture, exhibited many of the same elements that made up the slave communities, and, like the slave communities, was largely at the mercy of the whites who surrounded it. Without a centralized church, any school system worth the name, or any of the normal civic privileges that the average white citizens enjoyed, it was difficult for the free black communities to act as a vanguard for the slave communities.

Second, blacks in antebellum America were experiencing a complex form of cultural syncretism. It must be remembered that a number of ethnically diverse Africans were brought to the New World during the Atlantic slave trade so two simultaneous processes were taking place in the creation of black community. First, the Europeans worked assiduously to remove as many cultural props—language, religion, kinship rituals, rites of passage—that they could to make the Africans a less volatile, less warlike labor presence (which is why, in the end, the African was preferred to the Indian as a slave). Black community was always meant to be, in the eyes of whites, dependent, precarious, impoverished, an area or configuration to be policed and contained. Second, the Africans came to meld or distill the strands of cultural expressions that they were able to maintain to forge a new identity. So, true black community—independent, stabilized, and prosperous—was to become a subversive concept.

The most famous of the slave narratives were Frederick Douglass's 1845 *Narrative of the Life of Frederick Douglass, An American Slave* and his 1855 *My Bondage and My Freedom,* Harriet Jacobs's *Incidents in the Life of a Slave Girl,* published in 1861, *The Narrative of William Wells Brown,* published in 1846, *Running a Thousand Miles for Freedom* by William and Ellen Craft, published in 1860, *The Narrative of Henry Box Brown Who Escaped from Slavery in a Box Three Feet Long and Two Feet Wide; Written from a Statement of Facts by Himself,* published in 1849, *Life of Josiah Henson, formerly a Slave, Now an Inhabitant of Canada, Narrated by Himself,* published in 1849, and *Twelve Years a Slave: the Narrative of Solomon Northup, a Citizen of New York, Kidnapped in Washington City in 1841, and Rescued in 1853, from a Cotton Plantation Near Red River in Louisiana,* published in 1853. All of these works tried in various ways to create a sense of black community in the narratives by talking not only of the slave narrator's sense of connection to his or her own family (family piety was virtually a cliché in this works) but to the larger community of slaves, who often assisted the narrator in his escape. Moreover, the books tried to create a sense of connection through their texts between blacks in the North and South, slave and free. Of these, the works by Douglass, William Wells Brown, and Jacobs are considered by literary critics and African-American literary experts today to have the most value.

Indeed, Douglass and Brown, both escaped slaves who became veteran speakers on the abolition circuit, were true men of letters. Douglass ran a newspaper for many years, and Brown published several other works including the earliest black novel, *Clotel or the President's Daughter,* published in 1853, and *Three Years in Europe,* the first black travel book, published in 1852. Brown was to publish several more books, including some of the earliest full-scale black histories. Other early black novels published before 1860 were Frank J. Webb's *The Garies and Their Friends,* a novel about free blacks in Philadelphia, published in 1857, Martin R. Delany's *Blake: Or, the Huts of America,* a militant, highly polemical novel about black rebellion and emigration, published in 1859, and Harriet E. Wilson's *Our Nig,* an autobiographical novel about a biracial child's indentured servitude in a cruel white household, published in 1859. Most of these novels received little attention, at least from white audiences. Unquestionably, the most significant piece of racial fiction published during this period was written by a white woman. Harriet Beecher Stowe's epochal antislavery novel, *Uncle Tom's Cabin* was published in 1852 and had an influence that extended far beyond the immediate issue of slavery. The name of the title character was to become a hated epithet among blacks, and the long shelf life of the work as popular theater ensured that a number of troubling stereotypes endured as near myths in the American imagination. Novelist James Baldwin, in declaring his literary independence nearly one hundred years later, was to damn, in particular, the burden of this novel on the work of black writers.

TOWARD A BLACK LITERARY AESTHETIC

The slave narratives were, far and away, the most important and most developed black literature in the United States, indeed, in the Western world at that time. They were to establish two major trends in African-American literature: first, a preoccupation with autobiographical and confessional writing that remains to this day; and second, a strong tendency to bind social protest or explicit political consciousness with the aesthetic act of making literature. While the first trend has produced an extraordinarily rich vein of American writing, to Booker T. Washington's *Up From Slavery* to *The Autobiography of Malcolm X,* from Maya Angelou's *I Know Why The Caged Bird Sings* to James Weldon Johnson's *Along This Way,* from Ann Moody's *Coming of Age in Mississippi* to Langston Hughes's *The Big Sea,* the second has been far more problematical.

Black literature has been charged over the years by white critics with being nothing more than social protest, or "mere sociology," or a literature without technique, style, or innovation. It was not until the 1952 publication of Ralph Ellison's *Invisible Man,* nearly one hundred years after the publication of the first African-American novel, that a black fictional work was considered without question to be of superior literary merit, equal to the best white literature. This slow growth of recognition and of true achievement was, in some respects, inevitable. It took nearly two hundred years for white American literature to evolve from sermons and tracts to the works of Whitman, Hawthorne, Melville, and Poe. Black writers who were serious about the craft of making good literature have always been sensitive to the charge from whites of writing second-rate, race-bound works. But they have been equally sensitive to the needs of their black audience and of their group in general, understanding that African Americans would not be interested in a literature that was to given over to "mere aesthetics" or to the idea of art for art's sake, which most would think a frivolous indulgence and not a serious engagement with life and art as they saw those matters. Most black writers saw literature as something that represented their community, that was a force in the ideological and political construction of their community whether or not the literature actually depicted black community as a successfully working enterprise. One aspect of this problem is well captured in James Weldon Johnson's "The Dilemma of the Negro Author," published in the *American Mercury* in 1928 where he raised the issue of different audiences and the inability of the black author to reconcile their expectations, their needs, their perspectives. The reason for the severity of this problem stems in part from the nature of the black community itself and how, historically, it has been forced to function totally for the white community's convenience. The conflict about the purpose of African-American literature—for the question of its content and its craftsmanship comes down to the issue of function—in relation to the formation of community remains of great, even overriding, profundity for black writers and their audience as well as the larger society.

AFRICAN-AMERICAN LITERATURE IN THE AGE OF FREEDOM

Since the Civil War, there have been three crucial periods for African-American literature where the conflict about its purpose became explicit: the New Negro or Harlem Renaissance era, the early Civil Rights era of the 1950s, and the Black Arts movement of the late 1960s. Briefly considered, these periods coincide with certain extraordinary developments within the United States itself: Prohibition, urbanization; false prosperity; a new wave of black political consciousness; a rising interest in and concern about communism during the 1920s and 1930s; the cold war; prosperity; a national policy of racial integration; a new assertiveness among blacks; the rise of youth culture in the 1950s; an intense black militancy; a nation deeply divided over the Vietnam War; a rash of political assassinations; a national policy to wipe out poverty; questions about the extent and future of prosperity; and a sharply influential counterculture on the left during the late 1960s. It is important to note two things about these three eras: each occurred during or immediately after a major American war; and in each instance, as has been the case for African Americans in their struggle in the United States since the end of Reconstruction, the major political concerns about citizenship and community are tied, often expressly so, with the meaning and function of African-American art, generally, and African-American literature, in particular.

The era of the Harlem Renaissance, starting with the black migration to the North in 1915 and ending with the rise of Richard Wright—a southern migrant—in the late 1930s, revived the issue of African-American musical theater and African-American vernacular expression, which originated in the 1890s with the famous comedy team of Williams and Walker and the coon song, on the one hand, and the dialect poetry of Paul Laurence Dunbar, on the other. Indeed, James Weldon Johnson, who was such an important presence in both areas in the 1890s, was to be a prime mover and shaker during the Renaissance. African-American musical theater became very big in the 1920s as did experimentation in vernacular poetry leading, in one direction, to the blues lyrics of the young Langston Hughes, and, in another direction, to the sermonic cadences of Johnson's *God's Trombones.*

In each case, old-fashioned, overly sentimentalized, and crudish dialect was eschewed for something more subtle, richer, closer to the actual power and expressive range of black speech. The Renaissance brought together a number of forces: a large nationalist mass movement spearheaded by Marcus Garvey that made Africa and Pan-Africanism thought about in ways that far exceeded the intensity expressed in the 1890s black nationalist movements; the two large black middle-class organizations, the National Association for the Advancement of Colored People and the Urban League; a revolutionary black music called jazz and, in phonograph records, a new technology with which to hear it; an intense historical consciousness that resulted in the formation of the Association for the Study of Negro Life and History and a number of anthologies on black culture including Alain Locke's *The New Negro*, the most storied of the age. It is no surprise, therefore, that this era saw the publication of Jean Toomer's experimental work *Cane* (1923), Claude McKay's *Home to Harlem* (1928), Countee Cullen's *Color* (1925), Langston Hughes's *The Weary Blues* (1926), Nella Larsen's *Passing* (1929), Zora Neale Hurston's *Their Eyes Were Watching God* (1937), to name only a small number of works by authors who were to become principal names in African-American fiction and poetry. This could only have happened because the black community itself reached a certain level of strength and self-confidence.

Nonetheless, the Renaissance was considered a failure by many black writers and critics, including a number who lived through it. First, it was felt that much of the literature seemed preoccupied with middle-class concerns or with presenting blacks as exotics. This criticism was not entirely deserved, but certainly one of the burning questions of the age was "How Is the Negro to Be Depicted in Literature?" (A version of that question is still a vital concern for African Americans today.) Many white literary types thought this concern to be somewhere between philistine and infantile, but they hardly understood the sensitivity of a group that had been so viciously and persistently maligned by their culture. Second, compared to the incredible experimentation taking place in the best white literature of the day, from Hemingway to Stein, from Joyce to T. S. Eliot, African-American literature seemed tame, indeed, almost old-fashioned in some of its Victorian flavor. Third, the black community was still weak: no major black publishing houses were produced in this era, nor were there any successful black drama companies, despite black popularity on the Broadway musical stage. Indeed, this last point may be the most telling; for unlike white ethnic enclaves like the Jewish or Irish Catholic communities in the United States, the black community was constantly seen by whites as threatening if it were not rigidly controlled and contained. Whites also used the black community as the venue for their own crimes and vices. In short, the larger white community worked very hard to make sure that the black community could never fully function as a community.

Although Wright continued to produce much important work in the 1950s, including political works, a collection of short stories, and three new novels, the 1950s saw the end of the dominance of this artist, whose works largely ended the Harlem Renaissance by reinventing the black novel as a politically self-aware, proletariat mechanism for social criticism and engagement.

In fact, it ended, at least temporally, a black interest in Marxist-oriented art and sheer naturalistic writing. In the early 1950s came such writers as William Demby (*Beetlecreek*), James Baldwin (*Go Tell It On the Mountain, Giovanni's Room*), Ralph Ellison (*Invisible Man*), and Gwendolyn Brooks (*Annie Allen, Maud Martha*) who were to garner great critical recognition and respect from the white literary establishment. None of these novels was a purely naturalistic work and Brooks's poetry was demanding in a way unlike any Harlem Renaissance poet (except possibly the highly experimental Jean Toomer). Just a few years after Jackie Robinson integrated professional baseball, in an era of a more sensitive treatment of blacks in films like "Home of the Brave," "No Way Out," "Cry, The Beloved Country," and "Blackboard Jungle," and right around the time of the Supreme Court decision to desegregate public schools, there was a considerable willingness on the part of the liberal white intelligentsia to accept blacks into the American mainstream, not realizing that blacks, as Ralph Ellison was to argue so eloquently in his essays, helped to invent the mainstream that had denied them for so long.

Although much of this work still exhibited the despair, hopelessness, and violence that one found in Wright, some, like Baldwin and Ellison quite critically, muted elements of social protest by going off in new directions, writing more textured, densely complex works about the inner psychological life of black people. The end of the decade saw the rise of novelists Paule Marshall and William Melvin Kelly, poet LeRoi Jones, and playwright Lorraine Hansberry. The criticism of the literature of this period was that it was too assimilationist and far too concerned with technique, although these were, in fact, its strengths in moving black literature into the mainstream of American writing. But the movement was not quite as assimilationist as some critics thought. The black writers of the 1950s came to prominence during the liberation movements taking place in Africa and the concerted attacks against European imperialism by the Third World generally. Writers like Baldwin and Hansberry wrote about Africa as black writers have done since the days of Phillis Wheatley. Nearly all continued to attack racism vehemently. Several black writers of note found America so difficult to live in that they left the country, opting for Europe instead. The writing of this period certainly reflected not simply what the black bourgeoisie wanted but where the black community as a whole wished to go, not into a white world but away from the restrictions of a black one.

BLACK LITERATURE AND THE BLACK COMMUNITY

By the late 1960s, LeRoi Jones, having become a much-read poet (*The Dead Lecturer, Preface to a Twenty-Volume Suicide Note*), playwright (*Dutchman* and *The Slave*), and essayist (*Home: Social Essays*), changed his name to Imamu Amiri Baraka and launched the Black Arts movement, first in Harlem, then in Newark, New Jersey, in a period lasting roughly from 1965 to

1975. Partly in response to the strong assimilationist tendencies of the Civil Rights movement, partly in response to a growing and more radical black youth movement, partly in response to black nationalism's finally having, in the figure of the recently assassinated Malcolm X, a martyr upon which to hang myths, the Black Arts Movement invented a black nationalist value system called Kawaida. Inspired, in part, by the African socialist philosophy of Julius K. Nyerere, Kawaida spawned the popular black holiday Kwanzaa and insisted that all black art had to be explicitly political, aimed at the destruction of whites or white values, and preoccupied solely with the liberation of black people. Black art had to be aimed at the masses, thus the rise of black theater and an accessible, nearly didactic black poetry. It had to eschew white technique or an overly white, bourgeois concern with the problems of technique or formalistic meaning and process. Much of this work descended into a kind of black agitprop. Yet there was impressive work accomplished at this time including the establishment of several black publishing companies—Broadside in Detroit and Third World Press in Chicago; *Black Fire,* the epochal anthology edited by Baraka and Larry Neal; work by writers like Don L. Lee (Haki Madhubuti), Sonia Sanchez, Nikki Giovanni, Etheridge Knight, and Eldridge Cleaver. It was the time of the black exploitation movies (which spawned the incredible Melvin Van Peebles's film, "Sweet, Sweetback's Badass Song"), the emergence of black radio as a true force in American culture, and the rise of boxer Muhammad Ali (who had changed his name from Cassius Clay) as a black hero of resistance. Self-absorbed with its dramatic self-presentation, the Black Arts movement produced little fiction. The most important novelist of the period, John A. Williams, who wrote the defining work of the age, *The Man Who Cried I Am,* was not associated with the Black Arts movement, nor were Toni Morrison and Alice Walker, who both began their work at this time.

What might be said about all of these creative periods is that the black community evolved or changed in some vital ways or felt itself in a state of crisis. The literature tended not simply to reflect or merely respond to, but actually to be part of the change or crisis itself. How can writing, or literature, continue to serve the black community or help make it continue to function as community in its present condition? In each instance, innovations were produced. But there was also less dependence on the past, less self-conscious creation of tradition than there could have been. Perhaps in the 1920s or even in the 1950s, this was not possible. But in the 1960s, surely, one of the failures of the Black Arts movement to become what the Harlem Renaissance sought to be—a new black cultural-nationalist movement, a political movement for independence through the reinvention of culture—was the inability to formulate a usable black literary past of sufficient strength and diversity to support an atmosphere that would continue to generate innovation and enrichment. This is slowly but surely happening with African-American literature today, with a greater number of recognized writers than at any time in history.

THE FUTURE OF BLACK LITERATURE

It has been said that since the end of the Black Arts Movement, women have come to dominate African-American literature. Certainly, with the rise of feminism in the 1970s and a growing self-consciousness about gender on the part of black women, women's issues and concerns in African-American literature have received considerable prominence. Toni Morrison (the first black American to receive the Nobel Prize for literature), Alice Walker, Gloria Naylor, and even more recently, Terry McMillan and Bebe Campbell, have all become best-selling authors. Lesser known but equally well-regarded writers such as June Jordan, Audre Lorde, Octavia Butler, Gayle Jones, and Ntozake Shange have had a considerable impact on the present literary scene. Moreover, as more women—black and white—have become university professors and literary critics, there has been a growing intellectual and scholarly interest in the work of black women. Since the end of the Black Arts Movement, however, there have emerged several black male writers as well: Ernest Gaines, Ishmael Reed, James McPherson, David Bradley, Reginald McKnight, Charles Johnson, and Samuel Delany have all received a great deal of attention.

Moreover, the dominant black figures in public intellectual discourse these days, such as Henry Louis Gates Jr., Stanley Crouch, Houston Baker, Stephen Carter, Shelby Steele, Glenn Loury, and Cornell West, are men. The belief that black women and feminist issues dominate African-American literature today has led to a distinct undercurrent of tension between black men and black women, as the former accuse the latter of unfairly attacking and criticizing them, playing into the hands of the white power structure. This debate has been fueled as well by a concern over the survival of black men in American society, which some think has reached a crisis point.

Once again, these developments point to the burden that black literature, fraught with political and social significance, must bear in constructing the idea of black community and the difficulty it faces in trying to do so. These pressures also point to the problem of audience, as more black writers are currently being recognized and rewarded by the white literary establishment, although there is a more powerful black reading audience than ever. There is, finally, the question of precisely what black literature should be about, how much social protest or sociological weight it should carry, and how black people should be depicted in it. Despite these ongoing concerns, contemporary African-American writing is a richly diverse field and a compelling presence on the American literary scene.

FOR FURTHER READING

Angelou, Maya. *I Know Why the Caged Bird Sings.* New York: Bantam Books, 1983.

Asante, Molefi. *The Afrocentric Idea.* Rev. ed. Philadelphia: Temple University Press, 1998.

Baker, Houston A., Jr. *Blues, Ideology and Afro-American Literature: A Vernacular Theory.* Chicago: University of Chicago Press, 1987.

_____. *Long Black Song: Essays in Black Literature and Criticism.* Charlottesville: University of Virginia Press, 1990.

_____. *Singers of Daybreak: Studies in Black American Literature.* Washington, D.C.: Howard University Press, 1983.

Baraka, Imamu Amiri. *Home: Social Essays.* Hopewell, N.J.: The Ecco Press, 1998.

Braxton, Joanne M., and Andree Nicola McLaughlin, eds. *Wild Women in the Whirlwind: AFRA-American Culture and the Contemporary Literary Renaissance.* New Brunswick, N.J.: Rutgers University Press, 1990.

Carby, Hazel. *Reconstructing Womanhood: The Emergence of the Afro-American Woman Novelist.* New York: Oxford University Press, 1990.

Cooke, Michael G. *Afro-American Literature in the Twentieth Century: The Achievement of Intimacy.* New Haven, Conn.: Yale University Press, 1990.

Fischer, Dexter, and Robert Stepto, eds. *Afro-American Literature: A Vernacular Theory.* New York: Modern Language Association, 1979.

Gates, Henry Louis Jr., ed. *The Classic Slave Narratives.* New York: NAL/Dutton, 1987.

_____. *The Signifying Monkey: A Theory of African-American Literary Criticism.* New York: Oxford University Press, 1990.

Gates, Henry Louis Jr., and Sunday Ogbonna Anozie, eds. *Black Literature & Literary Theory.* New York: Routledge, 1990.

Huggins, Nathan I. *The Harlem Renaissance.* New York: Oxford University Press, 1973.

Hughes, Langston. *The Langston Hughes Reader.* New York: George Braziller, 1981.

Hurston, Zora Neale. *Their Eyes Were Watching God.* Reissue Ed. New York: Harper Collins, 1999.

Morrison, Toni. *Playing in the Dark: Whiteness and the Literary Imagination.* New York: Vintage, 1993.

Redding, J. Saunders. *A Scholar's Conscience: Selected Writings of J. Saunders Redding, 1942–1977.* Ed. Faith Berry. Lexington: University of Kentucky Press, 1992.

Smith, Valerie. *Self-Discovery and Authority in Afro-American Narrative.* Cambridge: Harvard University Press, 1991.

Stepto, Robert B. *From Behind the Veil: A Study of Afro-American Narrative.* 2nd ed. Urbana: University of Illinois Press, 1991.

Wright, Richard. *Early Works.* Ed. Arnold Ramersad. New York: Library of America, 1991.

READING 11

Baldwin's Reception and the Challenge of His Legacy

Lynn Orilla Scott

I.

When James Baldwin died in 1987, five thousand people attended his funeral at the Cathedral of St. John the Divine in Harlem. The people came to celebrate his life and to mourn his passing because he had changed their lives; he was "quite possibly for his times their most essential interpreter."[1] Literary agent Marie Brown described Baldwin's passing as "the end of an era." He was "the last survivor ... of those few most powerful moral articulators who could effectively lecture the society, among the very few whom we could quote almost daily as scripture of social consciousness."[2] A substantial number of leading American writers, intellectuals, and musicians came to pay tribute to Baldwin. Maya Angelou, Toni Morrison, and Amiri Baraka each gave eulogies, and many more wrote tributes to Baldwin's life and work that were published in newspapers around the world, some later in Quincy Troupe's *James Baldwin: The Legacy* and other venues. In her funeral address Toni Morrison said that Baldwin, like the Magi, had given her three gifts: a language to dwell in, the courage to transform the distances between people into intimacy, and the tenderness of vulnerability:

> No one possessed or inhabited language for me the way you did. You made American English honest—genuinely international. You exposed its secrets and reshaped it until it was truly modern dialogic, representative, humane. You stripped it of ease and false comfort and fake innocence and evasion and hypocrisy. And in place of deviousness was clarity. In place of soft plump lies was a lean, targeted power. In place of intellectual disingenuousness and what you called "exasperating egocentricity," you gave us undecorated truth. You replaced lumbering platitudes with an upright elegance. You went into that forbidden territory and decolonized it, "robbed it of the jewel of its naivete," and un-gated it for black people so that in your wake we could enter it, occupy it, restructure it in order to accommodate our complicated passion—not our vanities but our intricate, difficult, demanding beauty, our tragic, insistent knowledge, our sleek classical imagination—all the while

Lynn Orilla Scott, "Baldwin's Reception and the Challenge of His Legacy," *Witness to the Journey: James Baldwin's Later Fiction*, pp. 2-18, 177-181. Copyright © 2002 by Michigan State University Press. Reprinted with permission.

> refusing "to be defined by a language that has never been able to recognize [us]." In your hands language was handsome again. In your hands we saw how it was meant to be: neither bloodless nor bloody, and yet alive.[3]

Baldwin's funeral was a dramatic testament of his influence as a writer, thinker, friend, and social activist for the generation that followed him.

However, this funeral service, especially in its omissions, suggests the difficulties of interpreting Baldwin's legacy. Writing for the *Gay Community News,* Barbara Smith said: "Although Baldwin's funeral completely reinforced our Blackness, it tragically rendered his and our homosexuality completely invisible. In those two hours of remembrance and praise, not a syllable was breathed that this wonderful brother, this writer, this warrior, was also gay, that his being gay was indeed integral to his magnificence."[4] Baldwin wrote against a dominant strain of black nationalist thought which placed homosexuality in opposition to black resistance, an ideology that regarded homosexuality as a product of white oppression and evidence of internalized self-hatred. Given the homophobic climate, it is not surprising that interpretations of Baldwin's work that stress his contribution to representing black experience have, until quite recently, ignored or denied the importance of his homosexual themes and the homosexuality of his subjects, as if it were not possible to read his texts as expressions of both black and homosexual experience.[5]

Baldwin also wrote against an ideology that reified racial categories, insisting that "white" and "black" were inventions that oppressed blacks but also imprisoned whites in a false innocence that denied them self-knowledge. The only speaker at Baldwin's funeral who was not an African American was the French ambassador. Clyde Taylor found the irony inescapable: "Jimmy, like so many black artists, had been more fully honored and respected abroad than by his own society. France had given him its highest tribute, the Legion of Honor. By contrast, what had American society done?"[6] Perhaps the absence of an official honor from a representative of the American government was, finally, a testament to Baldwin's willingness to sharply criticize American institutions, and to his determination to be among the true poets who are "disturbers of the peace." Yet the absence of any American speaker of European descent is striking, given Baldwin's many white American friends and associates and the considerable impact Baldwin's writing had on the ways white Americans as well as black Americans think about race and sexuality.

Baldwin wrote that as a young man he left America in order to "prevent [himself] from becoming merely a Negro; or, even merely a Negro writer. [He] wanted to find out in what way the specialness of [his] experience could be made to connect [him] with other people instead of dividing [him] from them."[7] Later Baldwin would come to accept, even embrace, the designation of black writer and the enormous responsibility that went with it as part of the historical contingency within which he lived and worked. However, Baldwin never stopped exploring the "specialness" of his experience as it connected him to others. As an American, an African American, and a homosexual, Baldwin sought to provide a witness to overlapping but frequently incompatible experiences and communities. The challenge for writers who interpret his legacy is to find a language that doesn't reduce the complexity of Baldwin's art and vision. As Toni Morrison said in her funeral address: "The difficulty is your life refuses summation—it always did."[8]

At first glance it would seem that James Baldwin's life and work have received considerable attention. To date there have been eight biographies of Baldwin (four of which are for young readers);[9] eight book-length studies of Baldwin's work;[10] eight collections of critical essays; and three collections of tributes written shortly after Baldwin's death.[11] There has been significant bibliographic work done on Baldwin as well.[12] However, it becomes very clear after reviewing the critical output that comparatively little has been written on Baldwin's last three novels. The large majority of criticism has taken one or more of the first three novels as its focus or to a lesser extent the early essays through *The Fire Next Time*. Of the full-length studies only Carolyn Wedin Sylvander's discusses all of Baldwin's novels, and her book is primarily a reader's guide. Horace Porter's *Stealing the Fire* (1989) explores the influence of Henry James, Harriet Beecher Stowe, and Richard Wright on Baldwin's early essays and fiction, dismissing Baldwin's work after *The Fire Next Time* as unsuccessful. Porter's book is the most recent of the full-length critical studies (not including Bobia's book on Baldwin's reception in France), yet it is over ten years old. Trudier Harris's *Black Women in the Fiction of James Baldwin* (1985) provides close readings of *If Beale Street Could Talk* and *Just Above My Head* but omits any discussion of *Tell Me How Long the Train's Been Gone* since it has no major black women characters. Macebuh's, Möller's, and Pratt's studies were written prior to the publication of Baldwin's last novel or novels.

The critical collections have emphasized Baldwin's earlier work as well. Even D. Quentin Miller's recent *Reviewing James Baldwin: Things Not Seen* (1999), which purports to give attention to Baldwin's neglected later work, has no discussion of *Tell Me How Long the Train's Been Gone* or *If Beale Street Could Talk* and only one essay on *Just Above My Head*. Miller's collection does, however, include important work on some of Baldwin's lesser-known writing, some of which was written during the seventies and eighties.[13] A number of the contributors to Dwight McBride's *James Baldwin Now* see Baldwin's work as a progenitor to theoretical developments in gender and gay studies as well as to the study of the cultural construction of whiteness. These essays, on the whole, do a much more sophisticated job of analyzing Baldwin's work as it complicates and interimplicates categories of race, gender, and sexuality than early essays were able to do.[14] They replace the old image of the fifties Baldwin as a liberal humanist with a much more complex figure, one who intervened in, rather than merely reflected, the liberal discourse of the period. However, the focus of this collection is Baldwin's early work, particularly *Giovanni's Room* and *Another Country,* in the context of post–World War II American culture. As a result there is little discussion of Baldwin's response to the changing culture and conditions of the sixties and seventies, and there is little discussion of Baldwin's representations of black families and of black communities, since there is nothing on *Go Tell It on the Mountain, Tell Me How Long the Train's Been Gone, If Beale Street Could Talk*, or *Just Above My Head*.[15]

In her introduction to *Black Women in the Fiction of James Baldwin* (1985), Trudier Harris wrote that she was "surprised to discover that a writer of Baldwin's reputation evoked such vague memories from individuals in the scholarly community" and found it "discouraging ... that one of America's best-known writers, and certainly one of its best-known black writers, has not attained a more substantial place in the scholarship on Afro-American writers."[16] Although there was renewed interest in Baldwin's life and work in the late eighties following his death (as evidenced by the publication of James Campbell's and David Leeming's biographies, Quincy Troupe's *James Baldwin: The Legacy*, the published proceedings of a conference at the University of Massachusetts at Amherst, and the film *The Price of the Ticket*), the quantity of scholarship on Baldwin's writing has significantly lagged behind that of other well-known African American writers, such as Richard Wright, Ralph Ellison, or Toni Morrison. Moreover, Baldwin studies have not benefited from the presence of African American theory and scholarship in the academy. Craig Werner pointed out the extent to which Baldwin has been ignored:

> To be sure, Baldwin's name is occasionally invoked, generally as part of a trinity including Richard Wright and Ralph Ellison. But his work, much less his vision, is rarely discussed, even within the field of Afro-American Studies. Baldwin is conspicuous by his absence from recent (and valuable) books on cultural theory (Henry Louis Gates Jr.'s *The Signifying Monkey*, Robert Stepto's *From Behind the Veil*, Houston Baker's *Blues, Ideology, and Afro-American Literature: A Vernacular Theory*), intellectual history (Sterling Stuckey's *Slave Culture: Nationalist Theory and the Foundations of Black America*, Harold Cruse's *Plural But Equal: Black and Minorities in America's Plural Society*); literary criticism (Keith Byerman's *Fingering the Jagged Grain: Tradition and Form in Recent Black Fiction*, John Callahan's *In the African-American Grain: The Pursuit of Voice in Twentieth-Century Black Fiction*); and period history (David Garrow's *Bearing the Cross*, Doug McAdam's *Freedom Summer*). There are to be sure occasional exceptions, mostly [sic] notably Michael Cooke's *Afro-American Literature in the Twentieth Century* and Melvin Dixon's *Ride Out the Wilderness: Geography and Identity in Afro-American Literature*. Still, given Baldwin's central importance to the development of issues raised in all of the above work, the general silence suggests that the larger changes of intellectual fashion have influenced the internal dynamics of discourse on Afro-American culture.[17]

Werner attributes Baldwin's marginalization in the academy to the dominance of a post-structuralist critique which "resurrected an ironic sensibility that renders Baldwin's moral seriousness and his political activism nearly incomprehensible to literary intellectuals."[18]

While Baldwin's "concern with salvation" may have made him unfashionable, his incisive critique of racial and sexual categories in the formation of American identity certainly precede the poststructuralist critique of "identity." Eric Savoy has pointed out the limitation of a great deal of criticism that argues that Baldwin's main theme is "a search for identity." The direction of Baldwin's work is not toward the attainment of identity, but rather toward knowledge of self "as implicated, situated subject, but simultaneously as 'other' and therefore as resisting agent."[19] Baldwin's neglect by the academy may be explained by the dominance of an intellectual sensibility that rendered political activism and moral seriousness incomprehensible, as Werner claims. However, Baldwin's marginalization is also partly due to the pressures of canonizing black literature by defining a black difference. Baldwin's critique of racial representation—what Savoy has called his "double resistance" to both white, middle-class, heterosexual America and to the ways in which other black writers (especially Richard Wright) and gay writers (Andre Gide) brought their otherness to text—puts Baldwin at odds with at least some theories of black difference.

In Houston A. Baker Jr.'s influential *Blues, Ideology, and Afro-American Literature: A Vernacular Theory,* as well as in his earlier book *The Journey Back: Issues in Black Literature and Criticism,* Baldwin is not exactly ignored. He becomes the "other" in Baker's attempt to canonize Richard Wright as the writer whose work best reveals a distinctive and resistant African American discourse. Baker defends Wright from the negative critique of *Native Son* and of "protest fiction" in Baldwin's "Everybody's Protest Novel" and "Many Thousands Gone." According to Baker, Baldwin's criticism of Wright is based on a bourgeois aesthetic in which the artist is perceived to be above or separate from society.[20] While Baker's deconstruction of the binary "art" versus "protest" is useful in revealing the political motivation of 1950s "aesthetic" criticism, he reinstates the binary by portraying Wright as the black writer with a political consciousness and Baldwin as the writer who advocates "a theology of art," whose writing is "poetic, analytical, asocial."[21] However, Baldwin's criticism of *Native Son* was as much politically motivated as it was aesthetically motivated. His argument with Wright turned less on artistic flaws in the depiction of Bigger Thomas than on a racist representation of the black male in which Baldwin believed the novel to be implicated.[22]

One of the central problems of Baldwin's reception has been the way in which arguments over "art" and "politics" have misrepresented and marginalized his work. Baker's characterization of the difference between Wright and Baldwin mirrors and reverses the response of those New Critics who embraced Baldwin's criticism of Wright and read Baldwin's first novel as a vindication of their literary values, which emphasized formal structures over social criticism. Yet as Horace Porter, Craig Werner, and others have argued, Baldwin's early work, including *Go Tell It on the Mountain,* was not apolitical. As Werner points out, "Just as the original readers of *Native Son* simplified the work to accommodate their ideology, Baldwin's aesthetic defenders ignored major political elements of his novel."[23] Horace Porter's book (appropriately subtitled *The Art and Politics of James Baldwin*) makes this argument in detail by elaborating the intertexuality in Baldwin's early work with both Wright and Stowe.

While Baldwin has been criticized by some Marxist and some African American literary theorists for his alleged bourgeois aesthetics, with the publication of *Blues for Mister Charlie, Tell Me How Long the Train's Been Gone, No Name in the Street,* and *If Beale Street Could Talk* Baldwin came under attack in the liberal press by Mario Puzo, Pearl K. Bell, John Aldridge, and others for writing "propaganda." Using Baldwin's early statements on protest fiction against him, they argued that Baldwin was doing the very thing for which he had criticized Richard Wright: he was writing protest fiction with melodramatic plots and stereotypical characters. Moreover, taking offense at the occasional use of "street" language and the sharper, more militant tone, many of these critics argued that Baldwin's "bitterness" revealed that he was out of touch with American "progress" in race relations. Those who had embraced Baldwin's early work for aesthetic reasons felt betrayed.

To a large extent the scholarly community has agreed with the initial assessment of Baldwin's later novels. Horace Porter found Baldwin's later essays and fiction deeply disappointing:

> he moves from the promethean figure, the man who stole the fire of "Notes of a Native Son," the powerful writer of *The Fire Next Time*, to the embittered and self-indulgent nay-sayer of *No Name in the Street* and *Evidence of Things Not Seen*. None of Baldwin's later novels or essays rivals the narrative ingenuity and rhetorical power of *Go Tell It on the Mountain* and *Notes of a Native Son*, his first novel and his first collection of essays.[24]

Henry Louis Gates Jr. and Hilton Als concur with this evaluation of Baldwin's decline as an artist and place the blame on black militants (most notably Eldridge Cleaver), from whose criticism Baldwin allegedly never recovered. Gates views *No Name in the Street,* in particular, as a "capitulation" by a man who was desperate "to be loved by his own" and who "cared too much about what others wanted from him."[25] Reviewing the 1998 Library of America's two-volume selection of Baldwin's essays, early novels, and stories, Hilton Als reflects on "both [his] early infatuation and [his] later disaffection" with Baldwin's work. Because Baldwin "compromised" his unique perspective and "sacrificed his gifts to gain acceptance from the Black Power movement," Als sees Baldwin's career as "a cautionary tale ... a warning as well as an inspiration."[26]

Clearly Baldwin has been in the crossfire of arguments that assume certain artistic and social values and set them in contradistinction. In fact, it remains very difficult to sort out aesthetic from political judgments when discussing Baldwin's reception because they are so deeply interconnected. One of the aims of this book is to interrogate the assumption that Baldwin's increased political activism and militancy in the sixties led to his decline as an artist. The reading of Baldwin's later work as lacking aesthetic value is as problematic as the reading of his earlier work as lacking political value. As Craig Werner has pointed out, James Baldwin "asserted the ultimately moral connection of political and cultural experience."[27] There is no doubt that Baldwin's later work was influenced by the turbulent political and racial environment of the sixties and early seventies, as well as by the decline in economic and social conditions for urban black youth and families in the seventies. I wish to argue that his response to the events of the sixties and seventies was more complex than has been acknowledged and that his last three novels should be read not as evidence of either a political capitulation or an artistic decline, but as evidence of the ways Baldwin creatively responded to a changing racial environment and discourse in an attempt to communicate the story he wanted to tell.

As the only major African American writer whose career spanned the pre- and post-civil rights and black power period, Baldwin's historical position was unique. Richard Wright died in 1960; Langston Hughes died in 1967; Ralph Ellison survived Baldwin, but stopped writing (or at least publishing) fiction. The sensibilities of prominent contemporary African American writers, including Toni Morrison, Alice Walker, and Amiri Baraka, were formed in the crucible of the civil rights era. Baldwin's work from the middle sixties on reflected the dramatic shift in American racial and political discourse, symbolized by the positive signification of "black" and the deployment of a resistant identity politics. His work also reflected a racial and political reality that Baldwin read as increasingly repressive, even genocidal, for the majority of black Americans, a reading that put him at sharp odds with a liberal rhetoric of black progress.

Tell Me How Long the Train's Been Gone, If Beale Street Could Talk, and *Just Above My Head* are not flawless novels. There are some overwritten, even carelessly written passages and some inconsistencies in character and plot that are difficult to account for and that could have been corrected by more careful editing. Yet to focus solely on artistic faults (which the majority of reviewers did) is to ignore the power and vision present in these works. Moreover, what some reviewers described as artistic flaws were certainly aspects of Baldwin's intentional experimentation with voice and form. Baldwin took risks with his later work. He reframed his earlier stories to reflect his experience and, especially, his interest in reproducing in the novel a style of resistance that he found in African American music. Baldwin gave up the tighter, more formal structures of his earliest work. For example, the compartmentalized and isolated voices of the characters in Go *Tell It on the Mountain* give way to experiments in first-person narration. These novels demonstrate a relationship between author and character (i.e., Baldwin's relationship to Leo Proudhammer, Tish Rivers, and Hall Montana) that parallels a jazz musician's relationship to his instrument as an extension or elaboration of the performer's self.[28] Baldwin's narrators are instruments of self-expression who perform Baldwin's voice in different bodies—both male and female—and in different places—Harlem, the Village, Paris. They echo and revise the author's life. They suggest that "identity" is, indeed, a complex affair that involves a recognition of "others" and the presence of the "other" in the "self."

II.

In 1988, shortly after Baldwin's death, a conference at the University of Massachusetts at Amherst brought several eminent writers and scholars together to pay tribute to James Baldwin. The published proceedings of this conference gave voice to a deep concern with the type of criticism Baldwin had been receiving. Describing literary criticism as an open letter to an author, John Edgar Wideman said, "We're getting a species of letter which endangers my relationship to James Baldwin and James Baldwin's relationship to the tradition and to you and to your children." In these "poison pen letters," Baldwin is cast as "a kind of villain" who "does not appreciate progress. He is enraged and bitter. He lost his footing as an artist and simply became a propagandist. And that version of Baldwin's career is very dangerously being promulgated and it's being pushed in a kind of surreptitious way by these letters."[29] Chinua Achebe sought to clarify Baldwin's accomplishment. Responding to the frequent charge that Baldwin failed to recognize America's progress, Achebe pointed out that for Baldwin progress was not a matter of more black mayors and generals. Baldwin's project was to "redefine the struggle" by seeing it "from a whole range of perspectives at once—the historical, the psychological, the philosophical, which are not present in a handful of statistics of recent advances." Baldwin's strength was in his ability "to lift from the backs of Black people the burden of their race" and "to unmask the face of the oppressor, to see his face and to call him by name." Achebe concluded that "Baldwin, belongs to mankind's ancient tradition of storytelling, to the tradition of prophets who had the dual role to fore-tell and to forth-tell."[30]

Although the proceedings of the Amherst conference offer a corrective to the white liberal dismissal of Baldwin's work after the middle sixties, they completely ignore Baldwin's homosexual themes and, more important, the extent to which black and white homophobia affected Baldwin's reception. There was more than one version of the "poison-pen letter." Around the same time Baldwin was being condemned by white liberals for his black militancy, he was being condemned by black militants for his homosexuality. The most notorious example was Eldridge Cleaver's attack on Baldwin in *Soul on Ice:* "There is in James Baldwin's work the most grueling, agonizing, total hatred of the blacks, particularly of himself, and the most shameful, fanatical, fawning, sycophantic love of the whites that one can find in the writings of any black American writer of note in our time."[31]

Cleaver argues that there is a "decisive quirk" in Baldwin's writing that caused him to "slander Rufus Scott in *Another Country,* venerate Andre Gide, repudiate [Norman Mailer's] *The White Negro,* and drive the blade of Brutus into the corpse of Richard Wright."[32] Charging Baldwin with waging "a despicable underground guerrilla war ... against black masculinity" and calling "homosexuality a sickness, just as are baby-rape or wanting to become the head of General Motors,"[33] Cleaver expresses in virulent form a homophobia representative of some segments of the black community.

In Cleaver's analysis, which parallels that of conservative black critics such as Stanley Crouch, homosexuality is considered to be a remnant of slavery, a habit learned from whites and thus a symptom of internalized self-hatred. In this reading Baldwin's homosexuality necessarily negates any claim that Baldwin can speak to an authentic "black" experience. Of course homophobic responses to Baldwin's work are not limited to black critics. In writing about *Another Country,* Robert Bone said:

> Few will concede to a sense of reality, at least in the sexual realm, to one who regards heterosexual love as "a kind of superior calisthenics." To most, homosexuality will seem rather an evasion than an affirmation of human truth. Ostensibly the novel summons us to reality. Actually it substitutes for the illusions of white supremacy those of homosexual love.[34]

Although not exactly the same argument as Cleaver's, Bone's argument also links homosexuality with white supremacy as a travesty of truth. Numerous critics took the position that Baldwin's representations of bisexuality and homosexuality undermined his credibility as a novelist and as a spokesperson for blacks. In addition Baldwin's sexuality put him in a difficult relationship to other civil rights leaders; it was probably the main reason he was not invited to speak at the 1963 March on Washington.[35]

Emmanuel S. Nelson has effectively documented the homophobia in Baldwin's reception, in its silences as well as in its more obvious forms, and has suggested that the reason Baldwin has been more highly regarded as an essayist than as a novelist is related to the relative absence of homosexual themes in his essays compared with his novels.[36] Homophobia may also be at the center of the decline in Baldwin's reputation as a novelist since his later novels, with the exception of *If Beale Street Could Talk,* are increasingly positive and explicit in their representation of black homosexual relationships. Given this fact, the belief that Baldwin adapted his writing or "compromised" his vision to please critics such as Cleaver seems unfounded. In the face of black homophobia Baldwin responded by continuing to represent and even celebrate homosexuality in *Tell Me How Long the Trains' Been Gone* and *Just Above My Head.* Nelson calls for an analysis of Baldwin's work that explores both his "racial awareness and his homosexual consciousness on his literary imagination" without privileging one over the other.[37] Bryan R. Washington expresses caution over "politically fashionable" but hollow efforts to "recanonize" Baldwin by avoiding his "homopoetics (politics)." He argues that such avoidance "proceeds from a desire to keep the recanonizing train on track—a train driven by theories of race and writing designed to minimize difference, to promote the academic institutionalization of blackness by homogenizing it."[38]

Although Baldwin has been underrepresented in the field of African American studies compared to other black writers of his stature, he has received substantial treatment in many studies on gay male writing, including Georges-Michel Sarotte's *Like a Brother, Like a Lover* (1976, translated into English, 1978), Stephen Adams's *The Homosexual as Hero in Contemporary Fiction* (1980), Claude J. Summers's *Gay Fictions: Wilde to Stonewall* (1990), David Bergman's *Gaiety Transfigured: Gay Self-Representation in America* (1991), Mark Lilly's *Gay Men's Literature in the Twentieth Century* (1993), and Wilfrid R. Koponen's *Embracing a Gay*

Identity: Gay Novels as Guides (1993). Yet all of these studies ignore Baldwin's later fiction (and only Sarotte's book was published before Baldwin's last novel). None discuss *Just Above My Head,* and *Tell Me How Long the Train's Been Gone* receives only passing mention, if any at all. Summers and Koponen work strictly with *Giovanni's Room,* while Adams and Lilly work with both *Giovanni's Room* and *Another Country.*

In his substantial chapter on Baldwin, Stephen Adams argues that "the knowledge Baldwin claims of American masculinity—as one who has been menaced by it—has an authority which in turn menaces preferred images of manhood, both black and white. He puzzles over his own definitions in ways which explode the notions of narrowness in the experience of a racial or sexual minority."[39] Adams takes several of Baldwin's critics to task, including Irving Howe, who charges Baldwin with "whipped cream sentimentalism" in the portrayal of homosexual love in *Giovanni's Room,* and Sarotte, who reads *Giovanni's Room* as memoir and identifies David's position as a homophobic homophile with Baldwin's. While Adams develops careful and sympathetic readings of *Giovanni's Room* and *Another Country,* he dismisses *Tell Me How Long the Train's Been Gone* in the last paragraph, calling it Baldwin's endorsement of black militancy and describing the Leo-Christopher relationship as a product of Baldwin's "wishful thinking" that "rings false."[40] David Bergman's treatment of Baldwin occurs within a broad discussion of black discourse on racism and sexuality, evangelical Protestantism, Africa as racial homeland, and the coded discourse of earlier black homosexual writers, especially Alain Locke. What could be a promising approach to the intersection of race and homosexuality in Baldwin's writing is marred by Bergman's uninformed statements about Baldwin's work. For example, Bergman is seemingly unaware of Baldwin's theoretical and personal essays on homosexuality—"The Preservation of Innocence" and "There Be Dragons"—when he claims that Baldwin's only nonfiction on homosexuality is "The Male Prison."[41] In addition, Bergman's assertion that "after Cleaver's attack, Baldwin emphasized racial much more than sexual issues" is simply not supported by Baldwin's later work.[42]

That most gay studies ignore Baldwin's later novels adds weight to Nelson's observation that analyses which privilege Baldwin's homosexuality tend to ignore his blackness. Unlike *Giovanni's Room* and *Another Country,* the homosexuality of *Tell Me How Long the Train's Been Gone* and of *Just Above My Head* occurs within a specifically black context, making it impossible to explore the representation of homosexuality in these novels without also addressing the representation of race. Melvin Dixon's chapter on Baldwin in *Ride out the Wilderness* and Lee Edelman's essay, "The Part for the (W)hole: Baldwin, Homophobia, and the Fantasmatics of 'Race,'" in *Homographesis* are important exceptions to the tendency to privilege either "blackness" or "homosexuality" when reading Baldwin's texts, and both produce very interesting, although quite different, readings of *Just Above My Head*.[43]

In the history of twentieth-century American letters it would be hard to find another figure more simultaneously praised and damned, often by the same critic in the same essay, than James Baldwin. A remarkable aspect of Cleaver's response to Baldwin is its initial adulation of Baldwin's work and the way this adulation is expressed in clearly sexual terms.

From the beginning tone of Cleaver's essay, one would not expect the coming attack. Cleaver describes the "continuous delight" he felt reading "a couple of James Baldwin's books." He describes Baldwin's talent as "penetrating" and says he "lusted for anything Baldwin had written. It would have been a gas for [him] to sit on a pillow beneath the womb of Baldwin's typewriter and catch each newborn page as it entered this world of ours."[44] However, Cleaver begins to feel "an aversion in [his] heart to part of the song [Baldwin] sang" and after reading *Another Country* he "knew why [his] love for Baldwin's vision had become ambivalent."[45] This movement from praise and identification with Baldwin's work to ambivalence, disappointment, and rejection is the single most common characteristic of Baldwin criticism, regardless of the particular ideological, racial, or sexual orientation of the critic. (Noting the irony, Craig Werner has pointed out that "it is perhaps not surprising that Baldwin's blackness has never been clearer than in his rejection."[46])

Baldwin's work has presented problems to readers from almost every perspective—liberal, black nationalist, feminist, and homosexual—and to some extent each of these constituencies in their inability to accommodate Baldwin's complexity has helped to marginalize him. In addition to the previously discussed challenges he presents to both liberal and nationalist discourses, Baldwin's work gets an ambivalent response from feminist and gay criticism as well. Although Baldwin's female characters are numerous, varied, and complex, especially when compared to other black male writers of his generation, Trudier Harris, Hortense Spillers, and others have critiqued Baldwin's discourse for essentializing gender, and his female characters for their dependence on men and male values. While acknowledging Baldwin's tremendous contribution to making the representation of a gay black male sexuality possible, some pro-gay critics are uncomfortable with Baldwin's reluctance to discuss gay issues in his nonfiction or to assert a gay identity. (Baldwin insisted that "homosexual" was not a noun.) The predominance of bisexual characters in Baldwin's fiction and his use of a heterosexual narrator to describe homosexual experience in *Just Above My Head* is taken by some as evidence of the extent to which Baldwin is, himself, implicated by the homophobia he so trenchantly critiques.

What these narratives of disappointment suggest is that James Baldwin did not tell the story that various critical constituencies wanted him to tell. For the white liberal he did not confirm that the "success" of a talented black individual represented the "progress" of the race; for black and white integrationists he seemed to lose faith in the dream of interracial understanding; for the black nationalist his stories did not evoke masculine-individualist heroics (and thus were judged as stories of complicity rather than resistance); for the feminist his women characters were too traditional in their relationships to men, and his concern with reinventing "masculinity" appeared to construct the feminine as other; for the gay activist he did not assert a separate homosexual identity. The critical narratives of Baldwin's "unfulfilled potential" must be understood in terms of the critics' own desire for a particular kind of spokesperson, but they also must be understood in relationship to the "promise" that Baldwin presents to his readership and to his politics of "salvation."

(As Baldwin said in a 1987 interview, "I am working toward the New Jerusalem. That's true. I'm not joking. I won't live to see it but I do believe in it. I think we're going to be better than we are."[47]) While Baldwin's concern for salvation may make him incomprehensible to a certain poststructuralist sensibility, as Werner claims, it also raises expectations in readers who would probably not agree on just what the New Jerusalem should look like. Baldwin did not leave a map of his heavenly city, only a few trail markers to indicate the way.

Baldwin's work is wedded to the tradition of realistic fiction as well as to the tradition of the jeremiad, which seeks to call people to their better selves while warning them of the failings and the dangers of their current course. His work is driven by two traditions, which are not always compatible: the tradition of mimetic truth telling and the tradition of religious truth telling. The first called Baldwin to testify to the sorrows, joys, contingencies, and interruptions of everyday experience, while the second called him to exhort, to promise, and to create a vision of a new and better order out of the old, corrupt one. It is the balance Baldwin creates between these two impulses that make up his distinctive voice. His fidelity to lived experience and to representing human relationships in all their complexity signifies on what Baldwin called "the protest novel." His commitment to a moral vision also signifies on "the protest novel," requiring that he, too, protest, but in a different key.

NOTES

1. Clyde Taylor, "Celebrating Jimmy," in *James Baldwin: The Legacy*, ed. Quincy Troupe (New York: Touchstone-Simon and Schuster, 1989), 30.
2. Ibid., 37.
3. Toni Morrison, "Life in His Language," in *James Baldwin: The Legacy*, 76.
4. Barbara Smith, "We Must Always Bury Our Dead Twice," *Gay Community News*, 20–26 December 1987: center and 10.
5. Patricia Holland addresses the way in which discursive boundaries have made the black gay subject invisible: "The disciplines of feminist, lesbian-gay, and African American studies have imagined for themselves appropriate subjects to be removed, at least theoretically, from such a contentious space into the place of recognition. These bodies/subjects are either white but not heterosexual or black but not homosexual. In the crack between discourses, the black and queer subject resides." See "(Pro)Creating Imaginative Spaces and Other Queer Acts," in *James Baldwin Now*, ed. Dwight McBride (New York: New York University Press, 1999), 266.
6. Taylor, "Celebrating Jimmy," 33–34.
7. James Baldwin, "The Discovery of What It Means to Be an American," in *The Price of the Ticket: Collected Nonfiction, 1948–1985* (New York: St. Martin's and Marek, 1985), 171.
8. Morrison, "Life in His Language," 75.
9. Biographies of James Baldwin include David Leeming, *James Baldwin: A Biography* (New York: Alfred A. Knopf, 1994); James Campbell, *Talking at the Gates: A Life of James Baldwin* (New York: Penguin, 1991); W. J. Weatherby, *James Baldwin: Artist on Fire* (New York: Dell, 1989); and Fern Marja Eckman, *The Furious Passage of James Baldwin* (New York: M. Evans, 1966). Juvenile biographies include Lisa Rosset, *James Baldwin* (New York: Chelsea House, 1989); Randall Kenan, *James Baldwin* (New York: Chelsea House, 1994); Ted Gottfried, *James Baldwin: Voice from Harlem* (New York: F. Watts, 1997); and James Tachach, *James Baldwin* (San Diego: Lucent Books, 1997).
10. Single author, book-length studies that focus solely on Baldwin's work include Rosa Bobia, *The Critical Reception of James Baldwin in France* (New York: Peter Lang, 1997); Horace Porter, *Stealing the Fire: The Art and Protest of James Baldwin* (Middletown, Conn.: Wesleyan University Press, 1989); Trudier Harris, *Black Women in the Fiction of James Baldwin* (Knoxville, Tenn.: University of Tennessee Press, 1985); Carolyn Wedin Sylvander, *James Baldwin*

(New York: Frederick Ungar, 1980); Louis H. Pratt, *James Baldwin* (Boston: Twayne Publishers, 1978); and Stanley Macebuh, *James Baldwin: A Critical Study* (New York: Third Press, 1973). European monographs on Baldwin's work include Karin Möller, *The Theme of Identity in the Essays of James Baldwin: An Interpretation* (Goteborg, Sweden: Acta Universitatis Gothoburgensis, 1975); and Peter Bruck, *Von der "Storefront Church" zum "American Dream": James Baldwin und der amerikanische Rassenkonflikt* (Amsterdam: n.p., 1975).

11 Edited collections of critical essays on Baldwin's work include D. Quentin Miller, ed., *Re-viewing James Baldwin: Things Not Seen* (Philadelphia: Temple University Press, 2000); Dwight A. McBride, *ed.*, *James Baldwin Now* (New York: New York University Press, 1999); Trudier Harris, ed., *New Essays on "Go Tell It on the Mountain"* (New York: Cambridge University Press, 1999); Jakob Kollhofer, ed., *James Baldwin: His Place in American Literary History and His Reception in Europe* (New York: Peter Lang, 1991); Fred L. Standley and Nancy V. Burt, eds., *Critical Essays on James Baldwin* (Boston: G. K. Hall, 1988); Harold Bloom, *ed.*, *James Baldwin* (New York: Chelsea House Publishers, 1986); Therman B. O'Daniel, *ed.*, *James Baldwin: A Critical Evaluation* (Washington, D.C.: Howard University Press, 1977); and Keneth Kinnamon, ed., *James Baldwin: A Collection of Critical Essays* (Englewood Cliffs, N.J.: Prentice-Hall, 1974). Tributes to James Baldwin include Quincy Troupe, ed., *James Baldwin: The Legacy* (New York: Touchstone-Simon and Schuster, 1989); Jules Chametzky, ed., *Black Writers Redefine the Struggle: A Tribute to James Baldwin* (Amherst, Mass.: University of Massachusetts Press, 1989); and Ralph Reckley, ed., *James Baldwin in Memoriam: Proceedings of the Annual Conference of the Middle Atlantic Writers' Association, 1989* (Baltimore: Middle Atlantic Writers' Association Press, 1992).

12 For the most complete listing of Baldwin's published work, see David Leeming and Lisa Gitelman's "Chronological Bibliography of Printed Works by James Baldwin," in David Leeming's *James Baldwin*, 405–17. To get a picture of the initial reception of Baldwin's work through *If Beale Street Could Talk* and the first three decades of critical response, see Fred L. Standley and Nancy V. Standley's *James Baldwin: A Reference Guide* (Boston: G. K. Hall, 1980), which provides an annotated bibliography of writings about James Baldwin from 1946 to 1978. Also see Daryl Dance's "James Baldwin," in *Black American Writers Bibliographical Essays*, vol. 2, ed. Thomas Inge et al. (New York: St. Martin's, 1978), 73–119. While no one has matched the thoroughness of the Standleys' *Reference Guide*, there have been subsequent bibliographic lists and essays, including the introduction to Fred L. Standley and Nancy V. Burt's *Critical Essays on James Baldwin;* and Jeffrey W. Hole, "Select Bibliography of Works by and on James Baldwin," in *James Baldwin Now*, 393–409. Among other things, Hole lists seventy-five essays published on the work of James Baldwin between 1985 and 1997 and thirty-eight dissertations that include a significant discussion of Baldwin's work published during the same years.

13 See, for example, Cassandra M. Ellis, "The Black Boy Looks at the Silver Screen: Baldwin as Moviegoer," in *Re-viewing James Baldwin*, 190–214; and D. Quentin Miller, "James Baldwin, Poet," in *Re-viewing James Baldwin*, 233–54.

14 See, for example, Yasmin Y. DeGout, "'Masculinity' and (Im)maturity: 'The Man Child' and Other Stories in Baldwin's Gender Studies Enterprise," in *Re-viewing James Baldwin*, 134. De Gout argues that "any reading of Baldwin's fiction reveals him to be progenitor of many of the theoretical formulations currently associated with feminist, gay, and gender studies. … Baldwin ultimately reveals in his fiction how sexism and heterosexism affect women and men in a gendered society and how gender constructs are inseparably linked to race, class, and other identity categories."

15 An exception to the focus on Baldwin's earlier work is Nicholas Boggs, "Of Mimicry and (Little Man Little) Man: Toward a Queer Sighted Theory of Black Childhood," in *James Baldwin Now*, 122–60. Boggs reads Baldwin's 1976 *Little Man Little Man: A Story of Childhood* in the contexts of metaphors of African Americanist criticism and queer theory.

16 Harris, *Black Women in the Fiction of James Baldwin*, 3–4.

17 Craig Werner, "James Baldwin: Politics and the Gospel Impulse," *New Politics: A Journal of Socialist Thought* 2, no. 2 (1989): 107.

18 Ibid.

19 Eric Savoy, "Other(ed) Americans in Paris: Henry James, James Baldwin, and the Subversion of Identity," *English Studies in Canada* 18, no. 3 (1992): 3.

20 Houston A. Baker Jr., *Blues, Ideology, and Afro-American Literature: A Vernacular Theory* (Chicago: University of Chicago Press, 1984), 140–42.

21 Houston A. Baker Jr., *The Journey Back: Issues in Black Literature and Criticism* (Chicago: University of Chicago Press, 1980), 60–61.

22 Lawrie Balfour has also recently argued that Baldwin's critique of *Native Son* is not "purely an aesthetic one." Baldwin's objection is moral in that he argues the protest novel helps perpetuate what he has called "the myth of innocence." See her essay "Finding the Words: Baldwin, Race Consciousness, and Democratic Theory," in *James Baldwin Now,* 76–77.

23 Werner, "James Baldwin," 111.

24 Porter, *Stealing the Fire,* 160. Houston A. Baker Jr., however, came to the defense of Baldwin's later work. See "The Embattled Craftsman: An Essay on James Baldwin," *The Journal of African-Afro-American Affairs* 1, no. 1 (1977): 28–51, where Baker argues that Baldwin needs a new kind of critic who understands his relationship to African American literature and culture. See the following chapter for further discussion.

25 Henry Louis Gates Jr., "What James Baldwin Can and Can't Teach America," *New Republic,* 1 June 1992, 42.

26 Hilton Als, "The Enemy Within," *New Yorker,* 16 February 1998, 72, 78. Also see Henry Louis Gates Jr. and Nellie McKay's introduction to Baldwin in *The Norton Anthology of African American Literature* (New York: W. W. Norton and Co., 1997) for a summary of the negative assessment of Baldwin's later work.

27 Werner, "James Baldwin," 106.

28 In *Blues People: Negro Music in White America* (New York: William Morrow, 1963), 30–31, LeRoi Jones's description of Charlie Parker's relationship to his alto saxophone had great resonance for me as I thought about the relationship between Baldwin and many of the characters he created (especially the four autobiographical characters in *Just Above My Head,* each of whom are named after Baldwin).

Jones says, Parker produced a sound that "would literally imitate the human voice with his cries, swoops, squawks, and slurs. ... Parker did not admit that there was any separation between himself and the agent he had chosen as his means of self-expression."

29 Chametzky, *Black Writers Redefine the Struggle,* 66.

30 As quoted in ibid., 6–7.

31 Eldridge Cleaver, *Soul on Ice* (New York: Delta-Dell, 1968), 99.

32 Ibid., 105.

33 Ibid., 109–10.

34 Robert Bone as quoted in David Bergman, *Gaiety Transfigured: Gay Self-Representation in American Literature* (Madison: University of Wisconsin Press, 1991), 164–65.

35 David Leeming says that Baldwin knew that "people were wary of his reputation as a homosexual and he was disappointed that he had not been asked to participate [in the March on Washington] in any meaningful way" (*James Baldwin,* 228). Lee Edelman deconstructs the barely coded homophobic language that was used to describe Baldwin in *Time Magazine* and in other public arenas, language that marginalized or negated Baldwin's role as a civil rights leader. He points out that such "humorous" descriptions of Baldwin as "Martin Luther Queen" combined racism and homophobia to discredit King and the movement as well as Baldwin. See *Homographesis: Essays in Gay Literary and Cultural Theory* (New York: Routledge, 1994), 42—44.

36 Emmanuel S. Nelson, "Critical Deviance: Homophobia and the Reception of James Baldwin's Fiction," *Journal of American Culture* 14, no. 3 (1991): 91–96.

37 Ibid., 91.

38 Bryan R. Washington, *The Politics of Exile: Ideology in Henry James, F. Scott Fitzgerald, and James Baldwin* (Boston: Northeastern University Press, 1995), 97.

39 Stephen Adams, *The Homosexual as Hero in Contemporary Fiction* (New York: Harper and Row, 1980), 36.

40 Ibid., 54.

41 Bergman, *Gaiety Transfigured,* 168.

42 Ibid., 166.

43 Melvin Dixon, *Ride out the Wilderness: Geography and Identity in Afro-American Literature* (Urbana: University of Illinois, 1987); Edelman, *Homographesis.*

44 Cleaver, *Soul on Ice,* 97.

45 Ibid., 98.

46 Werner, "James Baldwin," 112.

47 James Baldwin, "The Last Interview (1987)," interview with Quincy Troupe, in *James Baldwin: The Legacy,* 184.

READING 12

Poet-Translators
Langston Hughes to Paul Blackburn

Jonathan Mayhew

The creative misreading of Lorca among American poets has a cultural, not a linguistic, cause. In my view, at least, the main issues involved have very little to do with the inherent differences between the Spanish and English languages, or even with the shortcomings of individual translators. The belief that relatively minor imperfections in a translation are serious obstacles to cross-cultural communication (or that an ideal translation would make all obstacles disappear) represents a kind of "magical thinking." Logically, even the most perfect rendering can do nothing in and of itself to prevent readers from seeing Lorca's poetry through an orientalist lens. While inadequate translations can perpetuate cultural misunderstandings, I prefer to see them more as a symptom than a cause.

The Lorca who influences American poetry of the postwar period is, however, a poet read *in translation*, and this fact has far reaching implications. In the first place, translation itself might be considered as a form of *apocryphal Lorquiana*, "the making finally of something that Lorca did not write."[1] To read poetry in translation, in fact, is always to read words that the poet did not write—except, of course, in cases of auto translation. A corollary of this principle is that to translate poetry in verse is to write poetry or, at the very least, to make a series of poetic choices.[2] Although some scholar-translators do not define themselves explicitly as poets, the versions they produce will inevitably be compared to those of poet-translators: there is no clear-cut distinction to be made between the work of poets and scholars, since translators in both categories employ a wide gamut of approaches.[3]

While all verse translation entails the creation of a new poem, the apocryphal nature of translation becomes especially pronounced whenever the process of translation itself becomes visible, whether in demonstrably weaker versions—those that unintentionally traduce the original text—or in those that deliberately eliminate "the translator's invisibility" through the use of modernist techniques.[4] Lorca translations produced before 1970 are variable in both approach and quality, and thus offer fertile ground for the study of this particular kind of apocrypha. Despite the oft-repeated claim that Lorca's poetry possesses a certain "clarity," many translators have had difficulty in finding an appropriate register in English. There has been no single leader in the field—a translator universally recognized as

Jonathan Mayhew, "Poet-Translators: Langston Hughes to Paul Blackburn," *Apocryphal Lorca: Translation, Parody, Kitsch*, pp. 53-59, 189-191. Copyright © 2009 by University of Chicago Press. Reprinted with permission.

both excellent and influential—and thus no consensus about what an acceptable translation of Lorca ought to look like. Even some expert readers of the period did not appear to differentiate strongly between translations of variable quality. Edwin Honig, for example, praised Ben Belitt's edition of *The Poet in New York* as "a model of scrupulous textual work and heroic translating."[5] This is wholly at odds with my own judgment, but it is hard to dismiss Honig, since he was himself one of the more adept translators during the same period. A retrospective look at Belitt's work reveals serious flaws, but in historical terms it cannot be denied that Belitt was influential in popularizing Lorca's New York poetry.

Instead of attempting a comprehensive evaluation of the entire corpus of Lorca translations, I have limited my discussion here to a few historically significant and influential cases.[6] The decade of the 1950s is a crucial one for the entry of Lorca into the mainstream of American poetry, so I begin with Langston Hughes's *Gypsy Ballads*, which he began to work on in Madrid during the Spanish civil war and published in 1951. The two translations that generated the most enthusiasm for Lorca in this decade were both published at the halfway point, in 1955: *The Selected Poems of Federico García Lorca*, a compendium of translations by various hands, and Ben Belitt's *The Poet in New York*. Paul Blackburn's *Lorca/Blackburn* did not have the historical impact of these other translations, since it was published posthumously in 1979. Blackburn's translation, however, was produced during the pivotal period of American Lorquismo and throws into relief some key issues about the practice of translation at midcentury.

I. VERNACULAR LORCA: LANGSTON HUGHES'S *GYPSY BALLADS*

Romancero gitano [Gypsy balladbook] is Lorca's best-known book in the Spanish-speaking world, containing some of the poet's most famous and most frequently translated poems. Rolfe Humphries, Carl Cobb, Robert Havard, Michael Hartnett, and Will Kirkland have all published translations of the complete work into English, while numerous other translators, including Bly, Lloyd, Spender and Gili, Blackburn, Merryn Williams, William Bryant Logan, and a probably a few others as well, have given us versions of individual poems. Only a very few works of twentieth-century European poetry, like Rilke's *Sonnets to Orpheus* and *The Duino Elegies*, have been translated more frequently than Lorca's *Ballads*.[7]

Lorca's *Romancero gitano* presents a set of unique challenges to the English-language translator. I believe it is harder to translate, in fact, than the notoriously difficult *Poeta en Nueva York*. The *Romancero*, because of the precision of its language, leaves much less room for error than the "surrealist" conundrums of Lorca's New York poetry. The first problem is metrical: Lorca's verse rhythms are too strong and distinctive simply to be ignored, but there is no ready-made equivalent in English. The use of the English-language ballad stanza might produce jarring effects like this:

> I took her to the river
> believing her unwed;

> the fact she had a husband
> was something left unsaid.[8]

Many of Lorca's individual lines, with their internal repetitions of words and sounds, have a distinctive, memorable quality in Spanish: "Huye, luna, luna, luna," "verde que te quiero verde," "por el monte, monte, monte," "noche que noche nochera." Rolfe Humphries translates Lorca's famous lines: "El niño la mira, mira, / el niño la está mirando" as "The child stares at the moon, / fixedly all the while," erasing the poetic effect that Lorca achieves through repetition of the verb.[9] Even lines without such repetition can be unforgiving in their strength and integrity, showing up any obviously weaker equivalent: Humphries renders "romano torso desnudo," creditably, as "A Roman torso, naked," but his additional comma needlessly breaks up the noun phrase.[10] Punctuation, since it is a marker of rhythm, is never a trivial matter in verse.

A related challenge is to maintain rhythmic and narrative momentum while doing justice to the metaphorical density of this poetry. The images flow in rapid succession, appealing to the five senses, and are of a baroque complexity in their elaboration. Lorca's four-part analogies are particularly tricky. Take the lines: "El jinete se acercaba / tocando el tambor del llano" [The horseman was drawing near / playing the drum of the plain]. Not only is the plain, metaphorically, a drum, but the horse's hooves become mallets or drumsticks. Will Kirkland's version—"Closer comes the horseman / drumming on the plain"—captures the speed of the lines, but blunts the force of the metaphor by using the verb *drum*, which in English usage is a dead metaphor (e.g., "*drumming* ones fingers on the table").[11] The plain has to *be* a drum. Humphries realizes this, but destroys the effect with verbose, explanatory writing that interrupts the continuity of the narrative: "Rider *and horse* appear / With a *long* roll of the drum, / The *great* drum of the plain.[12]

Langston Hughes, one of the most significant poets of the Harlem Renaissance, is also one of the earliest and most accomplished translators of Lorca into English, although his *Gypsy Ballads* did not appear in print until 1951.[13] (Like the British poet Ted Hughes, he also translated *Blood Wedding*.) In a short translator's note, Hughes gives this account of the stages through which his *Gypsy Ballads* passed:

> First translated at the "Alianza de Escritores" in Madrid during the civil war with the aid of the poets, Rafael Alberti, Manuel Altolaguirre, and other friends of Lorca's. Revised in New York, 1945, with the aid of Miguel Covarrubias; and in June, 1951, with the poet's brother, Francisco García Lorca, at Columbia University. Checked with the Lloyd, Spender, Humphries, and Berea versions of certain poems, also with published French and Italian translations. Final copy, June 10, 1951.[14]

Although the existence of Hughes's translation is no secret to scholars in the field, there has been no in-depth analysis of its strategies and successes. In my own judgment, *The Gypsy Ballads* has to be included among the best poetry that Hughes wrote. Just as Ezra Pound's translations of Chinese poetry (*Cathay*) and of a section of the Anglo-Saxon poem "The Seafarer" are classics of modernism, Hughes's Lorca translation must be considered a significant work of American poetry at midcentury. Nevertheless, the text of these translations appeared only as a chapbook of the *Beloit Poetry Review* and was never reprinted.[15] Until the advent of the Internet, it was available only to those with access to a good university library with back issues of the *Beloit Poetry Review*. It was left out of the volume of Hughes's *Collected Works* that included his versions of *Blood Wedding* and of poems by the Cuban poet Nicolás Guillén.

The main strengths of his *Gypsy Ballads* are its colloquial sharpness and its musicality. Unlike many other translators (Spender, Humphries, Kirkland), Hughes does not water down Lorca's language through redundancy or weak lexical choices.[16] He achieves a vernacular quality, but without evoking any *particular* dialect of the spoken language. There is no identifiable African American slang or dialect, for example. He is attentive to rhythm, but avoids the singsong effects that might result from a naive use of the English ballad-stanza. He is not afraid of assonance or alliteration: "Smoky anvils are her breasts / moaning round songs."[17] "Loosely luscious ladies pass /eating sunflower seeds."[18] Hughes also excels at translating Lorca's touchstone lines: "Fly, moon, moon, moon"; "When the night came, / that nightly comes nightly."[19] "Green as I would have you green," however, seems less satisfying: the ambiguity of Lorca's "Verde que te quiero verde" [Green I love {want} you green] is virtually untranslatable.[20]

The virtues of Hughes's method can be seen in passages likes these:

> Preciosa throws away her tambourine
> and runs off without stopping.
> The stud-wind pursues her
> with a hot sword.
> The sea scowls up its roar
> The olive trees grow pale.
> Flutes of forest shade sing,
> and the smooth gong of the snow.
> ...
> The judge, with the Civil Guards,
> comes through the olive groves.
> Slippery blood sings
> a silent song of serpents.
> Honorable Civil Guards:
> the same as usual—
> four Romans dead
> and five Carthaginians.[21]

The voice of the poet Langston Hughes can be heard in these translations. His intervention is not *invisible*, to use Venuti's criterion, but neither is it overly intrusive. One area where his presence is strongly felt is in a relatively direct treatment of sexuality and violence. His "*stud*-wind" and "*cocky* angel" accentuate the implied sexual force of Lorca's "viento-hombrón" and "ángel marchoso."[22] Where other translators blunt the force of Lorca's violence, Hughes's more colloquial and direct language allows it to come forward. He calls a *reyerta* a *brawl* rather than a mere *dispute* (9) and knows that the verb *cercar* means *lay siege*, not merely *surround* (29).[23] As with almost any translation, it would be possible to quibble with any number of Hughes's individual choices, but his overall approach reveals him to be a strong translator, in sympathy with Lorca's sensual directness.

Because his *Gyspy Ballads* was never published by a major publisher like New Directions, Grove, or Knopf, Langston Hughes has remained a largely forgotten link in the history of North American Lorquismo. He anticipates the later interest in Lorca among subsequent generations of African American poets, including Baraka, Kaufman, and Mackey, but his work as a translator is more often *mentioned* than read. Modern biographers also believe that Hughes was a closeted gay man, but the gay poets interested in Lorca in the 1950s—Duncan, Spicer, Ginsberg, O'Hara—would probably not have seen him in this light. Ironically, the Lorca boom of the 1950s often drew its inspiration from translations of indifferent quality rather than seeking out the work of Langston Hughes, the most prominent poet to have translated Lorca in the previous generation.

NOTES

1. García Lorca, *Poet in New York*, trans. Medina and Statman, xxii.
2. Prose translations of verse belong to a separate category, since the visual format might signal the absence of a specifically *poetic* intention.
3. The conventional notion is that scholars will produce dry and overliteral versions, while poets will be freer and less rigorous, but this division of labor does not necessarily obtain. Hyperliteralism, for example, can result from a weak grasp of the source language more characteristic of poets. Scholars can misconstrue and embellish the original text, while poets sometimes attain a high degree of scholarly expertise.
4. In *The Translator's Invisibility*, Lawrence Venuti frames the ongoing historical debate around translation as a conflict between "fluency" and "the translator's invisibility," on the one hand, and a "foreignizing" translation practice based on Schleiermacher's theory, on the other. Venuti strongly favors disruptions of the dominant (and ideological suspect) norm of fluency. My sympathies, too, lie with foreignizing translation, but I am also interested in exploring the norms of acceptability that allow a translation to reach its target audience.
5. Honig, "Lorca to Date," 122.
6. I have not been able to do justice to some earlier contributors to the translation of Lorca (Honig, Humphries, Lloyd, Campbell) or to the numerous translations that have been published since 1980. To do so would require two additional chapters of equivalent length. Robert Bly's contribution to the translation of Lorca will be treated in the context of the deep image school of poetry (chapter 4).
7. For a selected bibliography of Lorca in English see García Lorca, *Collected Poems*, 862–63. I will follow standard usage here and refer to Lorca's *romances* as *ballads*, since virtually every English-language translator and commentator before me has accepted this term as a functional equivalent. In my own mind, however, the *ballad* and the *romance* are two very different species of animal. Of course, the term *ballad* is a perfectly good one to apply to a *translation* of a Lorca poem into English.

8   García Lorca, *The Gypsy Ballads of Federico García Lorca*, trans. Humphries, 30.
9   Ibid., 19. Medina and Statman, in their otherwise acceptable translation of *Poet in New York*, persistently and perversely truncate Lorca's repetitions, translating "Negros, negros, negros, negros," for example, as "Blacks" (García Lorca, *Poet in New York*, trans. Medina and Statman, 26–27). Repetition is such a key device in Lorca's poetry that its omission in the translation is inexplicable. The translators justify this procedure as follows: "All this play, this erasure, has seemed necessary to retain the feeling, the power, the music of Lorca's work" (xxi). But how is the power of Lorca's music retained by the erasure of this musical device?
10 García Lorca, *Gypsy Ballads*, trans. Humphries, 36.
11 García Lorca, *Collected Poems*, 519.
12 García Lorca, *Gypsy Ballads*, trans. Humphries, 19; emphasis added. I have italicized extraneous elements added by the translator.
13 See Brent Hayes Edwards's account of Hughes's encounter with Lorca's poetry during the Spanish civil war in "Langston Hughes and the Futures of Diasporas."
14 García Lorca, *Gyspy Ballads*, trans. Hughes. Hughes's version is incomplete: he translated the first fifteen poems of Lorca's book, leaving out the three concluding "Romances históricos." For the relations between Hughes and Lorca, see María Paz Moreno, "Gyspy Moon over Harlem." I remain agnostic over the question of whether Lorca and Hughes met personally, as Moreno argues. If they had, Hughes would have probably mentioned this fact in his autobiography.
15 Literary history would have different if this volume had been published by a major New York trade publisher in the mid-1940s, but, according to Arnold Rampersad, "Alfred Knopf himself, advised by a senior editor, flatly rejected the Lorca book, without offering much of an explanation" (*Life of Langston Hughes*, 2:119–20).
16 Rolfe Humphries's 1953 version, published by Indiana University Press, is not consistently bad, but it ignores the importance of repetition in Lorca's poetry (as noted above), and introduces redundancies like "Worthy / of a queen or an empress," where Hughes has "worthy of an empress." Hughes's *Gypsy Ballads* is also superior, in my view, to Will Kirkland's acceptable but overly tame version. Kirkland, for example, translates "bellas de sangre *contraria*" as "lovely with the *other's* blood" (García Lorca, *Collected Poems*, 524–25; emphasis added), diluting the force of the adjective *contraria* [contrary, opposing, rival, enemy].
17 García Lorca, *Gypsy Ballads*, trans. Hughes, 18.
18 Ibid., 21.
19 Ibid., 6, 36.
20 Ibid., 10.
21 Ibid., 8–9.
22 Ibid., 8, 30.
23 Ibid., 9, 29.

READING 13

Harlem and the Renaissance
1920–1940

Cary D. Wintz

What was the Harlem Renaissance and when did it begin? This seemingly simple question reveals the complexities of the movement we know varyingly as the New Negro Renaissance, the New Negro movement, the Negro Renaissance, the Jazz Age, or the Harlem Renaissance. To answer the question it is necessary to place the movement within time and space, and then to define its nature. This task is much more complex than it might seem.

Traditionally the Harlem Renaissance was viewed primarily as a literary movement centered in Harlem and growing out of the black migration and the emergence of Harlem as the premier black metropolis. It was also traditionally viewed as a male-dominated movement, although it was acknowledged that women poets and writers played a role, but generally as second-tier talent. The names that dominated were male writers—Langston Hughes, Countee Cullen, Jean Toomer, Claude McKay, and others; promoting and guiding the movement were other men: Alain Locke, James Weldon Johnson, W. E. B. Du Bois, and Charles S. Johnson. Jessie Fauset was given some slight credit as a minor novelist, but little was said about her role in nurturing the movement. The significance of Nella Larsen and Zora Neale Hurston would not be fully acknowledged for a half century after the end of the Renaissance. Music and theater were mentioned briefly, more as background and local color, as providing inspiration for poetry and local color for fiction. However, there was no analysis of the developments in these fields. Likewise art was discussed mostly in terms of Aaron Douglas and his association with Langston Hughes and other young writers who produced *Fire!!* in 1926, but little or no analysis of the work of African American artists. And there was even less discussion or analysis of the work of women in the fields of art, music, and theater.

Fortunately this narrow view has changed. The Harlem Renaissance is increasingly viewed through a broader lens that recognizes it as a national movement with connections to international developments in art and culture that places increasing emphasis on the nonliterary aspects of the movement, and, of course, brings the participation of women more fully to the center of the movement.

In this essay, I will provide a brief introduction to the Harlem Renaissance, focusing largely on time and place in the emergence of the movement in literature, musical theater,

Cary D. Witz, "Harlem and the Renaissance: 1920-1940," *Women Artists of the Harlem Renaissance*, ed. Amy Helene Kirschke, pp. 3-21. Copyright © 2014 by University Press of Mississippi. Reprinted with permission.

music, and the visual arts. Although of necessity it is limited in scope and detail, I hope to bring awareness to the complexity of its subject.

TIME

First, to know when the Harlem Renaissance began, we must determine its origins. Understanding the origins depends on how we perceive the nature of the Renaissance. For those who view the Renaissance as primarily a literary movement, the Civic Club Dinner of March 21, 1924, signaled its emergence. This event did not occur in Harlem, but was held almost one hundred blocks south in Manhattan at the Civic Club on Twelfth Street off Fifth Avenue. Charles S. Johnson, the young editor of *Opportunity*, the National Urban League's monthly magazine, conceived the event to honor writer Jesse Fauset on the occasion of the publication of her novel, *There is Confusion*. Johnson planned a small dinner party with about twenty guests, a mix of white publishers, editors, and literary critics, black intellectuals, and young black writers. But, when he asked Alain Locke to preside over the event, he agreed only if the dinner honored African American writers in general rather than one novelist.

So the simple celebratory dinner morphed into a transformative event with over one hundred attendees. African Americans were represented by W. E. B. Du Bois, James Weldon Johnson, and others of the black intelligentsia, along with Fauset and a representative group of poets and authors. White guests predominately were publishers and critics; Carl Van Doren, editor of *Century* magazine, spoke for this group, calling upon the young writers in the audience to make their contribution to the "new literary age" emerging in America.[1]

The Civic Club dinner significantly accelerated the literary phase of the Harlem Renaissance. Frederick Allen, editor of *Harper's*, approached Countee Cullen, securing his poems for his magazine as soon as the poet finished reading them. As the dinner ended Paul Kellogg, editor of *Survey Graphic*, hung around talking to Cullen, Fauset, and several other young writers, then offered Charles S. Johnson a unique opportunity: an entire issue of *Survey Graphic* devoted to the Harlem literary movement. Under the editorship of Alain Locke, the "Harlem: Mecca of the New Negro" number of *Survey Graphic* hit the newsstands March 1, 1925.[2] It was an overnight sensation. Later that year Locke published a book-length version of the "Harlem" edition, expanded and re-titled *The New Negro: An Interpretation*.[3] In the anthology Locke laid down his vision of the aesthetic and the parameters for the emerging Harlem Renaissance; he also included a collection of poetry, fiction, graphic arts, and critical essays on art, literature, and music.

For those who viewed the Harlem Renaissance in terms of musical theater and entertainment, the birth occurred three years earlier when *Shuffle Along* opened at the Sixty-Third Street Musical Hall. *Shuffle Along* was a musical play written by a pair of veteran vaudeville acts—comedians Flournoy Miller and Aubrey Lyles and composers/singers Eubie Blake and Nobel Sissle. Most of its cast featured unknowns, but some, like Josephine Baker and Paul Robeson, who had only minor roles in the production, were on their way to international fame. Eubie Blake recalled the significance of the production, when he pointed out that he and Sissle and Lyles and Miller accomplished something that the other great African American performers—Cole and Johnson, Williams and Walker—had tried, but failed to achieve. "We did it, that's the story," he exclaimed, "*We* put *Negroes* back on Broadway!"[4]

Poet Langston Hughes also saw *Shuffle Along* as a seminal event in the emergence of the Harlem Renaissance. It introduced him to the creative world of New York, and it helped to redefine and energize music and nightlife in Harlem. In the process it introduced white New Yorkers to black music, theater, and entertainment and helped generate the white fascination with Harlem and the African American arts that was so much a part of the Harlem Renaissance. For the young Hughes, just arrived in the city, the long-range impact of *Shuffle Along* was not on his mind. In 1921 it was all about the show, and, as he wrote in his autobiography, it was "a honey of a show":

> Swift, bright, funny, rollicking, and gay, with a dozen danceable, singable tunes. Besides, look who were in it: The now famous choir director, Hall Johnson, and the composer, William Grant Still, were part of the orchestra. Eubie Blake and Nobel Sissle wrote the music and played and acted in the show. Miller and Lyles were the comics. Florence Mills skyrocketed to fame in the second act. Trixie Smith sang "He May Be Your Man, But He Comes to See Me Sometimes." And Caterina Jarbors, now a European prima donna, and the internationally celebrated Josephine Baker were merely in the chorus. Everybody was in the audience—including me. People came to see it innumerable times. It was always packed.[5]

Shuffle Along also brought jazz to Broadway. It combined jazz music with very creatively choreographed jazz dance to transform musical theater into something new, exciting, and daring. And, the show was a critical and financial success. It ran 474 performances on Broadway and spawned three touring companies. It was a hit show written, performed, and produced by blacks, and it generated a demand for more. Within three years nine other African American shows appeared on Broadway, and white writers and composers rushed to produce their versions of black musical comedies.

Music was also a prominent feature of African American culture during the Harlem Renaissance. The term *Jazz Age* was used by many who saw African American music, especially the blues and jazz, as defining features of the Renaissance. However, both jazz and the blues were imports to Harlem. They emerged out of the African American experience around the turn of the century in southern towns and cities, like New Orleans, Memphis, and St. Louis. From these origins these musical forms spread across the country, north to Chicago before arriving in New York a few years before to World War I.

Blues and black blues performers such as musician W. C. Handy and vocalist Ma Rainey were popular on the vaudeville circuit in the late nineteenth century. The publication of W. C. Handy's "Memphis Blues" in 1912 and the first recordings a few years later brought this genre into the mainstream of American popular culture. Jazz reportedly originated among the musicians who played in the bars and brothels of the infamous Storyville district of New Orleans. Jelly Roll Morton claimed to have invented jazz there in 1902, but it is doubtful that any one person holds that honor. According to James Weldon Johnson jazz reached New York in 1905 at Proctor's Twenty-Third Street Theater. Johnson described the band there as "a playing-singing-dancing orchestra, making dominant use of banjos, mandolins, guitars, saxophones, and drums in combination, and [it] was called the Memphis Students—a very good name, overlooking the fact that the performers were not students and were not from Memphis. There was also a violin, a couple of brass instruments, and a double-bass."[6] Seven years later composer and bandleader James Reese Europe, one of the "Memphis Students," took his Clef Club Orchestra to Carnegie Hall; during World War I, while serving as an officer for a machine-gun company in the famed 369th U.S. Infantry Division, James Europe, fellow officer Nobel Sissle, and the regimental band introduced the sounds of ragtime, jazz, and the blues to European audiences.

Following the war, black music, especially the blues and jazz, became increasingly popular with both black and white audiences. Europe continued his career as a successful bandleader until his untimely death in 1919. Ma Rainey and other jazz artists and blues singers began to sign recording contracts, initially with African American record companies like Black Swan Records, but very quickly with Paramount, Columbia, and other mainstream recording outlets. In Harlem one club opened after another, each featuring jazz orchestras or blues singers. Nobel Sissle, of course, was one of the team behind the production of *Shuffle Along*, which opened Broadway up to *Chocolate Dandies* and a series of other black musical comedies, featuring these new musical styles.

The visual arts, particularly painting, prints, and sculpture, emerged somewhat later in Harlem than did music, musical theater, and literature. One of the most notable visual artists of the Harlem Renaissance, Aaron Douglas, arrived in Harlem from Kansas City in 1925. Later that year his first pieces appeared in *Opportunity* and ten Douglas pieces appeared as "ten Decorative Designs" illustrating Locke's *The New Negro*. Early the next year, W. E. B. Du Bois published Douglas's first illustrations in the *Crisis*. Due to his personal association with Langston Hughes, Wallace Thurman, and other African American writers, his collaboration with them in the publication of their literary magazine *Fire!!*, and his role designing book jackets and illustrating literary works, Douglas was the most high-profile artist clearly connected to the Harlem Renaissance in the mid- to late 1920s. And while these connections to the literary part of the Renaissance were notable, they were not typical of the experience of other African American artists of this period.

More significant in launching the art phase of the Harlem Renaissance were the exhibits of African American art in Harlem and the funding and exhibits that the Harmon Foundation provided. The early stirrings of the African American art movement in Harlem followed a 1919 exhibit on the work of Henry Ossawa Tanner's work at a midtown gallery in New York, and an exhibit of African American artists two years later at the Harlem Branch of the

New York Public Library. Even more important to the nurturing and promotion of African American art were the activities of the Harmon Foundation. Beginning in 1926 the foundation awarded cash prizes for outstanding achievement by African Americans in eight fields, including fine arts. Additionally, from 1928 through 1933 the Harmon Foundation organized an annual exhibit of African American art. Initially the exhibits were held in New York, but beginning in 1929 the exhibits traveled across the country following their New York debut. Also the Harmon Foundation developed catalogs for the exhibits that attempted to define the nature and the appropriate aesthetic for black art. Alain Locke was influential in the activities of the Harmon Foundation. He served as a judge for the Harmon prizes and influenced the black aesthetic promoted by the foundation in their catalogs and exhibits. While some African American artists and intellectuals accused the Harmon Foundation of exerting undue influence on African American art, and harming young artists by prematurely displaying their works, the foundation's work certainly provided financial support for artists through its prizes and travel grants and effectively publicized African American visual arts through its exhibits and catalogs.

The Harlem Renaissance was also linked to the social and demographic changes impacting African Americans in the second and third decades of the twentieth century. The most visible of the social forces was the black migration that had begun in the early twentieth century, accelerated during the war, and continued through the 1920s, bringing from the South the hundred thousand or more who would transform Harlem into the Negro metropolis, and impacting cities across the country—north, south, and west. The result was an increasingly urbanized African American population that was national in scope rather than being largely confined to the old South. This migration directly impacted the Harlem Renaissance. Along with the thousands of mostly poor, working-class blacks coming north into Harlem were the musicians, writers, poets, artists, dancers, actors, editors, publishers, critics, businesspersons, professionals, and intellectuals who created and nurtured the Harlem Renaissance. This pattern was repeated in Chicago and other northern cities, as well as in Atlanta, Houston, Dallas, Kansas City, Los Angeles, and other cities of the South and West.

Adding to the creative ferment of the period was social and political upheaval. World War I brought in its wake a series of devastating race riots culminating in the 1919 outbreaks in Washington and Chicago, as well as the 1921 Tulsa riot. During this period traditional African American leadership was in a state of transition. The death of Booker T. Washington in 1915 had temporarily left Du Bois and the NAACP as the dominant political voice among African Americans. However, black politics shifted as Marcus Garvey mobilized tens of thousands of supporters and confronted the NAACP and the African American establishment with a mass political movement championing black nationalism and Pan-Africanism, while A. Philip Randolph and the *Messenger* challenged traditional black leadership from the socialist left. Du Bois, who had turned fifty in 1918, stumbled in his efforts to address issues raised by the world war, and largely failed to connect with the younger, more strident black voices emerging in politics and in the arts.

PLACE

Situating the Harlem Renaissance in space is almost as complex as defining its origins and time span. Certainly Harlem is central to the Harlem Renaissance, but it serves more as an anchor for the movement than as its sole location. In reality the Harlem Renaissance both drew from and spread its influence across the United States, the Caribbean, and the world. Only a handful of the writers, artists, musicians, and other figures of the Harlem Renaissance were native to Harlem or New York, and only a relatively small number lived in Harlem throughout the Renaissance period. And yet, Harlem impacted the art, music, and writing of virtually all of the participants in the Harlem Renaissance.

Harlem refers to that part of Manhattan Island north of Central Park and generally east of Eighth Avenue or St. Nicholas Avenue. Originally established in the seventeenth century as a Dutch village, it evolved over time. In the late seventeenth and early eighteenth centuries it housed the country estates of the rich, and it remained largely rural or semirural through the mid-nineteenth century, with a mix of poor squatters in the marshes and mudflats along the Harlem River, and weekend homes of the wealthy in the uplands. Following its annexation by the city in 1873 the marshes and mudflats were filled in and building lots were sold. The resulting Harlem real estate boom lasted about twenty years during which developers erected most of the physical structures that defined Harlem as late as the mid-twentieth century. They designed this new, urban Harlem primarily for the wealthy and the upper middle class; it contained broad avenues, a rail connection to the city on Eighth Avenue, and expensive homes and luxurious apartment buildings accompanied by commercial and retail structures, along with stately churches and synagogues, clubs, social organizations, and even the Harlem Philharmonic Orchestra.

By 1905 Harlem's boom turned into a bust. Excessive speculation and overbuilding resulted in empty apartments and houses that had to be leased out to renters or subdivided into multifamily units. Desperate white developers began to sell or rent to African Americans, often at greatly discounted prices, while black real estate firms provided the customers. At this time approximately 60,000 blacks lived in New York, scattered through the five boroughs, including a small community in Harlem. The largest concentration inhabited the overcrowded and congested Tenderloin and San Juan Hill sections of the west side of Manhattan. When New York's black population swelled in the twentieth century as newcomers from the South moved north and as redevelopment destroyed existing black neighborhoods, pressure for additional and hopefully better housing pushed blacks northward up the west side of Manhattan into Harlem.

Harlem's transition, once it began, followed fairly traditional patterns. As soon as blacks started moving onto a block, property values dropped further as whites began to leave. This process was especially evident in the early 1920s. Both black and white realtors took advantage of declining property values in Harlem, the panic selling that resulted when blacks moved in. Addressing the demand for housing generated by the city's rapidly growing black population, they acquired, subdivided, and leased Harlem property to black tenants.

Year by year the boundaries of black Harlem expanded, as blacks streamed into Harlem as quickly as they could find affordable housing. By 1910 they had become the majority group on the west side of Harlem north of 130th Street; by 1914 the population of black Harlem was estimated to be 50,000.

During the next two decades black Harlem continued to grow as tens of thousands of migrants from the South were joined by thousands of black immigrants from the West Indies. All seemed to find their way to Harlem's streets and tenements. In 1920 black Harlem extended from 130th Street to 145th Street and from Fifth to Eighth Avenue, and contained approximately 73,000 blacks; by 1930 black Harlem had expanded north ten blocks to 155th and south to 115th; it spread from the Harlem River to Amsterdam Avenue, and housed approximately 164,000 blacks. The core of this community, bounded roughly by 126th Street on the south, 159th Street on the north, the Harlem River and Park Avenue on the east, and Eighth Avenue on the west, was more than 95 percent black.

By 1920 Harlem, by virtue of the sheer size of its black population, had emerged as the virtual capital of black America; its name evoked a magic that lured all classes of blacks from all sections of the country to its streets. Impoverished southern farmers and sharecroppers made their way northward, where they were joined in Harlem by black intellectuals such as W. E. B. Du Bois and James Weldon Johnson. Although the old black social elites of Washington, DC, and Philadelphia were disdainful of Harlem's vulgar splendor, and while it housed no significant black university as did Washington, Philadelphia, Atlanta, and Nashville, Harlem still became the race's cultural center and a Mecca for its aspiring young. It housed the National Urban League, A. Philip Randolph's Brotherhood of Sleeping Car Porters, and the black leadership of the NAACP. Marcus Garvey launched his ill-fated black nationalist movement among its masses, and Harlem became the geographical focal point of African American literature, art, music, and theater. Its nightclubs, music halls, and jazz joints became the center of New York nightlife in the mid-1920s. Harlem, in short, was where the action was in black America during the decade following World War I.

Harlem and New York City also contained the infrastructure to support and sustain the arts. In the early twentieth century New York had replaced Boston as the center of the book publishing industry. Furthermore new publishing houses in the city, such as Alfred Knopf, Harper Bothers, and Harcourt Brace were open to adding greater diversity to their book lists by including works by African American writers. By the late nineteenth century, New York City housed Tin Pan Alley, the center of the music publishing industry. In the 1920s when recordings and broadcasting emerged, New York was again in the forefront. Broadway was the epicenter of American theater, and New York was the center of the American art world.

In short in the early twentieth century no other American city possessed the businesses and institutions to support literature and the arts that New York did.

In spite of its physical presence, size, and its literary and arts infrastructure, the nature of Harlem and its relation to the Renaissance are very complex. The word *Harlem* evoked strong and conflicting images among African Americans during the first half of the twentieth century. Was it the Negro metropolis, black Manhattan, the political, cultural, and spiritual center of African America, a land of plenty, a city of refuge, or a black ghetto and emerging slum? For some, the image of Harlem was more personal. King Solomon Gillis, the main character in Rudolph Fisher's "The City of Refuge," was one of these. Emerging out of the subway at 135th and Lennox Avenue, Gillis was transfixed:

> Clean air, blue sky, bright sunlight. Gillis set down his tan-cardboard extension-case and wiped his black, shining brow. Then slowly, spreadingly, he grinned at what he saw: Negroes at every turn; up and down Lenox Avenue, up and down One Hundred and Thirty-fifth Street; big, lanky Negroes, short, squat Negroes; black ones, brown ones, yellow ones; men standing idle on the curb, women, bundle-laden, trudging reluctantly homeward, children rattle-trapping about the sidewalks; here and there a white face drifting along, but Negroes predominantly, overwhelmingly everywhere. There was assuredly no doubt of his whereabouts. This was Negro Harlem.[7]

Gillis then noticed the commotion in the street as trucks and autos crowded into the intersection at the command of the traffic cop—an African American traffic cop.

> The Southern Negro's eyes opened wide; his mouth opened wider. ... For there stood a handsome, brass-buttoned giant directing the heaviest traffic Gillis had ever seen; halting unnumbered tons of automobiles and trucks and wagons and pushcarts and street-cars; holding them at bay with one hand while he swept similar tons peremptorily on with the other; ruling the wide crossing with supreme self-assurance; and he, too, was a Negro!
>
> Yet most of the vehicles that leaped or crouched at his bidding carried white passengers. One of these overdrove bounds a few feet and Gillis heard the officer's shrill whistle and gruff reproof, saw the driver's face turn red and his car draw back like a threatened pup. It was beyond belief—impossible. Black might be white, but it couldn't be that white!
>
> "Done died an' woke up in Heaven," thought King Solomon, watching, fascinated; and after a while, as if the wonder of it were too great to believe simply by seeing, "Cullud policemans!" he said, half aloud; then repeated over and over, with greater and greater conviction, "Even got cullud policemans."[8]

Gillis was one of those who sought refuge in Harlem. He fled North Carolina after shooting a white man. Now in Harlem the policeman was black. Not that this changed his fate.

At the end of the story, one of these black policemen dragged Gillis away in handcuffs. The reality of Harlem often contradicted the myth.

For poet Langston Hughes Harlem was also something of a refuge. Following a mostly unhappy childhood living at one time or another with his mother or father, grandmother, or neighbors, Hughes convinced his stern and foreboding father to finance his education at Columbia University. He recalled his 1921 arrival: "I went up the steps and out into the bright September sunlight. Harlem! I stood there, dropped my bags, took a deep breath and felt happy again. I registered at the Y. When college opened, I did not want to move into the dormitory at Columbia. I really did not want to go to college at all. I didn't want to do anything but live in Harlem, get a job and work there."[9] After a less than happy year at Columbia, Hughes did exactly that. He dropped out of school and moved into Harlem. Hughes, though, never lost sight that poverty, overcrowded and dilapidated housing, and racial prejudice were part of the daily experience of most Harlem residents.

For Hughes, too, the desire to just "live in Harlem" was as much myth as reality. After dropping out of Columbia and moving to Harlem he actually spent little time there. Until the late 1930s he was much more of a visitor or transient in Harlem than a resident. Typically he passed through, visited for weekends or several weeks, while his life and jobs took him away from Harlem. For example, he spent much of 1922 working on Staten Island and on ships anchored up the Hudson River. In 1923 and 1924 he worked on freighters sailing to Africa and Europe and spent several months in Paris and Italy. He returned to the United States in 1925 but spent the year in Washington, DC. From 1926 through 1929 he attended Lincoln University in Pennsylvania. From 1930 to 1938 he spent most of his time traveling, with extensive stays in the South, the Caribbean, the Soviet Union, and California, occasionally passing through New York and spending brief periods there. He again made Harlem his home in 1938. While Hughes spent many weekends and vacations in Harlem during his years at Lincoln University, during the height of the Renaissance, between 1923 and 1938 he was away from the city more than he was there, more a visitor than a full-time resident.

James Weldon Johnson saw a still different Harlem. In his 1930 book, *Black Manhattan*, he described the black metropolis in near utopian terms as the race's great hope and its grand social experiment: "So here we have Harlem—not merely a colony or a community or a settlement ... but a black city located in the heart of white Manhattan, and containing more Negroes to the square mile than any other spot on earth. It strikes the uninformed observer as a phenomenon, a miracle straight out of the skies."[10] When Johnson looked at Harlem, he did not see an emerging slum or a ghetto, but a black neighborhood north of Central Park that was "one of the most beautiful and healthful" in the city. "It is not a fringe, it is not a slum, nor is it a 'quarter' consisting of dilapidated tenements. It is a section of new-law apartment houses and handsome dwellings, with streets as well paved, as well lighted, and as well kept as in any other part of the city."[11]

Without question Harlem was a rapidly growing black metropolis, but what kind of city was it becoming? Harlem historian Gilbert Osofsky argued that "the most profound change that Harlem experienced in the 1920s was its emergence as a slum. Largely within the space of a single decade Harlem was transformed from a potentially ideal community to a neighborhood with manifold social and economic problems called 'deplorable,' 'unspeakable,' 'incredible.'"[12] Many problems contributed to Harlem's growing pathology. Housing, which had initially attracted blacks to the area, was, for most, overpriced, congested, and dilapidated. Jobs were scarce, in part because of the competition for jobs among the many migrants, but primarily due to job discrimination practiced even in the heart of Harlem. As a result most of Harlem's residents lived in poor housing, either in poverty or on the verge of poverty, in a neighborhood experiencing the typical results of poverty and discrimination: growing vice, crime, juvenile delinquency, and drug addiction.

In short, the day-to-day realities that most Harlemites faced differed dramatically from the image of Harlem life presented by James Weldon Johnson. Harlem was beset with contradictions. While it reflected the self-confidence, militancy, and pride of the New Negro in his or her demand for equality, and it reflected the aspirations and creative genius of the talented young people of the Harlem Renaissance along with the economic aspirations of the black migrants seeking a better life in the north, ultimately Harlem failed to resolve its problems and to fulfill these dreams.

The 1935 Harlem Race Riot put to rest the conflicting images of Harlem. On March 19, 1935, a young Puerto Rican boy was caught stealing a ten-cent pocketknife from the counter of a 135th Street five-and-dime store. Following the arrest, rumors spread that police had beaten the youth to death. A large crowd gathered, shouting "police brutality" and "racial discrimination." A window was smashed, looting began, and the riot spread throughout the night. The violence resulted in three blacks dead, two hundred stores trashed and burned, and more than $2,000,000 worth of destroyed property. The Puerto Rican youth whose arrest precipitated the riot had been released the previous evening when the merchant chose not to press charges. Shocked by the uprising Mayor Fiorello La Guardia established an interracial committee headed by E. Franklin Frazier, a professor of sociology at Howard University, to investigate the riot. They concluded the obvious: the riot resulted from a general frustration with racial discrimination and poverty.

What the committee failed to report was that the riot shattered once and for all James Weldon Johnson's image of Harlem as the African American urban utopia. In spite of the presence of artists and writers, nightclubs, music, and entertainment, Harlem was a slum, a black ghetto characterized by poverty and discrimination. Burned-out storefronts might be fertile ground for political action, but not for art, literature, and culture. Harlem would see new black writers in the years to come. Musicians, poets, and artists would continue to make their home there, but it never again served as the focal point of a creative movement with the national and international impact of the Harlem Renaissance.

Johnson did not personally witness the 1935 riot. He had left the city in 1931, the year after he published *Black Manhattan*, to take the Spence Chair in Creative Literature at Fisk University in Nashville. He lived there until his death in 1938.

RENAISSANCE

So, what was the Harlem Renaissance? The simple answer is that the Harlem Renaissance (or the New Negro movement, or whatever name is preferred) was the most important event in twentieth-century African American intellectual and cultural life. While best known for its literature, it touched every aspect of African American literary and artistic creativity from the end of World War I through the Great Depression. Literature, critical writing, music, theater, musical theater, and the visual arts were transformed by this movement; it also affected politics, social development, and almost every aspect of the African American experience from the mid-1920s through the mid-1930s.

But there was also something ephemeral about the Harlem Renaissance, something vague and hard to define. The Harlem Renaissance, then, was an African American literary and artistic movement anchored in Harlem, but drawing from, extending to, and influencing African American communities across the country and beyond. We date it roughly from the end of the First World War through the Great Depression, but its roots extend well before the war and its legacy continued many years beyond the 1930s. It had no clearly defined beginning or end, but emerged out of the social and intellectual upheaval in the African American community that followed World War I, blossomed in the 1920s, and then faded away in the mid- to late 1930s and early 1940s.

Likewise the Harlem Renaissance has no single defined ideological or stylistic standard that unified its participants and defined the movement. Instead, most participants in the movement resisted black or white efforts to define or narrowly categorize their art. For example, in 1926 a group of writers, spearheaded by writer Wallace Thurman and including Langston Hughes, Zora Neal Hurston, and artist Aaron Douglas, among others, produced their own literary magazine, *Fire!!* One purpose of this venture was the declaration of their intent to assume ownership of the literary Renaissance. In the process they turned their backs on Alain Locke and W. E. B. Du Bois and others who sought to channel black creativity into what they considered to be the proper aesthetic and political directions. Despite the efforts of Thurman and his young colleagues, *Fire!!* fizzled out after only one issue and the movement remained ill defined. In fact, this was its most distinguishing characteristic. There would be no common literary style or political ideology associated with the Harlem Renaissance. It was far more an identity than an ideology or a literary or artistic school. What united participants was their sense of taking part in a common endeavor and their commitment to giving artist expression to the African American experience. If there was a statement that defined the philosophy of the new literary movement it was Langston

Hughes's essay, "The Negro Artist and the Racial Mountain," published in the *Nation*, June 16, 1926:

> We younger Negro artists who create now intend to express our individual dark-skinned selves without fear or shame. If white people are pleased we are glad. If they are not, it doesn't matter. We know we are beautiful. And ugly, too. The tom-tom cries and the tom-tom laughs. If colored people are pleased we are glad. If they are not their displeasure doesn't matter either. We will build our temples for tomorrow, strong as we know how, and we will stand on top of the mountain, free within ourselves.[13]

Like *Fire!!* this essay was the movement's declaration of independence both from the stereotypes that whites held about African Americans and the expectations that they had for their literary works, and from the expectations that black leaders and black critics had for black writers, and the expectations that they placed on their work.

The determination of black writers to follow their own artistic vision and the diversity that this created was the principal characteristic of the Harlem Renaissance. This diversity is clearly evident in the poetry of the period where subject matter, style, and tone ranged from the traditional to the more inventive. Langston Hughes, for example, captured the life and language of the working class, and the rhythm and style of the blues in a number of his poems, none more so than "The Weary Blues." In contrast to Hughes's appropriation of the form of black music, especially jazz and the blues, and his use of the black vernacular, Claude McKay and Countee Cullen utilized more traditional and classical forms for their poetry. McKay used sonnets for much of his protest verse, while Cullen's poems relied both on classical literary allusions and symbols and standard poetic forms.

This diversity and experimentation also characterized music. This was evidenced in the blues of Bessie Smith, the range of jazz from the early rhythms of Jelly Roll Morton to the instrumentation of Louis Armstrong or the sophisticated orchestration of Duke Ellington. In art the soft colors and pastels Aaron Douglas used to create a veiled view for the African-inspired images in his paintings and murals contrasted sharply with Jacob Lawrence's use of bright colors and sharply defined images.

Within this diversity, several themes emerged that set the character of the Harlem Renaissance. No black writer, musician, or artist expressed all of these themes, but each did address one or more in his or her work. The first of these themes was the effort to recapture the African American past—its rural southern roots, urban experience, and African heritage. Interest in the African past corresponded with the rise of Pan-Africanism in African American politics, which was at the center of Marcus Garvey's ideology, and also a concern of W. E. B. Du Bois in the 1920s. Poets Countee Cullen and Langston Hughes addressed their African heritage in their works, while artist Aaron Douglas used African motifs in his art. A number of musicians, from the classical composer William Grant Still to jazz great Louis Armstrong, introduced African-inspired rhythms and themes in their compositions. The exploration of black southern heritage was reflected in novels by Jean Toomer and Zora Neale Hurston, as well as in Jacob Lawrence's art. Zora Neale Hurston used her experience as a folklorist as the basis for her extensive study of rural southern black life in her 1937 novel, *Their Eyes Were Watching God*. Jacob Lawrence turned to African American history for much of his work, including two of his multi-canvass series of paintings, the Harriett Tubman series and the one on the Black Migration.

Harlem Renaissance writers and artists also explored life in Harlem and other urban centers. Both Hughes and McKay drew on Harlem images for their poetry, and McKay used the ghetto as the setting for his first novel, *Home to Harlem*. Some black writers, including McKay and Hughes, as well as Rudolph Fisher and Wallace Thurman were accused of overemphasizing crime, sexuality, and other less-savory aspects of ghetto life in order to feed the voyeuristic desires of white readers and publishers, in imitation of white novelist Carl Van Vechten's exploitation of Harlem in his novel, *Nigger Heaven*.

A third major theme addressed by the literature of the Harlem Renaissance was race. Virtually every novel and play and most of the poetry explored race in America, especially the impact of race and racism on African Americans. In their simplest form these works protested racial injustice. Claude McKay's sonnet, "If We Must Die," was among the best of this genre. Langston Hughes also wrote protest pieces, as did almost every black writer at one time or another. Countee Cullen, not noted as a political activist, nevertheless addressed the theme of racism effectively in his poem, "Incident." The poem recounts an encounter on a train in Baltimore involving two eight-year-old children. Excited to be on the train ride, the black child saw the white child staring at him:

> Now I was eight and very small,
>   And he was no whit bigger,
> And so I smiled, but he poked out
>   His tongue and called me, "Nigger."

Of his eight-month stay in Baltimore that one incident was all that the child remembered.[14]

Among the visual artists Lawrence's historical series emphasized the racial struggle that dominated African American history, while Romare Bearden's early illustrative work often focused on racial politics. The struggle against lynching in the mid-1920s stimulated antilynching poetry as well as Walter White's carefully researched study of the subject, *Rope and Faggot*; in the early 1930s the Scottsboro incident stimulated considerable protest writing, as well as a 1934 anthology, *Negro*, which addressed race in an international context. Most of the literary efforts of the Harlem Renaissance avoided overt protest or propaganda, focusing instead on the psychological and social impact of race. Among the best of these studies were Nella Larsen's two novels, *Quicksand* in 1928 and, a year later, *Passing*; both explored characters of mixed racial heritage who struggled to define their racial identity in a world of prejudice and racism. Langston Hughes addressed similar themes in his poem "Cross" and his 1931 play, *Mulatto*, as did Jessie Fauset in her 1929 novel *Plum Bun*. That same year

Wallace Thurman made color discrimination within the urban black community the focus of his novel *The Blacker the Berry*.

Finally, the Harlem Renaissance incorporated all aspects of African American culture in its creative work. This ranged from the use of black music as an inspiration for poetry or black folklore as an inspiration for novels and short stories. Best known for this was Langston Hughes, who used the rhythms and styles of jazz and the blues in much of his early poetry. James Weldon Johnson, who published two collections of black spirituals in 1927 and 1928, and Sterling Brown, who used the blues and southern work songs in many of the poems in his 1932 book of poetry *Southern Road*, continued the practice that Hughes had initiated. Other writers exploited black religion as a literary source. Johnson made the black preacher and his sermons the basis for the poems in *God's Trombones*, while Hurston and Larsen used black religion and black preachers in their novels. Hurston's first novel, *Jonah's Gourd Vine* (1934), described the exploits of a southern black preacher, while in the last portion of *Quicksand* Larsen's heroine was ensnared by religion and a southern black preacher.

Through all of these themes Harlem Renaissance writers, musicians, and artists were determined to express the African American experience in all of its variety and complexity as realistically as possible. This commitment to realism ranged from the ghetto realism that created such controversy when writers exposed negative aspects of African American life, beautifully crafted and detailed portraits of black life in small towns such as in Hughes's novel, *Not Without Laughter*, or the witty and biting depiction of Harlem's black literati in Wallace Thurman's *Infants of the Spring*.

While these themes were shared across the various arts fields that made up the Harlem Renaissance, there was very little collaboration across the fields, and when collaboration existed, it was generally a one-way street. Poets and writers were most influenced by artists in other areas. The impact of black music on the work of Langston Hughes and James Weldon Johnson has been noted, but in a broader way music (including musical theater, jazz, blues, and the venues in which they are performed) is one of the elements that appears again and again in the literature and the visual arts of the Harlem Renaissance. Black writers were clearly aware of this arts genre, and they were consumers of the music. Black artists shared this concern. Black writers and artists frequented the clubs and joints and even the house rent parties where the musicians worked and played. To a lesser extent they were also aware of musical theater and theater. In contrast most black musicians seem to have expressed little concern or interest in the black literature of the period. As Cab Calloway noted in his autobiography, "Those of us in the music and entertainment business were vaguely aware that something exciting was happening, but we weren't directly involved … the two worlds, literature and entertainment, rarely crossed."[15]

Collaboration between black writers and artists was only marginally more common. Aaron Douglas was close friends with a number of Harlem Renaissance writers, participated actively in the production of *Fire!!*, and provided cover art and illustrations for a number of literary works, including those of Langston Hughes, Wallace Thurman, and James Weldon Johnson. In the mid-1930s artist Romare Bearden frequented the "306 House" where he met other artists as well as several Harlem Renaissance writers. Several years later Bearden and Jacob Lawrence each rented studio space in a building where Claude McKay lived; both young artists enjoyed the conversations with the older author, but there is no evidence that there was any collaboration. Years later Bearden would be involved in designing record album covers for jazz records. However, for the most part the practitioners of art, music, and literature operated separately. However, there is no indication that black literature deeply impacted the work of either artist, or that their art significantly impacted either music or literature.

* * *

The Harlem Renaissance appealed to and relied on a mixed audience—the African American middle class and white consumers of the arts. African American magazines such as the *Crisis* (the NAACP monthly journal) and *Opportunity* (the monthly publication of the Urban League) employed Harlem Renaissance writers on their editorial staff, published their poetry and short stories, and promoted African American literature through articles, reviews, and annual literary prizes. They also printed illustrations by black artists and used black artists in the layout design of their periodicals. Also, blacks attempted to produce their own literary and artistic venues. In addition to the short-lived *Fire!!*, Wallace Thurman spearheaded another single-issue literary magazine, *Harlem*, in 1927, while poet Countee Cullen edited a "Negro Poets" issue of the avant-garde poetry magazine *Palms* in 1926, and brought out an anthology of African American poetry, *Caroling Dusk*, in 1927.

As important as these literary outlets were, they were not sufficient to support a literary movement. Consequently the Harlem Renaissance relied heavily on white-owned enterprises for its creative works. Publishing houses, magazines, recording companies, theaters, and art galleries were primarily white owned, and financial support through grants, prizes, and awards generally involved white money. In fact, one of the major accomplishments of the Renaissance was to push open the door to mainstream periodicals, publishing houses, and funding sources. African American music also played to mixed audiences. Harlem's cabarets attracted both Harlem residents and white New Yorkers seeking out Harlem nightlife. The famous Cotton Club carried this to a bizarre extreme by providing black entertainment for exclusively white audiences. Ultimately, the more successful black musicians and entertainers moved their performances downtown.

The relationship of the Harlem Renaissance to white venues and white audiences created controversy. While most African American critics strongly supported the movement, others like Benjamin Brawley and even W. E. B. Du Bois were sharply critical and accused Renaissance writers of reinforcing negative African American stereotypes. Langston Hughes's assertion that black artists intended to express themselves freely, no matter what the black public or white public thought, accurately reflected the attitude of most writers and artists.

* * *

The end of the Harlem Renaissance is as difficult to define as its beginnings. It varies somewhat from one artistic field to another. In musical theater, the popularity of black musical reviews died out by the early 1930s, although there were occasional efforts, mostly unsuccessful, to revive the genre. However, black performers and musicians continued to work, although not so often in all-black shows. Black music continued into the World War II era, but the popularity of blues singers waned somewhat, and jazz changed as the big band style became popular. Literature also changed, and a new generation of black writers like Richard Wright and Ralph Ellison emerged with little interest or connection with the Harlem Renaissance. In art, a number of artists who had emerged in the 1930s continued to work, but again with no connection to a broader African American movement. Also, a number of Harlem Renaissance literary figures went silent, left Harlem, or died. Some, including Langston Hughes and Zora Neale Hurston, continued to write and publish into the 1940s and beyond, although there was no longer any sense that they were connected to a literary movement. And Harlem lost some of its magic following the 1935 race riot. In any case few, if any people were talking about a Harlem Renaissance by 1940.

NOTES

1. Carl Van Doren, "The Younger Generation of Negro Writers," *Opportunity* 2 (1924): 144–45. Van Doren's Civic Club Dinner address was reprinted in *Opportunity*.
2. *Survey Graphic, Harlem: Mecca of the New Negro* 6 (March 1925).
3. Alain Locke, ed., *The New Negro: An Interpretation* (New York: Atheneum, 1969).
4. See Terry Waldo, "Eubie Blake," in *Harlem Speaks: A Living History of the Harlem Renaissance*, ed. Cary D. Wintz (Naperville, IL: Sourcebooks, 2007), 151–65.
5. Langston Hughes, *The Big Sea* (New York: Hill and Wang, 1963), 223–24.
6. James Weldon Johnson, *Black Manhattan* (New York: Atheneum, 1968), 120–21.
7. Rudolph Fisher, "The City of Refuge," in *The New Negro*, 57–58. "The City of Refuge" was first published in *Atlantic Monthly*, February 1925.
8. Fisher, "The City of Refuge," 58–59.
9. Hughes, *Big Sea*, 81–82.
10. Johnson, *Black Manhattan*, 3–4.
11. Ibid., 146. Johnson also expresses this view of Harlem in "The Making of Harlem," *Survey Graphic* 6 (March 1925), 635–39.
12. Gilbert Osofsky, *Harlem: The Making of a Ghetto: Negro New York, 1890–1930* (New York: Harper & Row, 1963), 135.
13. Langston Hughes, "The Negro Artist and the Racial Mountain," *Nation*, June 16, 1926, 694.
14. Countee Cullen, "Incident," *My Soul's High Song: The Collected Writings of Countee Cullen*, ed. Gerald Early (New York: Anchor, 1990).
15. Cab Calloway and Bryant Rollins, *Of Minnie the Moocher and Me* (New York: Thomas Y. Crowell Company, 1976), 105.

READING 14

Reading the Harlem Renaissance into Public Policy

Lessons from the Past to the Present

Renata Harden, Christopher K. Jackson, and Berlethia J. Pitts

> Harlem. 1917. Music bursting from the seams, the wondrous sounds of Cab Calloway's "scat" singing, and the majestic melody of Duke Ellington and his Cotton Club orchestra. The cool crisp air is almost perfectly aligned to the tunes of the jazz that captivates the night air.
>
> Lights, camera, action—The "Queen of Happiness," Florence Mills takes center stage at the Alhambra Theater on Seventh Avenue for her performance in the musical Blackbirds while Anita Bush's, The Lafayette Players, the first African American acting company, prepares its 300 performers for the stage.
>
> At a small outdoor café, straddled alongside broad sidewalks and newly constructed homes, amidst the sounds of voices and the echoes of the city, sit four brightly colored chairs, each in its own lavish raiment. Here we see Countee Cullen, Langston Hughes, Zora Neale Hurston, and Claude McKay sharing a literary moment, a moment that would eventually develop into a profound cultural and artistic expression, a decade of prominent and expressive publications by African Americans, the Harlem Renaissance.

The Harlem Renaissance is a product of African American culture and history, as Gates and McKay describe it as "the irresistible impulse of blacks to create boldly expressive art of a high quality as a primary response to their social conditions, as an affirmation of their dignity and humanity in the face of poverty and racism."[1] This period represents the beauty, strength, and intelligence of an oppressed people.[2] The term "renaissance" is used by historians to characterize some moment when a culture, once dormant, has been reawakened. It is during this time that the world saw a plethora of publications by African American authors, including Countee Cullen's *Color*, whose work became the first African American book of prose to be published by a major American publishing house, as well as Jean Toomer's *Cane*, which is a book of fiction published by DoubleDay. These works follow the poetic and artistic approaches of Claude McKay, a Jamaican-born immigrant to the United States,

Renata Harden, Christopher K. Jackson, and Berlethia J. Pitts, "Reading the Harlem Renaissance into Public Policy: Lessons from the Past to the Present," *Afro-Americans in New York Life and History*, vol. 36, no. 2, pp. 7-30, 34-36. Copyright © 2012 by Afro-American Historical Association of the Niagara Frontier. Reprinted with permission. Provided by ProQuest LLC. All rights reserved.

who is believed to be the first major poet of the Harlem Renaissance. The ability of Claude McKay to become one of the most prominent figures of the Harlem Renaissance speaks to the systematic conditions of racism and discrimination that linked black people all over the world. French-speaking blacks were uniting themselves with the Negritude movement while the British West Indies saw an explosion of literary achievements, especially through the literary work of Derek Walcott.

Yet, there was something about Harlem, New York, that made the renaissance become one of the most acclaimed literary and artistic movements in the history of the United States. Harlem, per se, and its strategic location as the home of the National Association for the Advancement of Colored People (NAACP), Marcus Garvey's Universal Negro Improvement Association, W.E.B. Du Bois' *Crisis* and other prominent literary, cultural, and political magazines and newspapers, and jazz legends such as Bessie Smith, Cab Calloway and Duke Ellington, was a haven for black folks, or as the title of the March 1925 issue of *Survey Graphic* proclaimed, "Harlem: Mecca of the New Negro." The subtitle was designated by Alain Locke, whose later work, *The New Negro,* is said to be the text that actually launched the Harlem Renaissance. Although later criticized for some of his decisive editorial judgments as editor of *The New Negro,* Locke's work helped to propel the idea that a cultural awakening, a new spirit, was emerging among African Americans in Harlem. Locke viewed the Harlem Renaissance as a "belief in the efficacy of collective effort in race co-operation."[3]

The goal of this collective effort was to use art as a vehicle for knowledge, understanding, and change. In his pivotal work, *The New Negro: Voices of the Harlem Renaissance,* Locke makes the distinction between the "Old Negro" and the "New Negro." The "Old Negro" was marred with historical controversy and moral debate. The "Old Negro" was a "something ... to be kept down, or in his place. ..." The humanistic attributes of the "Old Negro" were not at all present. Nonetheless, the "New Negro" represents that of "self-reliance," and "self-respect." According to Locke, the writing of this period demonstrates a "rise from social disillusionment to race pride, from the sense of social debt to the responsibilities of social contribution, and offsetting the necessary working and commonsense acceptance of restricted conditions, the belief in ultimate esteem and recognition."[4] Harlem became the symbol for African Americans' coming of age.

These developments were taking place in the midst of a changing geographical climate in which African Americans from the south were migrating north. A large number of Blacks streamed into the northern cities in the first years of the new century, forced out by the poverty of southern agriculture and the mean brutality of southern racial bigotry. The Great Migration included masses of black folks who were tired of the segregated south, its ties and enforcement of Jim Crow laws, its broken promises after the Civil War and during Reconstruction, and its bitter living conditions that had helped to sustain and maintain a poor quality of life for them. Lynching of African Americans and the denial of basic human rights under the protection of the law made the south a very difficult place to live. So, upon hearing of the better conditions of the industrial north and its factories and industries that were willing to hire African Americans, especially due to the fact that World War I had begun and, thus, White Americans were fighting abroad, Black Southerners left the south and all its baggage and journeyed to a new beginning.

Although they were met with harsh realities and conditions of the North, including residential segregation, they found Harlem, a place that welcomed them with open arms. Black Southerners found quality homes in a cosmopolitan atmosphere that far exceeded their expectations. They were surrounded by the leading writers, artists, jazz musicians, and performers of their time. Drawn to Harlem, others joined in this mass exodus from all over the United States, including, Langston Hughes from Kansas and later Illinois, Gwendolyn Bennett from Texas, Arna Bontemps from Los Angeles, Wallace Thurman from Washington, D.C., and Helene Johnson and Dorothy West from New England. The center of attraction, Harlem became the pivotal point from which the renaissance occurred, or as James Weldon Johnson so eloquently stated regarding Harlem as "the Negro capital of the world."

What we gain from this cultural phenomenon is the ability to understand the plight and conditions of African Americans during this time. Not only do we ingest their attitude towards racism and discrimination in the United States, we also learn of their responses to discrimination and their proliferation of "Black is Beautiful." The literature, in particular, is less attached to the earlier forms of dialectal writing and more attuned to the thoughts, emotions, aspirations, and pathos of African Americans. Poets and writers sought a freer, looser style of verse and language that reflected African American life in the 1920s.

Hence, from the literature of the Harlem Renaissance emerged themes of hope and oppression, the urban atmosphere, as well as racial pride and solidarity, and social and economic self-sufficiency. There can be no doubt that the emergence of Negro writers in the postwar period stemmed, in part, from the fact that they were inclined to exploit the opportunity to write about themselves. The growth of the Harlem Renaissance was fostered by two factors: (1) the migration that began during the war inspired blacks to develop a responsibility and a self-confidence that they had not previously known—they became defiant, bitter, and impatient; and (2) the riots that followed World War I. Blacks fought with audacity. They had achieved a level of articulation that made it possible for them to transfer their feelings into a variety of literary forms—they possessed enough restraint and objectivity to use their materials artistically. The writers of the Harlem Renaissance were not so much as revolting against the system as they were protesting the unjust operation of the system. The greatness of blacks during this period highlights a critical but intellectual juncture in American culture. At the height of the Great Depression in the 1930s, Blacks produced some of the most timeless works that spoke to their issues and provided an outlook for future generations.

Therefore, this article focuses on key themes that dominated this time period, hope and oppression, urban neighborhood-ghetto, embracing blackness, and social and political equality. More importantly, this writing will highlight the ways in which the literature of the Harlem Renaissance speaks to the social problems in the African American community today. The authors contend that there is a clear relationship between the cultural landscape and experiences of African Americans in the 1920s to those of today. In many regards, the problems that African Americans faced in their community in the 1920s are much of the same ones facing the community today. In other ways, the literature of the Harlem Renaissance speaks to the creation of problems that would be confined to later generations. As such, the authors will attempt to connect and show the severity of the issues as they particularly affect the African American community.

The specific works that have been selected for this article range from both fiction and non-fiction essays and prose. This conscious decision is due in part to highlight the diverse literature that was produced during the Harlem Renaissance. Moreover, the selection of these artifacts also reflects the teaching of these different works in an undergraduate classroom setting. It is important to draw a connection to the works and signify their relevance in today's society. As such, specific themes of the Harlem Renaissance will be examined in their original context first. After a clear and critical analysis is offered, the authors will draw a direct correlation to the social problems that still plague the African American community in today's society.

Furthermore, as the authors are teachers of English and African American Literature, they subscribe to the belief that the literature of the Harlem Renaissance rivals and is just as important as other literary periods. As such, their teaching of the material in the academic classroom is sometimes challenging, and oftentimes tumultuous, due to the Eurocentric worldview and perspectives that have come to frame the thinking processes of many African American students. Thus, this article will also focus on the lessons the authors have learned from teaching the works in the academic classroom and how those lessons can be applied to different scenarios.

HOPE AND OPPRESSION

At this time in American history, black people found themselves on the outskirts of U.S. society. It is this marginality that ultimately influences the writing of this time, and thus, creates an environment for the free expression of those ideals. Being on the periphery of American society gave the writers a keen insight into the world from which they had been forbidden. Take, for example, Claude McKay's lines in "The White House"[5]:

> *Your door is shut against my tightened face,*
> *And I am sharp as steel with discontent;*
> *But I possess the courage and the grace*
> *To bear my anger proudly and unbent.*

In these few lines, McKay's anger is only masked by his valor and poise, as his unhappiness from being barred from the White House has caused him to remain firm in his demeanor. He later exclaims in the poem:

> *Oh, I must keep my heart inviolate*

Against the potent poison of your hate.

McKay, known for his ability to use the Shakespearean sonnet to write passionately about Black injustice, remains steadfast in spite of the hatred that abounds.

McKay's poem echoes the sentiments of Zora Neale Hurston, one of the most prominent female writers of the time. Born in Eatonville, Florida, and later educated at Barnard College, her novels, including *Their Eyes Were Watching God, Dust Tracks on a Road, Mules and Men,* among other works, demonstrate her ability to explore and capture Black cultural reality. She describes her feelings of marginality in "How It Feels to Be Colored Me." She writes:

"I feel most colored when I am thrown against a sharp white background. For instance at Barnard. 'Besides the water of the Hudson' I feel my race. Among the thousand white persons, I am a dark rock surged upon, and overswept, but through it all, I remain myself. When covered by the waters, I am; and the ebb but reveals me again.[6]

In this passage, Hurston highlights the ways in which her color, her blackness, seems to stand out most when in an all-white environment. It is in this environment that she is submerged in whiteness, but she does not allow her surroundings to destroy her black identity.

Marita Bonner's work exhibits the interconnections of race, class, and gender. Her phenomenal essay, "On Being Young—a Woman—and Colored" made a powerful debut in the *Crisis*. It demonstrates the ways in which certain prejudices can marginalize an individual's way of life. She writes, "Why do they see a colored woman only as a gross collection of desires, all uncontrolled, reaching out for their Apollos and the Quasimodos with avid discrimination."[7] It is this sort of discrimination and the impending marginality and limitations that it causes that Bonner tackles throughout this pivotal essay.

Bonner's work highlights the gendered aspect of racial discrimination. But, it is Langston Hughes' "I, Too"[8] that establishes the connection between black racial identity and American nationality. Hughes, one of the premier writers of the time, eloquently describes the ways in which African Americans have a marginal position in American society, but will, one day, be included in the fabric of American national identity. He writes:

I, too, sing America
I am the darker brother.
They send me to eat in the kitchen
When company comes.
But I laugh,
And eat well,
And grow strong.
Tomorrow,
I'll be at the table

When company comes.
Nobody 'll dare Say to me,
"Eat in the kitchen,"
Then.
Besides,
They 'll see how beautiful I am
And be ashamed—

I, too, am America.

Hughes' poem demonstrates that hope can be silently manifested in spite of overt oppression.

From the discussion thus far, it is clear that the writers of the Harlem Renaissance were able to carefully observe their status in American society. Yet, occupying a peripheral position did not deter them or prevent them from recognizing the benefits of full integration into the larger society. In fact, their marginal position gave them keen insight into the problems afflicting the Negro race, let alone America in general. And they approached these problems with hope and optimism, despite their circumstances, as in Angelina Weld Grimke's poem, "The Black Finger"[9]:

I have just seen a beautiful thing
Slim and still,
Against a gold, gold sky,
A straight cypress,
Sensitive
Exquisite,
A black finger
Pointing upwards.
Why, beautiful, still finger are you black?
And why are you pointing upwards?

It is no wonder, then, that the writings came to define an era and the plight of black Americans. It is from the visions articulated through their writings that we are able to paint a clear portrait of black life in the 1920s.

URBAN NEIGHBORHOOD-GHETTO

The etymological definition of the word "ghetto" traces back to Rome in the early 15th century as an obligatory place for Jews. Though, today the term and area is known as a form of segregation for an ethnic minority.[10] The marginal position that African Americans occupied was influenced by both their class standing and racial discrimination, which directly affected their overall livelihood. Although Harlem, in particular, offered a chance for African Americans to live in a better quality of homes and neighborhoods than those found in the South, it still was consumed by the temptations of the ghetto—drugs, gambling, prostitution, just a name a few. The writers of the Harlem Renaissance used these distractions as muses for writing to describe their environment. Consider the first stanza of Claude McKay's "Harlem Shadows"[11]:

> I hear the halting footsteps of a lass
> In Negro Harlem when the night lets fall
> Its veil. I see the shapes of girls who pass
> To bend and barter at desire's call.
> Ah, little dark girls who in slippered feet
> Go prowling through the night from street to street!

In this stanza, McKay describes the women he observes as prostitutes who sell themselves at night. They tirelessly go throughout the neighborhood to offer their services to anyone who will purchase them. Later, in the last stanza, McKay has pity for these women, writing:

> Ah, stern harsh world, that in the wretched way
> Of poverty, dishonor and disgrace,
> Has pushed the timid little feet of clay,
> The sacred brown feet of my fallen race!
> Ah, heart of me, the weary, weary feet
> In Harlem wandering from street to street.

Moreover, he notes that the "harsh world" has created the situation for this, causing these women to have no other options but to exhaustively sell themselves for profit, and thereby, disgrace themselves.

This situation calls attention to the unequal economic status that African American women occupied at the time. In fact, a lot of black women held domestic occupational status, i.e., maids, housekeepers, nannies, etc. Being a servant for rich white people was a very common profession for many African Americans. Hughes describes the daily routine of a servant in "Negro Servant". He begins:

> All day subdued, polite,
> Kind, thoughtful to the faces that are white.

He later continues in the poem:

> At six o'clock, or seven, or eight,
> You 're through.
> You've worked all day.
> Dark Harlem waits for you.
> The bus, the sub

> *Pay-nights a taxi*
> *Through the park*

He ends with:

> *O, sweet relief from faces that are white!*

The urban images given above are quite a stretch from the rural settings of a lot of American poetry. Instead of highlighting pastoral, quite rural towns of the South, they highlighted city life, especially the vibrant streets of Harlem. Nella Larsen's widely acclaimed novel *Quicksand* describes the flamboyant life of black Harlem. The protagonist of the work, Helga Crane, makes Harlem her home. Larsen describes the magic of Harlem and its affect on Helga Crane: "Her existence was bounded by Central Park, Fifth Avenue, St. Nicholas Park, and One Hundred and Forty-fifth street. Not all a narrow life, as Negroes live it, as Helga Crane knew it. Everything was there, vice and goodness, sadness and gayety, ignorance and wisdom, ugliness and beauty, poverty and richness."[13]

One of the defining aspects of the urban-neighborhood ghetto is that it is predominately black. Although whites may patron some local businesses or entertainment arenas found within the black neighborhood, seldom do they live within the black community. Thus, the black community, plagued by its educational ailments, poor housing establishments, unemployment, crime, and poverty, is disproportionally and negatively affected by these circumstances, which ultimately affects their way of life. Rudolph Fisher's short story, "The City of Refuge" speaks to the black urban life found within Harlem. The main character is a southerner, King Solomon Gillis, who is fascinated by Harlem. Before leaving North Carolina for Harlem, New York, Gillis believes that "in Harlem, black was white. You had rights that could not be denied you; you had privileges, protected by law. And you had money. Everybody in Harlem had money. It was the land of plenty."[14] Yet, the reality of Harlem, and other predominately black neighborhood, is that they are strategically separated from predominately white neighborhoods, a kind of geographical racial division. Plus, they are plagued by certain urban ailments confined to city life, and those confined to being black. Racial segregation abound, the city suffered from the racial division experienced in the rest of the country.

EMBRACING BLACKNESS

Although the writers of the Harlem Renaissance tackled themes of hope and oppression as well as the urban environment, they also managed to embrace their black identity despite the overwhelming burdens of race in American society. The issue of race has and will continue to be the most highly debated and contested sociological variable that America has had to deal with. In 1903, W.E.B. Du Bois in his pivotal work, *The Souls of Black Folk,* asserted that, "The problem with the twentieth century is the problem of the colorline ..."[13] This statement not only proved to be true for the 20th century, it is a still a reoccurring problem within the 21st century as well. However, although this problem has been prevalent ever since the slaves first arrived in Virginia in 1619, during the Harlem Renaissance, there was a sense of racial solidarity and cooperation that existed that is not easily noticed in today's time.

The theme of one embracing their blackness can be seen in Langston Hughes poem "Negro," in which he affirms his blackness and sense of humanity by establishing his cultural roots to Africa. Throughout the poem, Hughes juxtaposes the great contributions the Negro has made to the world with that of brutality that he has also endured. Though, there is a strong connection and homage paid to Africa. This greatness is also evident in "Black Majesty[16]" by Countee Cullen:

> *These men were kings, albeit they were black,*
> *Christophe and Dessalines and L 'Ouverture;*
> *Their majesty has made me turn my back*
> *Upon a plaint I once shaped to endure.*

Davis contends that Cullen's poetry viewed the Negro as an alien in America who has been taken out of his beautiful homeland of Africa to endure "insult, humiliation, and injustice."[17] As the sonnet continues Cullen details the image of the Negro in America. Yet, he juxtaposes this image with that of the kings in which the Negro was once King and can be again.

> *Dark gutter-snipe, black sprawler-in-the-mud,*
> *A thing men did may do again.*
> *What answer filters through your sluggish blood*
> *To these dark ghosts who knew so bright a reign?*
> *"Lo, I am dark, but comely, " Sheba sings*
> *"And we were black, " three shades reply, "but kings. "*

These poems highlight the importance of one embracing their blackness and are used in the classroom setting to demonstrate to students that they come from greatness. They share the same sentiments of Marcus Garvey and his mission of the Universal Negro Improvement Association (UNIA) and his widespread "Back to Africa" campaign. Garvey not only embraced his blackness, he also embraced Africa as a whole. He describes the purpose of the UNIA association "to have established in Africa that brotherly co-operation which will make the interests of the African native and the American and West Indian Negro one and the same, ... we shall enter into a common partnership to build up Africa in the interests of our race."[18]

Gwendolyn Bennett's poem, "To a Dark Girl,"[19] promotes the beauty and distinctive features of being a Black girl. This poem is written like a personal letter to all Black girls, who in spite of whatever hardships, have a distinctive beauty in their brownness. The beauty and strength of a Black girl can be seen in the opening lines.

> *I love you for your brownness,*
> *And the rounded darkness of your breast,*
> *I love you for the breaking sadness in your voice*
> *And shadows where your wayward eyelids rest.*

The words "breaking sadness" and "wayward eyelids" are allusions to the struggles that Black girls have to endure. Bennett continues with this love letter by asserting that Black girls are like "forgotten queens," which is present in the grace of their walk. This poem is a testament for Black girls to embrace their heritage of

> *Something of old forgotten queens*
> *Lurks in the lithe abandon of your walk*
> *And something of the shackled slave*
> *Sob in the rhythm of your talk*
>
> *Oh, little brown girl, born for sorrow's mate,*
> *Keep all you have of queenliness,*
> *Forgetting that you once were slave,*
> *And let your full lips laugh at Fate!*

These ending lines represent a sign of transcendence from a Black girl's struggle to her "queenliness." Hence, her beauty is in her walk, talk, and full lips. In this poem, Bennett urges Black girls to embrace their distinctive features as a testament to their heritage.

SOCIAL AND POLITICAL EQUALITY

Another dominant theme of the Harlem Renaissance included social and political equality. Claude McKay tackled the issue of social and political equality in his poetry. Asserting a strong anger and revolution in the poem "If We Must Die," or the apparent disdain that America treats the Negro in "America." McKay's poetry calls direct attention to the societal ills that have and continue to plague the black community. Charles Johnson argues that McKay's poem "If We Must Die," is "one of stoical defiance which held behind it a spirit magnificent and glowing."[20] After beginning the poem with the symbol that Blacks were seen as "hogs" and "dogs," McKay outlines the greatness and nobility of the Negro.

> *If we must die, O let us nobly die,*
> *So that our precious blood may not be shed*
> *In vain; then even the monsters we defy*
> *Shall be constrained to honor us though dead!*

These lines allude to the use of Christian imagery and Christ's crucifixion. The "O" is like a cry out to Christ in a time of suffering and strength, which is reflective of Negro spirituals.

Religion was seen as a symbol of justice in a world that lacked it.[21] Langston Hughes does well to utilize these images to highlight the problem of lynching, which was a significant social problem at the time. He writes in the first stanza of "Christ in Alabama"[22]:

> *Christ is a nigger,*
> *Beaten and black:*
> *Oh, bare your back!*

Hughes continues, with the last stanza:

> *Most holy bastard*
> *Of the bleeding mouth,*
> *Nigger Christ*
> *On the cross*
> *Of the south.*

Clearly, Hughes is drawing a connection between the lynching of African Americans and the crucifixion of Christ. In *Returning Soldiers*[23], Du Bois outlined problems Blacks faced in America after returning from World War 1. Problems such as lynching, disfranchisement, ignorance, etc. In this essay, Du Bois contends:

> *We return.*
> *We return from fighting.*
> *We return fighting.*

World War I, in fact, highlighted certain issues for African Americans, especially the hypocrisy of fighting in a war abroad when freedom was unattainable at home. Although McKay, Hughes, and Du Bois take a militant, and in some ways, graphic approach to the problems Blacks faced, their work called attention to the need for change and the urgency for it.

It is important to note that Du Bois philosophy of "double-consciousness" overshadows some of the major works of this period. Du Bois contends that double-consciousness:

> *... is a peculiar sensation ... this sense of always looking at one self through the eyes of others, of measuring one's soul by the tape of a world that looks on in amused contempt and pity. One ever feels his two-ness,—an American a Negro; two souls two thoughts, two unreconciled strivings; two warring ideals in one dark body, whose dogged strength alone keeps it from being torn asunder.*[24]

The problem of being Black and American are highlighted in the poems of Hughes, Cullen and many others. In "America"[25] Hughes compares the struggles of Blacks and Jews in this country. The opening lines present the problem of being Black or Jewish in America and to be seen as an outcast.

> *Little dark baby,*
> *Little Jew baby,*
> *Little outcast,*

Cullen's "Incident"[26] written like a nursery rhyme, shows how a child is impacted by racism when he was in Baltimore and called a "nigger" by a young White boy on the train.

> *Now I was eight and very small,*
> *And he was no whit bigger,*
> *And so I smiled, but he poked out*
> *His tongue, and call me, "Nigger."*

The prosody in this poem by Cullen has a traditional pattern, simple language, and a regular beat; but it also addresses the problem of prejudice and racism from a child's perspective. These poems, among many others during this period, deal with the duality of being an American and being Black.

Although there are many more writers that spoke out against the social and political conditions that they faced, what is of critical importance here is that their art and/or craft in letters was used as a vehicle to call attention to these problems. Baraka believes that the writing during this period was revolutionary and reflects the "struggle to speak out against imperialism."[27]

FROM THE PAST TO THE PRESENT

The themes presented above speak volumes to the lives of African Americans today. Although a challenging economic time, African Americans have seen measurable progress, one that includes the election of the first African American president, President Barack Hussein Obama. His election alone is a testament to the hope and oppression that characterized the Harlem Renaissance. Obama was able to overcome vast challenges, including a single-parent household and an absentee father, coupled with the racial discrimination that continues to plague American society, to attain educational achievements and eventually the status of president of the United States. The election of this president symbolizes the promises of the nation and the ability to overcome obstacles to achieve a dream. This is reminiscent of Claude McKay's message in "America"[28]:

> *Although she feeds me bread of bitterness*
> *And sinks into my throat her tiger's tooth,*
> *Stealing my breath of life, I will confess*
> *I love this cultured hell that tests my youth! ... .*

The stanza above shows an undeniable love and affection for America, despite the challenges she presents to him. This is a common tendency among African Americans: to overcome adversity with dignity, grace, and a little bit of love, as exhibited during the Civil Rights Movement. Still, the nation has not come so far as to distance itself from racism, as the issue of being black is evident with the recent reports regarding the legitimacy of President Obama's birth in Hawaii, and the constant and degrading stereotypes that follow Black people in media.

Economically, African Americans have grown substantially in terms of monetary advancement, which has allowed many of them to move into historically white suburbs. Yet, the policy implication for this is drastic, as the political clout of African American middle class comes in question. The move from the city to the suburbs can affect the census results and weaken the suburban black vote. The President of the National Urban League, Marc Morial says "African-Americans must be vigilant against subtle discrimination when states redraw their political maps."[29] Hence, it is important that African Americans are counted, regardless of their location. An under count could possibly result in policy implications that hinder the progress of African Americans. It has already been determined that there was an under count in the 2000 census by 2.8 percent. According to the Associated Press, "New York Mayor Michael Bloomberg and Detroit Mayor Dave Bing already have said they will contest the 2010 counts for their cities. Those challenges are mostly aimed at getting a higher population count that would bring a larger share of federal dollars to their cities for schools, roads and health care."[30] Thus, although some blacks have migrated to suburbs, they have not escaped the challenges that come with being black in America.

Those blacks that are confined to the city still face massive unemployment and are usually relegated to low-paying jobs, representative of the urban neighborhood-ghetto written about during the Harlem Renaissance. At 15.3 percent, the unemployment rate for African Americans is much higher than for other groups. As it was then, and still today, many African Americans live in densely populated areas comprised with inadequate schools. This often culminates into a disastrous spiral of crime and a cycle of imprisonment, which impedes political and economic participation.

The writers of the Harlem Renaissance expressed their ideas in a segregated society. Integration had not occurred yet, and so the overt racism of the 1920s is masked in today's society in other ways. Yet, the writers were able to give an accurate portrayal of life during this time, in which class issues had just begun to affect the way of life for many African Americans, especially those that migrated from the south to the north. Now we can see the manifestations of class issues in the black community, especially in terms of the migration from the city to the suburb and the mass reverse exodus from the north to the south. The issue of class was clearly articulated in the writings of E. Franklin Frazier. His writings reflect that of a man who spoke out about "America's racial injustice, the Negro's reluctance to measure up to national standards ... and the false ideals of Black middle class."[31] In his work *La Bourgeoisie Noire,* Frazier argues that the Negro is not a homogeneous group. The issue of class-consciousness is examined and explained to dispel the notion that all Blacks share the same economic interests. Some from the Black middle class have bought into the capitalistic system that is not concerned about culture but of "work and wealth."

Differences in class status ultimately affect the ways in which some blacks experience racial discrimination. Thus, the racial solidarity and cooperation that existed during the Harlem Renaissance has been altered in this new generation, as many blacks are guided by their own economic interests. And since many are now in white neighborhoods, their class interests usually aligns with their white neighbors. Consequently, even the "Black is beautiful" motto has been challenged, seeing that with racial integration came new standards of beauty, life, and education. [...].

CONCLUSION

The writers of the Harlem Renaissance were able to carefully articulate and portray the life of African Americans during the 1920s. They highlighted the issues and concerns that were prevalent in their life. It is from their works that we learned how they dealt with massive oppression and discrimination as well as poverty and racism. Moreover, their work also called attention to the problems that would eventually affect later generations. It is also through their work and their articulation of their trials that we, as educators, have "instructions" as to how we can, and must, address the cyclical issues that plague our communities: those past, those present and those to come.

ENDNOTES

1. Henry Louis Gates and Nellie Y. McKay, eds. *The Norton Anthology of African American Literature* (New York: Norton, 2004), 953.
2. Imara A. Baraka, *Daggers and Javelins Essays, 1974–1979* (New York: William Morrow and Co., 1984).
3. Alaine Locke., ed., *The New Negro: Voices of the Harlem Renaissance* (New York: Antheneum, 1925/1992), 11.
4. Locke, *The New Negro*, 11.
5. Claude McKay, "The White House," in *The Norton Anthology of African American Literature*, eds. Henry Louis Gates and Nellie Y. McKay (New York: Norton, 2004), 1009.
6. Zora Neale Hurston, "How It Feels to be Colored Me," in *The Norton Anthology of African American Literature*, eds Henry Louis Gates and Nellie Y. McKay (New York: Norton, 2004), 1031.
7. Marita Bonner, "On Being Young—a Woman—and Colored," in *The Norton Anthology of African American Literature*, eds, Henry Louis Gates and Nellie Y. McKay (New York: Norton, 2004), 1246.
8. Langston Hughes, "I, Too," in *The Norton Anthology of African American Literature*, eds. Henry Louis Gates and Nellie Y. McKay (New York: Norton, 2004), 1295.
9. Angelina Weld Grimke, "The Black Finger," in *The Norton Anthology of African American Literature*, eds. Henry Louis Gates and Nellie Y. McKay (New York: Norton, 2004), 969.
10. Sandra Debenedetti-Stow, "The Etymology of 'Ghetto': New Evidence from Rome," in *Jewish History* 6, no. 1–2 (1992): 79–85.
11. Claude McKay, "Harlem Shadows," in *The Norton Anthology of African American Literature*, eds. Henry Louis Gates and Nellie Y. McKay (New York: Norton, 2004), 1006.
12. Langston Hughes, "Negro Servant," in *The Norton Anthology of African American Literature*, eds. Henry Louis Gates and Nellie Y. McKay (New York: Norton, 2004), 1301.

13 Nella Larsen, "Quicksand," in *The Norton Anthology of African American Literature,* eds. Henry Louis Gates and Nellie Y. McKay (New York: Norton, 2004), 1113.
14 Rudolph Fisher, "The City of Refuge," in *The Norton Anthology of African American Literature,* eds. Henry Louis Gates and Nellie Y McKay (New York: Norton, 2004), 1225.
15 W. E. B. Du Bois, *The Souls of Black Folks* (New York: Signet, 1903), 17.
16 Chris Berg, "Black Majesty," Poem of the Moment Blog, March 23, 2006, accessed May 26, 2011, http://poeminstant.blogspot.eom/2006/03/countee-cullen.html.
17 Arthur P. Davis, "The Alien-and-Exile Theme in Countee Cullen's Racial Poems," *Phylon* 14, no. 14(1953): 390.
18 Marcus Garvey, "Africa for the Africans," in *The Norton Anthology of African American Literature,* eds. Henry Louis Gates and Nellie Y. McKay (New York: Norton, 2004), 998
19 Gwendolyn Brooks, "To a Dark Girl," in *The Norton Anthology of African American Literature,* eds. Henry Louis Gates and Nellie Y. McKay (New York: Norton, 2004), 1268.
20 David Lewis, ed., *The Portable Harlem Renaissance Reader* (New York: Penguin, 1995), 209.
21 Lawrence W. Levine, *Black Culture and Black Consciousness: Afro-American Folk Thought from Slavery to Freedom,* 30th Anniversary Edition (New York. Oxford University Press, 2007.
22 Langston Hughes, "Christ in Alabama," in *The Norton Anthology of African American Literature,* eds. Henry Louis Gates and Nellie Y. McKay (New York Norton, 2004), 1301.
23 W. E. B. Du Bois, "Returning Soldiers," *The Crisis,* XVIII (1919): 13.
24 Du Bois, *Souls,* 11.
25 Langston Hughes, "America," Vintage Hughes, accessed May 26, 2011, http://www.randomhouse.com/highschool/catalog/display.pperl?isbn=9781400034024&view=printexcerpt.
26 Countee Cullen, "Incident," in *The Norton Anthology of African American Literature,* eds. Henry Louis Gates and Nellie Y. McKay (New York: Norton, 2004), 1342.
27 *Baraka, Daggers and Javelins,* 144.
28 Claude McKay, "America," in *The Norton Anthology of African American Literature,* eds. Henry Louis Gates and Nellie Y. McKay (New York: Norton, 2004), 1008.
29 "New State of Black America report expresses concern about black clout in once white suburbs," Nola.com, March 31, 2011, accessed on May 25, 2011, http://www.nola.com/news/index.ssf2011/03/new state of black america rep.html.
30 Ibid.
31 Davis, *The Alien,* 390–400.

PART V

The Civil Rights Movement, 1955–1970

READING 15

The Origins and Causes of the Civil Rights Movement

David Levering Lewis

If it is venturesome to suppose that anything analytically new may be offered as to the origins and causes of the Civil Rights Movement of the 1960s, it is equally true that the demography of this phenomenon is fundamental to its deepest comprehension. In this case, political demographics may truly be said to be racial destiny. In the two decades immediately following the outbreak of World War Two, almost three times as many Afro-Americans departed the South as had left during the Great Migration of the century's second decade—with 1,599,000 moving mostly North during the period 1940–1950, and 1,473,000 during the next ten years. The decade of the Sixties saw continued high migration, with some 1,380,000 more southern Afro-Americans outmigrating.

The political implications of this huge population shift were apparent to astute political observers as early as the 1928 presidential election, when the normally "solid" South divided its support between Herbert Hoover and Alfred E. Smith. For some Democrats, winning Afro-American voters in the urban North and East was seen as vital to garnering sufficient electoral votes to upset Hoover. Smith's campaign manager, the resourceful Mrs. Belle Moskovitz, persuaded him to offer the young assistant executive secretary of the National Association for the Advancement of Colored People (NAACP), Walter White, direction of the Smith-for-President Colored League. White and the NAACP leadership were assured that the Democratic standard bearer would adopt, publicly, a rhetoric of racial tolerance and, privately, a policy of seeking the counsel of and making federal appointments from the ranks of the civil rights establishment. Ultimately, white southern pressures forced Smith to renege. Walter White regretfully declined.[1] Nevertheless, about 20 percent of the Afro-American electorate voted for the Democrats, eight percent more than in previous elections.

Robert L. Vann, publisher of the Pittsburgh *Courier,* predicted that millions of his people would turn "the pictures of Abraham Lincoln to the wall" in the 1932 presidential election. With the unique exception, however, of Democratic Harlem, an even greater percentage voted for Hoover than before. What Walter White called the Afro-American's "chronic Republicanism" seemed fully reconfirmed with the rejection of Franklin D. Roosevelt. In fact, this was the last act in a drama of hidden attitudinal and political developments. The

David Levering Lewis, "The Origins and Causes of the Civil Rights Movement," *The Civil Rights Movement in America,* ed. Charles W. Eagles, pp. 3-17, 157-159. Copyright © 2012 by University Press of Mississippi. Reprinted with permission.

racial realignment was to come in the congressional elections two years later, when FDR's party won a majority of Afro-American voters for the first time in history. Howard University political philosopher Kelly Miller's pronouncement that the "Negro is no longer the wheel-horse of the Republican Party" fulfilled Robert Vann's prediction.

By 1936, the strategy pursued under Hoover to turn the southern GOP "lily white" was as dead as Prohibition—not to return until the Eisenhower Fifties. Alfred M. Landon wrapped himself in the mantle of Lincoln and Frederick Douglass, and Republicans inserted a fine-sounding civil rights plank in the national platform that year. Big city Democratic machines—Tammany in New York, Kelly-Nash in Chicago, Dickmann in St. Louis, Pendergast in Kansas City—lavished patronage on the black community. As Nancy Weiss shows, the Party effectively reminded Afro-Americans how well they had fared under FDR, after the misery caused by Hoover. "Let Jesus lead you, and Roosevelt feed you!" one popular slogan exhorted.[2]

Pat Watters and Reese Cleghorn observed of the years after 1934, "It was in this period that Negro votes and public policy at the presidential level became, in significant degree, cause and effect."[3] Northward migration reinforced the labor-urban-based wing of the Democratic Party, the wing in sympathy with the broader economic and social objectives of the New Deal. Southern Democrats in senior congressional positions not only meant disenfranchisement and segregation for Afro-Americans, but legislative obstructionism in the service of economic conservatism and regional parochialism. These were the Party satraps whom FDR finally publicly denounced as "feudal oligarchs" (Ellison Smith of South Carolina, Walter George of Georgia, Millard Tydings of Maryland, Martin Dies of Texas, Theodore Bilbo of Mississippi) and appealed directly but altogether unsuccessfully to their constituents to unseat some of them in the 1938 congressional elections. In matters of maximum importance to it, the South remained well in control of partisan and even national politics, but the emergence of countervailing forces within the Democratic Party was unmistakable.

As one of the key elements in this new coalition of power, Afro-Americans did, in fact, increase their advantages during the so-called Second New Deal (1936–1940). The new, more responsive Attorney General created the civil rights section in the Justice Department; the Department of Interior imposed racial quotas on WPA contractors; the Civilian Conservation Corps augmented Afro-American enrollment from 6 to 11 percent; other alphabet agencies recruited some 100 of the best and brightest Afro-American university graduates as midlevel bureaucrats (Ralph Bunche, William Hastie, Rayford Logan, et al.); finally, somewhat assuaging Afro-American anguish about his waffling over poll tax repeal and public silence about federal antilynching legislation, FDR delivered at Howard University his symbolic "no forgotten men and no forgotten races" speech. In 1940, the Democratic platform addressed itself directly for the first time to equal protection under law and due process rights for Afro-Americans.

By then, 48 percent of the Afro-American population was urban; and, although only about 23 percent of it resided outside the South, its concentration in key northern cities was imposing—13 percent of Philadelphia's total population; 13.5 percent of Detroit's; 13 percent of Indianapolis's; 8.3 percent of Chicago's (for a total of nearly 300,000); and 6.4 percent of New York's (477,000, a treble increase over the 1920 census). *Time* magazine had noted four years previously, if erroneously, "In no national election since 1860 have politicians been so Negro-minded as in 1936."[4] More significantly, in 1941, Ralph Bunche's *Journal of Negro Education* article, "A Critical Analysis of the Tactical Programs of Minority Groups," gave preliminary formulation to the crucial "balance of power" concept, to which NAACP publicist Henry Lee Moon devoted booklength treatment seven years later, and by which more than a generation of Afro-American policymakers and politicians have since been guided (sometimes overambitiously).[5]

Although isolation of any single election factor risks presenting a false picture, the reality that Afro-American votes were now potentially determinative in 16 non-South states with 278 electoral votes escaped no serious political strategist.[6] Thus, in the 1944 FDR-Dewey contest, Thomas E. Dewey would unquestionably have won if his percentage of Afro-American votes had been equivalent to Hoover's in 1932. Thus, once again, as at its historic 1936 national convention, the Democratic Party's presidential decisionmakers successfully calculated the risks of offending the South with Hubert Humphrey's strong 1948 civil rights plank. Four southern states went Dixiecrat, while Harry S. Truman narrowly defeated Dewey because, as historians August Meier and Elliott Rudwick state, 1948 was "the first election since Reconstruction in which the Negro's status was a major issue and in which his political power was a critical factor in the outcome."[7] Nevertheless, massive Afro-American support for Adlai Stevenson was irrelevant to the outcome four years later—a perfect object lesson in the limitations of the balance of power paradigm. Under Dwight D. Eisenhower, the Hoover strategy of winning the lily white South was again regnant. This devastating limitation aside—and it is the one by which Afro-Americans are currently bedeviled—"there had been," as Watters and Cleghorn affirm, "a revolution in the power to obtain results."[8]

A reductionist interpretation of postwar liberalism both distorts and disserves the considerable reserve of moral and constitutional principles by which that liberalism was powered. Fascism's doctrinal depravity, the solidarism of the war effort, and the trauma of the Holocaust deeply affected the collective American mind. There were not a few white southerners, and probably a majority of white northerners, who would have wished to say to the first sit-in students, as did the woman in the Greensboro Woolworth's, "you should have done this ten years ago."[9] George Fredrickson's *White Supremacy* has masterfully shown the potential for political and social inclusion of racial minorities that a constitutional commitment to egalitarian democracy can sustain and mobilize, even in the face of its longstanding nullification by formal and informal arrangements and compromises.[10] The official creeds of societies matter a great deal.

That said, it would be equally imperceptive to downplay the high degree of correspondence between the Afro-American's urbanization and outmigration from the South and the postwar mentality of racial meliorism. By 1950, the "power to obtain results" of

Afro-Americans was running dangerously far ahead of the South's intellectual and institutional power to react constructively. Simultaneously, the racial attitudes in much of the rest of the nation were being transformed by that same potential power. Even the most casual reference to Tocqueville or Crane Brinton must have indicated a situation in which rising expectations and very slow social change presented the classic formula for upheaval, if not revolution—those flashpoint conjunctions which Ted Robert Gurr's work usefully assembles for our retrospective examination.[11] Was it not significant in this regard that the Carnegie Foundation, which had financed the massive study of another evolving racial crisis (that arising from unrest among South Africa's Afrikaner poor), produced, through Gunnar Myrdal and his regiment of social scientists, the ultimate liberal conceptualization of and prescription for the American dilemma?[12]

The impact of *An American Dilemma* was so potent that it controlled racial thought and policy for at least a decade. For all its impressive sociological panoply and perdurable insights, the Myrdalian analysis was imbedded in Hegelian idealism. Right ideas would gradually transform wrong institutions; the American Creed would ultimately reify itself because the compounding tensions between high ideals and ignoble realities would compel white Americans to reexamine the racial status quo. "The moral dilemma of the American [is] the conflict between his moral valuations on various levels of consciousness and generality," Myrdal writes.[13] If, as I believe, Stanford Lyman's contention is correct that the "entire body of Myrdal's argument is open to question" because of the explicit assumption that" 'higher values' generally win out in the long run over 'lower' ones," all this matters rather less than the transformative power that *An American Dilemma* attained principally by legitimizing debate about the dilemma.[14]

Its publication came in the same year as the Supreme Court, after a twelve-year toleration of the fiction that southern white primaries were privately organized occasions, found its rare Fifteenth Amendment voice in *Smith v. Allwright*, definitively striking down this major franchise impediment. Two years later, came the presidentially impanelled Committee on Civil Rights, whose eloquent, comprehensive report was ready for publication in late 1947. *To Secure These Rights* spoke in Myrdalese of the moral imperatives of the American Creed, but it introduced a significant new reason for its fulfillment: "The United States is not so strong, the final triumph of the democratic ideal is not so inevitable that we can ignore what the world thinks of us or our record."[15] Another blue-ribbon, presidential committee produced, in time for the 1948 election, a searing expose of the social consequences of segregated education and a recommendation that all forms of educational segregation end as soon as possible. Finally, Harry Truman gave Afro-Americans the long-awaited presidential rhetoric, calling on Congress in his State of the Union message to enact significant civil rights legislation.

In all of these developments there was the resonance of political demography; but neither the reality nor the prospect of Afro-American votes counting heavily in close elections would have sufficed alone to produce the civil rights advances ahead. By the early Fifties, demographics had also yielded impressive economic benefits. Despite severe employment dislocation caused by temporary dismantlement of defense industries and two punishing recessions in 1953–54 and 1957–58, Afro-Americans generally prospered in the score of years after the War. During the period 1947 to 1974, according to the U.S. Census Bureau's global study, "the median income of Black families more than doubled," rising from 51 to 62 percent of white family income, with 51 percent becoming white collar.[16] During the late 1940's and early 1950's, the black unemployment rate of less than 2 percent was at its lowest relative to the white rate (which it otherwise tends to double).[17] *Jet* and *Ebony,* and a number of mainstream popular magazines, ballyhooed the new black purchasing power, calculated to be larger than the gross national product of several European nations.

Rising incomes also meant a tripling of the college population, with prewar Afro-American invisibility at northern white universities giving way to dramatic increase.[18] Predictably, there was now a steady supply of "exemplary" Afro-Americans (athlete Jackie Robinson joining the Dodgers in 1947, poet Gwendolyn Brooks winning a Pulitzer and jurist William Hastie appointed to a federal judgeship in 1949, diplomat Ralph Bunche receiving the Nobel Peace Prize in 1950)—racial paragons whose lives rebutted inferiority stereotypes, on the one hand, and, on the other, diverted attention from the distressing Marxism of W.E.B. Du Bois, Paul Robeson, and Benjamin Davis, Jr. Thus, in the Myrdalian decade after 1944, that article of faith of such civil rights leaders as James Weldon Johnson, Charles S. Johnson, and Walter White that the race problem was essentially not so much institutional or even economic but, rather, a phenomenon of collective psychology, now seemed verified.[19] Many white and black civil libertarians began to believe that those rhetorical taboos—usually beginning, "Would you want your daughter ... ?"—might now be answered affirmatively, if the subject were Ralph Bunche, Jr., or Jackie Robinson, Jr.

In the case of the Supreme Court, the two taboo questions concerned housing and education. Richard Bardolph and Richard Kluger have amply documented the granite conservatism and infinite civil rights evasions of the Court during the administrations of FDR and Truman.[20] But New Deal and Fair Deal ideologies, reinforced by the Afro-American's increasingly credible political and economic presence, began the slow reversal of *Plessy v. Ferguson* in the late 1930's. The NAACP litigation strategy, conceived in 1931 during Nathan Margold's brief tenure as the first salaried legal counsel, produced, under Charles Hamilton Houston's inspired direction, a trickle and then a stream of Supreme Court victories. Beginning with *Missouri ex rel Gaines* e. *Canada,* the 1938 decision requiring University of Missouri Law School either to admit a single qualified applicant or build him a law school, continuing with the 1947 *Sweatt v. Painter* and 1948 *Sipuel v. Oklahoma* decisions, and climaxing with *McLaurin v. Oklahoma State Regents* in 1950, mandating truly equal professional school facilities, NAACP Lawyers had almost achieved their goal of making separate-but-equal higher education too expensive for the South.[21] In *McLaurin,* Chief Justice Fred M. Vinson's opinion had gone so far as to speculate on the possibility that separateness might be incompatible with equality. That same year, the NAACP filed its first public school segregation case before

Judge J. Waties Waring of Charleston, South Carolina, contesting the educational policies in Clarendon County.

From one perspective, NAACP tactics simply made a virtue of necessity: litigation focusing on higher education raised constitutional issues whose validation involved, as a practical matter, only a finite cohort of Afro-Americans. From another perspective—that of class interests—the NAACP's tactics, as well as those of the National Urban League and other major civil rights organizations, betrayed a consistent elitism. Martin Kilson reminds us that, until the mid-1960's, "civil rights politics was largely a middle-class affair, and the Negro lower strata had little political relationship to civil rights politics."[22] However finite the cohort, white, law, dental, and business school admissions were bread-and-butter exigencies to the civil rights establishment and its dues-paying supporters.

To be sure, quality public-school education was one of their paramount concerns, but, to a considerable extent, E. Franklin Frazier's black bourgeoisie had carved out tolerable enclaves for its children either in the urban public school systems of the South or through private means there.[23] Furthermore, for much of the Afro-American civil rights rank and file, there was a vested interest in separate equality in public school education (principalships, teaching positions, the two-income-per-family necessity). In this regard, it is worth a good Marxist speculation about the surprising fact revealed by Kluger that it was Judge Waring of South Carolina who persuaded Thurgood Marshall to withdraw and amend the NAACP's petition so as to challenge head-on the constitutionality of racial segregation.[24] There were good reasons why just plain folk called it the "National Association for the Advancement of *Certain* People."

It was this "certain people" syndrome that had caused the NAACP to be roundly criticized by many of the younger Afro-American intellectuals during the Du Bois-sponsored 1933 Amenia Conference—particularly the Association's hostility to organized labor and relative indifference to economic issues.[25] Here again, migration north generated an important alliance. So long as most Afro-Americans remained in the South (the majority of them as peasant farmers), locked into the Republican Party, they remained irrelevant to the concerns of organized labor. The shift to the Democrats made a labor-black alliance at least a possibility; although, with the important exception of A. Philip Randolph of the Brotherhood of Sleeping Car Porters, Afro-American leadership during much of the Thirties regarded organized labor as the prime enemy. As Herbert Hill has shown, the racial exclusivity of the AFL was endemic and chronic, "from Gompers to benign William Green to the current era of sophisticated public relations under George Meany. ..."[26] But rampant mechanization of southern agriculture during the New Deal drove hundreds of thousands more unskilled Afro-Americans into northern industrial centers where fierce working-class white hostility to them as "scabs" was gradually attenuated, after the 1935 founding of the CIO, by a strategy of cooptation.

The collapse of such great labor strikes as Homestead in 1892 and the "Red Scare" steel strikes of 1919, as well as the 1927 United Mine Workers failure to organize the southern fields, was said to be attributable to black strike breakers.[27] With four out of five black workers unskilled, the Congress of Industrial Organization's John L. Lewis, Philip Murray, and David Dubinsky proclaimed the brotherhood of all and energetically set about organizing black coal miners, steel workers, and auto workers. The role of "SWOC" (the Steel Workers Organizing Committee) in cementing the new interracial alliance was crucial, SWOC funds flowed into the NAACP treasury, where they went to finance litigation and antilynch lobbying. In 1941, the longlived marriage of the NAACP and the United Automobile Workers occurred dramatically when patrician Walter White stood at the gate to Henry Ford's River Rouge plant with a bullhorn, exhorting black workers to join the union.[28] Weiss finds that CIO funds also struck a positive response from the deeply conservative National Urban League.[29]

While the American Federation of Labor remained as lily white as before, even its leadership soon found it useful to support rhetorically and financially the civil rights agenda, as well as to take such specific public relations steps as full admission of Randolph's Brotherhood of Sleeping Car Porters and official participation in Scottsboro and Angelo Herndon rallies.[30] Unskilled and skilled organized labor courted Afro-Americans for their own interests (interests largely coinciding with those of the Democratic Party), and Afro-Americans rallied to both from symmetrical motives. The very aggressive recruitment by communist unions of Afro-American membership and infiltration of Afro-American organizations, such as the National Negro Congress and Scottsboro defense groups, contributed a positive legacy of interracial activism. If, by 1940, the civil rights militancy of Harry Bridges's Marine Workers Industrial Union, Mike Quill's Transport Workers Union, and H. L. Mitchell's socialist-inspired Southern Tenant Farmers Union deadended in the debacle of the Popular Front, historians Harvard Sitkoff, Mark Naison, Nell Painter, Dan Carter, and Donald Grubbs *inter alia,* have shown how durably educative and energizing communist unionism could be.[31]

By the early 1950's, the cumulative impact of balance of power politics, rising incomes, federal court decisions, coalition with organized labor, and the string of exemplary racial "firsts," had primed much of the nation for an end to segregation. There was change even in the South, where *Smith v. Allwright* brought Afro-American registration from a mere 250,000 in 1944 to 1,008,614 by 1952—still only 20 percent of its voting age population there.[32] For a brief, incredible period, it seemed possible that gubernatorial politics might replicate Democratic presidential politics in Georgia and Alabama. In Georgia, former governor Ellis Arnall's protege, James Carmichael (candidate of urban, business, and progressive forces), polled more ballots than Eugene Talmadge in 1946, with the help of an overwhelming black vote—only to be denied office because of that state's infamous, rural-loaded "county unit" system.[33] In Alabama, populist Governor James Folsom opposed the Strom Thurmond Dixiecrats, courted "Nigra" votes, and stupefied white Alabamians with a 1949 Christmas message, declaring, "As long as the Negroes are held down by deprivation and lack of opportunity, all the other people will be held down alongside them."[34] Folsoms protege, George C. Wallace, later took the state in a different direction.

But Morton Sosna's "silent South" occasionally found its voice. Ralph McGill of the Atlanta *Constitution* and Virginius Dabney of the Richmond *Times-Dispatch,* while meticulously eschewing advocacy of racial integration, cautiously urged the abandonment of Jim Crow public transportation. The Chapel Hill sociologists, led by Howard W. Odum, and the Chapel Hill artists, influenced by Paul Green, expended much conscience-stricken passion, if not light, over the race problem. The Southern Regional Council, a gentlemanly, slightly interracial group of southern educators, debated, temporized, and finally, in 1951, authorized Arthur Fleming, its president, to state that it was "neither reasonable nor right that colored citizens of the United States should be subjected to the humiliation of being segregated by law." Of course, the loudest voice in the muted, Deep South was not a man's but Lillian Smith's whose novels and editorials in her *North Georgia Review* pricked the conscience of the white South. Fairly undetected, there were, as Aldon Morris's recent study reveals, highly significant civil rights developments occurring at the grass roots in numerous southern cities and towns. A new Afro-American leadership—ministerial and populist—was taking shape below the traditional oligarchic, white-black leadership configuration. Still, one had to have, as a reading of Sosna and Harry Ashmore indicates, the most restrained expectations for efficacious white southern liberalism in the 1950's.[35]

The stage was now set for decision in the five cases grouped as *Brown v. the Board of Education of Topeka, Kansas.* The sudden death of Chief Justice Vinson permitted the jurisprudentially radical reasoning—theories from sociology and psychology—leading to the Court's unanimous May 17, 1954 decision. In retrospect, the civil rights revolution appears to have been the inevitable consequence of *Brown.* "Revolution" here denotes social upheaval accompanied by collective citizen violence and extraordinary state intervention. Yet, at the risk of sinning counterfactually, it seems that the revolutionary character of civil rights might very well have been different—have been much more evolutionary—but for three interdependent factors. In order of ascending causal importance, those factors were: first, the internal politics of the Warren Supreme Court dictating, as the price of unanimity in *Brown,* a one-year stay of implementation and the enunciation of the anticlimactic, "all deliberate speed" doctrine; second, the collpase and supplanting of responsible southern white leadership in virtually every domain (religion, politics, business, education) by opportunists and extremists; and, third and decisively, the southern politics of the Eisenhower White House and the Presidents own race relations convictions.[36]

Eisenhower's well-known reactions—that Earl Warren's appointment had been a mistake and the decision foolish—and his refusal to endorse *Brown,* except in the negative sense of stating that it was law, was, as Ashmore, Kluger, Sitkoff, Anthony Lewis, and Steven Lawson among others have argued, calamitous.[37] It should be recalled that, for about two years after *Brown,* "all deliberate speed" meant just that in much of the South. About 700 of the 3000 southern school districts quietly desegregated, including, significantly, that of Hoxie township in rural Lawrence County, Arkansas. The governors of South Carolina and Virginia initially appealed for calm and promised dutiful compliance. "We will consider the matter and work toward a plan which will be acceptable to our citizens and in keeping with the edict of the Court," Virginia's governor promised.[38] If the white South was hardly enthusiastic about school desegregation and if, as the so-called 1956 Southern Manifesto attested, most of its leaders were plotting to retard implementation through legal casuistry and administrative procrastination, a course of outright white defiance and violence was probably not inevitable until Little Rock.

Here was the great political miscalculation. The Eisenhower White House, with its eyes on 1956, had no intention of forfeiting a large, grateful southern white vote, despite its secret deal with Democrat Adam Clayton Powell to press for a civil rights act in exchange for the Harlem Congressman's endorsement of the President.[39] Ignorant of the Souths cultural and political atavisms, White House evasions and silences were bound to produce the very no-holds-barred crisis they hoped to avoid. Laissez-faire that had worked with Senator Joseph McCarthy was mistaken. Some 530 cases of recorded violence and reprisals against southern Afro-Americans were recorded between 1955–1958. The 1955 Interstate Commerce Commissions order banning segregation in interstate travel had no writ in the Deep South. School integration was nonexistent in Virginia, Georgia, Alabama, Louisiana, Mississippi, and South Carolina. In eight Deep South states, 45,845 fewer Afro-Americans registered to vote between 1956 and 1958 because of intimidation.[40]

But a primary contribution of the white South to the civil rights revolution was its assault upon the NAACP. Texas and Alabama's injunctions, Georgia's annulment of tax exemption, Virginia's sedition acts, South Carolina's public employment prohibitions decimated the Association's chapters and made outlaws of the stalwarts. The Alabama NAACP could support Arthurine Lucy's successful admission to the University of Alabama; but it looked impotent when she was speciously expelled a few days later, while a local mob hooted. In this climate, Monroe County, North Carolina, NAACP chapter president Robert Williams, expelled by the national executive secretary for arming and drilling his members, was a predictable phenomenon. Little Rock, the South's 1957 redneck edition of Fort Sumter, was equally predictable. Scenting victory, Yale law professor Alexander Bickel wrote, "the southern leaders, or at least a sufficient number of them, sought to assure it by turning from litigation and agitation to direct action by the use of mobs."[41]

Meanwhile, Afro-American leadership was undergoing radical transformation. Southern Baptist preachers, conspicuous in the past for their civic parochialism and cautiousness, were leading desegregation boycotts—boycotts in which, for the first time, poor folk participated in large numbers. Audible above the din of demonstration was heard the baritone of a new leadership voice. "Give us the ballot," Martin Luther King, Jr., demanded from the Lincoln Memorial, during the May 1957 Prayer Pilgrimage to Washington:

> Give us the ballot and we will no longer have to worry the federal government about our rights. ... Give us the ballot and we will get the people judges who love mercy. Give us the ballot and we will quietly, lawfully, and nonviolently,

without rancor or bitterness, implement the May 17, 1954, decision of the Supreme Court.[42]

The students who listened to Martin Luther King concluded that what was not given would have to be taken.

NOTES

1. Cf., David Levering Lewis, *When Harlem Was in Vogue* (New York: Knopf, 1981), 205-6.
2. Nancy J. Weiss, *Farewell to the Party of Lincoln: Black Politics in the Age of FDR* (Princeton: Princeton University Press, 1983), 202.
3. Pat Watters and Reese Cleghorn, *Climbing Jacob's Ladder: The Arrival of Negroes in Southern Politics* (New York: Harcourt, Brace and World, 1967), 10.
4. Quoted in Harvard Sitkoff, *A New Deal for Blacks: The Emergence of Civil Rights as a National Issue—The Depression Decade* (New York: Oxford University Press, 1981), 91.
5. Ralph Bunche, "A Critical Analysis of the Tactical Programs of Minority Groups," *Journal of Negro Education*, IV (July 1935), 308-20; Henry Lee Moon, *Balance of Power: The Negro Vote* (Garden City: Doubleday, 1948).
6. Watters and Cleghorn, *Climbing Jacob's Ladder*, 21.
7. August Meier and Elliott M. Rudwick, *From Plantation to Ghetto*, (3rd ed.; New York: Hill and Wang, 1976), 279.
8. Quoted in Watters and Cleghorn, *Climbing Jacob's Ladder*, 12.
9. Quoted in Harvard Sitkoff, *The Struggle for Black Equality, 1954-1980* (New York: Hill and Wang, 1981), 70.
10. George M. Fredrickson, *White Supremacy: A Comparative Study in American and South African History* (New York: Oxford University Press, 1982), esp. chapter 6.
11. Crane Brinton, *Anatomy of a Revolution* (1938; reprint ed., New York: Vintage, 1965); Ted Robert Gurr, *Why Men Rebel* (Princeton: Princeton University Press, 1970). Alexis de Tocqueville, *L'Ancien Regime et la Revolution* (Paris, 1856).
12. Cf., seminal controversial essay by Ralph Ellison, "An American Dilemma: A Review," *Shadow and Act* (New York: Random House, 1964), 303-17.
13. Gunnar Myrdal, An *American Dilemma: The Negro Problem and Modern Democracy* (New York: Harper and Row, 1944), I, lxxi.
14. Stanford M. Lyman, *The Black American in Sociological Thought: A Failure of Perspective* (New York: Putnam, 1972), 113.
15. Albert P. Blaustein and Robert L. Zangrando, eds., *Civil Rights and the American Negro: A Documentary History* (New York: Trident, 1968), 379.
16. *The Social and Economic Status of the Black Population* in *the United States: An Historical View, 1790-1978* (Washington, D.C.: Government Printing Office, 1979), 379; William H. Harris, *The Harder We Run: Black Workers Since the Civil War* (New York: Oxford University Press, 1982), 127.
17. *The Social and Economic Status*, 61.
18. *Ibid.*, 93.
19. Cf., Lewis, *When Harlem Was* in Vogue, 93, and "Parallels and Divergences: Assimilationist Strategies of Afro-American and Jewish Elites from 1910 to the Early 1930s," *Journal of American History*, 73 (December 1984), 543-64, esp. 548-51.
20. Richard Bardolph, *The Civil Rights Record: Black Americans and the Law, 1849-1970* (New York: Crowell, 1970); Richard Kluger, *Simple Justice: The History of Brown v. Board of Education and Black America's Struggle for Equality* (New York: Knopf, 1975).
21. Kluger, *Simple Justice*, 133-8, 274-84.
22. Martin Kilson, "Black Politics: A New Power," *Dissent*, 18 (August 1971), 333-45, 337.
23. Cf., Kluger, *Simple Justice*, 329; Constance McLaughlin Green, *The Secret City: A History of Race Relations in the Nations Capital* (Princeton: Princeton University Press, 1967), 209-12; Mamie Garvin Fields with Karen Fields,

Lemon Swamp and Other Places: A Carolina Memoir (New York: Free Press, 1983), chapters 3 and 4; August Meier and David L. Lewis, "History of the Negro Upper Class in Atlanta, Georgia, 1890–1959," *Journal of Negro Education,* 28 (Spring 1959), 128–39.

24 Kluger, *Simple Justice,* 304.

25 Sitkoff, *A New Deal for Blacks,* 251; B. Joyce Ross, *J. E. Spingarn and the Rise of the NAACP, 1911–1939* (New York: Atheneum, 1972), 182.

26 Herbert Hill, "The Racial Practices of Organized Labor: The Contemporary Record," in Julius Jacobson, ed., *The Negro and the American Labor Movement* (Garden City: Anchor, 1968), chapter 8, esp. 287.

27 Ray Marshall, "The Negro in Southern Unions," in Jacobson, ed., *The Negro and the American Labor Movement,* 138; Sitkoff, *A New Deal for Blacks,* 179.

28 August Meier and Elliott M. Rudwick, *Black Detroit and the Rise of the UAW* (New York: Oxford University Press, 1979), 100.

29 *Nancy J. Weiss, The National Urban League, 1910–1940* (New York: Oxford University Press, 1974), 291.

30 William H. Harris, *Keeping the Faith: A Philip Randolph, Milton P. Webster, and the Brotherhood of Sleeping Car Porters, 1925–37* (Urbana: University of Illinois Press, 1977), chapter 7.

31 Sitkoff, *A New Deal for Blacks,* chapter 6; Mark Naison, *Communists in Harlem During the Depression* (Urbana: University of Illinois Press, 1983); Nell Painter, *The Narrative of Hosea Hudson: His Life as a Negro Communist in the South* (Cambridge: Harvard University Press, 1979); Donald H. Grubbs, *Cry from the Cotton: The STFU and the New Deal* (Chapel Hill: University of North Carolina Press, 1971).

32 Watters and Cleghorn, *Climbing Jacob's Ladder,* 27.

33 *Ibid.,* 30.

34 Marshall Frady, *Wallace* (New York: World, 1968), 102.

35 Aldon Morris, *The Origins of the Civil Rights Movement: Black Communities Organizing for Change* (New York: Free Press, 1984); Morton Sosna, *In Search of the Silent South: Southern Liberals and the Race Issue* (New York: Columbia University Press, 1977); Harry Ashmore, *Hearts and Minds: The Anatomy of Racism from Roosevelt to Reagan* (New York: McGraw-Hill, 1982).

36 Kluger, *Simple Justice,* chapter 25; Steven F. Lawson, *Black Ballots: Voting Rights in the South, 1944–1969* (New York: Columbia University Press, 1976), chapter 6.

37 Anthony Lewis, *Portrait of a Decade: The Second American Revolution* (New York: Random House, 1964), chapter 4.

38 Quoted in *ibid.,* 29.

39 Maurine Christopher, *America's Black Congressmen* (New York: Crowell, 1971), 200.

40 Watters and Cleghorn, *Climbing Jacob's Ladder,* 28.

41 Lewis, Portrait *of a Decade,* 40.

42 David Levering Lewis, *King; A Biography* (Urbana: University of Illinois Press, 1978), 93.

READING 16

Civil Rights Reform and the Black Freedom Struggle

Clayborne Carson

Social movements ultimately fail, at least in minds of many committed participants. As radicals and revolutionaries have discovered throughout history, even the most successful movements generate aspirations that cannot be fulfilled. Activists, particularly those in social movements that are driven by democratic ideals, often do not regard the achievement of political reform as conclusive evidence of success. Their activism drives them toward values that cannot be fully implemented except within the activist community. Thus, although American social movements provided a major impetus for the extension of civil rights to previously excluded groups, many abolitionists struggled for more radical transformation than was achieved through the Fourteenth and Fifteenth Amendments, and many feminists wanted more than the Nineteenth Amendment or the Equal Rights Amendment. Similarly, many black activists of the 1960s came to see themselves as seeking more than the civil rights acts of 1964 and 1965.

Because the emergent goals of American social movements have usually not been fulfilled, scholars have found it difficult to determine their political significance. Institutionalized political behavior rather than mass movements are the central focus of studies on American politics. Historians have portrayed social movements as important forces on behalf of reform but not as the decisive shapers of the reforms themselves. They typically devote little attention to the internal processes of social movements and view activists only as harbingers of change—colorful, politically impotent, socially isolated idealists and malcontents who play only fleeting roles in the drama of American political history.

Center stage is reserved for the realistic professional reformers who remain at the edges of movements and for politicians who respond to mass activism by channeling otherwise diffuse popular energies into effective reform strategies. Abolitionist activists, historians have suggested, did not free blacks from bondage through moral suasion or through other distinctive forms of antislavery militancy; instead, the Republican Party transformed abolitionist sentiments into a viable political program. Similarly, historians have noted that the initial Populist platform, itself a tepid manifestation of late-nineteenth century agrarian radicalism, was enacted by later generations of unradical reformers. Historians, in short, typically view social reform movements from a distance and see mass activism as significant

Clayborne Carson, "Civil Rights Reform and the Black Freedom Struggle," *The Civil Rights Movement in America*, ed. Charles W. Eagles, pp. 19-32, 159-160. Copyright © 2012 by University Press of Mississippi. Reprinted with permission.

only to the extent that it contributes to successful reform efforts using institutionalized strategies and tactics.

This view of mass activism reflects sociological approaches to the study of social movements that downplay their political functions. American sociologists of the 1950s and 1960s explained that social movements served to relieve widely shared discontents that resulted from strains in the social system. Implicit or explicit in most sociological studies of American social movements was the notion that they were more likely to serve psychological rather than instrumental functions, that they manifested inchoate, individual discontent rather than serious, even if unsuccessful, political strategies involving organized groups. Historians influenced by sociological studies of social movements have argued, for example, that the abolitionists were psychologically abnormal or that populists were reacting against the passing of a familiar agrarian society.

Until recent years, the classical sociological view of social movements prevailed in the study of what is generally called the civil rights movement. Use of the term "civil rights" itself is based on the assumption that the southern black movements of the 1960s remained within the ideological boundaries of previous civil rights activism. Many social scientists studying black protest participation insisted that activism resulted from a distinctive psychological state that was shared by activists. According to an extensive literature, based largely on survey data rather than field observation of ongoing struggles, protest participation was most likely among blacks who had become increasingly aware of the discrepancies, or dissonance, between their conditions of life and the alternatives made possible by the rapidly changing surrounding society. As one sociologist put it, black protesters were distinguished from other blacks by a "higher awareness of the wider society" which made them "more prone to develop the particular set of attitudes and perceptions that lead to protest."[1]

Social scientists found it much easier to offer such analyses of the black struggle during the first half of the 1960s, when there were few signs of dissension within the movement over integrationist goals. During the last half of the decade, however, it became increasingly difficult to explain black power militancy as the outgrowth of the frustrated integrationist desires of blacks. Nevertheless, the classical sociological perspective continued to dominate scholarly writings regarding black militancy. If mass black activism could not be understood as a somewhat unwieldy tactic for achieving longstanding civil rights objectives, it was still possible to portray it as a politically unproductive or even counterproductive expression of mass frustration. Few scholars have been willing to study the internal dynamics of black social movements or to examine their varied and constantly changing strategies, tactics, and styles of leadership. As the nonviolent struggles of the early 1960s gave way to the violent racial conflicts of the late 1960s, the understandable reluctance of scholars, most of whom were white, to study black movements close up rather than from afar became more and more evident.

Thus, until recently, the civil rights literature was comprised mainly of studies of the major national civil rights leaders and their organizations. Following the lead of sociologists, most historians assumed that the black insurgences of the decade after the Montgomery bus boycott could best be understood within the context of a national campaign for civil rights reform. They saw mass activism among blacks as an extension of previous institutionalized civil rights reform efforts. To be sure, historians recognized that the new activism went beyond the once dominant NAACP tactics of litigation, lobbying, and propagandizing, but they saw increased black activism as a new tactic within a familiar strategy based on appeals to power. Protest was a product of widespread black dissatisfaction with the pace of racial change rather than with underlying strategies to achieve change. Instead of viewing mass activism as an independent social force, with its own emergent values and ideology, scholars were more likely to see it as an amorphous source of social energy that could be directed by the leaders of national civil rights organizations.

Indeed, some historical accounts have stressed the decisive role of white politicians rather than civil rights leaders in guiding the effort to achieve civil rights reforms. Thus, Arthur M. Schlesinger's account of the Kennedy presidency illustrated a common theme in surveys of the 1960s when it described Kennedy as a leader seeking to "keep control over the demand for civil rights" through timely concessions which would "hold the confidence of the Negro community." In broader terms, Schlesinger portrays Kennedy as moving "to incorporate the Negro revolution into the democratic coalition and thereby [helping] it serve the future of American freedom."[2] More recently, Carl M. Brauer gave more attention to the black protest movement as an independent force for change, but he too concluded that Kennedy usually maintained the initiative, driven by his need "to feel that he was leading rather than being swept along by events." When black militancy threatened to get out of hand in the spring of 1963, Brauer recounts, the President "boldly reached out to grasp [the reins of leadership] once again."[3]

Studies of civil rights organizations and their leaders understandably give more emphasis to the role of these organizations and their leaders than do studies of presidential leadership, but nonetheless these writings are ambiguous regarding the extent to which organizations and leaders were able to mobilize and direct the course of black militancy. They have focused on the strategies developed by national civil rights groups, while portraying mass activism as a new instrument in the arsenal of national civil rights leaders. The result has been that we have many studies of national civil rights leaders, particularly Martin Luther King, Jr., but few that attempt to determine the extent to which civil rights leaders reflected the aspirations of participants in black struggles.

This failure to clarify the shifting relationship between leadership and mass struggle is a glaring deficiency of studies that imply that national civil rights organizations and leaders played decisive roles in mobilizing southern blacks as a force for change during the 1950s and 1960s. Although the scholarship of the last five years has begun to rectify this deficiency, the perspective of the previous civil rights literature continues to reflect as well as shape the prevailing popular conception of the black struggle.

Embedded in this literature is the assumption that the black struggle can best be understood as a protest movement, orchestrated by national leaders in order to achieve national civil rights legislation. As already noted, use of the term civil rights movement, rather than such alternatives as black freedom struggle, reflects the misleading assumption that the black insurgences of the 1950s and 1960s were part of a coordinated national campaign. Viewing the black struggle as a national civil rights reform effort rather than a locally-based social movement has caused scholars to see Birmingham in the spring of 1963 and Selma in the winter and spring of 1965 as the prototypical black protest movements of the decade. In reality, however, hundreds of southern communities were disrupted by sustained protest movements that lasted, in some cases, for years.

These local protest movements involved thousands of protesters, including large numbers of working class blacks, and local organizers who were more concerned with local issues, including employment opportunities and political power, than with achieving national legislation. Rather than remaining within the ideological confines of the integrationism or Kings Christian-Gandhianism, the local movements displayed a wide range of ideologies and proto-ideologies, involving militant racial or class consciousness.[4] Self-reliant indigenous leaders who headed autonomous local protest organizations have been incorrectly portrayed as King's lieutenants or followers even when they adopted nonviolence as a political weapon rather than a philosophy of life and were clearly acting independently of King or of the Southern Christian Leadership Conference, which he headed.

At present, few detailed studies of these sustained local movements have appeared, but William Chafe's study of Greensboro and Robert J. Norrell's study of the Tuskegee black movement, to cite two examples, reveal that local black movements were unique and developed independently of the national civil rights organizations.[5] Blacks in these communities developed their own goals and strategies which bore little relation to national campaigns for civil rights legislation. King was the pre-eminent national black leader, the exemplar of Gandhian ideals, but in Greensboro, Tuskegee, and many other communities, local leaders and organizers played dominant roles in mobilizing blacks and articulating the emergent values of the local struggles.

Careful examinations of local movements, therefore, challenge the assumption that national leaders, notably Martin Luther King, orchestrated local protest movements in their efforts to alter national public opinion and national policy. There is much to suggest that national civil rights organizations and their leaders played only minor roles in bringing about most local insurgences. It was more often the case that local black movements produced their own distinctive ideas and indigenous leadership rather than that these movements resulted from initiative of national leaders.

The Montgomery bus boycott, for example, began in 1955 as the result of an unplanned act of defiance by Rosa Parks. Martin Luther King, Jr., emerged as a spokesman and as a nationally-known proponent of nonviolent resistance only after Montgomery blacks had launched their movement and formed their own local organization—the Montgomery

Improvement Association. King's organization, the Southern Christian Leadership Conference, was formed only after the boycott ended. To be sure, the Montgomery struggle was an extension of previous civil rights reform efforts, but it began as an outgrowth of local institutional networks rather than as a project of any national civil rights organization.[6]

Similarly, no national organization or leader initiated the next major stage of the black struggle, the lunch counter sit-ins of 1960. SCLC, CORE, and the NAACP attempted to provide ideological and tactical guidance for student protesters after the initial sit-in in Greensboro, but student activists insisted on forming their own local groups under student leadership. Even the Student Nonviolent Coordinating Committee, which was founded by student protest leaders, was unable to guide the sit-in movement—a fact that contributed to SNCC's subsequent support for the principle of local autonomy.[7]

CORE initiated the Freedom Rides of 1961, but this desegregation effort did not become a major social movement until CORE abandoned the rides after protesters were attacked by whites in Alabama. Student militants formed their own organizations. Hundreds of student freedom riders then brought the movement into Mississippi and later to other parts of the South.[8]

The Freedom Rides provided a stimulus for the massive Albany protests of December 1961, which became a model for mass mobilizations of black communities elsewhere in the South. Each of the national civil rights organizations tried to offer guidance for the mass marches and demonstrations which culminated in the Birmingham protests of spring 1963, but by the summer of that year it had become clear to national black leaders that the black struggle had acquired a momentum over which they had little control. A. Philip Randolph, the black leader who proposed a march on Washington, told President Kennedy, "The Negroes are already in the streets. It is very likely impossible to get them off. If they are bound to be in the streets in any case, is it not better that they be led by organizations dedicated to civil rights and disciplined by struggle rather than to leave them to other leaders who care neither about civil rights nor about nonviolence?"[9] Malcolm X recognized and identified with the local black leadership that mobilized the black insurgencies of 1963: "In Cambridge, Maryland, Gloria Richardson; in Danville, Virginia, and other parts of the country, local leaders began to stir up our people at the grass-roots level. This was never done by these Negroes of national stature."[10]

Even this brief discussion of the early history of the southern black struggle should reveal a major weakness of studies that assumed that King played a dominant initiating role in southern protests. These studies have not determined the extent to which King was actually able to implement his nonviolent strategy in specific places. Studies focused on civil rights leaders and organizations, rather than on local movements, often give the impression that King was not only the major national spokesman for the black struggle but also its prime instigator.

During the period from 1956 to 1961, however, King played only a minor role as a protest mobilizer as opposed to his role as a national symbol of the black struggle. Acknowledgement that King had limited control over the southern struggle should not detract from his historical importance as a heroic and intellectually seminal leader; recognition of King's actual role instead reminds us that his greatness was rooted in a momentous social movement. Numerous black communities organized bus boycotts and, later, sit-in movements with little direct involvement by King, who was seen by many black activists as a source of inspiration rather than of tactical direction. Even in Albany, where he played a major role in the 1961 and 1962 protests, he joined a movement that was already in progress and worked alongside indigenous leaders who often accepted but sometimes rejected his advice. In St. Augustine, Birmingham, and Selma, he also assisted movements that had existed before his arrival. In numerous other communities, movements arose and were sustained over long periods with little or no involvement by King or his organization.

Moreover, these local movements should not be viewed as protest activity designed to persuade and coerce the federal government to act on behalf of black civil rights. There was a constant tension between the national black leaders, who saw mass protest as an instrument for reform, and local leaders and organizers who were often more interested in building enduring local institutions rather than staging marches and rallies for a national audience. Local black leadership sought goals that were quite distinct from the national civil rights agenda. Even in communities where King played a major role, as in Albany, Birmingham, and Selma, he was compelled to work with local leaders who were reluctant, to say the least, to implement strategies developed by outsiders.

Black communities mobilized not merely to prod the federal government into action on behalf of blacks but to create new social identities for participants and for all Afro-Americans. The prevailing scholarly conception of the civil rights movement suggests a movement that ended in 1965, when one of the last major campaigns led by a civil rights organization prompted the passage of the Voting Rights Act. The notion of a black freedom struggle seeking a broad range of goals suggests, in contrast, that there was much continuity between the period before 1965 and the period after. Contrary to the oft-expressed view that the civil rights movement died during the mid-1960s, we find that many local activists stressed the continuity between the struggles to gain political rights for southern blacks and the struggles to exercise them in productive ways. Rather than claiming that a black power movement displaced the civil rights movement, they would argue that a black freedom movement seeking generalized racial advancement evolved into a black power movement toward the unachieved goals of the earlier movement.

In summary, scholars have portrayed the black struggle as an augmentation of traditional civil rights reform strategies directed by national civil rights organizations. They have stressed the extent to which national civil rights leaders were able to transform otherwise undirected mass discontent into an effective instrument to speed the pace of reform.

This conception of the black struggle has encountered a strong challenge from a new generation of scholars who have closely examined the internal dynamics of the black struggle in order to determine its sources and emergent norms. As suggested above, previous scholarly studies become increasingly deficient in explanatory power as scholars move nearer to the black struggle itself. If the black struggle were to be seen as a series of concentric circles, with liberal supporters on the outside and fulltime activists at the center, the older scholarly literature would appear adequate in its description of dramatic, highly-publicized confrontations in Albany, Birmingham, and Selma and its treatment of the impact of these confrontations on public opinion and the national government. But the literature fails, for the most part, to explain what occurred at the core of the black struggle where deeply committed activists sustained local movements and acquired distinctive tactics, strategies, leadership styles, and ideologies. It was among activists at the core of the struggle that new radical conceptions of American society and black identity emerged. The scholarly literature helps in explaining why a black person gained new rights, but this literature has been less successful in explaining why a black person is now likely to bring quite different attitudes to whatever he or she does than would have been the case before the black struggle began.

Among the recently published works that offer appealing new perspectives for viewing the black struggle as a social movement are the historical studies of specific local movements, such as those of Chafe, Norrell, and those currently being written by J. Mills Thornton on Montgomery and John Dittmer on Mississippi. These and other studies should provide a fuller understanding of the local context of the black struggle.

Several young sociologists have also charted some promising new directions in the civil rights literature. Doug McAdam[11] delivered the most sweeping assault yet on the theoretical underpinnings of the previous civil rights literature. He recognized that this literature was rooted in inappropriate classical sociological theories of social movements that focus attention on discontented individuals seeking to manage the psychological strains associated with temporary disruptions of the social equilibrium. His alternative perspective points to the political character of the black struggle, which, he argues, arises not simply from increasing discontent, but from a growing recognition among discontented people that they have the power to alter their conditions of life.

Yet, although McAdam s political process model can serve as a useful way to examine the black struggle, his use of historical evidence remains open to question. Rather than beginning with a broad definition of indigenous organization among blacks, he attempts to demonstrate the importance of indigenous organizations by pointing to the role played by the major civil rights organizations in the black insurgences of the 1960's. After examining the *New York Times* index, he comes to the unsurprising conclusion that most of the *Times'* reports mentioned the involvement of the major civil rights groups in protest activity. McAdam should be troubled by the fact that the civil rights groups may have influenced the news reporting by directing reporters' attention to activities in which the group was involved and that the reporters themselves may have had difficulty assessing the nature of organizational involvement in protest activity. The utility of McAdam's model would have been even more convincingly demonstrated if he had recognized that political processes take unique forms in each local context and that extensive research is needed to determine what roles particular types of national and local institutions play in a specific social movement.

Aldon Morris[12] offers a perspective similar in many respects to McAdam's, although he is more concerned with studying the social context of the black struggle than with carrying on a dialogue with previous civil rights scholarship. Morris makes an admirable attempt to do something that the previous generation of scholars neglected to do—that is, to determine how as well as why movements arise and to do this by actually undertaking serious historical research. His original interviews with many of the leaders of the black struggle are themselves wonderful contributions to historical scholarship. Just as McAdam's historical sources do not always serve his analytical purposes, however, so Morris's interviews provide an insufficient base on which to rest his argument.

On the one hand, Morris seeks to demonstrate that indigenous black institutional and leadership networks played major roles in sustaining the black struggle; this is a notion I have no difficulty accepting. On the other hand, he also wants to show that preexisting black institutions invariably initiated and sustained those struggles. His evidence demonstrates that these organizations provided vital resources for those individuals who initiated the local movements, but far more careful research into documentary evidence from the period would be needed to assess the role played by civil rights organizations as opposed to individuals acting independently of those organizations. In some instances, my own interviews with the same individuals placed greater emphasis on the restraining influence on black activism of preexisting organizations. In numerous instances, isolated individuals engaged in protest-intiating actions that were unauthorized by any organization, and these voluntary actions served as catalysts for mobilizing existing institutions into action. To conclude, for example, that spontaneity played little role in the sit-ins of 1960s because many individuals involved in initiating the sit-ins were affiliated with organizations is to downplay the disruptive impact of the sit-ins on those organizations.

Both McAdam, because of his reliance upon newspaper sources, and Morris, because of his insufficient use of primary sources from the period under examination, do not give sufficient attention to the importance of institutional transformation as basic themes in local black struggles. While it is true that the national civil rights organizations played major roles in the southern struggle, it is also the case that these organizations operated in a constantly changing context to which they were forced to respond. Morris relies upon the useful concept of "local movement center" to describe the "dynamic form of social organization" that sustained the struggle, but, surprisingly, his use of the concept conveys little of the dynamism that actually made such centers sources of tactical and ideological innovation.

It should be possible to direct attention to the fact that preexisting institutions, leaders, and organizations were critically involved in all phases of the struggle without losing sight of the numerous ways in which activism served to challenge existing arrangements in black communities. To maintain, for example, that existing black church networks were vital to the struggle should not lead us to ignore the fact that many black churches did little to aid the struggle, did not join the umbrella organizations that came into being to sustain protest activity, and often were unwilling even to allow civil rights meetings to take place inside their buildings. To maintain that pre-existing civil rights groups played crucial roles in the struggle should not lead us to conclude that they always did so without prodding from activists or without considerable internal policy conflicts. To maintain that many black protest leaders were already part of the leadership structure of black communities is to ignore the extent to which the sudden rise to prominence of a leader such a King disrupted existing patterns of leadership.

Despite these criticisms, McAdam, Morris, and the historians who have done careful study of local movements have offered us important insights which correct the still-dominant view that movements are typically peripheral to institutionalized structures and to the process of political change. But this insight needs to be combined with an understanding of the capacities of social movements to transform the structures that created them, to generate new ideas and values, and to transform the people who become involved in them. Careful study of the internal dynamics of the black struggle will make us more aware of the ways in which institutions of various types can sustain movements or can kill them. Studies of the historical black struggles of 1960's currently being conducted by the many talented scholars entering this exciting field might also suggest how the vastly greater resources of contemporary black communities might be mobilized to renew the struggle.

NOTES

1   John Orbell, "Protest Participation among Southern Negro College Students," *American Political Science Review,* 61 (June 1967), 554–555. Cf. Ruth Searles and J. Allen Williams, Jr., "Negro College Students' Participation in Sit-ins," *Social Forces,* 40 (March 1962), 215–220; James A. Geschwender, "Social Structure and the Negro Revolt: An Examination of Some Hypotheses," *Social Forces* 43, (December 1964), 250–256; and Anthony M. Orum and Amy M. Orum, "Class and Status Bases of Negro Student Protest," *Social Science Quarterly,* 49 (December 1968), 521–533. This literature is more fully discussed in my paper, "The Civil Rights Movement and the Transformation of American Racial Thought," delivered at annual meeting of the Organization of American Historians, Los Angeles, April 5, 1984.

2   Arthur M. Schlesinger, Jr., *A Thousand Days: John F. Kennedy in the White House* (Boston: Houghton Mifflin, 1965), 850, 892.

3   Carl F. Brauer, *John F. Kennedy and the Second Reconstruction* (New York: Columbia University Press, 1977), 318.

4   Havard Sitkoff's survey of the black struggle reflects the common journalistic emphasis on King and the local movements he initiated but nonetheless notes the ideological diversity that accompanied the increasing scale of activism during and after 1963: "The unemployed and working poor had little interest in ... symbolic and status gains. ... They had even less sympathy for, or knowledge of, the spirit of *Satyagraha.* King's talk of love left them cold. ... As the black struggle became more massive and encompassing, impatience multiplied, disobedience became barely civil, and nonviolence often a mere stratagem." Sitkoff, *The Struggle for Black Equality, 1954–1980* (New York: Hill and Wang, 1981), 145.

5   William H. Chafe, *Civilities and Civil Rights: Greensboro, North Carolina, and the Black Struggle for Freedom* (New York: Oxford University Press, 1980); and Robert J. Norrell, *Reaping the Whirlwind: The Civil Rights Movement in Tuskegee* (New York: Knopf, 1985). Norrell comments: "[The civil rights movement] had a different experience in each place and no place was the same after it left. Each community now has a story to tell about the movement, and only when many of those stories are told will the South's great social upheaval be well understood" [p. ix].

6 Cf. J. Mills Thornton III, "Challenge and Response in the Montgomery Bus Boycott," *The Alabama Review,* 33 (July 1980), 163–235; and Aldon D. Morris, *The Origins of the Civil Rights Movement: Black Communities Organizing for Change* (New York: The Free Press, 1984).

7 Cf. August Meier and Elliot Rudwick, *CORE: A Study in the Civil Rights Movement, 1942–1968* (New York: Oxford University Press, 1973), chapter 4; and Carson, *In Struggle: SNCC and the Black Awakening of the 1960s* (Cambridge: Harvard University Press, 1981), chapters 1 and 2.

8 Cf. Meier and Rudwick, CORE, chapter 5; and Carson, *In Struggle,* chapter 6.

9 Schlesinger, *Thousand Days,* 854–855.

10 George Breitman, ed., *Malcolm X Speaks: Selected Speeches and Statements* (New York: Merit Publishers, 1965), 13.

11 Doug McAdam, *Political Process and the Development of Black Insurgency, 1930–1970* (Chicago: University of Chicago Press, 1982).

12 Morris, Origins *of the Civil Rights Movement,* 284.

READING 17

Dr. Martin Luther King, Jr. and the African-American Religious Origins of the Beloved Community

Anthony E. Cook

The life and works of Dr. Martin Luther King, Jr. were significantly influenced by the social gospel of Walter Rauschenbusch. While Rauschenbusch wrote during the tumultuous but promising times of the progressive era, King later led a civil rights movement no less transformative than the progressive era of the early twentieth century. As stated above, Rauschenbusch modernized Christianity in the same way Dewey modernized philosophy, adapting it to the conditions and possibilities of American society. Rauschenbusch's social gospel answered the major problems raised by Dewey's critique of traditional religion, problems that ultimately necessitated Dewey's rejection of supernatural faith in favor of a naturalist Common Faith.

Had Dewey incorporated some of the progressive understandings of religion being developed during his lifetime, progressive liberal thought might have developed differently than it did. As it turned out, both the pragmatist and realist variants of progressive liberalism were too utilitarian to appeal to that deep yearning for a spiritually affirming and just community.

King was obviously influenced by Rauschenbusch's theology of the social gospel as well as the work of Reinhold Niebuhr, Martin Buber and Gandhi. Most often forgotten or ignored by King scholars and biographers, however, is the profound influence of the African-American religious tradition on his theology and activism. An understanding of this influence is essential to grasping King's approach to theology, politics and social reform. It is through this tradition that he developed an understanding of the "Beloved Community," his response to the problems facing the "least of these" in American society.

It was the influence of this African-American religious tradition on King's thought and work that significantly laid the foundation for his religiospiritual understanding of liberal tenets, an understanding I believe is crucial to the resurrection of the progressive liberal vision in American politics and culture. King's appropriation of the African-American religious tradition led him to a spirituality of reconstruction that he did not fully elaborate in

---

Anthony E. Cook, "Dr. Martin Luther King, Jr. and the African-American Religious Origins of the Beloved Community," *The Least of These: Race, Law, and Religion in American Culture*, pp. 97-110, 236-237. Copyright © 1997 by Taylor & Francis Group. Reprinted with permission.

his lifetime but which is there, like a seed beneath the surface of all he said and did, awaiting our attention and cultivation.

A. THE ROLE OF THE AFRICAN-AMERICAN CHURCH IN THE AMERICAN SLAVE EXPERIENCE

In order to fully understand the influence of the African-American religious tradition on King's thought, one must understand the vital role African-American religion played in the community-building enterprise necessitated by the social disintegration and chaos of the American slavery experience. Confronted by practices of social control that destroyed or suppressed their West African heritage, language and traditions, Africans were expected to conform to a community created by their slave-masters. Slave-masters attempted to refashion the African's identity through the eradication of collective memory. In the void created by the socially imposed atomization and amnesia of the African community, the African-American Church served both to legitimate and delegitimate the moral authority of a slave-owning society. An understanding of both effects is essential for understanding King's theology and process of interpretation.

1. THE ROLE OF RELIGION IN THE LEGITIMATION OF AUTHORITY

Slave-masters believed Christianity had a stabilizing and disciplining influence on the slaves' dispositions, and they thought it would foster consent by Africans to their exploitation and oppression. The conservative evangelicalism intended to convince Africans of their subordinate status, however, possessed qualities that would eventually allow many slaves to turn its use as a rationalization of slavery against slavery itself. The rationalization of slavery generally went along the following lines: Africans were a heathen class of humans, pagans outside the Christian community. Slavery was, therefore, an institution established principally for the benefit of Africans, intended to save them from God's wrath against pagan worshippers. Through the beneficent institution of slavery, these heathens might gradually be converted from their sinful and evil ways and made fit for the Kingdom of God.

The concern for salvation under this conservative evangelicalism was, of course, a spiritual and not an earthly salvation. Bringing salvation to the slaves was premised on five basic assumptions of a conservative Christian orthodoxy later challenged by Rauschenbusch and King. The first was the fallen nature of human beings—the pervasiveness of human depravity and sin. The second was the need for contrition—a period of mourning characterized by feelings of personal guilt and sorrow for sins. The third was the need for conversion—an intensely personal experience with God in which the burdens of sin were lifted and the soul cleansed and made fit for the Kingdom of God. The fourth was the necessity of coming out of the world—the sometimes-physical but usually psychological separation of the community of believers from sinful, worldly concerns and pursuits. The last was a deference to the state and existing social order—rendering unto God that which was God's and unto

Caesar that which was Caesar's. Such an understanding of separation of church and state was predicated on a belief that God had duly appointed civil government to constrain the sinful nature of earthly beings.

These features of conservative evangelicalism were considered rooted in an infallible scripture representing the untainted word of God. They legitimated slave-masters' authority in several ways. Southern evangelicals elaborated the scriptural justifications for slavery and invoked the will of God to reconcile slaves to their subordinate status. Slavery could not be sin, they reasoned, since God sanctioned it in his infallible Word. Evangelicals frequently cited the Old Testament story of Noah's son, Ham, whose progeny God supposedly condemned to a legacy of servitude for Ham's indiscretion. These and other scriptural evidences were, to the proslavery evangelicals, conclusive proof of God's authorization of African slavery.

Having provided the moral justification for slavery through scripture, evangelicals constructed an argument designed to avert any effort by the Church to transform the institution. Because the scripture supported slavery, and secular authority established and protected it under state law, the Church, mindful of its commitment to the separation of church and state, could not condemn slavery. Because slavery did not constitute sin, God's law did not contradict the civil law. Slavery fell under the latter, and the scriptures dictated obedience to secular authority.

Moreover, conservative evangelicalism dictated that because God would deal with the evil of Southern slavery and apartheid in His own way and time, the eradication of those institutions should await His divine deliverance as evidenced by the changed hearts and minds of men. Like the apostle Paul's letter to the master of the slave named Onesimus in the New Testament, persuasion and not coercion was the preferred strategy for dealing with the slavery question. Thus patience and the implicit acceptance of a slave's subordinate status were exalted as the highest of Christian virtues.

Conservative evangelicalism had made its position on the morality of slavery quite clear. Unresolved, however, was whether the separation of church and state permitted the Church to play any role at all in the relationship between masters and slaves. Although scripture exhorted masters to provide their slaves with instruction sufficient for salvation, evangelicals emphasized that salvation was the sole purpose of giving slaves the Gospel. The evangelical message was that if slaves were faithful to the Gospel—humble and obedient, faithfully serving in the station to which providence had assigned them—they too could enter the Kingdom of God. As one evangelical contended: "Our design in giving them [the slaves] the Gospel, is not to civilize them—not to change their social condition—not to exalt them into citizens or freemen—it is to save them."[1]

2. THE ROLE OF RELIGION IN THE DELEGITIMATION OF AUTHORITY

Although the use of religion as an instrument of social control often necessitated oversight by white masters, strict enforcement was not maintained, and slaves often met separately for religious services, including weekly and Sunday evening services. It was within the freedom provided for religious worship that Africans began to assert some control over how the void created by the disintegration of their cultural identities and communities would be filled. In this small space of freedom, an alternative conception of community was defined, and the history of a new American people emerged. African-American religion and its central vehicle of expression, the African-American Church, supplied the needed catalyst for the reconstruction of community destroyed by slavery.

Although slave-masters and evangelicals attempted to limit the transmission of counter-hegemonic interpretations of scripture, their efforts were often met with quiet defiance and limited success. African gospel preachers and slaves who learned to read against their masters' wishes (and, many times, against state law as well) were determined to read the Bible in light of their own experiences. Many slaves realized that the message of submission, docility and absolute obedience to the master was a distorted picture of the Bible's eternal truths.

The Africans' appropriation of conservative evangelicalism as a bulwark against the degradation and countless microaggressions of slavery proved that there were alternate interpretations of the texts that supposedly justified their subjugation. Slaves demonstrated that scripture was subject to an alternative interpretation that called for the eradication of the very social structure evangelicals sought to legitimate. In short, in their monumental struggles against oppression, slaves deconstructed and reconstructed religious ideology to reflect their deepest yearnings for freedom and community. To the surprise and fear of many whites, slaves transformed an ideology intended to reconcile them to a subordinate status into a manifesto of their God-given equality. This theological reconstruction was both prophetic and pragmatic in orientation.

Prophetic Christianity involved a critical application of religious principles to the social context of oppression. It measured and judged that context by the normative standards derived from the religious tradition. Thus prophetic Christianity always presupposed a normative or ideal conception of community as a standard from which deviation might be judged, challenged and transformed. For prophetic Christians, slavery might at times have to be tolerated but it could never be accepted. One was obligated to proclaim God's judgment on such an evil and to offer oneself as an instrument through which God's deliverance from slavery might be wrought.

Like the prophets of the Old Testament, prophetic Christians restored the connection between religious devotion and social justice. Under the judgment of God expressed through the prophet, one could not simultaneously claim to be faithful to God and also be an exploiter of the weak and vulnerable. Protection and just treatment of the most powerless segments of the community were inextricably connected to righteousness, and, thus, a devotee of the faith could not have one without the other. Those who maintained otherwise were hypocrites, vipers and the true sinners against God and humanity.

Conservative evangelicalism taught that slavery was a divinely ordained practice instituted by the master race for the benefit of morally deficient Africans. But slaves read of

Moses, the Hebrew children and God's mighty deliverance from the hardships of Egyptian slavery. The story provided proof of God's intolerance of American slavery and his intention someday to divide the Red Sea of Southern oppression and lead His people out of Pharaoh's land.

Many slaves found in the Judeo-Christian tradition, then, and particularly in the historical Jesus of early Christianity, a call to revolutionary action. They read of a Jesus who proclaimed that God had anointed Him to "preach the gospel to the poor; ... to preach deliverance to the captives, and ... to set at liberty them that are bruised";[2] who commanded those who would follow him to care for "the least of these": the hungry, naked, sick, and those in prison; who entered Jerusalem to the revolutionary cry of Hosannah; and who defiantly asserted "[t]hink not that I am come to send peace on earth: I came not to send peace, but a sword."[3] Denmark Vessey and Nat Turner, for example, recognized the revolutionary potential of Christianity: "since God is on our side, we strike for freedom, confident in his protection."[4] The Reverend Henry Highland Garnet contended: "'To such degradation [as slavery] it is sinful in the extreme for you to make voluntary submission. ... Brethren arise, arise! Strike for your lives and liberties. Now is the day and the hour. ... Rather die freemen than live to be slaves'."[5]

Pragmatic Christianity was a functional religion, very much resembling Dewey's pragmatism. It was improvisational, experimental and open to revision. Beliefs, rituals and practices were valued according to their utility in restoring a sense of community to a people whose community cohesiveness had been weakened and destroyed by a relentless persecution. In short, pragmatic Christianity was concerned with the development of understandings that permitted an oppressed people to survive from day to day and maintain a faith in ultimate deliverance, if not in this life, then in the one to come.

Pragmatic Christianity found scriptural support for a more patient opposition to slavery that fostered and preserved a healthy sense of self-worth. It was not focused, as was prophetic Christianity, on openly proclaiming judgment on the evil system of slavery and utilizing every opportunity to defy it. Instead, pragmatic Christianity focused on the internal development of spiritual resources needed to survive slavery.

Against the formidable oppression of slavery, segregation and contemporary forms of subjugation, this pragmatic Christianity would provide the means by which African-Americans could survive their daily travails. Its emphasis on personal faith nurtured a forward-looking people who could sing with conviction the words "I'm so glad that trouble won't last always."[6] Its emphasis on love bolstered a sense of self-esteem diminished by the debilitating and degrading practices of a culture that relegated them to the status of objects. It nurtured an inward-looking people who could sing with reassurance the words "The trumpet sounds within my soul. I know I ain't got long to stay here."[7]

Conservative religious ideology portrayed slaves as inherently inferior and unequal creatures in need of white paternalism. But slaves heard of a God who gave His only Son to die for all humanity. They heard that God did not discriminate among persons—that in Him there was neither Jew nor Gentile, slave nor free—that all were brothers in Christ Jesus. Slave-masters and evangelical preachers admonished slaves to render absolute obedience to their masters and to serve cheerfully in the position to which they were destined. But slaves read of and believed in a master superior to their earthly masters—a master to whom their own masters were held in submission, and whose commandments their masters were obligated to obey. The belief in Jesus as ultimate master undermined the suggestion that complete submission was owed to one's earthly master.

The disparity between what slaves read and heard from their own preachers and the practices of whites in the slave system had two important consequences. First, it preserved and enhanced the self-esteem of the slaves; the realization that some whites were not faithful to the Word provided them with a sense of moral superiority. Even in slavery, slaves could be the light unto the sinner's path.

Second, it provided a standard against which they could measure whites individually, rather than collectively by their social status as master race. It provided a framework for understanding the differences between cruel white overseers and whites who worked on the underground railroad to freedom. Even when the institutions of oppression seemed most intractable, understanding their oppression as the sin of unfaithful whites maintained for the Africans a sense of sanity and hope occasionally given new meaning by the prophetic focus on power and immediate liberation. In short, the pragmatic appropriation of Christian ideology by the African-Americans provided the basis for their survival of slavery's many brutalities and indignities.

Although this appropriation helped to restore the dignity of the African slave, it also had paradoxical effects. Pragmatic Christianity admirably served the cause of survival, but its eschatological and inward orientation simultaneously served the function of social control. It saved black Christians from a debilitating hatred which, if permitted to fester, would have created a pervasive sense of despair and hopelessness that would have substantially impaired the moral will to survive. However, it also promoted as virtues patience and tolerance of the social institutions of oppression. Viewing morality in terms of individual character thus undermined the possibilities of a sustained Christian radicalism against what was perhaps the most debilitating and sustained system of subordination known to the modern world—American slavery.

3. THE ROLE OF RELIGION IN THE SHAPING OF ALTERNATIVE CONCEPTIONS OF COMMUNITY

The unique synthesis of prophetic and pragmatic Christianity drawn from slave religion was the African-American religious tradition that significantly shaped King's theology and praxis. This synthesis drew heavily on the interplay between the individualist and spiritual orientation of pragmatic Christianity and the collectivist and social orientation of prophetic Christianity. It encouraged an intensely personal relationship with God while nurturing the possibilities of collective defiance and transformation. I will argue shortly that this synthesis formed the foundation of King's conception of the Beloved Community. But first, let us explore more closely the alternative conception of community implied by the prophetic and pragmatic conceptions of Christianity developed above.

The African-American Church rejected white Christianity's claim that the law and order of a slave society were necessary to constrain the evil proclivities of human nature and should be obeyed. Furthermore, most slaves probably never accepted the view that slavery was justified on grounds of black inferiority and white superiority. For these slaves, the spiritual freedom and sense of equality that accompanied religious conversion threw into question the morality of the social order in which they lived. Conversion was an experience of unconditional love and acceptance from God and those involved in the process. No earthly slave society or system of oppression could refute such a cosmic affirmation of one's inherent worth. One student of this period writes:

> Contradicting a system that valued him like a beast for his labor, conversion *experientially* confirmed the slave's value as a human person, indeed attested to his ultimate worth as one of the chosen of God. ... [M]eetings encouraged participants to include references to individual misfortunes and problems in their prayers and songs, so that they might be shared by all. This type of consolation ... [was] the answer to the crucial need of individuals for community.[8]

The religious experience of conversion was central to the alternative belief system of slaves and the alternative community that belief system implied. The process of conversion in African-American religion involved a period of sustained mourning in which the contrite sinner would assemble with worshipers in prayer for as many successive meetings as required to "bring the sinner through"—a phrase used to express the sinner's completion of a right of passage from the alienated existence of sinner to the bonds of Christian fellowship and community. The process of conversion often resulted in a cataclysmic seizure of the person by the Holy Spirit that catapulted all into a rapture of ecstatic joy and praise. The experience was collectively cathartic. In the slave community, uninhibited shouting and praise temporarily obliterated secular distinctions in status between the slaves. It was a process in which personalities disintegrated by the social chaos of oppression found meaning and commonality by fusing with others in a collective act of self-affirmation and even defiance.

The African-American Christianity that resulted from this synthesis between prophetic and pragmatic variants offered the alternative conception of community that would inspire King to struggle to redeem American society from its racist and oppressive history. King's aspiration to rebuild community from the social death of slavery and segregation paralleled the conversion experience in slavery. Nonviolent direct action would inaugurate a period of societal mourning and repentance for the sins of the past. From this collective contrition redemption would follow. New individuals would be forged in the crucible of redemptive suffering. A new community, a beloved community, would evolve from a righteous struggle for the soul of America.

The struggle for a sense of collective as well as individual self-worth was essential to any social conversion; segregation laws and impoverished conditions that diminished not only self-worth but a community's sense of itself as well had to be challenged and abolished. The objective was to break down the barriers of hatred and misunderstanding that prevented individuals from seeing and respecting the God-given humanity of all.

But King knew that only collective action and peaceful defiance of the status quo could achieve the destruction of such barriers and simultaneously engender the formation of a beloved community founded on love and justice. A redistribution of wealth and power through the collectively cathartic experience of social conversion was a necessary part of this conception of community.

In this social conversion, law would have to assist in the obliteration and amelioration of many of the secular distinctions founded on race, class and the deprivation of fundamental human rights. Like the alternative conception of community implied by the conversion experience in African-American religion, social conversion would strive for a universal sense of oneness that appreciated the particularity of the African-American experience. This social conversion of the American culture would require people to change their hearts and minds as well as behaviors. While law could not alone transform hearts and minds, it could edify. It could encourage the kind of introspection that makes such change possible.

I believe King's synthesis of pragmatic and prophetic Christianity drew from the concrete experiences of the African-American struggle for liberation. The communal or social possibilities of religious conversion greatly impressed him in this regard. In the conversion experience of the African-American religious tradition, previously alienated individuals saw themselves as inextricably connected through prayer and praise that placed them on one accord. In the call and response of conversion a special solidarity was forged which, at least for this moment of resplendent rapture, harmoniously integrated class, gender and regional distinctions. Difference became an asset rather than a liabilty, an opportunity to see the same God variously expressed through the particularities of community. King sought to bring this experience of textured solidarity from the shout circle of the African-American religious tradition to the larger American society. Through a social conversion that emulated religious conversions, the Beloved Community might be born. Alienated individuals might be able to glimpse the inter-relatedness of their being and begin to act from an orientation of love rather than fear as they worked out their own textured solidarity.

To foster this spiritual and social solidarity, King masterfully used narrative, the story-telling that had long been a cornerstone of African culture in general and the African-American religious tradition in particular. A major attribute of narrative is that it gives voice to those rendered voiceless by discourses, ideologies and institutional practices that objectify them as things to be possessed rather than beings to be revered. It sets forth the irreducible essence of one's humanity and disperses the dark shadows that shroud its beauty from view. Through narrative mere footnotes in history are lifted into the text and read as agents in the making of history and not mere passive appendages to the histories of others. We gain through the stories of those made voiceless by a stultifying cultural imperialism, a picture more complete than before, a chorus of human experience richer than the monotone of the conqueror's refrain.

Another attribute of narrative is that it explains how ideologies, discourses and social orderings are experienced by the oppressed. To be sure, oppression breeds pathologies that the oppressed must strive to overcome, but it also spawns more positive and creative responses. Narrative often provides insight into these more positive responses, the ways marginalized groups transform hopeless conditions into powerful possibilities that might benefit us all. Such understanding informs a more complex reconstructive vision of community than the myopic insights of one-dimensional histories permit. In other words, contained within the harrowing experiences of oppression are rich alternative conceptions of community developed by the oppressed to make sense of their worlds and to inspire their struggle for better worlds still. By examining the concrete ways people have responded to oppression, we often find the proverbial diamond in the rough—the nuanced ways people have reconstructed community from chaos and hope from despair. The theoretical possibilities presented by a conception like the Beloved Community are given practical guidance by the elaboration of such experiences through narrative.

Finally, narrative makes an epistemological claim. We know first and best through experience, emotion and feeling. Only later is this knowledge given expression by the abstract categories of mind that detach it from its true source of creation. Narrative is the language of spirit speaking to spirit, that ineffable sixth sense connecting us with the other through the often different stories we tell of our struggles to be free from and yet belong to something. Through stories we come to know the other not as other but as self waiting to be claimed. Through stories we bridge, even if temporarily, the chasms that seemingly separate our plights, and we know, even if we cannot long sustain its awareness, that we are not alone.

King realized that many African-Americans probably never believed that the assumptions of conservative evangelicalism logically compelled their submission to authority. Their submission was not based on consent to a social order they believed to be legitimate. Rather, coercion and its constant threat of death, injury, humiliation or impoverishment compelled their submission. Individuals may have fully agreed with the theoretical critique of conservative religious ideology and yet been constrained by existential limitations that made collective struggle to attain alternative conceptions of community difficult if not impossible. King eloquently describes these existential limitations through a moving use of narrative:

> [W]hen you have seen vicious mobs lynch your mothers and fathers at will and drown your sisters and brothers at whim; when you have seen hate-filled policemen curse, kick, brutalize and even kill your black brothers and sisters with impunity; when you see the vast majority of your twenty million Negro

brothers smothering in an airtight cage of poverty in the midst of an affluent society; ... when you take a crosscountry drive and find it necessary to sleep night after night in the uncomfortable corners of your automobile because no motel will accept you; when you are humiliated day in and day out by nagging signs reading "white" and "colored"; when your first name becomes "nigger" and your middle name becomes "boy" (however old you are) and your last name becomes "John," and when your wife and mother are never given the respected title "Mrs."; when you are harried by day and haunted by night by the fact that you are a Negro, living constantly at tiptoe stance never quite knowing what to expect next, and plagued with inner fears and outer resentments; when you are forever fighting a degenerating sense of "nobodiness"; then you will understand why we find it difficult to wait.[9]

Through such moving narrative as this, King bridged the gap between those who had and had not experienced the brutalities of slavery and segregation. These experiences necessitated his eclectic appropriation of various theologies and philosophies, which he constantly American life. As I have pointed out, King drew inspiration from the African-American religious tradition, a tradition allowing him to develop innovative approaches to the problems facing oppressed people.

In summary, the history and experiences of African-Americans under oppression taught King several valuable lessons. First, submission to illegitimate authority did not derive exclusively from a hegemonic ideology such as the conservative evangelicalism of slavery and segregation. Public and private coercion played a significant role in maintaining submission. Second, far from being duped by the political and religious ideologies intended to oppress them, African-Americans had often successfully turned those ideologies on their heads and used them as instruments of survival and liberation. Third, within the space created by the interplay of coercion and consent, African-Americans evolved and implemented conceptions of community important to broader visions of a reconstructed society. The interdependency, love, equality and hope that characterized the best of those communities were particularly attractive to King and greatly informed his conception of a Beloved Community.

NOTES

1 Anne C. Loveland, Southern Evangelicals and the Social Order, 1800–1860, at 206 (1980).
2 *Luke* 4:18 (King James).
3 *Matthew* 10:34 (KingJames).
4 Albert J. Raboteau, *The Black Experience in American Evangelicalism: The Meaning of Slavery*, in The Evangelical Tradition in America 180, 190 (L. Sweet ed., 1984).
5 Id. (footnote omitted) (quoting Garnet, *An Address to the Slaves of the United States of America* (1843), reprinted in Sterling Stuckey, The Ideological Origins of Black Nationalism 165, 168–72 [1972]).
6 *Hush, Hush Somebody's Calling My Name, in* Songs of Zion 125 (Abbingdon 1981).

7 *Steal Away to Jesus,* in Songs of Zion, *supra* note 6, at 180.
8 Raboteau, *supra* note 4, at 193–94 (emphasis in original).
9 Martin Luther King, Jr., *Letter from Birmingham City Jail* (1963), reprinted in A Testament of Hope: The Essential Writings of Martin Luther King, Jr. 292–93 (James M. Washington ed. 1986) [hereinafter A Testament of Hope].

PART VI

Post-Racial America in the Age of Barack Obama

READING 18

Race and Multiraciality
From Barack Obama to Trayvon Martin

Reginald Daniel

RACE, IDENTITY, AND THE ONE-DROP RULE: A THEORETICAL PERSPECTIVE

The rule of hypodescent is a social code designating racial group membership of first-generation offspring of unions between European Americans and Americans of color exclusively based on their background of color. Successive generations of individuals who have European American ancestry combined with a background of color have more flexibility in terms of self-identification. The one-drop rule of hypodescent designates as black everyone with any African American ancestry ("one-drop of blood"). It precludes any choice in self-identification and ensures that all future offspring of African American ancestry are socially designated and self-identified as black (Daniel 2002, ix–xi, 16–17, 37; Davis 1991, 9, 15, 118).[1] Beginning in the late sixteenth century, the dominant European Americans began enforcing rules of hypodescent as part of anti-miscegenation statutes aimed at punishing and eventually prohibiting interracial intimacy, as well as defining multiracial offspring as black in an attempt to preserve white racial "purity" and privilege. By the middle of the eighteenth century, interracial marriages in the Southern and some Northern colonies (and eventually states) in Anglo-North America were proscribed and stigmatized where they were not legally prohibited (Barthé, Jr. 2012, 83–85; Daniel 2006, 89–92).

During the early seventeenth century, African Americans were comparatively small in numbers and the distinction between the white indentured servant and the black slave was less precise than that between bonded and free. There were no laws against miscegenation despite strong prejudice against interracial intimacy (Daniel 2002, 87; Hodes 1997, 1–15; Spickard 1989, 237; Tenzer 1990, 56–68). Consequently, a small, but not insignificant, number of European indentures and African slaves intermarried or formed common-law unions of some duration. They had legitimate offspring, alongside more widespread clandestine and fleeting liaisons involving births outside of wedlock. Most of the latter were between white masters and indentured or slave women of African descent, and involved coercive sexual relations as in extended concubinage or rape. The offspring of these unions were slaves contingent upon the slave status of the mother, not the rule of hypodescent. Accordingly,

G. Reginald Daniel, "Race and Multiraciality: From Barack Obama to Trayvon Martin," *Race and the Obama Phenomenon: The Vision of a More Perfect Multiracial Union*, ed. G. Reginald Daniel and Hettie V. Williams, pp. 3-15, 36-38, 339-384. Copyright © 2014 by University Press of Mississippi. Reprinted with permission.

the rule did not increase the numbers of slaves, but rather, the numbers of blacks whether slave or free. Still hypodescent did conveniently function to exempt white landowners (particularly slaveholders) from the legal obligation of passing on inheritance and other benefits of paternity to their multiracial progeny (Davis 1991, 9, 15, 118).

The ancestral quanta defining legal blackness have varied over time and according to locale. There is evidence of perceptions and practices that were normative long before they were formalized in law. Statutes and court decisions were inevitably more precise than social custom (Jordan 2014, 73). The one-drop rule gained currency as the informal or "commonsense" (Omi and Winant 1994, 106) definition of blackness between the seventeenth and nineteenth centuries. It did not become a customary part of the legal apparatus until the early twentieth century (circa 1915) (Daniel 2002, 34–42; 2006, viii–ix; Davis 1991, 9–11, 55–58). The rule has supported legal and informal barriers to racial equality in most aspects of social life. At the turn of the twentieth century, these restrictions culminated with the institutionalization of Jim Crow segregation.

Beginning in the mid-1950s, those proscriptions were dismantled and accompanied by the passage of historic civil rights legislation in the 1960s, including the 1967 *Loving v. Virginia* decision, which removed the last laws prohibiting interracial marriage. Notions of racial purity that supported the ideology of white supremacy were increasingly repudiated. Rules of hypodescent have been removed from all state statutes. European Americans, nevertheless, have maintained identities and privileges based on white racial exclusivity originating in hypodescent. According to Lipsitz, European Americans continue to uphold a "possessive investment in whiteness" (Lipsitz 1998, 2). This manifests itself by means of a matrix of practices that leads to significantly different life chances along racial lines. These outcomes are not merely the byproducts of benign neglect. They are also the cumulation of the purposeful designs of whites that assign people of different racial groups to different social spaces. This, in turn, results in grossly inequitable access to education, employment, transportation, and housing (Lipsitz 2011, 6).

Hypodescent had unintended consequences for groups of color, especially blacks. By drawing boundaries that excluded blacks from having contact as equals with whites, it legitimated and forged group identities among the former. Consequently, blacks hold on tenaciously to the onedrop rule. It is considered a necessary, if originally oppressive, means of maintaining the integrity of the black community and mobilizing in the continuing struggle against racial inequality (Daniel 2006, 217). Yet the rule has become so accepted in the U.S. that its oppressive origins are largely obscured and its logic never questioned. It is part of what Bourdieu defines as the "doxa" (Bourdieu 1977, 159)—the sphere of sacrosanct or unquestioned social dogmas that have acquired the force of nature. Individuals reinforce, if only unwittingly, blackness and whiteness or any other racial designations as if they were mutually exclusive, if not hierarchical categories of experience, as well as objective phenomena with an independent existence of their own.

Hypodescent is the lynchpin of U.S. constructions of whiteness, including notions of white racial purity, which have been critical to maintaining white racial privilege. It is also the basis of monoraciality and its associated advantages that accrue to European Americans as well as groups of color ("monoracial privilege") (Nadal 2011, 43). Consequently, monoraciality has been internalized as the normative pattern of identification. It has suppressed a multiracial identity through macroagressions and mezzoagressions involving institutions and organizations respectively that structure the behavior of actors in the political and cultural economy. Johnston and Nadal argue that monoraciality has also sustained microaggressions in the sphere of interpersonal relations, where individuals are the perpetrators (Johnston and Nadal 2010, 123–44). Whether intentional or unintentional, these discriminatory attitudes and practices form part of what they refer to as "monoracism" (Johnston and Nadal 2011, 127; Nadal 2011, 43).

A critique of monoraciality should not be understood as a dismissal of monoracial forms of identification as illegitimate. Rather, it interrogates the external ascription of monoracial categories of identification that delegitimizes all other forms of identification. Monoraciality is itself reflective of a broader "monological" paradigm premised on an "either/or" mentation, which seeks to erase complexity, multiplicity, and ambiguity. Singularity is the norm in terms of the construction of all categories of difference encompassing race, gender, sexuality, and a host of others including one's stance on critical social issues relating to morality and politics (Colker 1996, 1–10; Daniel 2012, 244; Wilber 1997, 71–92; Wilber 1998, 141; Wilber 2000, 278).

This chapter explores several questions. First, to what extent has the U.S. racial order become more willing to bend or break the one-drop rule, as indicated by the election to the nation's highest office the first African-descent American, who is also the multiracial offspring of an African father and European American mother? In other words, to what extent does the election of Barack Obama indicate a decrease in the rigid enforcement of the one-drop rule as the primary factor determining the social location of African-descent Americans? Finally, to what extent is Obama's election emblematic of increasing inclusiveness of African-descent Americans as equals more generally in the U.S. racial order?

BLACK AND MORE THAN BLACK: TOWARD A MORE PERFECT UNION

On March 18, 2008, at the National Constitution Center in Philadelphia, Pennsylvania, presidential candidate, then senator Barack Obama delivered a speech entitled "A More Perfect Union." Since announcing his candidacy, Obama sought to maintain a "race-neutral" campaign. He was forced to address racial concerns in response to the controversy surrounding Reverend Jeremiah Wright, the pastor of his church in Chicago, Trinity United Church of Christ. In several sermons, Wright made what some considered inflammatory remarks about U.S. race relations and foreign policy (Ross and el-Buri 2008). Obama's thirty-minute speech was a persuasive piece of oratory on race relations unlike anything one customarily hears from politicians.[2] It was more analogous to a thoughtful history and sociology lesson. On several occasions, Obama addressed the topic of multiraciality (Ponder 2012, 62). He mentioned his interracial parentage and noted that some commentators questioned whether he is either "too black" or "not black enough" (Obama 2008b). He stated that Michelle Obama is the descendent of slaveowners and slaves, a heritage that has been passed on to their two daughters; and finally, Obama acknowledged his large international family that includes individuals scattered across several continents.

Obama also contextualized Wright's remarks. He discussed white racism, white privilege, racial inequality, and provided a nuanced framing of "black anger" and "white resentment" (Obama 2008b). He acknowledged these phenomena as expressions of the racial and class strife that has marred the egalitarian principles set forth in the nation's founding documents. The title and sentiment of Obama's speech were thus taken from the U.S. Constitution and, by extension, the Bill of Rights. The speech also called to mind the Declaration of Independence by symbolically offering a "Declaration of Interdependence,"[3] which could bring the nation closer to perfecting the union envisioned in its originating principles. Obama's address also hearkened back to Dr. Martin Luther King, Jr.'s "I Have a Dream" speech, which he presented at the August 28, 1963, March on Washington. King called upon the nation to live out the meaning of its founding documents and judge individuals by the content of their character rather than by the color of their skin.

Reverend Jesse Jackson's 1984 and 1988 presidential campaigns—particularly his 1984 speech, which laid the foundation for his even more successful 1988 campaign—is perhaps the most immediate precursor of Obama's Philadelphia speech. Obama distanced himself from Reverends Jackson and Al Sharpton,[4] as well as other black political figures whose worldviews were informed by the mass protests against Jim Crow segregation.[5] Yet Jackson's speech demonstrated the effectiveness of moving beyond calls simply for black mobilization to include appeals that would resonate with a substantial plurality of white voters as well as other communities of color (Walters 2005, 133–44; Walters 2007, 15–16). Obama's speech demonstrated "the transformative ability of oratory to infuse familiar ideas with new meanings" (Carson 2009).[6]

Obama's Philadelphia address, like his other speeches and writings, was a masterful example of what Frank and McPhail call the "rhetoric of consilience" (Frank and McPhail 2005, 571–94). In this strategy, "understanding results through translation, mediation, and an embrace of different languages, values, and traditions" (Frank and McPhail 2005, 578). Obama juxtaposes the trials and tribulations of blacks with those of other racial groups, including whites, but without equating them. He conceptualizes a race-neutral space where they may share common principles and the "transcendent value" of equity and justice (Shafer 2008).

Yet black public figures, particularly individuals seeking elective office, often studiously avoid or minimize the topic of race in order to appeal to a larger, particularly white, constituency (Davis 2011, 48–49). Steele refers to this racial diplomacy as "bargaining" (Steele 2004, 73). Bargaining seeks to disarm race for whites by extending them racial redemption from the historical injustices inflicted on blacks. It also holds out the promise of race-neutrality in addressing contemporary inequality and the pursuit of social justice. But bargaining trusts that whites will reciprocate by not holding the bargainers' race against them given the magnanimity of the original gesture (Steele 2004, 74–75; Wingfield and Feagin 2009, 33; Wingfield and Feagin 2012, 1–29). On the other hand, "challenging" (Steele 2004, 73), embodied in the civil rights tradition of leadership personified by Reverend Wright, confronts whites with the injustices perpetuated against blacks. An expectation is that whites take some ownership of corrective and compensatory measures, legal and otherwise, to help eliminate racial inequality (Steele 2004, 77–78: Wingfield and Feagin 2009, 4).[7]

Obama sought to differentiate himself from the civil rights tradition of leadership but conveyed respect for it. Indeed, the civil rights struggle contributed to social advances that made possible his nomination and eventual election (Sugrue 2012, 13–16). Obama provided a compassionate explanation for Wright's comments without justifying them, and denounced them without rejecting the minister himself (Obama 2008b, 17–23). Obama eventually severed ties with Wright and his church by virtue of additional controversial assertions he made in an interview on *Bill Moyers Journal* and in speeches at the National Association for the Advancement of Colored People (NAACP) in Detroit and the National Press Club in Washington, D.C. (Johnson 2008; Neumeister 2010).[8] The delicate task of bargaining, apart from Obama's intense campaign schedule, may, in part, explain why he declined to appear at Tavis Smiley's "State of the Black Union" symposium in New Orleans in February 2008 (Mitchell 2008)[9] and at the Lorraine Motel in Memphis on the anniversary of Dr. Martin Luther King Jr.'s assassination in April 2008 (MacGillis 2008).

Obama's skillful deployment of bargaining and consilience is integrally connected to his experience as the son of a white mother from Kansas, the heartland of the United States, and black father from Kenya, the African homeland of humanity. Obama has stated, "I am rooted in the African-American community. But I'm not defined by it. I am comfortable in my racial identity. But that's not all I am" (CBS 2007a). In his autobiography *Dreams from My Father: A Story of Race and Inheritance*, Obama maintains, "I learned to slip back and forth between my black and white worlds, understanding that each possessed its own language and customs and structures of meaning, convinced that with a bit of translation on my part the two worlds would eventually cohere" (Obama 1995, 82).

The immediacy of Obama's interracial parentage and rearing outside the continental United States, in Hawai'i and Indonesia, by his white mother and her relatives, along with his Indonesian stepfather (Obama 1995, xv, 23–25, 30–33), has imbued his consciousness with a broader vision and wider ranging sympathies in forming an identity. This enhances his image as the physical embodiment of the principles of inclusiveness and equity. Yet Obama has never said he *identifies* as multiracial (Dariotis and Yoo 2012, 99, 105; Jeffries 2014, 64–70; King-O'Riain 2013, 114; Miletsky 2012, 142; Ponder 2012, 76).[10] This was underscored when he checked only the "Black, African American, or Negro" box on the 2010 census race question even though, since 2000, respondents have been allowed to check more than one box (Roberts and Baker 2010). To the disappointment of MAVIN, one of the nation's multiracial advocacy groups, Obama cautioned about a multiracial identity in conversation with organization representatives who were hoping to capitalize on his celebrity for their documentary film "Chasing Day Break" (Elam 2011, 35–36).

For all his hybridity, Obama's identity is situated in the black community and extends outward from that location (Collins 2012, 169–90). This differs from a multiracial identity, which manifests itself "betwixt and between" the boundaries of traditional U.S. racial groups (Turner 1969, 97). It extends outward from this liminal location depending upon individuals' orientation toward the groups that compose their background (Anzaldúa 1987, 77–91; Daniel 2002, 93–113; Renn 2004, 67–93; Rockquemore and Brunsma 2002, 40–52; Rockquemore, Brunsma, and Delgado 2009, 13–34; Wallace 2001, 121–25, 147–52). Despite myriad backgrounds, experiences, and identities, the shared liminality based on identification with more than one racial background becomes an integral part of the self-conception of multiracial-identified individuals, and a defining component of the multiracial experience (Cornell and Hartmann 1998, 86, 96). This identity interrogates the "either/or" thinking that underpins U.S. racial formation and seeks to shift to a "both/neither" mindset (Daniel 2002, 3, 10, 111).

Since the late 1960s, growing numbers of individuals have challenged hypodescent and its proscriptions. This is related to the dismantling of Jim Crow segregation and implementation of civil rights legislation during the 1950s and 1960s. More specifically, it is attributable to the landmark 1967 decision in *Loving v. Virginia*, which overturned statutes in the remaining sixteen states prohibiting racial intermarriage. Previously, the racial state regarded interracial intimacy as a private rather than public matter. This was part of the state's tactic of deflecting attention away from the contradictions between its espousal of freedom and justice and the empirical realities of Jim Crow segregation, including anti-miscegenation statutes.

Interracial intimacy thus became central to the debate on the relationship of private matters to the public sphere of civil rights activism. Many activists wanted interracial intimacy to be considered a public matter as part of the promotion of equal rights and social justice, particularly in terms of black-white relations. They endeavored to achieve this primarily through popular culture, but also through litigation. Activists hoped to expose the pervasive racism in the legal system of a nation that trumpeted itself as the arsenal of democracy to the rest of the world (Lubin 2005, ix–xxi, 66–95, 151–59; Moran 2007, 239, 249–50). The *Loving* decision did not, however, derive from the civil rights movement itself although the changing climate engendered by the movement paved the way. It originated in a lawsuit filed by an interracial couple, Richard Loving, who was European American, and his wife Mildred Jeter, who was an African-descent American. They took their case to the Supreme Court, which ruled anti-miscegenation laws unconstitutional (Daniel 2002, 97).

In 1961, when Barack Obama was born, twenty-one states still maintained anti-miscegenation laws, the majority of whites disapproved of racial intermarriage (96 percent according to survey research), and individuals who dared cross the racial divide were considered deviants (Altman and Klinkner 2006, 299–315; Dedman 2008; Rockquemore and Brunsma, 21). Furthermore, Obama grew up in an era when a multiracial identity was not an option. This identity is more common among offspring of interracial marriages, including black-white individuals, born in the post–civil rights era. Many individuals display traditional monoracial identities. Increasing numbers exhibit a multiracial consciousness based on identification with more than one racial background (Binning, Unzueta, Huo, and Molina 2009, 36–36, 44–46; Korgen 1998, 9–56; Renn 2004, 67–94; Rockquemore and Brunsma 21, 41–48).

Beginning in the late 1970s, this consciousness emerged in a movement seeking to change official racial-data collection standards that required individuals to identify with only one racial background (DaCosta 2007, 21–46; Daniel 2002, 125–54; Williams 2006, 1–64). By the 2000 census, this movement succeeded in making it possible for individuals to express a multiracial identity by checking more than one box in the race question (DaCosta 2007, 2–4, 21–46; Daniel 2002, 125–51; Williams 2008, 39–84). Consequently, many scholars argue that the one-drop rule has less impact on identity formation of multiracials of partial African descent. Others contend it still influences identity formation through external imposition as well as self-ascription (Jeffries 2014, 64–70; Khanna 2010, 96–121; Rockquemore and Brunsma 2002, 45–46).

BLACK, WHITE, AND MULTIRACIAL: A MORE PERFECT UNION

Barack Obama's significance as the first African-descent American elected to the nation's highest office cannot be underestimated. It demonstrates the considerable gains some blacks have made since the 1960s. Obama's election has transformed the aesthetic of the nation's political landscape and instilled a sense of pride and optimism in African Americans while inspiring more black youth to realize their potential for advancement. If Obama has significance for African Americans, he has special meaning for the growing population of multiracial-identified Americans (Jeffries 2014, 64–70). Multiracials totaled 7 million on the 2000 census (Stuckey 2008; Jones 2005). Based on 2010 census data, their numbers increased to 9 million—or 2.9 percent of the population. Although they still make up only a fraction of the total population, this is a growth rate of about 32 percent since 2000, when multiracials composed 2.4 percent of the population (Humes, Jones, and Ramirez 2011, 6–7).

Although Obama does not identify as multiracial, his public success, loving extended interracial family, and comfort as an African American who acknowledges his multiracial background indicates how much things have changed since he was born (Dedman 2008). During his first news conference as president-elect, Obama conveyed this comfort with the throwaway response "mutts like me" when asked by reporters what types of puppies he would consider getting for his daughters. This was a more personalized reference to

Obama's multiracial background than his typically more oblique reference to it by mentioning his parents.[11] Moreover, Obama's open discussion of his multiracial background, along with heightened interest among lay and professional genealogists, has provided the U.S. with an opportunity to embrace itself as a more complex and interconnected racial terrain. In the past, few records were available and only enthusiasts made the effort to do genealogical research. The abundance of information on the Internet, including Ancestry.com's massive data base in Provo, Utah, as well as information publically available on family genealogy websites, coupled with the ease and increased sophistication of DNA testing, now makes it possible to verify the centuries of extensive racial intermingling (Stolberg 2012).

For example, Lynne Cheney, in doing research for *Blue Skies, No Fences*, a memoir about growing up in Wyoming, discovered that Obama and then-Vice President Dick Cheney share a seventeenth-century white male ancestor, which makes them eighth cousins (Associated Press 2007). Billionaire financier Warren Buffett and Obama are seventh cousins, three times removed. Obama and the former Republican senator from Massachusetts, Scott Brown, are tenth cousins. Actor Brad Pitt and Obama are ninth cousins. Sarah Palin and Barack Obama are tenth cousins. The president is also tenth cousins (once removed) with Rush Limbaugh (Rose 2010). Obama's other distant cousins include former President George W. Bush and his father, George H. W. Bush, Gerald Ford, Lyndon Johnson, Harry S. Truman, James Madison, British prime minister Sir Winston Churchill, and Civil War general Robert E. Lee (Johnson 2010; Jones 2009; Lavoie 2008).

In September 2009, former professional African American boxer Muhammad Ali visited Ennis, Ireland, to celebrate his Irish ancestry. A plaque was unveiled in the city to honor Ali's ancestors, particularly the ancestors and descendants of his great-grandfather Abe Grady, who immigrated to the United States in the 1860s and married a black woman (Associated Press 2009a; Pogatchnik 2009). Some of Senator McCain's white male ancestors reportedly not only owned slaves but also fathered children with slave women. These individuals have living descendants as do many others who were enslaved on the McCain plantation.[12]

Michelle Obama has Native American ancestry and her maternal third great-grandfather was European American. This individual fathered a biracial son, Dolphus T. Shields, with Melvina Shields, who was the First Lady's maternal third great-grandmother. Both Melvina and Dolphus were slaves. Consequently, the latter was born outside of wedlock, and may have been the product of rape. These findings substantiate a longstanding family rumor about a white forebear (Smolenyak 2009; Swarns 2012a, 210; Swarns and Kantor 2009). Anyone familiar with U.S. history would not be startled by these revelations. While blacks are monoracially identified, most have African, European, and in many cases, Native American ancestry, although the actual combination varies from individual to individual. Furthermore, for several centuries many blacks who are predominantly European in ancestry have displayed phenotypes that have made it possible for them to "pass for white." Whites with African ancestry inherited from these individuals number in the millions (Davis 1991, 52).

The public disclosure and discussion of Michelle Obama's genealogy provides a direct link between her ancestors' journey from servitude and her seat in the Office of the First Lady (Swarns and Kantor 2009). It is also another opportunity for increased openness and honesty in discussing multiraciality as an integral part of the nation's history, which has been obscured by centuries of racism. A requisite component of this conversation would involve acknowledging that the multiracial phenomenon in the U.S. historically originated in interracial relationships largely consummated more through coercion and violence during slavery, as was most likely the case with Michelle Obama's third great-grandparents, than mutual consent and peaceful means, as in the case of Barack Obama's parents.

If Barack Obama's biography has suggested his background does not include slave ancestors, genealogists of Ancestry.com have discovered marriage and property records, which, along with DNA evidence, challenge that assumption. Their findings indicate Obama's maternal lineage may include an individual of African descent in colonial Virginia named John Punch. In 1640, Punch was an indentured servant who escaped from Virginia to Maryland. He was captured in Maryland, along with two white servants who also escaped, and was put on trial. Punch's punishment—servitude for life—was harsher than that of the white servants. This was years before Virginia legalized slavery, which held individuals in bondage in perpetuity. Historians have never been able to pinpoint an exact date for the beginning of African slavery in the U.S. Some now regard Punch as the first individual of African descent to be legally enslaved (Stolberg 2012).

Records suggest Punch fathered children with a white woman, who passed her free status on to them. This gave rise to a family with a slightly different name, Bunch, of which Obama's mother, Stanley Ann Dunham, is a descendent. The genealogists traced two major Bunch family lineages, one that migrated to North Carolina, where they were recorded as "mulatto" in early records. The other lineage remained in Virginia, continued to intermarry, became prominent landowners, and was considered white. Obama descends from the Virginia line, which eventually migrated to Tennessee, where his great-great-great-great-grandmother Anna Bunch was born. Her daughter, Frances Allred, who was born in 1834, moved to Kansas where Dunham was born in 1942. There is no indication Dunham knew about her African American ancestry. Because many records have been destroyed, researches could not make a definitive determination of whether John Punch, the slave, is a Bunch ancestor. However, the Bunch family maintains an online database that traces their genealogy. It is supplemented with DNA tests indicating the men in the family have genetic markers consistent with sub-Saharan African ancestry (Stolberg 2012).

In the media Obama is generally referred to as black or African American, less frequently as multiracial or biracial. Yet individuals have displayed varying responses in terms of how he is viewed racially. Data on these attitudes were collected for Mark Williams by Zogby International in a November 2006 Internet poll of 2,155 people. Individuals were told Obama's parents' background, and then were asked to identify Obama's race. Obama was identified as black by 66 percent of African Americans, 9 percent of Latinas/os, 8 percent of whites, and 8 percent of Asian Americans. He was designated with multiracial-identifiers by 88 percent of Latinas/os, 80 percent of whites, 77 percent of Asian Americans, and 34 percent of African Americans.[13]

Obama's multiracial background has made it possible for a wide range of individuals to feel comfortable with him, which was instrumental in building an impressive voter coalition in 2008. According to election polls, this included 95 percent of blacks and a 2-1 advantage among all other racial groups, including Latinas/os, Asian Americans, and others. In addition, Obama carried every age group other than those sixty-five and older (Mercurio 2008). Young people of all racial groups born roughly between 1982 and 2003—the "Millennial generation" (Apollon 2011, 1; Winograd and Hais 2008, 66–67)—have been among Obama's most ardent supporters. According to figures from the 2008 Current Population Survey, slightly more than half of Millennials—56 percent—are European American. The remaining 44 percent are Latina/o (20 percent), African American (15 percent), Asian American (5 percent), multiracial (3 percent), and Native American (1), with a significantly larger share of blacks and multiracials than previous generations. This population is the most racially diverse cohort in U.S. history and has been exposed to a comparatively more racially diverse society than any previous generations (Apollon 2011, 3–28; Tseng 2008).

That said, Senator McCain led Obama by twelve points among white voters. However, this is hardly the anticipated "Bradley Effect"[14] in which whites, who oppose a black politician, mislead pollsters about the candidate for whom they will vote in order to appear racially unbiased (Mercurio 2008). Obama won decisively in the electoral vote (Obama 365, McCain 173). The popular vote was considerably closer (Obama 66, 882, 230, McCain, 58, 343, 671). Obama garnered 53 percent and McCain 46 percent (CNN 2008). Pre-election polls were generally accurate in reflecting voters' preference for Obama. The recent economic crisis supplanted Iraq as the dominant campaign issue (MacAskill 2008). A candidate's perceived ability to handle that turmoil, along with widespread dissatisfaction with the Bush administration, was a deciding factor in the election. Those sentiments, apart from questions of race, gave Obama an edge over McCain despite the latter's strength in national security (Feldman 2008).

In the 2012 election, Obama's showing of 93 percent among blacks, who turned out in record numbers, was all but guaranteed. The true game changer came with garnering 73 percent of the Asian American vote and 71 percent of the Latina/o vote. Asian Americans in particular have remained an elusive voter bloc. Support from these communities is attributable in part to massive organizing in response to voter suppression efforts in more than a dozen states. Republicans passed restrictions aimed at reducing the turnout of Obama's "coalition of the ascendant"—young voters, African Americans, and Latinas/os (Berman 2012). According to 2012 exit polls, nationally Romney won 60 percent of the white vote; Obama garnered 40 percent (Scocca 2012). However, 60 percent of Obama's supporters were 18–29 years of age, and 54 percent of females voted for him (Murray 2012). A newly released voter poll found that feminists, not simply women in general, were critical to Obama's 2012 re-election (Plank 2013).[15]

NOTES

Earlier versions of this chapter appeared in *The Black Scholar* 39, no. 1 (Fall/Winter 2009), 51–59, and *Barack Obama and the Biracial Factor: The Battle for a New American Majority*, ed. Andrew J. Jolivétte (Bristol, UK: Polity Press, 2012), 21–59.

1. U.S. attitudes toward the offspring of unions between blacks and other groups of color (e.g., Native Americans) have varied. More often than not, these individuals have been subject to the one-drop rule.

2. Houston Baker was less sanguine about Obama's speech. He states:

   > *Sen. Obama's race speech at the National Constitution Center, draped in American flags, was reminiscent of the Parthenon concluding scene of Robert Altman's Nashville: a bizarre moment of mimicry, aping Martin Luther King Jr., while even further distancing himself from the real, economic, religious and political issues so courageously articulated by King from a Birmingham jail. In brief, Obama's speech was a pandering disaster that threw, once again, his pastor under the bus." "What Should Obama Do About Rev. Jeremiah Wright?"* (Salon.com. 2008)

   Utley and Heyse in this volume argue that Obama's speech was an appropriate and successful response to a political-personal crisis. He negotiated the controversy surrounding his personal relationship with Rev. Wright by acknowledging racial disparities in the U.S. without placing blame for those disparities. Accordingly, Obama maintained a post-racial rhetorical stance that appealed to extremely diverse audiences. They argue, however, that the speech failed to accurately represent a racially differentiated United States. By sanitizing the nation's histories of chattel slavery and racism, Obama's speech reified many harmful racial tropes.

3. The Declaration of Interdependence was a movement spearheaded in the 1940s by Pulitzer Prize-winning philosopher Will Durant. A primary goal was to reduce racial hostility by promoting human tolerance, fellowship, and mutual respect. Will Durant Foundation, http://www.willdurant.com/interdependence.htm.

4. Sharpton stated he has strategically underplayed his hand, avoiding public appearances with Obama during the election campaigns since it could be used by his opponents to discredit him. However, Sharpton has been to the White House at least eight times since Obama's 2008 election. Todd Boyd, a professor of African American studies at the University of Southern California, sees a cynical ploy by Obama to use Sharpton as a foil to Jackson, embracing what he considers the lesser of two evils (Samuels and Adler 2010).

5. Yet, since 2008 the Obama administration has worked closely with the National Association for the Advancement of Colored People (NAACP) under the leadership of Ben Jealous. The organization expanded its focus to include immigration, gay rights, and voting rights, which have been among Obama's leading priorities. Jealous was instrumental in helping ex-felons, many of them African American, obtain voting rights. Jealous and his colleagues thus had ready access to Obama, which opened the door for the organization to raise money to dig out of a gaping financial hole. The group was criticized for working so closely with the Obama Administration that it was unable to effectively criticize the latter ("NAACP President Ben Jealous Abruptly Announces His Resignation," *Your Black World*, September 8, 2013. http://www.yourblackworld.net/2013/09/black-news/naacp-president-ben-jealous-abruptly-announces-his-resignation/).

6. One also hears echoes of Senator Barbara Jordan's "We the People" speech, which she delivered at the 1974 Watergate Hearings concerning the impeachment of President Nixon, as well as her keynote address at the 1967 Democratic Convention.

7. Both tactics may be employed by anyone seeking inclusion in the white male-dominated mainstream of society. Also, they are applicable to aggrieved groups besides blacks.

8. In a 2010 letter obtained by the Associated Press, Wright told a group seeking to raise funds for African relief that his pleas to release frozen funds for use in earthquake-ravaged Haiti would likely be ignored. "No one in the Obama administration will respond to me, listen to me, talk to me or read anything that I write to them." He said he is "toxic" to the Obama administration and that President Obama "threw me under the bus" (Schapiro 2010).

9. Obama asked that his wife, Michelle, be allowed to speak on his behalf.

10 Jeffries conducted in-depth interviews with multiracial-identified college students to determine their perceptions of Barack Obama. Interviews examined the influence of race on Obama's identity management and political career, the relationship between Obama and respondents' multiracial identity, and Obama's impact on U.S. race relations. Notwithstanding the fact that Obama does not embrace a multiracial identity, respondents held favorable opinions of him and respected his right to identify as black. Though sometimes deeply disappointed in that choice, they believed emphasis on Obama's blackness, rather than his multiraciality, is the outcome of personal choice and political pressure. That said, they emphasized that racism remains a significant factor in Obama's career and in the United States more generally (Jeffries 2012, 49–79, 183–200).

11 This comment was not unanimously considered positive. Some individuals viewed it as a re-articulation of previous pathological images of multiracials as social misfits and genetically inferior (Fram 2008; Graham 2008).

12 The tradition among the black McCains is that they have biological ties to the white McCains. The latter say they are unaware of this connection (Blackmon 2008).

13 Most respondents designated Obama with multiracial-identifiers. Small percentages responded with "white," "none of the above," and "not sure." Blacks upheld the one-drop rule. See Johnson 2010; Williams 2006.

14 This trend is named after Democratic candidate Tom Bradley, a former black mayor of Los Angeles, who lost the 1982 California gubernatorial election after leading in the polls. Exit polls indicated Bradley leading by a wide margin. He thought there would be an early election night. However, Bradley lost to Republican candidate George Deukmejian. Subsequently, other black candidates who were comfortably ahead in polls lost or narrowly won the elections. For example, in the 1989 Virginia gubernatorial race, Democrat L. Douglas Wilder, who is black, won by less than half of 1 percent over Marshall Coleman, the Republican candidate, who is white. However, pre-election exit polls showed Wilder on average with a comfortable 9 percent lead over Coleman. Other elections cited as possible indications of the Bradley effect include the 1983 and 1989 mayoral elections, respectively, in Chicago and New York City (Associated Press 2008b).

15 A record number of deportations during Obama's first administration have left many immigrants, largely people of color, and others ambivalent about his policies (Shalal-Esa 2012). Obama appointed individuals of color and women to important governmental positions during his first administration, and many of his top advisers and staffers in the White House are women. Obama's cabinet has been largely composed of white males (Lawrence 2013; K. Liptak 2013).

REFERENCES

Altman, Micah, and Philip A. Klinkner, 2006. "Measuring the Difference between White Voting and Polling on Interracial Marriage." *Du Bois Review* 3(2)(September): 299–315.

Anzaldúa, Gloria. 1987. *Borderlands: La Frontera—The New Mestiza*. San Francisco: Spinsters/Aunt Lute.

Apollon, Dominique. 2011. "Don't Call Them 'Post-Racial.' Millennials' Attitudes on Race, Racism, and Key Systems in Our Society." Applied Research Center. June 7. http://www.racialequitytools.org/resourcefiles/ARC_Millennials_Report_June_2011.pdf.

Associated Press. 2007. "Lynne Cheney: VP, Obama Are Eighth Cousins." MSNBC, October 17. http://www.msnbc.msn.com/id/21340764/.

———. 2008b. "What Bradley Effect? No Hidden Bias Seen in '08." MSNBC, November 7. http://www.msnbc.msn.com/id/27589729/from/ET/.

———. 2009a. "Ali Visiting Irish Home of His Ancestors, Boxing Legend Meets Distant Relatives During Celebrations." MSNBC, September 1. http://nbcsports.msnbc.com/ id/32640853/ns/sports-other_sports/.

Barthé, Darryl G., Jr. 2012. "Racial Revisionism, Caste Revisited: Whiteness, Blackness, and Barack Obama." In *Obama and the Biracial Factor: The Battle for a New American Majority*, ed. Andrew J. Jolivétte, 81–98. Bristol, UK: Policy Press.

Berman, Ari. 2012. "Tea Party and the Right, the GOP's Voter Suppression Strategy." *Alternet*, November 26. http://www.alternet.org/tea-party-and-right/gops-voter-suppression-strategy?akid=9721.3701.g43T5R&rd=1&src=newsletter750513&t=14.

Binning, Kevin R., Miguel M. Unzueta, Yuen J. Huo, and Ludwin E. Molina. 2009. "The Interpretation of Multiracial Status and Its Relation to Social Engagement and Psychological Well-being." *Journal of Social Issues* 65(1): 35–49.

Blackmon, Douglas A. 2008. "Two Families Named McCain: Candidate's Kin Share a History with Descendants of Slaves." *Wall Street Journal*, October 17. http://online.wsj.com/article/SB122419511761942501.html.

Bourdieu, Pierre. 1977. *Outline of a Theory of Practice*. Trans. Richard Nice. New York: Cambridge University Press.

Carson, Clayborne. 2009, "King, Obama, and the Great American Dialogue: What Would Martin Luther King Jr.—Had He Been Alive Today—Have Thought of Our Latest President's Oratory?" *American Heritage People*, May 25. http://www.americanheritage.com/articles/web/20090525-President-Civil-Rights-Martin-Luther-King-Jr-Barack-Obama-Speech-I-Have-A-Dream.shtml>.

CBS. 2007a. "Candidate Obama's Sense of Urgency." *60 Minutes*, February 11.

CNN.com. 2008. "Election Center 2008, President Full Results." November 17. http://www.cnn.com/ELECTION/2008/results/president/.

Colker, Ruth. 1996. *Hybrid: Bisexuals, Multiracials, and Other Misfits under American Law*. New York: New York University Press.

Collins, Robert Keith. 2012. "A Different Kind of Blackness: The Question of Obama's Blackness and Intraracial Variation Among African Americans." In *Obama and the Biracial Factor: The Battle for a New American Majority*, ed. Andrew J. Jolivétte, 169–90. Bristol, UK: Policy Press.

Cornell, Stephen, and Douglas Hartmann. 1998. *Ethnicity and Race: Making Identities in a Changing World*. Thousand Oaks, CA: Pine Forge Press

DaCosta, Kimberly McClain. 2007. *Making Multiracials: State, Family, and Market in the Redrawing of the Color Line*. Palo Alto: Stanford University Press.

Daniel, G. Reginald. 2002. *More Than Black?: Multiracial identity and the New Racial Order*. Philadelphia: Temple University Press.

_____. 2006. *Race and Multiraciality in Brazil and the United States: Converging Paths?* University Park: Pennsylvania State University Press.

_____. 2012. *Machado de Assis: Multiracial Identity and the Brazilian Novelist*. University Park: Pennsylvania State University Press.

Dariotis, Wei Ming, and Grace J. Yoo. 2012. "Obama Mamas and Mixed Race: Hoping for 'A More Perfect Union.'" In *Obama and the Biracial Factor: The Battle for a New American Majority*, ed. Andrew J. Jolivétte, 99–112. Bristol, UK: Policy Press.

Davis, F. James. 1991. *Who is Black? One Nation's Definition*. University Park: Pennsylvania State University Press.

Davis, John. 2011. *The Barack Obama Presidency: A Two Year Assessment*. New York: Palgrave Macmillan.

Dedman, Bill. 2008. "Historians Write 1st Draft on Obama Victory." MSNBC, November 5. http://www.msnbc.msn.com/id/27539416/from/ET.

Elam, Michele. 2011. *The Souls of Mixed Folk: Race, Politics, and Aesthetics in the New Millennium*. Palo Alto, CA: Stanford University Press.

Feldman, Stanley. 2008. "Why Obama Won." CBS News, November 5. http://www.cbsnews.com/stories/2008/11/05/politics/main4572555.shtml.

Fram, Alan. 2008. "'Mutts Like Me' Shows Obama's Racial Comfort." MSNBC, November 8. http://www.msnbc.msn.com/id/27606637/.

Frank, David A., and Mark Lawrence McPhail. 2005. "Barack Obama's address to the 2004 Democratic National Convention: Trauma, Compromise, Consilience, and the (Im) possibility of Racial Reconciliation." *Rhetoric and Public Affairs* 8(4): 571–94.

Graham, Susan. 2008. "Dogs Are Mutts; People Are Multiracial." November 21. http://www.projectrace.com/fromthedirector/archive/112108_obama_mutt_multiracial.php.

Hodes, Martha. 1997. *White Women, Black Men: Illicit Sex in the Nineteenth-Century South*. New Haven: Yale University Press.

Humes, Karen R., Nicholas A. Jones, and Roberto R. Ramirez. 2011. "Overview of Race and Hispanic Origin: 2010." 2010 Census Briefs. Washington, D.C.: U.S. Census Bureau, March 2011. http://www.census.gov/prod/cen2010/briefs/c2010br-02.pdf.

Jeffries, Michael P. 2013. *Paint the White House Black: Barack Obama and the Meaning of Race in America*. Palo Alto, CA: Stanford University Press.

Johnson, Glen. 2010. "President Obama, Scott Brown Related, Genealogists Say." *Huffington Post*, January 29. http://www.huffingtonpost.com/2010/01/29/president-obama-scott-bro_n_441754.html.

Johnson, L. A. 2008. "Obama Candidacy Raises Old Questions about What Is Black." *Pittsburgh Post-Gazette*, March 8. http://www.post-gazette.com/pg/08129/879988-176.stm.

Johnston, Marc P., and Kevin L. Nadal. 2010. "Multiracial Microaggressions: Exposing Monoracism." In *Microaggressions and Marginality: Manifestation, Dynamics, and Impact*, ed. Derald Wing Sue, 123–44. Hoboken, NJ: John Wiley and Sons.

Jolivétte, Andrew J. "Obama and the Biracial Factor: An Introduction." In *Obama and the Biracial Factor: The Battle for a New American Majority*, ed. Andrew J. Jolivétte, 3–30. Bristol, UK: Policy Press.

Jones, Nicholas A. 2005. "We the People of More Than One Race in the United States." Census 2000 Special Reports, CENSR-22. Washington, D.C.: U.S. Census Bureau, April. http://www.census.gov/prod/2005pubs/censr-22.pdf.

Jones, Stephanie J., ed. 2009. *The State of Black America 2009: Message to the President*. New York: National Urban League.

Jordan, Winthrop D. 2014. "Historical Origins of the One-Drop Racial Rule in the United States." *Journal of Critical Mixed Race Studies* 1(1): 98–132.

Khanna, Nikki. 2010. "'If You're Half Black, You're Just Black': Reflected Appraisals and the Persistence of the One-drop Rule.'" *Sociological Quarterly* 51(1): 96–121.

King-O'Riain, Rebecca Chiyoko. 2012. "Is 'No One as Irish as Barack O'Bama?'" In *Obama and the Biracial Factor: The Battle for a New American Majority*, ed. Andrew J. Jolivétte, 113–28. Bristol, UK: Policy Press.

Korgen, Kathleen O. 1998. *From Black to Biracial: Transforming Racial Identity Among Americans*, Westport, CT: Praeger.

Lavoie, Denise. 2008. "Barack Obama and Brad Pitt Are Cousins, Hillary Clinton and Angelina Jolie Are Also Cousins, Study Says." *Huffington Post*, March 25. http://www.huffingtonpost.com/2008/03/25/barack-obama-and-brad-pit_n_93356.html.

Lawrence, Jill. 2013. "Why Obama's White-Guy Problem Seems Worse Than It Is." *National Journal*, May 30. http://www.nationaljournal.com/whitehouse/why-obama-s-white-guy-problem-seems-worse-than-it-is-20130109.

Lipsitz, George. 1998. *The Possessive Investment in Whiteness: How White People Profit from Identity Politics*. Philadelphia: Temple University Press.

_____. 2011. *How Racism Takes Place*. Philadelphia: Temple University Press.

Liptak, Kevin. 2013. "Obama Urges Patience to Critics of White Male Nominees." *Political-ticker*, January 14. http://political-ticker.blogs.cnn.com/2013/01/14/obama-urges-patience-to-critics-of-white-male-nominees/.

Lubin, Alex. 2005. *Romance and Rights: The Politics of Interracial Intimacy, 1945–1954*. Jackson: University Press of Mississippi.

MacAskill, Ewen. 2008. "US Election: Buffett Joins Obama to Solve Economic Crisis." *Guardian*, July 29. http://www.guardian.co.uk/world/2008/jul/29/barackobama.uselections2008.

MacGillis, Alec. 2008. "Obama Recalls a Fuller History." *Washington Post*, April 4. http://blog.washingtonpost.com/the-trail/2008/04/04/obama_recalls_a_fuller_history.html.

Mercurio, John. 2008. "The Final Surprise: Obama's Key Groups." MSNBC, November 5. http://www.msnbc.msn.com/id/27557327/.

Miletsky, Zebulon Vance. 2013. "Mutt Like Me: Barack Obama and the Mixed Race Experience in Historical Perspective." In *Obama and the Biracial Factor: The Battle for a New American Majority*, ed. Andrew J. Jolivétte, 141–68. Bristol, UK: Policy Press.

Mitchell, Mary. 2008. "Discussions Across the Racial Divide." *Chicago Sun-Times*, February 14. http://blogs.suntimes.com/mitchell/2008/02/sen_barack_obamas_letter_to_ta_1.html.

Moran, Rachel F. 2007. "*Loving* and the Legacy of Unintended Consequences." *Wisconsin Law Review* 2: 239–81.

Murray, Mark. 2012. "One Month Later, Republicans Find Plenty of Blame for Election Loss." MSNBC, December 4. http://firstread.nbcnews.com/_news/2012/12/04/15677908-one-month-later-republicans-find-plenty-of-blame-for-election-loss?lite&ocid=msnhp&pos=1.

Nadal, Kevin L. 2011. "Microaggressions and the Multiracial Experience." *International Journal of Humanities and Social Science* 1(7)(June): 36–44.

Neumeister, Larry. 2010, "Rev. Wright: 'Obama Threw Me Under the Bus' President's Former Pastor Complains He Is Being Ignored by the White House." MSNBC, May 18. http:// www.nbcnews.com/id/37208439/ns/politics-white_house/

Obama, Barack. 1995. *Dreams from My Father: A Story of Race and Inheritance*. New York: Times Books.

_____. 2008b. "A More Perfect Union." *American Rhetoric*, March 18. http://www.american rhetoric.com/speeches/barackobamaperfectunion.htm.

Omi, Michael, and Howard Winant. 1994. *Racial Formation: From the 1980s to the 1990s*. 2nd ed. New York: Routledge.

Plank, Elizabeth. 2013. "New Study Finds More Than Half of Female Voters Are Feminist." *Policymic*, March 19. http://www.policymic.com/articles/30270/new-study-finds-more-than-half-of-female-voters-are-feminists.

Pogatchnik, Shawn. 2009. "Boxing Legend Ali Traces Roots to Irish Town Ali the Irishman: Fans Cheer Boxing Icon as He Finds Irish Roots in Great-Granddad's Hometown." Associated Press, September 1. http://abcnews.go.com/International/wire Story?id=8460201.

Ponder, Justin. 2012. "'A Patchwork Heritage': Multiracial Citation in Barack Obama's *Dreams from My Father*." In *Obama and the Biracial Factor: The Battle for a New American Majority*, ed. Andrew J. Jolivétte, 61–80. Bristol, UK: Policy Press.

Renn, Kristin A. 2004. *Mixed Race Students in College: The Ecology of Race, Identity, and Community on Campus*. Albany: State University of New York Press.

Roberts, Sam, and Peter Baker. 2010. "Asked to Declare His Race, Obama Checks 'Black.'" *New York Times*, April 2. http://www.nytimes.com/2010/04/03/us/politics/03census.html?_r=0.

Rockquemore, Kerry Ann, and David L. Brunsma. 2002. *Beyond Black: Biracial Identity in America*. Thousand Oaks, CA: Sage.

Rockquemore, Kerry Ann, David L. Brunsma, and Daniel J. Delgado. 2009. "Racing to Theory or Retheorizing Race? Understanding the Struggle to Build a Multiracial Identity Theory." *Journal of Social Issues* 65(1): 13–34.

Rose, Adam. 2010. "Obama and Palin Related? Website Claims President Also Has Ties to Limbaugh, Bush Family." *Huffington Post*, September 13. http://www.huffingtonpost.com/2010/10/13/obama-and-palin-related-w_n_760689.html.

Ross, Brian, and Rehab el-Buri. 2008. "Obama's Pastor: God Damn America, U.S. to Blame for 9/11." ABC News, March 13. http://abcnews.go.com/Blotter/story?id=4443788.

Salon.com. 2008. "What Should Obama Do About Rev. Jeremiah Wright?" April 29. http:// www.salon.com/2008/04/29/obama_wright/.

Samuels, Allison, and Jerry Adler. 2010. "The Reinvention of the Reverend." *Newsweek*, July 25. http://www.newsweek.com/2010/07/25/the-reinvention-of-the-reverend.html.

Schapiro, Rich. 2010. "Rev. Jeremiah Wright Claims President Obama 'Threw Me Under the Bus' in Letter to African Aid Group." *New York Daily News*, May 18. http://www.nydailynews.com/news/politics/rev-jeremiah-wright-claims-president-obama-threw-bus-letter-african-aid-group-article-1.447986#ixzz2ZMIg5fon.

Scocca, Tom. 2012. "Eighty-Eight Percent of Romney Voters Were White: The GOP Candidate's Race-based, Monochromatic Campaign Made Him a Loser." *Salon.com*, November 7. http://www.slate.com/articles/news_and_politics/scocca/2012/11/mitt_romney_white_voters_the_gop_candidate_s_race_based_monochromatic_campaign.html

Shafer, Jack. 2008. "How Obama Does that Thing He Does: A Professor of Rhetoric Cracks the Candidate's Code." *Slate*, February 14. http://www.slate.com/id/2184480/.

Smolenyak, Megan. 2009. "Michelle Obama's Roots." *Megan TV*, August. http://www.hon oringourancestors.com/megan-tv.html.

Spickard, Paul. 1989. *Mixed Blood: Intermarriage and Ethnic Identity in Twentieth-Century America*. Madison: University of Wisconsin Press.

Steele, Shelby. 2004. *Bound Man: Why We Are Excited about Obama and Why He Can't Win*. New York: Free Press.

Stolberg, Sheryl Gay. 2012. "Obama Has Ties to Slavery Not by His Father but His Mother, Research Suggests." *New York Times* July 30. http://www.nytimes.com/2012/07/30/us/obamas-mother-had-african-forebear-study-suggests.html?pagewanted=all.

Stuckey, Mike. 2008. "Multiracial Americans Surge in Number, Voice: Obama Candidacy Focuses New Attention on Their Quest for Understanding." MSNBC, May 28. http:// www.msnbc.msn.com/id/24542138/.

Sugrue, Thomas. 2010. *Not Even Past: Barack Obama and the Burden of Race*. Princeton, NJ: Princeton University Press.

Swarns, Rachel L. 2012. *American Tapestry: The Story of the Black, White, and Multiracial Ancestors of Michelle Obama*. New York: Amistad.

Swarns, Rachel L., and Jodi Kantor. 2009. "In First Lady's Roots, a Complex Path from Slavery." *New York Times*, October 7. http://www.nytimes.com/2009/10/08/us/politics/08genealogy.html?_r=1.

Tenzer, Laurence R. 1990. *A Completely New Look at Interracial Sexuality: Public Opinions and Select Commentaries*. Manahawkin, NJ: Scholar's Publishing House.

Tseng, Thomas. 2008. "Millennials: Key to Post-Ethnic America?" *New Geography*, July 30. http://www.newgeography.com/content/00137-millennials-key-post-ethnic-america.

Turner, Victor W. 1969. *The Ritual Process: Structure and Anti-structure*. New York: Cornell University Press.

Wallace, Kendra R. 2001. *Relative/Outsider: The Art and Politics of Identity among Mixed Heritage Students*. Westport, CT: Greenwood.

Walters, Ronald. 2005. *Freedom Is Not Enough: Black Voters, Black Candidates and American Presidential Politics*. Lanham, MD: Rowman & Littlefield.

_____. 2007. "Barack Obama and the Politics of Blackness." *Journal of Black Studies* 38(1): 7–29.

Wilber, Ken. 1997. "An Integral Theory of Consciousness." *Journal of Consciousness Studies* 4(1)(February): 71–92.

_____. 1998. *The Marriage of Sense and Soul: Integrating Science and Religion*. New York: Random House.

_____. 2000. *Integral Psychology: Consciousness, Spirit, Psychology, Therapy*. Boston: Shambhala Publications.

Williams, Kimberly M. 2008. *Mark One of More: Civil Rights in Multiracial America*. Ann Arbor: University of Michigan Press.

Williams, Mark. 2006. "Williams Identity Survey 11/1/06 thru 11/2/06." Zogby International.

Wingfield, Adia Harvey, and Joe R. Feagin. 2009. *Yes We Can: White Racial Framing and the Obama Presidency Campaign*. First edition. New York: Routledge.

_____. 2012. *Yes We Can: White Racial Framing and the Obama Presidency Campaign*. Second edition. New York: Routledge.

Winograd, Morley, and Michael D. Hais. 2008. *Millennial Makeover: MySpace, YouTube, and the Future of American Politics*. Piscataway, NJ: Rutgers University Press.

READING 19

Analyzing the Dream
Racism and America's Social Cancer

Stephen Balkaran

> "We must recognize that we can't solve our problem now until there is a radical redistribution of economic and political power ... this means a revolution of values and other things. We must see now that the evils of racism, economic exploitation and militarism are all tied together ... you can't really get rid of one without getting rid of the others ... the whole structure of American life must be changed. America is a hypocritical nation and [we] must put [our] own house in order."
>
> —Martin Luther King, Jr. (May 1967)

Recent discussions on race and America's post-racial society has left a silence gap in one of most debatable topics to emerge in the twenty-first century, that is, post-racial America in the age of President Barack Obama. This debate has neither materialized nor even blossomed. Racism continues to be a significant factor as we delve into the deep waters of race in America. As we conclude the Obama presidency, there are several important questions that continue to haunt our society; that is, race and politics are alive and well in America, and the fact that we are not living in a post-racial era continues to be a major disappointment in our society. The phrase "Can't Legislate Morality," coined by the late racist senator and presidential candidate Barry Goldwater, remains a message that is lost in today's society. Despite the passing of several important civil rights laws, he argued that it's still imbedded in our consciousness to discriminate against African Americans and other minority groups, that the American racist frame of mind cannot be changed. The idea that America in the post-Obama era would become a melting pot that we are constantly reminded of and often embrace remains a distant dream. Failure to talk about race and racism, and the failure to acknowledge that racism exists in the twenty-first century, are what fuel one of the most debatable topics in America, and it constantly reminds us that racism is alive and well.

HISTORICAL CONTEXT

At no other time in our country's great history has the idea of a post-racial society caught the eye of so many Americans. Many argue that the emergence of an African American candidate has fueled the debate regarding where do the politics of race fit in America. As Barack Obama's presidency concluded, one of the fundamental disappointments was his lack of any commitment to discuss race; this indicated that neither America nor the President was ready to have a constructive dialogue on race, despite the election of our first African American president. The fundamental question remains: why hasn't America gone beyond the issue of race in post-2018? Simply put, the history of America has been closely pegged with racism and discrimination against African Americans since its inception. It's an issue the founding fathers struggled to address in the early stages of this great nation, and as a result, it has continued to haunt our society through slavery, Jim Crow segregation, the Civil Rights movement, and modern-day legalized and systemic racism.

As we enter the twenty-first century, there are still many facets of oppression that exist and are prevalent in American society. Since the inception of America, the house of democracy has been plagued with cracks of racism and discrimination against African Americans and women. During the last 300 years, we have made little attempt to fix these cracks, and as a result, we have struggled with a defective foundation. Here lies the problem of why race still matters in America. Many Americans refuse to come to terms with the fact that the history of African Americans is a struggle against racism and oppression in a country that still today refuses to either acknowledge or apologize for its wrongdoing. Any discussion of race among white Americans evokes a very cautious and complicated reaction, and many often shy away from any constructive dialogue. Many Americans refuse to acknowledge that racism is a societal problem that can be only resolved by having a more open dialogue on race and discussion on diversity in America. Only conversations about truth, the need for reconciliation, and America's acknowledgment of its wrongdoing can lead to a more racially tolerant country, where the American dream can be enjoyed by all despite their race or color.

As we all looked on in January 2009, when much of the world watched the swearing in of the first African American US president into office, the idea that America was willing to put its ugly past behind and move toward a post-racial society and a more tolerable nation where Dr. Martin Luther. King's dream would be fulfilled enlightened all of us. Our expectations increased that America would transcend race and that both white and black racial attitudes would undergo a fundamental change, but this has not happened. The presence of the first African American president and the first family has not alleviated racial stereotypes, nor have the first family engaged in any constructive dialogue on race in America.

America continues to grapple with the issue of why race is still an important element in our society. As America slowly but surely confronts the issue of race, it becomes quite clear that race still matters in America. As our nation's economy entered an economic recession, caused by increased unemployment rates, failing housing markets, the financial crisis, and a nation indebted by the war in Iraq, the main concern by many Americans was, can an

African American president lead our great nation out of the depths of despair? Would he be judged as simply a president or as an African American president? This issue of race is a topic that America has struggled to confront and refused to come to terms with. The election of President Barack Obama called into question many people's views of the salience of race in American culture.

A recent Gallup poll, dated July 17L 2013, looked at racial and ethnic relations in the United States. The poll found that when asked, "Do you think that race relations between whites and blacks will always be a problem?" some 40 percent of Americans says that race and black-white relations will always be a problem in the United States. Comparatively, the same question was posed to Americans in another survey conducted by Gallup in 1964. Some 42 percent then believed that race and black-white relations would always be a problem in the United States.[1] This illustrates clearly that very little if any progress has occurred in the last 50 years when it comes to race relations as we enter into the twenty-first century.

The Civil Rights Act of 1964, arguably one of the most important acts of legislation in our country's history, ensured that legal barriers be torn down, which, theoretically, should eliminate barriers of discrimination against African Americans, women, and other minority groups in our society. Despite this law, today many groups, including Hispanics, Asian Americans, women, individuals with disabilities, members of the LGBT community, homeless, and other minorities, are still challenging our government for basic civil rights. Attacks on affirmative action, civil liberties, immigration watch groups, and other legislation have in many ways questioned our government's commitment to protect and guarantee civil rights in times of need. Some 50 years after the passage of the Civil Rights Act of 1964, has our government defaulted on that promise? African Americans remain one of the most underrepresented communities in schools, the workforce, and other sectors in the American society. The idea of Americans living in a post-racial society where all races are guaranteed the benefits of the American Dream and where racism no longer exists has almost disappeared in many minority communities.

WHERE ARE WE?

Gone are the days of former Alabama Governor George C. Wallace, who famously preached, "Segregation now! Segregation tomorrow! Segregation forever!" to resounding applause in 1963. Gone are the days when the "Whites only" and "Colored" signs lurked over water fountains, bathrooms, and restaurant counters. But as we enter the twenty-first century, silent and not overt segregation exists and is evident in our school systems, employment, poverty, healthcare, prison system, immigrant communities, and other sectors of society. It also permeates our society in ways we don't even realize. As a result, we must critically evaluate the legacy of the civil rights movement. Its main goal was primarily advancing the opportunities of African Americans, guaranteeing their constitutional rights, and eradicating legalized and systemic racism in the Jim Crow south, but more so, leveling the playing field for everyone in America.

Yet as we acknowledge the 50th anniversary of the Civil Rights Act of 1964, the question still remains: how far has America moved beyond the issue of race since the Civil Rights movement? How would Dr. King view the struggle today? Would he be happy or disappointed, or would he be outraged at the current status of African Americans and other minority groups? This controversial question can only be answered by looking at some disturbing facts on poverty, healthcare, the criminal justice system, education, and other facets of society in which race continues to play an important role. Would Dr. King be appalled to find out that the current situation of African Americans has not improved to the standards we all hoped would exist in today's society?

I will be the first to admit that the election of the nation's first African American president showed the racial progress that has been made in America. The fact that some 56 percent of white Americans voted for an African American candidate showed our progress in racial healing and tolerance. Yet despite this historic achievement, many of the goals of Dr. King and the Civil Rights movement remain unfinished, and in many cases, African Americans have continued to fall behind in public policies.

EDUCATION

The landmark Supreme Court case of Brown v. Board of Education in 1954 brought an end to any laws that established school segregation by deeming those laws unconstitutional, thus ending racial segregation in public schools. In this case, the Supreme Court established that the state laws that had created separate public schools for African American and white students were unconstitutional and would no longer be part of American society. The decision made in Brown v. Board of Education overturned the 1896 ruling on Plessy v. Ferguson, which had upheld the state laws requiring racial segregation as long as the facilities were "separate but equal." The Brown decision was supposed to end segregation within American public schools and ultimately led to the destruction of racial discrimination in other areas of American life. The idea of an integrated society where all colors can become one and enjoy the benefits of this great nation remains lost, and non-overt segregation continues to be embedded into the notion of race-based education.

The issue of school desegregation has been one of the foremost issues of the Civil Rights agenda. The notion of separate but equal was finally struck down in 1954 in Brown v. Board of Education. The former notion of "separate but equal" was built on tenets of white supremacy, which provided legal justification for the Jim Crow laws, which required separate accommodations for whites and blacks in many US states and cities and continued right into the 1960s. Yet despite the legalized eradication of school segregation, Harvard University's Civil Rights Project reported that schools today are more segregated than they were in the past. The report shows that US schools are becoming more segregated in all regions for both African American and Latino students. The Civil Rights Project reported that we are celebrating a victory over segregation at a time when schools across the nation are becoming increasingly segregated.[2]

Some 50 years after the March on Washington and the Brown v Board of Education decision, some 76 percent of African Americans attend segregated schools, according to The Civil Rights Project at UCLA, which reported that "across the country, 43 percent of Latinos and 38 percent of blacks attend schools where fewer than 10 percent of their classmates are whites."[3] The Civil Rights Project also reported that more than one in seven black and Latino students attend schools where less than 1 percent of their classmates are white. According to a *New York Times* article by N. R. Kleinfield, in the 2009/10 school year, half of New York City's public schools were 90-percent black and Hispanic. Progress has been limited since the days of the Little Rock Nine. Your quality of education depends on the zip code that you live in, and white suburban students remain ever more isolated from interactions with students of other races and classes.[4]

Segregation of Latino students is most pronounced in California, New York, and Texas, while in some states, inner-city schools are mostly black or brown. The most segregated cities for blacks include Atlanta, Chicago, Detroit, Houston, Philadelphia, and Washington, DC. Gary Orfield, director of the Civil Rights Project, indicated that "Extreme segregation is becoming more common."[5] According to Professors Feagin and Barnett, "despite the positive effects in education and other areas resulting from the Court's Brown decision, the decision has by no means been successful in dismantling institutionalized racism in American education. The Civil Rights Project note that although schools may be officially desegregated, they nevertheless remain effectively segregated due to the following: discrimination in schools by administrators, teachers, and students; racial bias in school curriculum; the separation of students into different ability tracks reflecting racial, class, and gender stratification; and the use of standardized testing that contains significant racial and class bias."[6]

According to author Gene A. Budig, measuring educational achievement in 2010 is important not only of itself but also because it directly correlates to levels of health, employment, income, and civic engagement. Average public high school graduation rates for whites are 83 percent; for blacks, 66.1 percent; and for Hispanics, 71.4 percent. Low-income, Hispanic, and African American students are more likely to need remediation than their wealthier, white peers (41 percent of Hispanic students and 42 percent of African American students require remediation, compared to 31 percent of white students). The percentage of 25- to 29-year-olds who have a bachelor's degree is 39 percent for whites, 20 percent for blacks, and 13 percent for Hispanics. The study also indicates that National Assessment of Student Progress score gaps between blacks and whites in mathematics and reading have not changed in 20 years. Schools are becoming more segregated: approximately 4 percent of black and Hispanic students attend schools that are more than 90-percent minority, up from less than a third in 1988.[7]

This continued racial inequality in educational opportunities can be attributed to a number of factors: (1) underperforming, poorly financed schools characterized by low quality of teaching, large class sizes, and inadequate facilities that perpetuate underachievement by minority students; (2) school assignment policies that promote segregation; (3) school district boundaries that are coterminous with town boundaries and local land use, zoning, and taxation powers; (4) systems of ability grouping and tracking that consistently retain or place minority students in lower-level classes with less exposure to curriculum that builds critical analytical skills; (5) failure to counteract differences in parental income and educational attainment—factors that impact a child's development and often correlate with race; and (6) lower teacher and administrator expectations of minority students.[8]

Furthermore the issue of race, racism, and education is exacerbated by white flight, also known as defector racial segregation. In fact, education for white, black, and brown students depends on the zip codes they live in. Today, the average white child attends a school where 77 percent of the other students are white. The average black student attends a high school where only 30 percent of the other students are white. For example, in New York State, 60 percent of all black students, including those in New York City, attend schools that are at least 90-percent black. Nationally, 76 percent of Latinos attend predominantly minority schools.[9] This increased segregation is problematic for a number of reasons. Racially segregated minority schools tend to have dramatically fewer resources and employ less experienced teachers. These disparate educational resources lead to larger class sizes, substandard facilities, lower per-pupil spending, and fewer counseling services. Furthermore, segregated minority schools are more likely to be housed in high-poverty neighborhoods that have high crime rates and limited access to community resources that enhance learning and development.[10]

The implementation of Brown v. Board of Education remains one of the most disappointing policy failures in America's civil rights history and continues to show why race still matters in America. Education has become the civil rights issue of the twenty-first century. Education disparities in America remains one of our most debated subjects, so why are there such huge educational disparities between white suburban and inner-city black and brown students?

POVERTY

Some 50 years ago, President Lyndon B. Johnson declared a "War on Poverty," making poverty in America one of his top priorities. He focused on not only raising awareness of the effects of poverty on black, brown, and white communities, but ensuring that government programs, head starts, and food stamps would help reduce poverty and assist America's poor. Yet despite his great intention to raise this issue of poverty, some 50 years after Dr. Martin L. King's poor people's campaign, poverty continues to be the cancer that threatens our society and also remains a significant factor in black and brown communities. One of the most promising of Dr. King's hopes was the equal opportunity for blacks to share in the nation's economic prosperity; his transition from civil rights to human rights reminds us of his commitment to equality for all in America despite what racial background we belong to.

As Dr. King reminded us in his "I Have a Dream" speech, the US Constitution contained "the promise that all men would be guaranteed the inalienable rights of life, liberty, and the pursuit of happiness. It is obvious today that America has defaulted on this promissory note insofar as her citizens of color are concerned. Instead of honoring this sacred obligation, America has given the Negro people a bad check which has come back marked 'insufficient funds.' But we refuse to believe that the bank of justice is bankrupt. We refuse to believe that there are insufficient funds in the great vaults of opportunity of this nation."[11] Some 50 years after the March on Washington, African Americans and other minority groups lag far behind their white counterparts in enjoying a piece of America's economic pie and the American dream.

According the US Census Bureau 2016 report on poverty in America, the poverty rate for all African Americans in 2016 was 22.1 percent, the highest of all races. The report indicated that the poverty rate increased between 2005 and 2016 for every demographic of African American families. Black families with children under 18 headed by a single mother have the highest rate of poverty, at 46.5 percent, compared to only 8.6 percent of married-couple black families.[12] The 2012 Census Bureau report showed that the poverty rate was 27.2 percent among African Americans and 25.6 percent among Hispanics. For non-Hispanic whites, the 2012 poverty rate was 9.7 percent. For Asians, it was 11.7 percent.[13] The 2016 Census report indicates that the numbers have not improved among the races. America continues to see a sharp racial divide in the crisis of poverty.

According to Annie Lowrey of the *New York Times*, the median income in 2012 for Asian households was $68,600. For non-Hispanic whites, it was about $57,000, while the typical Hispanic household had an income of $39,000, and blacks were at $33,300.[14] The "wealth gap" measures the difference between the median wealth of blacks versus the median wealth of whites. Almost all studies calculate wealth by adding up total assets (e.g., cash, retirement accounts, home, etc.), then subtracting liabilities (e.g., credit card debt, student loans, mortgage, etc.). The resulting figure is a household's net worth. *Forbes* magazine reports:

- According to the New York Times, for every $100 in white family wealth, black families hold just $5.04.
- The Economic Policy Institute found that more than one in four black households have zero or negative net worth, compared to less than one in ten white families without wealth.[15]

A recent report by the Institute for Policy Studies showed that between 1983 and 2013, the wealth of the median black household declined 75 percent (from $6,800 to $1,700), and the wealth of the median Latino household declined 50 percent (from $4,000 to $2,000).

At the same time, wealth for the median white household increased 14 percent, from $102,000 to $116,800.[16] While the Great Recession amplified the gap, much of the income disparity was due to intergenerational wealth through inheritance, social networks, the ability to make a down payment on a home, the ability to pay for college tuition, and so forth.

The emergence of a small but powerful African American middle class that has enjoy the fruits of its hard work and investments, like its white counterpart, must be acknowledged. Yet despite this amazing example of class mobility, many African Americans continue to lag far behind the other races. According to the Urban Institute, a nonpartisan research organization, blacks have poverty rates almost three times as high as whites. What is more disturbing is the poverty rate among young African Americans. According to the US Census Bureau 2012 Report, over one-third of black children are living in poverty today (37.9 percent).[17] This is the highest of all race groups, and this sharp upward trend has continued. In fact, reports have suggested that many young African American children are living in economic conditions equivalent to that of third-world countries.

Race continues to be a factor in the economic empowerment of the ethnic races in the twenty-first century. Legalized and systemic discrimination and lack of access to opportunities continue to hamper the dream of economic prosperity among the minority groups.

THE CRIMINAL JUSTICE SYSTEM

One of the best-kept secrets in America is our nation's race-based criminal justice system, in which people of color continue to be disproportionately incarcerated, profiled, and sentenced to death at significantly higher rates than their white counterparts, usually for the same crimes. Not only are more people of color locked away, but lack of basic civil rights, opportunities to vote, access to college financial aid, and job opportunities continue to plague minority communities in the twenty-first century. In light of these disparities, it is imperative that criminal justice reform evolve as the civil rights issue of the twenty-first century. According to the Sentencing Project, "So long as racism exists within society at large, it will be found within the criminal justice system. Racism fuels the overt bias which can show in the language, attitudes, conduct, assumptions, strategies and policies of criminal justice agencies. Instances of overt bias can lead in turn to the improper use of discretion among actors in the criminal justice system." Despite the fact that whites engage in drug offenses and criminal activities at a higher rate than African Americans, African Americans are incarcerated at a rate that is 10 times greater than that of whites.[18]

The Center for American Progress outlines several facts about the criminal justice system, civil rights, and minority communities. They list as follows:

1. **While people of color make up about 30 percent of the United States' population, they account for 60 percent of those imprisoned.** The prison population grew by 700 percent from 1970 to 2005, a rate that is outpacing crime and population rates.

The incarceration rates disproportionately impact men of color: 1 in every 15 African American men and 1 in every 36 Hispanic men are incarcerated in comparison to 1 in every 106 white men.

2. **According to the Bureau of Justice Statistics, one in three black men can expect to go to prison in their lifetime.** Individuals of color have a disproportionate number of encounters with law enforcement, indicating that racial profiling continues to be a problem. A report by the Department of Justice found that blacks and Hispanics were approximately three times more likely to be searched during a traffic stop than white motorists. African Americans were twice as likely to be arrested and almost four times as likely to experience the use of force during encounters with the police.

3. **Students of color face harsher punishments in school than their white peers, leading to a higher number of youth of color incarcerated.** Black and Hispanic students represent more than 70 percent of those involved in school-related arrests or referrals to law enforcement. Currently, African Americans make up two-fifths and Hispanics one-fifth of confined youth today.

4. **According to recent data by the Department of Education, African American students are arrested far more often than their white classmates.** The data showed that 96,000 students were arrested and 242,000 referred to law enforcement by schools during the 2009-10 school year. Of those students, black and Hispanic students made up more than 70 percent of arrested or referred students. Harsh school punishments, from suspensions to arrests, have led to high numbers of youth of color coming into contact with the juvenile-justice system and at an earlier age. ...

5. **Once convicted, black offenders receive longer sentences compared to white offenders.** The U.S. Sentencing Commission stated that in the federal system black offenders receive sentences that are 10 percent longer than white offenders for the same crimes. The Sentencing Project reports that African Americans are 21 percent more likely to receive mandatory-minimum sentences than white defendants and are 20 percent more like to be sentenced to prison.

6. **Voter laws that prohibit people with felony convictions to vote disproportionately impact men of color.** An estimated 5.3 million Americans are denied the right to vote based on a past felony conviction. Felony disenfranchisement is exaggerated by racial disparities in the criminal-justice system, ultimately denying 13 percent of African American men the right to vote. Felony-disenfranchisement policies have led to 11 states denying the right to vote to more than 10 percent of their African American population.[19]

It is generally agreed that discrimination based on race or ethnic origin is morally wrong and a violation of the principle of equality. The equality principle requires that those who are equal be treated equally based on similarities and that race not be a relevant consideration in that assessment.[20] The report shows a number of biases in our criminal justice system, such that one can only conclude that race continues to define the role of our criminal justice system in the twenty-first century. According to Michael Sclafani, "In the year 2010 there were 220,700 black individuals that were incarcerated for some reason, compared to 38,000 white people during the same year."[21] These numbers are astounding, especially when compared to the entire population of African Americans in the country. With these statistics, you would never think that this big of a gap would exist in the number of people who are incarcerated. There is a difference of 182,700 blacks compared to whites in prison, which shows that the rate of African Americans being incarcerated is exponentially higher than the rate of white American incarcerations. All these statistics on African American incarcerations show that there is a major difference between African Americans being arrested and imprisoned compared to other races.

According to the Sentencing Project in 2016, "One in every three black males born today can expect to go to prison at some point in their life, compared with one in every six Latino males, and one in every 17 white males, if current incarceration trends continue."[18] The source of such disparities is deeper and more systemic than explicit racial discrimination. The United States operates, in effect, two distinct criminal justice systems: one for wealthy people and another for poor people and people of color. The wealthy can access a vigorous advocacy system replete with constitutional protections for defendants. Yet the experiences of poor and minority defendants within the criminal justice system often differ substantially from that model due to a number of factors, each of which contributes to the overrepresentation of such individuals incarcerated in the system. As former Georgetown law professor David Cole states in his book, *No Equal Justice*, "These double standards are not, of course, explicit; on the face of it, the criminal law is color-blind and class-blind. But in a sense, this only makes the problem worse. The rhetoric of the criminal justice system sends the message that our society carefully protects everyone's constitutional rights, but in practice the rules assure that law enforcement prerogatives will generally prevail over the rights of minorities and the poor. By affording criminal suspects substantial constitutional protections in theory, the Supreme Court validates the results of the criminal justice system as fair. That formal fairness obscures the systemic concerns that ought to be raised by the fact that the prison population is overwhelmingly poor and disproportionately black."[22]

Whatever the arguments are, there is a direct connection to race and racism in our criminal justice system, and the underlying issue remains that race continues to play an important part in all public policy implementation. Not only in poverty, education and criminal justice—the topics I have thus far addressed—but in so many other facets of American society, race continues to define who we are as Americans and takes away the best of what we can become.

IMMIGRATION

At no other time our country's great history has a debate on immigration so divided the nation on its true value and rich tradition in welcoming immigrants with open arms. Not only has the debate gone into the presidential political spectrum, it has become the civil rights issue that will define the future America. The political debacle of the current civil rights issue has left the United States of America divided along racial, ethnic, and political lines as never before seen in our great country. Donald Trump's racist remarks during his political campaigns reminded us that hatred toward immigrants is alive and well in a country that preaches integration and acceptance of all. President Trump, while preparing a speech to Congress, reminded his staff that he had consistently delighted crowds with his racist diatribes. Acting as if he were at a rally, he then read aloud a few made-up Hispanic names and described potential crimes they could have committed, like rape or murder.

There hasn't been a time our country's great history that a debate on immigration has divided the nation as it has recently done, leaving us searching for an identity as to who we are and what we stand for. Undocumented immigrants have become the most convenient scapegoat for America's social problems; thus, anti-immigrant rhetoric has become prevalent and a norm within our political spectrum.

Central to the immigration debate are amnesty and pathway to citizenship for the 12 million human beings who are often referred to as "undocumented immigrants." This issue of immigration reform has become the focal point of all, immigrants and Americans alike, but none is it more important to than the Hispanic population. The "browning of America" and the continual reshaping of America by Hispanics continue to define who we are and enhance the best of what we can become as a nation of immigrants. The political importance of the Hispanic vote is closely tied to immigration reform, and whether or not we admit it, the American presidency will soon be dictated by the Hispanic vote. The recent immigration laws in Arizona, Mississippi, Pennsylvania, and other states have raised several important questions regarding the role of the federal government, civil rights, public policy decision making processes, and, more so, the role of race in many of the decision-making processes. The immigration debate has now generated so many divisions in our society that it has become the "civil rights debate of the twenty-first century"; never in American history has immigration become such a divisive issue, where policymaking and the electoral process go hand in hand.

Immigrants and immigration have played and will continue to play an important role in our country's rich diverse culture, yet that rich culture has been tested by the guarantee of one's civil rights. The economic, political, and social clout of current immigrants and the immigration debate are far more beneficial to the nation than their critics point them out to be. Hispanics are fast becoming the new cornerstone of this country's economic, political, and social power, and based on their potential, no other immigrant group in the history of our great nation has had such potential to redefine America and make us great.

CONCLUSION

America truly has come a long way in the last 50 years. The hard work and dedication of Dr. King and other civil rights leaders, activists, and common citizens have attempted to level the playing field for African Americans, women, members of the LGBT community, Hispanics, Native Americans, and others considerably. The election of our first African American president showed that America has made great strides toward a racially harmonious society, wherein we respect all contributions to our great country. We should be very proud of these accomplishments and civil rights gains, but it is also important that we do not become complacent with that progress.

In the Kerner Report, which represented the findings of an official government commission that studied the reasons behind the urban riots in 1969, the major conclusion was that "America is still two nations: one white and one black"; where are we today, in 2018?[23]

ENDNOTES

1. Gallup, "Americans Rate Racial and Ethnic Relations in U.S. Positively," July 17th, 2013, https://news.gallup.com/poll/163535/americans-rate-racial-ethnic-relations-positively.aspx.
2. Harvard University, "School Segregation on the Rise Despite Growing Diversity Among School-Aged Children," *Harvard Ed News*, July 17, 2001, https://www.gse.harvard.edu/news/school-segregation-rise-despite-growing-diversity-among-school-aged-children.
3. UCLA, "Civil Rights Project Reports Deepening Segregation and Challenges Educators and Political Leaders to Develop Positive Policies," The Civil Rights Project, September 19, 2012, https://civilrightsproject.ucla.edu/news/press-releases/crp-press-releases-2012/civil-rights-project-reports-deepening-segregation-and-challenges-educators-and-political-leaders-to-develop-positive-policies.
4. N. R. Klienfield, "'Why Don't We Have Any White Kids?'" *New York Times*, May 11, 2012, nytimes.com/2012/05/13/education/at-explore-charter-school-a-portrait-of-segregated-education.html
5. UCLA, "Civil Rights Project Reports Deepening Segregation and Challenges Educators and Political Leaders to Develop Positive Policies," The Civil Rights Project, September 19, 2012, https://civilrightsproject.ucla.edu/news/press-releases/crp-press-releases-2012/civil-rights-project-reports-deepening-segregation-and-challenges-educators-and-political-leaders-to-develop-positive-policies.
6. Joe R. Feagin and Berenice McNair Barnett. "Success *and* Failure: How Systematic Racism Trumped the *Brown v Board of* Education Decision," *University of Illinois Law Review*, 2004.
7. Gene A. Budig, "No simple answers to racial inequality," *USA Today*, September 2013.
8. John Brittan and Callie Kozlak, "Racial Disparities in Educational Opportunities in the United States, *Seattle Journal of Science* 6, no. 2 (Spring 2008): 596.
9. Ibid., 597
10. Ibid., 591.
11. Martin Luther King, Jr., "I Have A Dream," address delivered August 28, 1963.
12. United States Census Bureau, "Income and Poverty in the United States: 2016," Report Number P60-259, September 12, 2017, https://www.census.gov/library/publications/2017/demo/p60-259.html.
13. United States Census Bureau, "Income and Poverty in the United States: 2016," Report Number P60-259, September 2013, https://www.census.gov/library/publications/2013/demo/p60-245.html
14. Annie Lowrey, "Household Incomes Remain Flat Despite Improving Economy," *New York Times*, September 17 2013, https://www.nytimes.com/2013/09/18/us/median-income-and-poverty-rate-hold-steady-census-bureau-finds.html.

15 Brian Thompson, "The Racial Wealth Gap: Addressing America's Most Pressing Epidemic," *Forbes*, February 18, 2018, *https*://www.forbes.com/sites/brianthompson1/2018/02/18/the-racial-wealth-gap-addressing-americas-most-pressing-epidemic/#4e6b597e7a48. The Racial Gap. America's Epidemic.

16 Chuck Collins, Dedrick Asante-Muhammed, Emanuel Nieves, and Josh Hoxie, "Report: The Road to Zero Wealth," Institute for Policy Studies, September 11, 2017, https://ips-dc.org/report-the-road-to-zero-wealth/.

17 Diana Elliott, "Two American experiences: The racial divide of poverty," *Urban Institute*, July 21, 2016, https://www.urban.org/urban-wire/two-american-experiences-racial-divide-poverty.

18 The Sentencing Project, "Reducing Racial Disparity in the Criminal Justice System," 2008, https://www.sentencingproject.org/criminal-justice-facts/.

19 Sophia Kerby, "The Top 10 Most Startling Facts About People of Color and Criminal Justice in the United States," Center for American Progress, March 13, 2012, https://www.americanprogress.org/issues/race/news/2012/03/13/11351/the-top-10-most-startling-facts-about-people-of-color-and-criminal-justice-in-the-united-states.

20 May and Sharratt 1994: 317.

21 Michael Sclafani, Civil Rights in Present Day America, 2013.

22 David Cole, *No Equal Justice* (New York: The New Press, 1999), xvi.

23 Haas Institute, "1968 Kerner Report: Executive Summary,"1968, https://haasinstitute.berkeley.edu/1968-kerner-report.

READING 20

Black Lives, the Flag, and the Continued Racial Hatred

Stephen Balkaran

> "This is something that is deeply rooted in our society, it's deeply rooted in our history. ... When you're dealing with something as deeply rooted as racism or bias in any society, you've got to have vigilance, but you have to recognize that it's going to take some time, and you just have to be steady so you don't give up when we don't get all the way there."
>
> —President Barack Obama[1]

Continued racial and hate crime events have taken away the basic foundation of what our democracy stands for: life, liberty, and the pursuit of happiness, which are guaranteed to all who live in this promised land. The Charlottesville race riots in 2017 showed that continued racial hatred and bigotry are alive and well in our society. This race-based tragic event has only reminded us that there is a need for a more constructive, open dialogue on America's social cancer: racism. This social cancer needs to be address in a very cautious but sensitive way, in which all Americans can have a constructive, meaningful dialogue but at the same time come to a more proactive resolution. This dialogue must take place throughout all avenues of society, not only when a racial event stirs up racial hatred in our nation. This racial hatred leads to a racially sensitive nation in the short term, and lost in the dialogue is the long-term solution to America's race problem, which has been around for the last 300 years.

Defined by the Department of Justice, "hate crimes is the violence of intolerance and bigotry, intended to hurt and intimidate someone because of their race, ethnicity, national origin, religion, sexual orientation, or disability. The purveyors of hate use explosives, arson, weapons, vandalism, physical violence, and verbal threats of violence to instill fear in their victims, leaving them vulnerable to more attacks and feeling alienated, helpless, suspicious and fearful."[2] According to the head of the NAACP, Cornell Williams Brooks, "The level of hate crimes in this country has remained constant over years. We have to allocate resources to address these hate groups and these hate crimes. The fact of the matter is, the Justice Department underestimates the degree of hate crimes in this country because they have to rely on self-reporting. That is a challenge. And the fact that we have at least 200,000 to

300,000 hate crimes in a given year is unconscionable and inconsistent with our values as Americans."[3] Racial events and hate-based protests in many cities continue to remind us that hatred, racism, and bigotry are still part of our culture and fuel much of the ignorance that defines who we are and what we claim to stand for: a nation that preaches tolerance and respect.

According to a report released by the Southern Poverty Law Center (SPLC), a prominent civil rights organization based in Montgomery, Alabama, the number of domestic hate and extremist groups in the United States grew to record levels in 2011. This growth was led by a surge in antigovernment radicalism. In 2011, America had 1,018 hate groups nationwide, representing a slight increase from the previous record in 2010, when America had 1,002 hate groups.[4] This continued increase directly coincides with the election of the nation's first African American president, which led to increased hatred and bigotry against people of color and homosexuals. According to a *Huffington Post* report, "Perhaps more disturbing than the small, yet sustained rise in hate groups, is the parabolic growth over the last few years in the number of anti-government 'Patriot' and militia groups reported by the SPLC. These groups, which are categorized separately from hate groups, grew 55% to 1,274 in 2011, up from 824 in 2010. In 2008 such groups totaled only 149, while in 2009 the total increased to 512."[5] The notion of leaving our racial hatred past of the '50s, and '60s has always been met with great expectation and optimism. This dream that America would transcend race and that racial attitudes would undergo a fundamental change has not materialized in the twenty-first century. Events in Charlottesville, Ferguson, New York City, Baltimore, and Charleston have only reinforced the immense racial hatred and distrust in African American communities of white America. This dream that we are living in a post-racial society where all are guaranteed the benefits of our democracy has been lost in translation, and dialogue about our continued racial reconciliation remains a silent debate unless another racial events stir our nation's consciousness.

MEDIA BIAS

The love-hate relationship with mass media plays a crucial role in the way white Americans perceive African Americans. As a result of the overwhelming media focus on "crime, drug use, gang violence, welfare, prison incarceration rates, school dropout rates, music and other forms of anti-social behavior among African-Americans, the media have fostered a distorted and pernicious public perception of African-Americans."[6] The media has not studied either important events in the African American community today or this community's immense contributions to American society. Continued racial hatred has been fueled by the media and its negative role in portrayal of African Americans. The media have played a key role in perpetuating the effects of this historical oppression and contributed to African Americans' continuing status as second-class citizens into the twenty-first century. As a result, white America has suffered from a deep uncertainty as to who African Americans really are.

Despite this racial divide, something indisputably American about African Americans has raised doubts about the white man's value system. Indeed, it has also aroused the troubling suspicion that whatever else the true American is, he is also somehow black.

The media have taken a step further in Hollywood. Here, the portrayal of young African American males (involved in gangs and other deviant acts of violence) has become a multimillion dollar industry. American society has now accepted these stereotypes, which the film media have ascribed to the black community. Films such as *Boyz in the Hood* and *Menace II Society* have become multimillion dollar success stories with criminal portrayals of young blacks.

This portrayal, over time, has fostered false beliefs within white America regarding the way we perceive and view blacks. What the media refuse to acknowledge is that the vast majority of blacks are employed, attend school, and are not involved in gangs or other criminal activities. It is now quite common for young African American males to be stopped and questioned by cops if they don't fir the status quo hence the racial stereotypes. One of the main reasons for the inadequate coverage of the underlying causes of racial stereotypes in the United States is that the condition of blacks itself is not a matter of high interest to the white majority. Their interest in black America is focused on situations in which their imagined fear becomes a real problem. Events like boycotts, pickets, civil rights demonstrations, and particularly racial violence mark the point at which black activity impinges on white concerns. It is not surprising that the white-oriented media seek to satisfy the needs of their white audience and reflect this pattern of attention to these selected events. The tendency to characterize all African American males as criminals continues in our society. It is now common for law officers to stop young black males and to harass them as a result of this stereotype.

The solution to the great American media dilemma can be addressed by the following solutions. One, there is a need for America to have a more constructive dialogue on race; this has not come to fruition because any discussion of race among white Americans elicits a very cautious and complicated reaction, and many often shy away from any constructive dialogue. Second, we must admit we have a media bias problem; a nation that is in denial and is sleepwalking will never wake up. Many Americans refuse to acknowledge that racism is a societal problem that can only be resolved by having more open dialogue on race and discussion on diversity in America. Racial hatred and media biases continues to permeate our society in ways we don't even realize, and it has continued to define who we are and what we stand for as a nation that leads the free world and preaches democracy.

RIOTS AND BLACK LIVES MATTER

Recent race-based events throughout the nation have once again left us scrambling for a solution to America's race problem, not only the earthshaking events of violence, destruction, and disregard for human life, but more so the frustration in many African American communities. The riots take us back to the 1960s, when many African Americans were frustrated with the economic, social, and political disenfranchisement of their American dream. Yes, race was a factor, but it was not the main underlying source of the frustration in many African American communities. Baltimore and other poor cities have become the flagships of many poor urban communities. The lack of economic mobility, community policing, poverty, drugs, deviant behavior, a failed education system, and police brutality have continued to plague many inner-city African American communities. Yes, race was a catalyst, but it was not the underlying factor of these riots. The national debate that should be taking place is not what threat African Americans pose to police and society, but how we can correct a history of exclusion, oppression, and legal and systemic racism against a community that remains loyal to a country that has treated them as outsiders. Racism and race riots have taken away the best of who we are as Americans and what we can become as a society. The idea of Americans living in a post-racial society, where all races are guaranteed the benefits of the American dream and racism no longer exists, has almost disappeared in many urban minority communities.

The failure to have a constructive dialogue on the economic urban issues that affect many African American communities is the underlying cause of the frustration among many inner-city urban dwellers. The lack of modern-day policing techniques, community involvement, and communication, but more so trust and faith in police, fuels much of the debates that should be taking place today. Historical racism between police forces and African Americans throughout the country has led to a climate of distrust, hate, and disregard for black lives that has fueled much of the frustration that is being depicted today. Black lives matters because American lives matter; the recent events have only reinforced the idea that race continues to define who we are as Americans and perpetuate the fact that we are still not living in a post-racial era.

Baltimore and other black and brown cities should not be held as the scapegoat for America's socioeconomic, political, and race-based problems, but they should be held as a leader for the national dialogue that should be taking place. Baltimore represents much of what it is to be black in America—frustration among America's urban dwellers and poor socioeconomic conditions that have led to this dilemma of anger and frustration among its residents. There needs to be a national discussion that should not be taking place only in black and brown cities but throughout the nation on America's social ills. Evaluating the series of constant protests throughout the country, at times violent but mostly nonviolent, has left a deep uncertainty over the role of rage, race, and rebellion that continue to plague many African American communities. These events continue to give voice to the frustration of upward economic mobility, social despair, disregard for black lives, police brutality, and many other social ills that many African American communities are embedded in.

The recent riots only addressed police brutality, but gone from the discussion that should be taking place is the continued economic class warfare that has plagued many of these inner-city communities. The lack of access to upward economic mobility in many African

American communities is the underlying cause of their frustration, which has manifested itself in race rebellions and riots. The discussion that America must address is how we increase upward economic mobility in a community that has been denied their rightful piece of the American pie. Gone from the dialogue is upward economic mobility and its impact on the riots; gone from the dialogue is the continued social oppression that plagues these inner cities; gone from the dialogue is the question, why are many African Americans and their communities continuing to be plagued with economic starvation and poverty? These frustrations played an important role in many of the riots in the 1960s, which were often labeled race riots and not class rebellions. The social uprising was part of the economic warfare because of disparities that haunted many African American communities. Yes, race was a factor in the 1960s, but it was not the main underlying source of the frustration found in many African American communities.

African Americans remain one of the most underrepresented communities in schools, the workforce, and other sectors in American society, due to the direct result of economic racism, class discrimination, and, more so, their exclusion from American economic prosperity. Whatever the arguments are, there is a direct connection to race, racism, and the economic system, and the underlying issue remains that race continues to play an important part in all public policy implementation. Economic mobility is the main factor that continues to define many African American communities. It has continued to define who we are as Americans and has often taken away the best of what we can become as a nation. Yes, race remains an important factor in many of our social ills, but correcting racism must start with the economic empowerment that is so deeply needed in many inner-city communities.

Recent race riots throughout the country have left many questions that continue to haunt our society: community policing and trust in law enforcement, but more so the continuing significance of race in America. The recent riots that surrounded the death of Michael Brown and others have continued to open the debates about the discussions on race, criminal justice, and America's post-racial society. Whether we admit it or not, racism continues to be a significant factor that haunts our great country as we delve into the deep waters of race in America. A recent poll suggested that there is a deep divide on the Black Lives Matter movement: "Black and white opinion is sharply divided on the aims and the approach of the Black Lives Matter movement. Seventy percent of African-Americans are sympathetic to the movement, compared with only 37 percent of whites. Among all Americans, 41 percent agree with the movement, 25 percent disagree and 29 percent do not have an opinion either way."[7] In fact, the new Civil Rights movement, "Black Lives Matter," seems to be more generational than objective, according to the responses by Americans. The same poll found that "Support for Black Lives Matter correlates directly to age, with 50 percent of all adults younger than 30 saying they agree with the movement, compared with 20 percent who disagree with it. Among those 45 and older, 36 percent agree and 29 percent disagree."[8]

The race riots in many black and brown cities can be traced to economic, social, and racial factors that continue to haunt many poor African American communities: distrust in policing and stereotypes of young black males, but more so the failure to talk about race and the acknowledgment that race still plays an important role in our society. The riots brought many debates to the forefront of America, showing that in the twenty-first century, oppression continues to exist and is prevalent in American society.

Michael Brown's death (along with those of other African Americans), race riots, and peaceful social protest have become another part of the puzzle of why race matters in America. The fact that many Americans refuse to come to terms with the fact that the history of African Americans is a struggle against racism and oppression in a country that still today refuses to acknowledge and apologize for its actions and wrongdoing. As a result, lack of discussion of race among law enforcement, community engagement organizations, and white Americans fuels our greatest enemy. Any discussions of race among white Americans elicits a very cautious and complicated reaction, and many often shy away from any constructive dialogue. The race riots have brought many factors to the forefront, none more important that the fact that we need to acknowledge that racism is a societal problem that can be only resolved by having more open dialogue on race and discussion of diversity in America. Only conversations about the truth, the need for reconciliation, and America's acknowledgment of its wrongdoing can lead to a more racially tolerant country where the American dream can be enjoyed by all, despite race or color.

The stereotyping of young black males continues to be a major disappointment in society. Michael Brown became another element that defines our racial perception of who black men are. The idea that Michael Brown, a young black male, might be a threat to law enforcement, a thug, and just an outright deviant member of society reinforces the racial stereotype of how we view young black men and race in America. Michael Brown's death fuels the debate on what happened to the idea that America would become a melting pot that we are constantly reminded of and often embrace. His death reminds us that this melting pot did not melt, and it remains a distant dream. The fact is that the failure to talk about race and racism, and the failure to acknowledge that racism exists in the twenty-first century, is what fuels one of the most debatable topics in America. The events like those in Ferguson, Missouri, and other parts of America constantly remind us that we have a long way to go to achieve a post-racial society and a melting pot that is sought after in America. These recent earth-shaking events throughout the country have left us gasping for a solution to America's problem. Only conversations about the truth, the need for reconciliation, America's acknowledgment of its past wrongdoing, and access to economic opportunities for all can lead to a more racially tolerant society. These riots have only reinforced that white and black racial attitudes have not undergone a fundamental change and that race continues to be a catalyst that fuels much of the debates that are taking place today.

In the twenty-first century, there are still many facets of oppression that exist and are prevalent in many African American communities. Silent and not overt racism is evident in their school systems, employment, poverty, healthcare, the prison system, and other sectors of their communities.[9] Class disparity continues to be an important element that defines many black and brown inner-city communities, and combined with the lack of upward economic mobility opportunities, this can be easily used to gauge many African American communities. These economic and class disparities permeate our society in ways we don't even realize and play an important role in the frustration that plagues the inner-city urban communities that many African Americans call home. This access to upward economic mobility is more important today than at any other time in our history and will be the key to bridging the gaps in many of America's socioeconomic and racial dilemmas.

We as a nation must critically evaluate the legacy of tolerance. Have we forgotten this message? Have we forgotten the message of hope, the foundations of our democracy? Are we as a nation suffering from amnesia? America is still two nations: one white and one black. There needs to be a national discussion on racial hatred that should not be taking place only in Charlottesville, Baltimore, or New York City, but throughout the nation, focusing on America's social ill.

THE FLAG

Recent protests by African American athletes with regard to respecting the American national anthem and flag have once again left us as a nation searching for an identity. Who are we, and where do the roles of racial politics and African American patriotism fit in with the nation? The continued debates regarding African American athletes kneeling and the national anthem have once again left us debating the continuing significance of race, politics, and American democratic ideals. This debate has generated so much confusion, it has left a nation divided along racial lines and patriotism. Lost in the debates is the true nature of freedom of expression that is guaranteed by the same ideals the flag stands for: freedom and liberty.

Our national anthem, "The Star-Spangled Banner," has been the unifying symbol that binds a nation of immigrants, those of low socioeconomic classes, multiethnic groups, religious groups, and just simply Americans. Despite these attributes, "The Star-Spangled Banner" often reminds certain ethnic groups—African Americans and Native Americans— of the history of exclusion and oppression under the watchful words of freedom and liberty. That freedom and liberty that is manifested by the anthem and flag give us the right to protest—many African American athletes who protest the anthem and flag are simply saying to America, be true to yourself, practice what you preach. The greatest promise of America, our flag, and our anthem is the right to protest for our rights. The media and presidential critics that point to the lack of patriotism among the athletes toward the flag, the anthem, military personnel, and their families have been misguided, misinformed, and misinterpretive. There has never been any hatred toward any of the above-mentioned groups; the issue at heart has been lost in translation, and that is the continued racism and exclusion that are still prominent in our society and affect many African Americans simply because of their color. The hype saying that African Americans are not loyal to America, the flag, and the anthem is a message that is completely unfounded and can be debunked by the longstanding African American experience.

First, African Americans have had a long historical commitment toward protecting American democracy and freedom, the basic watch-words of the anthem and symbol of the flag. Tracing their commitment in the Revolutionary War, the Civil War, World War I, World War II, Korea, Vietnam, and present-day Iraq and Afghanistan, African Americans have always served America with great pride and dedication. Secondly, the debates revolve around Francis Scott Key and his famous words overlooking the Baltimore Harbor in 1812. Scott Key, like many Americans, was a man of his time and, like many before him, owned and profited from the institution of slavery. His famous words, "land of the free, and the home of the brave," immediately announced the hypocrisy of this nation, and it is a song that reveals the two Americas. "The Star-Spangled Banner" reveals the gross contradiction of many of the foundations of American society, in which African Americans have been the constant victims of hypocrisy and hatred. His famous words were written in a time when the majority of African Americans were embodied in the institution of slavery, when slaves were not considered human beings. The idea of white supremacy meant excluding and oppressing African Americans and became an integral part of the *Land of the Free, Home of the Brave*. Hence, the point is, America has always been a country of contradictions, in its founding values, leaders, symbols, and the way they have treated African Americans.

There has always been a love-hate relationship between America and African Americans, the debate over the national anthem and the flag is just another twist in this longstanding feud. This relationship stems from the contradiction of our basic watch-words and foundations, which is manifested in our national anthem and flag. Where to protest, when to protest, and how to protest are all irrelevant until a nation of contradictions makes amends with the African American community for the centuries of exclusion and oppression and lives up to the true values of the flag and the anthem: *Land of the Free, Home of the Brave*.

The dialogue on continued racial events must include different races, police, community activists, political leaders, clergy, and any other members of society. Only conversations about the truth, the need for reconciliation, and America's acknowledgment of its wrongdoing can lead to a more tolerant society where the American dream can be enjoyed by all. All lives matter, because American lives matter.

ENDNOTES

1. Breitbart, "Obama: Racism Deeply Rooted in US," Breitbart TV, December 7, 2014, http://www.breitbart.com/video/2014/12/07/obama-racism-deeply-rooted-in-us.
2. https://www.justice.gov/archive/crs/pubs/crs_pub_hate_crime_bulletin_1201.htm
3. CBS News, "Face the Nation Transcripts June 21, 2015: Brooks, Scott, Nunes, June 21, 2015, http://www.cbsnews.com/news/face-the-nation-transcripts-june-21-2015-brooks-scott-nunes.
4. https://www.fbi.gov/about-us/investigate/civilrights/hate_crimes

5 Brian Levin, "U.S. Hate and Extremist Groups Hit Record Levels, New Report Says," *HuffPost*, March 8, 2012, http://www.huffingtonpost.com/brian-levin-jd/hate-groups-splc_b_1331318.html.

6 R. Taylor, "The harm brought by racial stereotype. *Hartford Courant*, March 19, 1995, p. D4.

7 Giovanni Russonello, "Race Relations Are at Lowest Point in Obama Presidency, Poll Finds," *New York Times*, July 13, 2016, http://www.nytimes.com/2016/07/14/us/most-americans-hold-grim-view-of-race-relations-poll-finds.html?_r=1.

8 Ibid.

9 Stephen Balkaran, "Why Race Matters: America's 21st Century Social Cancer," *International Journal of Education and Science* 2, no. 2 (February 2015), http://www.ijessnet.com/wp-content/uploads/2015/02/9.pdf.

READING 21

Letter from the Birmingham Jail

Dr. Martin Luther King

Martin Luther King, Jr.
Birmingham City Jail
April 16, 1963

My dear Fellow Clergymen,

While confined here in the Birmingham City Jail, I came across your recent statement calling our present activities "unwise and untimely." Seldom, if ever, do I pause to answer criticism of my work and ideas. If I sought to answer all the criticisms that cross my desk, my secretaries would be engaged in little else in the course of the day and I would have no time for constructive work. But since I feel that you are men of genuine goodwill and your criticisms are sincerely set forth, I would like to answer your statement in what I hope will be patient and reasonable terms.

   I think I should give the reason for my being in Birmingham, since you have been influenced by the argument of "outsiders coming in." I have the honor of serving as president of the Southern Christian Leadership Conference, an organization operating in every Southern state with headquarters in Atlanta, Georgia. We have some eighty-five affiliate organizations all across the South—one being the Alabama Christian Movement for Human Rights. Whenever necessary and possible we share staff, educational, and financial resources with our affiliates. Several months ago our local affiliate here in Birmingham invited us to be on call to engage in a nonviolent direct action program if such were deemed necessary. We readily consented and when the hour came we lived up to our promises. So I am here, along with several members of my staff, because we were invited here. I am here because I have basic organizational ties here. Beyond this, I am in Birmingham because injustice is here. Just as the eighth century prophets left their little villages and carried their "thus saith the Lord" far beyond the boundaries of their home town, and just as the Apostle Paul left his little village of Tarsus and carried the gospel of Jesus Christ to practically every hamlet and city of the Graeco-Roman world, I too am compelled to carry the gospel of freedom beyond my particular home town. Like Paul, I must constantly respond to the Macedonian call for aid.

Martin Luther King, Jr., "Letter from a Birmingham Jail." 1963.

Moreover, I am cognizant of the interrelatedness of all communities and states. I cannot sit idly by in Atlanta and not be concerned about what happens in Birmingham. Injustice anywhere is a threat to justice everywhere. We are caught in an inescapable network of mutuality tied in a single garment of destiny. Whatever affects one directly affects all indirectly. Never again can we afford to live with the narrow, provincial "outside agitator" idea. Anyone who lives inside the United States can never be considered an outsider anywhere in this country.

You deplore the demonstrations that are presently taking place in Birmingham. But I am sorry that your statement did not express a similar concern for the conditions that brought the demonstrations into being. I am sure that each of you would want to go beyond the superficial social analyst who looks merely at effects, and does not grapple with underlying causes. I would not hesitate to say that it is unfortunate that so-called demonstrations are taking place in Birmingham at this time, but I would say in more emphatic terms that it is even more unfortunate that the white power structure of this city left the Negro community with no other alternative.

In any nonviolent campaign there are four basic steps: (1) Collection of the facts to determine whether injustices are alive; (2) Negotiation; (3) Self-purification; and (4) Direct action. We have gone through all of these steps in Birmingham. There can be no gainsaying of the fact that racial injustice engulfs this community. Birmingham is probably the most thoroughly segregated city in the United States. Its ugly record of police brutality is known in every section of this country. Its unjust treatment of Negroes in the courts is a notorious reality. There have been more unsolved bombings of Negro homes and churches in Birmingham than any city in this nation. These are the hard, brutal, and unbelievable facts. On the basis of these conditions Negro leaders sought to negotiate with the city fathers. But the political leaders consistently refused to engage in good faith negotiation.

Then came the opportunity last September to talk with some of the leaders of the economic community. In these negotiating sessions certain promises were made by the merchants—such as the promise to remove the humiliating racial signs from the stores. On the basis of these promises Rev. Shuttlesworth and the leaders of the Alabama Christian Movement for Human Rights agreed to call a moratorium on any type of demonstrations. As the weeks and months unfolded we realized that we were the victims of a broken promise. The signs remained. As in so many experiences of the past we were confronted with blasted hopes, and the dark shadow of a deep disappointment settled upon us. So we had no alternative except that of preparing for direct action, whereby we would present our very bodies as a means of laying our case before the conscience of the local and national community. We were not unmindful of the difficulties involved. So we decided to go through a process of self-purification. We started having workshops on nonviolence and repeatedly asked ourselves the questions, "Are you able to accept blows without retaliating?" "Are you able to endure the ordeals of jail?"

We decided to set our direct-action program around the Easter season, realizing that with the exception of Christmas, this was the largest shopping period of the year. Knowing that a strong economic withdrawal program would be the by-product of direct action, we felt that this was the best time to bring pressure on the merchants for the needed changes. Then it occurred to us that the March election was ahead, and so we speedily decided to postpone action until after election day. When we discovered that Mr. Connor was in the run-off, we decided again to postpone action so that the demonstrations could not be used to cloud the issues. At this time we agreed to begin our nonviolent witness the day after the run-off.

This reveals that we did not move irresponsibly into direct action. We too wanted to see Mr. Connor defeated; so we went through postponement after postponement to aid in this community need. After this we felt that direct action could be delayed no longer.

You may well ask, Why direct action? Why sit-ins, marches, etc.? Isn't negotiation a better path?" You are exactly right in your call for negotiation. Indeed, this is the purpose of direct action. Nonviolent direct action seeks to create such a crisis and establish such creative tension that a community that has constantly refused to negotiate is forced to confront the issue. It seeks so to dramatize the issue that it can no longer be ignored. I just referred to the creation of tension as a part of the work of the nonviolent resister. This may sound rather shocking. But I must confess that I am not afraid of the word tension. I have earnestly worked and preached against violent tension, but there is a type of constructive nonviolent tension that is necessary for growth. Just as Socrates felt that it was necessary to create a tension in the mind so that individuals could rise from the bondage of myths and half-truths to the unfettered realm of creative analysis and objective appraisal, we must see the need of having nonviolent gadflies to create the kind of tension in society that will help men rise from the dark depths of prejudice and racism to the majestic heights of understanding and brotherhood. So the purpose of the direct action is to create a situation so crisis-packed that it will inevitably open the door to negotiation. We, therefore, concur with you in your call for negotiation. Too long has our beloved Southland been bogged down in the tragic attempt to live in monologue rather than dialogue.

One of the basic points in your statement is that our acts are untimely. Some have asked, "Why didn't you give the new administration time to act?" The only answer that I can give to this inquiry is that the new administration must be prodded about as much as the outgoing one before it acts. We will be sadly mistaken if we feel that the election of Mr. Boutwell will bring the millennium to Birmingham. While Mr. Boutwell is much more articulate and gentle than Mr. Connor, they are both segregationists dedicated to the task of maintaining the status quo. The hope I see in Mr. Boutwell is that he will be reasonable enough to see the futility of massive resistance to desegregation. But he will not see this without pressure from the devotees of civil rights. My friends, I must say to you that we have not made a single gain in civil rights without determined legal and nonviolent pressure. History is the long and tragic story of the fact that privileged groups seldom give up their privileges voluntarily.

Individuals may see the moral light and voluntarily give up their unjust posture; but as Reinhold Niebuhr has reminded us, groups are more immoral than individuals.

We know through painful experience that freedom is never voluntarily given by the oppressor; it must be demanded by the oppressed. Frankly I have never yet engaged in a direct action movement that was "well timed," according to the timetable of those who have not suffered unduly from the disease of segregation. For years now I have heard the word "Wait!" It rings in the ear of every Negro with a piercing familiarity. This "wait" has almost always meant "never." It has been a tranquilizing thalidomide, relieving the emotional stress for a moment, only to give birth to an ill-formed infant of frustration. We must come to see with the distinguished jurist of yesterday that "justice too long delayed is justice denied." We have waited for more than three hundred and forty years for our constitutional and God-given rights. The nations of Asia and Africa are moving with jet-like speed toward the goal of political independence, and we still creep at horse and buggy pace toward the gaining of a cup of coffee at a lunch counter.

I guess it is easy for those who have never felt the stinging darts of segregation to say wait. But when you have seen vicious mobs lynch your mothers and fathers at will and drown your sisters and brothers at whim; when you have seen hate filled policemen curse, kick, brutalize, and even kill your black brothers and sisters with impunity; when you see the vast majority of your twenty million Negro brothers smothering in an air-tight cage of poverty in the midst of an affluent society; when you suddenly find your tongue twisted and your speech stammering as you seek to explain to your six-year-old daughter why she can't go to the public amusement park that has just been advertised on television, and see tears welling up in her little eyes when she is told that Funtown is closed to colored children, and see the depressing clouds of inferiority begin to form in her little mental sky, and see her begin to distort her little personality by unconsciously developing a bitterness toward white people; when you have to concoct an answer for a five-year-old son asking in agonizing pathos: "Daddy, why do white people treat colored people so mean?"; when you take a cross-country drive and find it necessary to sleep night after night in the uncomfortable corners of your automobile because no motel will accept you; when you are humiliated day in and day out by nagging signs reading "white" men and "colored"; when your first name becomes "nigger" and your middle name becomes "boy" (however old you are) and your last name becomes "John," and when your wife and mother are never given the respected title "Mrs."; when you are harried by day and haunted by night by the fact that you are a Negro, living constantly at tip-toe stance never quite knowing what to expect next, and plagued with inner fears and outer resentments; when you are forever fighting a degenerating sense of "nobodiness"—then you will understand why we find it difficult to wait. There comes a time when the cup of endurance runs over, and men are no longer willing to be plunged into an abyss of injustice where they experience the bleakness of corroding despair. I hope, sirs, you can understand our legitimate and unavoidable impatience.

You express a great deal of anxiety over our willingness to break laws. This is certainly a legitimate concern. Since we so diligently urge people to obey the Supreme Court's decision of 1954 outlawing segregation in the public schools, it is rather strange and paradoxical to find us consciously breaking laws. One may well ask: "How can you advocate breaking some laws and obeying others?" The answer is found in the fact that there are two types of laws: There are just laws and there are unjust laws. I would be the first to advocate obeying just laws. One has not only a legal but moral responsibility to obey just laws. Conversely, one has a moral responsibility to disobey unjust laws. I would agree with Saint Augustine that "An unjust law is no law at all."

Now what is the difference between the two? How does one determine when a law is just or unjust? A just law is a man-made code that squares with the moral law or the law of God. An unjust law is a code that is out of harmony with the moral law. To put it in the terms of Saint Thomas Aquinas, an unjust law is a human law that is not rooted in eternal and natural law. Any law that uplifts human personality is just. Any law that degrades human personality is unjust. All segregation statutes are unjust because segregation distorts the soul and damages the personality. It gives the segregator a false sense of superiority and the segregated a false sense of inferiority. To use the words of Martin Buber, the great Jewish philosopher, segregation substitutes an "I-it" relationship for an "I-thou" relationship, and ends up relegating persons to the status of things. So segregation is not only politically, economically, and sociologically unsound, but it is morally wrong and sinful. Paul Tillich has said that sin is separation. Isn't segregation an existential expression of man's tragic separation, an expression of his awful estrangement, his terrible sinfulness? So I can urge men to obey the 1954 decision of the Supreme Court because it is morally right, and I can urge them to disobey segregation ordinances because they are morally wrong.

Let us turn to a more concrete example of just and unjust laws. An unjust law is a code that a majority inflicts on a minority that is not binding on itself. This is difference made legal. On the other hand a just law is a code that a majority compels a minority to follow that it is willing to follow itself. This is sameness made legal.

Let me give another explanation. An unjust law is a code inflicted upon a minority which that minority had no part in enacting or creating because they did not have the unhampered right to vote. Who can say that the legislature of Alabama which set up the segregation laws was democratically elected? Throughout the state of Alabama all types of conniving methods are used to prevent Negroes from becoming registered voters and there are some counties without a single Negro registered to vote despite the fact that the Negro constitutes a majority of the population. Can any law set up in such a state be considered democratically structured?

These are just a few examples of unjust and just laws. There are some instances when a law is just on its face but unjust in its application. For instance, I was arrested Friday on a charge of parading without a permit. Now there is nothing wrong with an ordinance which requires a permit for a parade, but when the ordinance is used to preserve segregation and to deny citizens the First Amendment privilege of peaceful assembly and peaceful protest, then it becomes unjust.

I hope you can see the distinction I am trying to point out. In no sense do I advocate evading or defying the law as the rabid segregationist would do. This would lead to anarchy. One who breaks an unjust law must do it openly, lovingly (not hatefully as the white mothers did in New Orleans when they were seen on television screaming "nigger, nigger, nigger") and with a willingness to accept the penalty. I submit that an individual who breaks a law that conscience tells him is unjust, and willingly accepts the penalty by staying in jail to arouse the conscience of the community over its injustice, is in reality expressing the very highest respect for law.

Of course there is nothing new about this kind of civil disobedience. It was seen sublimely in the refusal of Shadrach, Meshach, and Abednego to obey the laws of Nebuchadnezzar because a higher moral law was involved. It was practiced superbly by the early Christians who were willing to face hungry lions and the excruciating pain of chopping blocks, before submitting to certain unjust laws of the Roman Empire. To a degree academic freedom is a reality today because Socrates practiced civil disobedience.

We can never forget that everything Hitler did in Germany was "legal" and everything the Hungarian freedom fighters did in Hungary was "illegal." It was "illegal" to aid and comfort a Jew in Hitler's Germany. But I am sure that, if I had lived in Germany during that time, I would have aided and comforted my Jewish brothers even though it was illegal. If I lived in a communist country today where certain principles dear to the Christian faith are suppressed, I believe I would openly advocate disobeying these anti-religious laws.

I must make two honest confessions to you, my Christian and Jewish brothers. First, I must confess that over the last few years I have been gravely disappointed with the white moderate. I have almost reached the regrettable conclusion that the Negroes' great stumbling block in the stride toward freedom is not the White Citizen's "Counciler" or the Ku Klux Klanner, but the white moderate who is more devoted to "order" than to justice; who prefers a negative peace which is the absence of tension to a positive peace which is the presence of justice; who constantly says "I agree with you in the goal you seek, but I can't agree with your methods of direct action"; who paternalistically feels that he can set the timetable for another man's freedom; who lives by the myth of time and who constantly advises the Negro to wait until a "more convenient season." Shallow understanding from people of good will is more frustrating than absolute misunderstanding from people of ill will. Lukewarm acceptance is much more bewildering than outright rejection.

I had hoped that the white moderate would understand that law and order exist for the purpose of establishing justice, and that when they fail to do this they become dangerously structured dams that block the flow of social progress. I had hoped that the white moderate would understand that the present tension in the South is merely a necessary phase of the transition from an obnoxious negative peace, where the Negro passively accepted his unjust plight, to a substance-filled positive peace, where all men will respect the dignity and worth of human personality. Actually, we who engage in nonviolent direct action are not the creators of tension. We merely bring to the surface the hidden tension that is already alive. We bring it out in the open where it can be seen and dealt with. Like a boil that can never be cured as long as it is covered up but must be opened with all its pus-flowing ugliness to the natural medicines of air and light, injustice must likewise be exposed, with all of the tension its exposing creates, to the light of human conscience and the air of national opinion before it can be cured.

In your statement you asserted that our actions, even though peaceful, must be condemned because they precipitate violence. But can this assertion be logically made? Isn't this like condemning the robbed man because his possession of money precipitated the evil act of robbery? Isn't this like condemning Socrates because his unswerving commitment to truth and his philosophical delvings precipitated the misguided popular mind to make him drink the hemlock? Isn't this like condemning Jesus because His unique God consciousness and never-ceasing devotion to His will precipitated the evil act of crucifixion? We must come to see, as federal courts have consistently affirmed, that it is immoral to urge an individual to withdraw his efforts to gain his basic constitutional rights because the quest precipitates violence. Society must protect the robbed and punish the robber.

I had also hoped that the white moderate would reject the myth of time. I received a letter this morning from a white brother in Texas which said: "All Christians know that the colored people will receive equal rights eventually, but is it possible that you are in too great of a religious hurry? It has taken Christianity almost 2,000 years to accomplish what it has. The teachings of Christ take time to come to earth." All that is said here grows out of a tragic misconception of time. It is the strangely irrational notion that there is something in the very flow of time that will inevitably cure all ills. Actually time is neutral. It can be used either destructively or constructively. I am coming to feel that the people of ill will have used time much more effectively than the people of good will. We will have to repent in this generation not merely for the vitriolic words and actions of the bad people, but for the appalling silence of the good people. We must come to see that human progress never rolls in on wheels of inevitability. It comes through the tireless efforts and persistent work of men willing to be co-workers with God, and without this hard work time itself becomes an ally of the forces of social stagnation.

We must use time creatively, and forever realize that the time is always ripe to do right. Now is the time to make real the promise of democracy, and transform our pending national elegy into a creative psalm of brotherhood. Now is the time to lift our national policy from the quicksand of racial injustice to the solid rock of human dignity.

You spoke of our activity in Birmingham as extreme. At first I was rather disappointed that fellow clergymen would see my nonviolent efforts as those of the extremist. I started thinking about the fact that I stand in the middle of two opposing forces in the Negro community. One is a force of complacency made up of Negroes who, as a result of long years of oppression, have been so completely drained of self-respect and a sense of "somebodiness" that they have adjusted to segregation, and of a few Negroes in the middle class who, because of a degree of academic and economic security, and because at points they profit by segregation, have unconsciously become insensitive to the problems of the masses. The other force is one of bitterness and hatred and comes perilously close to advocating violence. It is expressed in the various black nationalist groups that are springing up over the nation, the largest and best known being Elijah Muhammad's Muslim movement. This movement is nourished by the contemporary frustration over the continued existence of racial discrimination. It is made up of people who have lost faith in America, who have absolutely repudiated Christianity, and who have concluded that the white man is an incurable "devil." I have tried to stand between these two forces saying that we need not follow the "do-nothingism" of the complacent or the hatred and despair of the black nationalist. There is the more excellent way of love and nonviolent protest. I'm grateful to God that, through the Negro church, the dimension of nonviolence entered our struggle. If this philosophy had not emerged I am convinced that by now many streets of the South would be flowing with floods of blood. And I am further convinced that if our white brothers dismiss us as "rabble rousers" and "outside agitators"—those of us who are working through the channels of nonviolent direct action—and refuse to support our nonviolent efforts, millions of Negroes, out of frustration and despair, will seek solace and security in black-nationalist ideologies, a development that will lead inevitably to a frightening racial nightmare.

Oppressed people cannot remain oppressed forever. The urge for freedom will eventually come. This is what has happened to the American Negro. Something within has reminded him of his birthright of freedom; something without has reminded him that he can gain it. Consciously and unconsciously, he has been swept in by what the Germans call the Zeitgeist, and with his black brothers of Africa, and his brown and yellow brothers of Asia, South America, and the Caribbean, he is moving with a sense of cosmic urgency toward the promised land of racial justice. Recognizing this vital urge that has engulfed the Negro community, one should readily understand public demonstrations. The Negro has many pent-up resentments and latent frustrations. He has to get them out. So let him march sometime; let him have his prayer pilgrimages to the city hall; understand why he must have sit-ins and freedom rides. If his repressed emotions do not come out in these nonviolent ways, they will come out in ominous expressions of violence. This is not a threat; it is a fact of history. So I have not said to my people, "Get rid of your discontent." But I have tried to say that this normal and healthy discontent can be channeled through the creative outlet of nonviolent direct action. Now this approach is being dismissed as extremist. I must admit that I was initially disappointed in being so categorized.

But as I continued to think about the matter I gradually gained a bit of satisfaction from being considered an extremist. Was not Jesus an extremist in love? "Love your enemies, bless them that curse you, pray for them that despitefully use you." Was not Amos an extremist for justice—"Let justice roll down like waters and righteousness like a mighty stream." Was not Paul an extremist for the gospel of Jesus Christ—"I bear in my body the marks of the

Lord Jesus." Was not Martin Luther an extremist—"Here I stand; I can do none other so help me God." Was not John Bunyan an extremist—"I will stay in jail to the end of my days before I make a butchery of my conscience." Was not Abraham Lincoln an extremist—"This nation cannot survive half slave and half free." Was not Thomas Jefferson an extremist—"We hold these truths to be self-evident, that all men are created equal." So the question is not whether we will be extremist but what kind of extremist will we be. Will we be extremists for hate or will we be extremists for love? Will we be extremists for the preservation of injustice—or will we be extremists for the cause of justice? In that dramatic scene on Calvary's hill three men were crucified. We must never forget that all three were crucified for the same crime—the crime of extremism. Two were extremists for immorality, and thus fell below their environment. The other, Jesus Christ, was an extremist for love, truth, and goodness, and thereby rose above His environment. So, after all, maybe the South, the nation, and the world are in dire need of creative extremists.

I had hoped that the white moderate would see this. Maybe I was too optimistic. Maybe I expected too much. I guess I should have realized that few members of a race that has oppressed another race can understand or appreciate the deep groans and passionate yearnings of those that have been oppressed, and still fewer have the vision to see that injustice must be rooted out by strong, persistent, and determined action. I am thankful, however, that some of our white brothers have grasped the meaning of this social revolution and committed themselves to it. They are still all too small in quantity, but they are big in quality. Some like Ralph McGill, Lillian Smith, Harry Golden, and James Dabbs have written about our struggle in eloquent, prophetic, and understanding terms. Others have marched with us down nameless streets of the South. They have languished in filthy, roach-infested jails, suffering the abuse and brutality of angry policemen who see them as "dirty nigger lovers." They, unlike so many of their moderate brothers and sisters, have recognized the urgency of the moment and sensed the need for powerful "action" antidotes to combat the disease of segregation.

Let me rush on to mention my other disappointment. I have been so greatly disappointed with the white Church and its leadership. Of course there are some notable exceptions. I am not unmindful of the fact that each of you has taken some significant stands on this issue. I commend you, Rev. Stallings, for your Christian stand on this past Sunday, in welcoming Negroes to your worship service on a non-segregated basis. I commend the Catholic leaders of this state for integrating Spring Hill College several years ago.

But despite these notable exceptions I must honestly reiterate that I have been disappointed with the Church. I do not say that as one of those negative critics who can always find something wrong with the Church. I say it as a minister of the gospel, who loves the Church; who was nurtured in its bosom; who has been sustained by its spiritual blessings and who will remain true to it as long as the cord of life shall lengthen.

I had the strange feeling when I was suddenly catapulted into the leadership of the bus protest in Montgomery several years ago that we would have the support of the white

Church. I felt that the white ministers, priests, and rabbis of the South would be some of our strongest allies. Instead, some have been outright opponents, refusing to understand the freedom movement and misrepresenting its leaders; all too many others have been more cautious than courageous and have remained silent behind the anesthetizing security of the stained glass windows.

In spite of my shattered dreams of the past, I came to Birmingham with the hope that the white religious leadership of this community would see the justice of our cause and with deep moral concern, serve as the channel through which our just grievances could get to the power structure. I had hoped that each of you would understand. But again I have been disappointed.

I have heard numerous religious leaders of the South call upon their worshippers to comply with a desegregation decision because it is the law, but I have longed to hear white ministers say follow this decree because integration is morally right and the Negro is your brother. In the midst of blatant injustices inflicted upon the Negro, I have watched white churches stand on the sideline and merely mouth pious irrelevancies and sanctimonious trivialities. In the midst of a mighty struggle to rid our nation of racial and economic injustice, I have heard so many ministers say, "Those are social issues with which the gospel has no real concern," and I have watched so many churches commit themselves to a completely other-worldly religion which made a strange distinction between body and soul, the sacred and the secular.

So here we are moving toward the exit of the twentieth century with a religious community largely adjusted to the status quo, standing as a tail-light behind other community agencies rather than a headlight leading men to higher levels of justice.

I have travelled the length and breadth of Alabama, Mississippi and all the other southern states. On sweltering summer days and crisp autumn mornings I have looked at her beautiful churches with their spires pointing heavenward. I have beheld the impressive outlay of her massive religious education buildings. Over and over again I have found myself asking: "Who worships here? Who is their God? Where were their voices when the lips of Governor Barnett dripped with words of interposition and nullification? Where were they when Governor Wallace gave the clarion call for defiance and hatred? Where were their voices of support when tired, bruised, and weary Negro men and women decided to rise from the dark dungeons of complacency to the bright hills of creative protest?"

Yes, these questions are still in my mind. In deep disappointment, I have wept over the laxity of the church. But be assured that my tears have been tears of love. There can be no deep disappointment where there is not deep love. Yes, I love the Church; I love her sacred walls. How could I do otherwise? I am in the rather unique position of being the son, the grandson, and the great-grandson of preachers. Yes, I see the Church as the body of Christ. But, oh! How we have blemished and scarred that body through social neglect and fear of being nonconformist.

There was a time when the Church was very powerful. It was during that period when the early Christians rejoiced when they were deemed worthy to suffer for what they believed. In those days the Church was not merely a thermometer that recorded the ideas and principles of popular opinion; it was a thermostat that transformed the mores of society. Wherever the early Christians entered a town the power structure got disturbed and immediately sought to convict them for being "disturbers of the peace" and "outside agitators." But they went on with the conviction that they were "a colony of heaven" and had to obey God rather than man. They were small in number but big in commitment. They were too God-intoxicated to be "astronomically intimidated." They brought an end to such ancient evils as infanticide and gladiatorial contest.

Things are different now. The contemporary Church is so often a weak, ineffectual voice with an uncertain sound. It is so often the arch-supporter of the status quo. Far from being disturbed by the presence of the Church, the power structure of the average community is consoled by the Church's silent and often vocal sanction of things as they are.

But the judgment of God is upon the Church as never before. If the Church of today does not recapture the sacrificial spirit of the early Church, it will lose its authentic ring, forfeit the loyalty of millions, and be dismissed as an irrelevant social club with no meaning for the twentieth century. I am meeting young people every day whose disappointment with the Church has risen to outright disgust.

Maybe again I have been too optimistic. Is organized religion too inextricably bound to the status quo to save our nation and the world? Maybe I must turn my faith to the inner spiritual Church, the church within the Church, as the true ecclesia and the hope of the world. But again I am thankful to God that some noble souls from the ranks of organized religion have broken loose from the paralyzing chains of conformity and joined us as active partners in the struggle for freedom. They have left their secure congregations and walked the streets of Albany, Georgia, with us. They have gone through the highways of the South on torturous rides for freedom. Yes, they have gone to jail with us. Some have been kicked out of their churches and lost the support of their bishops and fellow ministers. But they have gone with the faith that right defeated is stronger than evil triumphant. These men have been the leaven in the lump of the race. Their witness has been the spiritual salt that has preserved the true meaning of the Gospel in these troubled times. They have carved a tunnel of hope through the dark mountain of disappointment.

I hope the Church as a whole will meet the challenge of this decisive hour. But even if the Church does not come to the aid of justice, I have no despair about the future. I have no fear about the outcome of our struggle in Birmingham, even if our motives are presently misunderstood. We will reach the goal of freedom in Birmingham and all over the nation, because the goal of America is freedom. Abused and scorned though we may be, our destiny is tied up with the destiny of America. Before the pilgrims landed at Plymouth, we were here. Before the pen of Jefferson etched across the pages of history the majestic words of the Declaration of Independence, we were here. For more than two centuries our foreparents labored in this country without wages; they made cotton "king"; and they built the homes of their masters in the midst of brutal injustice and shameful humiliation—and yet out of a bottomless vitality they continued to thrive and develop. If the inexpressible cruelties of slavery could not stop us, the opposition we now face will surely fail. We will win our freedom because the sacred heritage of our nation and the eternal will of God are embodied in our echoing demands.

I must close now. But before closing I am impelled to mention one other point in your statement that troubled me profoundly. You warmly commend the Birmingham police force for keeping "order" and "preventing violence." I don't believe you would have so warmly commended the police force if you had seen its angry violent dogs literally biting six unarmed, nonviolent Negroes. I don't believe you would so quickly commend the policemen if you would observe their ugly and inhuman treatment of Negroes here in the city jail; if you would watch them push and curse old Negro women and young Negro girls; if you would see them slap and kick old Negro men and young Negro boys; if you will observe them, as they did on two occasions, refuse to give us food because we wanted to sing our grace together. I'm sorry that I can't join you in your praise for the police department.

It is true that they have been rather disciplined in their public handling of the demonstrators. In this sense they have been rather publicly "nonviolent." But for what purpose? To preserve the evil system of segregation. Over the last few years I have consistently preached that nonviolence demands the means we use must be as pure as the ends we seek. So I have tried to make it clear that it is wrong to use immoral means to attain moral ends. But now I must affirm that it is just as wrong or even more so to use moral means to preserve immoral ends. Maybe Mr. Connor and his policemen have been rather publicly nonviolent, as Chief Pritchett was in Albany, Georgia, but they have used the moral means of nonviolence to maintain the immoral end of flagrant injustice. T. S. Eliot has said that there is no greater treason than to do the right deed for the wrong reason.

I wish you had commended the Negro sit-inners and demonstrators of Birmingham for their sublime courage, their willingness to suffer, and their amazing discipline in the midst of the most inhuman provocation. One day the South will recognize its real heroes. They will be the James Merediths, courageously and with a majestic sense of purpose, facing jeering and hostile mobs and the agonizing loneliness that characterizes the life of the pioneer. They will be old, oppressed, battered Negro women, symbolized in a seventy-two year old woman of Montgomery, Alabama, who rose up with a sense of dignity and with her people decided not to ride the segregated buses, and responded to one who inquired about her tiredness with ungrammatical profundity: "My feets is tired, but my soul is rested." They will be the young high school and college students, young ministers of the gospel and a host of their elders courageously and nonviolently sitting-in at lunch counters and willingly going to jail for conscience sake. One day the South will know that when these disinherited children of God sat down at lunch counters they were in reality standing up for the best in the American dream and the most sacred values in our Judaeo-Christian heritage, and thus carrying our whole nation back to great wells of democracy which were dug deep by the founding fathers in the formulation of the Constitution and the Declaration of Independence.

Never before have I written a letter this long (or should I say a book?). I'm afraid it is much too long to take your precious time. I can assure you that it would have been much shorter if I had been writing from a comfortable desk, but what else is there to do when you are alone for days in the dull monotony of a narrow jail cell other than write long letters, think strange thoughts, and pray long prayers?

If I have said anything in this letter that is an overstatement of the truth and is indicative of an unreasonable impatience, I beg you to forgive me. If I have said anything in this letter that is an understatement of the truth and is indicative of my having a patience that makes me patient with anything less than brotherhood, I beg God to forgive me.

I hope this letter finds you strong in the faith. I also hope that circumstances will soon make it possible for me to meet each of you, not as an integrationist or a civil rights leader, but as a fellow clergyman and a Christian brother. Let us all hope that the dark clouds of racial prejudice will soon pass away and the deep fog of misunderstanding will be lifted from our fear-drenched communities and in some not too distant tomorrow the radiant stars of love and brotherhood will shine over our great nation with all their scintillating beauty.

Yours for the cause of
Peace and Brotherhood,

Martin Luther King, Jr.

CONCLUSION

As we reflect on the African American experience, we delve into the achievements, contributions, struggle, and progress of African Americans in our society. Despite this acknowledgment, we must continue to be vigilant and cautious in how we respect one of our country's greatest stories—that of the black experience. I am always disappointed when critics pose the dueling question, why do we need to celebrate African Americans or Black History Month? Though I seldom argue with such critics, I do feel compelled to inform such masses about our sad history with regard to the treatment of African Americans, but more so, to share the significance of their achievements and contributions in America. The contributions of African Americans are more important today than at any other time in our country's history. Not only has the country elected its first African American President, Barack Obama, but the contributions of African Americans are far reached: including those of civil rights leaders, educators, architects, inventors, scientists, sports heroes, and others. Yet, despite their commitment to America, there has remained a deep uncertainty as to who African Americans really are?

The African American experience is a 300-year struggle against racism and oppression in a country that still today refuses to acknowledge or apologize for its wrongdoing, we must acknowledge that African Americans were an integral part of shaping American history and that our history would not be the same without the black experience. Many of us are unaware that history books have left out the fact that one of George Washington's closest confidants was an African American named Samuel Fraunces, who advised him on many of his battles, and that Crispus Attucks, a fugitive slave in Massachusetts, became the first martyr of the American revolution. The African American slave trade played a key economic element in the American Revolutionary war and built large-scale economies in England, America, Holland, and many other European countries, all who benefited directly and indirectly from the African American slave industry.

Americans refuse to acknowledge that racism is a societal problem that can only be resolved by having a more open dialogue on race and discussion about diversity in America. Only conversations about the truth, the need for reconciliation, and America's acknowledgment of its wrongdoing can lead to a more racially tolerant country, where the American dream can be enjoyed by all despite their race or color. As we enter the twenty-first century, silent and not overt racism and segregation still exist and are evident in our school systems, employment, poverty, healthcare, prison system, immigrant communities, and other sectors of society. These also permeate our society in ways we don't even realize and take away the best of who we are as Americans and what we can become.

The election of the nation's first African-American president also led to the increased expectation that Americans will put our ugly racial past behind and move forward into a more racially sensitive and tolerant society. It seemed to offer the promise that America would transcend race and that both white and black racial attitudes would undergo a fundamental change, but it has NOT. The need for America to have a more constructive dialogue on race has not come to fruition for several factors. First, any discussion of race among white Americans elicits a very cautious and complicated reaction; many whites shy away from any racial dialogue. Second is the fact that we need to admit we have a problem; a nation that is in denial and is sleepwalking will never wake up.

Having an African-American president shows our ability to move beyond race and achieve racial reconciliation, but that will not solve neither heal our racial past nor solve America's greatest social cancer: the issue of race and racial discrimination. In spite of the unquestioned greatness of America, there must be a conscious effort by all Americans to achieve reconciliation; we must acknowledge our past wrongdoing and engage in conversations that can lead to a more racially tolerant society, wherein America can be enjoyed by all. America truly has come a long way in the last 50 years. The hard work and dedication of Dr. King and other civil rights leaders, activists, and common citizens have attempted to level the playing field for African Americans, women, members of the LGBT community, Hispanics, Native Americans, and others considerably. The election of our first African American president has helped us make great strides toward a racially harmonious society, wherein we respect all contributions to our great country. We should be very proud of these accomplishments and civil rights gains, but it is also important that we do not become complacent with that progress. As we reflect on the African American experience, we must truly be proud of their contributions in every aspect of our society. The legacies of Dr. King, other civil rights leaders, scientists, educators, inventors, sports heroes, and common citizens have played a key role in the development of American history and society. The need to persist for greater economic prosperity, pride, and independence. We must keep a promise to ourselves that the African American experience is much more than Black History Month; it is celebrating our past and present, but also paving our future.

ABOUT THE AUTHOR

Stephen Balkaran is currently an instructor of African American studies at Central Connecticut State University, where he initiated, developed, and coordinated a Civil Rights Project (2006-present). He also serves as an instructor of political science at Quinnipiac University (2011-present), the University of Connecticut-Tri Campus (2005-06), Post University (2003-04), and Capital Community College (1999-2003). Before launching his academic career, Mr. Balkaran worked for the African National Congress (Nelson Mandela's ruling party in South Africa), in partnership with the University of Connecticut. He was also a research associate for the United Nations in New York and a former aide to the Connecticut Secretary of State.

He has authored 6 books: *America's Promise: Chasing the Dream of Civil Rights* (2019); *Broken Promises, Broken Dreams: Disparities and Disappointments. Civil Rights in the 21st Century* (2017); *Before We Were Called Hispanics: Conversations on Race, Politics, and Immigration Reform* (2016); *The Continuing Significance of Race: An American Dilemma* (2014); and *Retracing the Movement: Photobiography of the Civil Rights Movement* (2011). His seventh and forthcoming book is entitled *Trouble in Paradise: The African American Experience in Key West*. He has also authored over 70 articles in academic journals, and magazines, as well as opinion editorials on race relations, diversity and inclusion, American foreign policy, and public policy. He has also given over 100 speeches on his research, publications, and books throughout the United States.

Mr. Balkaran's educational background spans the Presentation College in Trinidad, the University of Connecticut, and Quinnipiac University School of Law, including fellowship at Yale University, where he served as a research fellow for The Human Rights Research Fund at Yale University, working under Black Panther and Yale professor of African American studies Mrs. Kathleen Cleaver. Mr. Balkaran currently resides in Hartford, Connecticut.